T0003985

HELLO, GOODBYE

HELLO,
GOODBYE

75 RITUALS *for* TIMES *of* LOSS, CELEBRATION, *and* CHANGE

DAY SCHILDKRET

SIMON ELEMENT

NEW YORK   LONDON   TORONTO   SYDNEY   NEW DELHI

**SIMON
ELEMENT**

An Imprint of Simon & Schuster, Inc.
1230 Avenue of the Americas
New York, NY 10020

Copyright © 2022 by Day Schildkret

This publication contains the opinions and ideas of its author. It is intended to provide helpful and informative material on the subjects addressed in the publication. It is sold with the understanding that the author and publisher are not engaged in rendering medical, health, or any other kind of personal professional services in the book. The reader should consult his or her medical, health, or other competent professional before adopting any of the suggestions in this book or drawing inferences from it.

The author and publisher specifically disclaim all responsibility for any liability, loss, or risk, personal or otherwise, that is incurred as a consequence, directly or indirectly, of the use and application of any of the contents of this book.

All rights reserved, including the right to reproduce this book or portions thereof in any form whatsoever. For information, address Simon Element Subsidiary Rights Department, 1230 Avenue of the Americas, New York, NY 10020.

First Simon Element paperback edition January 2023

SIMON ELEMENT is a trademark of Simon & Schuster, Inc.

For information about special discounts for bulk purchases, please contact Simon & Schuster Special Sales at 1-866-506-1949 or business@simonandschuster.com.

The Simon & Schuster Speakers Bureau can bring authors to your live event. For more information or to book an event, contact the Simon & Schuster Speakers Bureau at 1-866-248-3049 or visit our website at www.simonspeakers.com.

Manufactured in the United States of America

1   3   5   7   9   10   8   6   4   2

Library of Congress Cataloging-in-Publication Data has been applied for.

ISBN 978-1-9821-7093-6
ISBN 978-1-9821-7094-3 (pbk)
ISBN 978-1-9821-7095-0 (ebook)

Quote from *The Fellowship of the Ring* on p. 395 reprinted by permission of HarperCollins Publishers Ltd. © 1955 J. R. R. Tolkien. Excerpts from *Braiding Sweetgrass* by Robin Wall Kimmerer reprinted by permission of Milkweed Editions. Copyright © 2013 by Robin Wall Kimmerer. Quote from *Breaking the Watch: The Meanings of Retirement in America* by Joel S. Savishinsky reprinted by permission of Cornell University Press. Copyright © 2000 by Joel S. Savishinsky. Quotes from David Whyte reprinted by permission of Many Rivers Press. Copyright © Many Rivers Press.

Names and identifying characteristics of some individuals have been changed.

To the last three years on the long road, and the many places and people who opened their hearts and homes.

And to this chapter of wandering coming to a close and the new unknown one just beginning.

CONTENTS

RITUALS *for* EVERY DAY

RITUALS *for the* YEAR

RITUALS *for* LETTING GO

RITUALS *for a* CRISIS

FOREWORD

"*Where am I? Who am I? Who are you? What do I do now? What was isn't any longer. Someone left. Someone arrived. Something broke. Something repaired. Life changed. Now, what can you do to mark this moment and find yourself again, to recognize that this is no longer that?*"

You and I are asking these questions now more than ever. What can we do to mark the often-unspoken moments our society urges us to ignore? Are we to simply pass them by, glossing over and moving on from the miscarriage, the breakup, the coming out, the move, the loss of a loved one, the healing of an illness? What about when we find a new love, a nourishing friendship, a job, a surge of creativity?

Instead of muscling our way through difficulty or numbing ourselves when things feel fantastic, what might help us pay attention and grant appropriate significance to these thresholds? How can we note these moments, learn from what's arduous, and honor holiness?

In 2016, there was a forty-eight-hour period between my mom's entering the hospital and her sudden passing. Calling in wisdom from dear teachers and my rabbi, I created personal rituals for nearly every hour during that time. A tiny altar was arranged in the room where my son and I slept, in front of which I would sit whenever I wasn't at the hospital. From a lifetime of images, I crafted a digital altar in my phone.

Then I made myself into an altar, wrapping myself in my mom's scarves, her jewelry, her favorite shirts.

Standing at her kitchen sink during that time, staring at her yard and her garden, feeling her presence, taking immense, full breaths, I would whisper mantras to comfort myself, moving slowly to ensure that I would feel every ounce of grief as it moved through me in waves. Those breaths and chants, I now see, were rituals I used to find resilience and fortitude as she slipped away from me.

Since her death, I continue to create these informal sacred spaces where I have time to quietly connect with her; sometimes aloud, often silently. It takes only a few seconds of sitting still to hear the singsong way in which she would call my name from the bottom of the stairs. Often I'll put on a piece of her clothing in order to feel her energetically holding me, surrounding me.

Similarly, as a parent of a teenager, my aim is to give my son as much space as possible, even though I wish I could shrink him back down and fold him and his curls back into my arms. Some evenings I'll use the teacup he made in pottery class to drink my tea, a tiny ritual that helps me steady myself as my role in his life shifts, giving him much-needed solo time while tending to my own heart. It's the small things.

If you're sensing it's your time to stop turning away and start venerating the shifts in consciousness you might be experiencing in your own life, this is your sign. No matter what's happening for you right now, the book you hold in your hands is here to help you pay attention, slow down, and listen differently.

Day's first book, *Morning Altars*, illustrates his colossal capacity for alchemizing ordinary bits of nature into an experience of quiet, prodigious respect. *Hello, Goodbye* takes this element of transformation to another stratosphere, elevating each moment to new relevance. Day steeps us in ancient understandings, inspiring us to cultivate conscious rapture and true respect with each suggestion. He reminds us that there are simple, profound ways to manage and mark the moments in time that seem small but mean the most.

Day reminds us to stop and recognize that something is happening. To feel. To create distinctions. To be discerning. To remember. To grieve. To heal. To begin again. To know that our heartbreak is actually a form of love, worth our reverence.

—Elena Brower
Santa Fe, New Mexico
June 2021

You say goodbye
and I say hello.

—Lennon–McCartney

HELLO.

his book is a child of change. Its first words were conceived at the onset of a global pandemic. Chapters formed as markets crashed, unemployment skyrocketed, and uncertainty descended on the world like a thick fog. I pursued the writing even as I anxiously watched the ground fall out from under me—my mother's lockdown in her memory-care facility, my grandmother's COVID infection and hospitalization, and all of my employment vanishing within one week. It's certainly ironic to write a book on marking change while swimming or sometimes even flailing in its abyss.

But perhaps it couldn't be any other way.

What kept me afloat every day was a quiet morning ritual. Before any coffee was ground, before any word typed, I would head to the sea. The tiny home that this book was written in is a stone's throw from a small beach named Seabright. I visited Seabright every morning before anything else in order to feel human again.

It took real discipline to keep to this ritual. My attention was being pulled in a hundred other directions during those early days of the pandemic. Each morning would kick-start with another fire to extinguish or emergency to tend to, and honestly, going to the sea felt frivolous. But a voice within me knew better. This voice said: *Going to the sea will let you not lose yourself.* So, I made a nonnegotiable agreement to head to Seabright first before looking at any email, answering any call, or responding to any worried text message—and this granted me the capacity to face that day's shit show. Going to the sea wasn't a beach visit. It was a ritual—a way to remember and feel connected again. Every morning, I'd grab my coat and my basket, slip into rubber rain boots, and head outside. Along the way I collected whatever caught my eye—golden cedar cones, old man's beard, dried maple helicopters, lush spongy moss, fallen snowdrop petals—all depending on the season, of course. As I crossed the small footbridge and climbed down the rickety stairs, I came to an expanse of stone, water, and islands. Some days, just glimpsing that deep green gulf would break me down in grief and relief, as if I was in the presence of something that could hold me so I could finally collapse. On those tender mornings, it was enough to let myself just be a fragile human, unsure and undone, mingling my tears with the salty Salish sea.

Most mornings, however, I'd get on my hands and knees and listen to the symphony of the place: the tide raising and lowering the shore's pebbles; the sounds of a distant seal's bobbing head and the gruff of his heavy breath; a family of geese honking incessantly overhead, flying with haste beyond the grand firs. No matter how much my world was spinning, no matter how the pandemic had undone everything I took for granted, these sounds oriented me. Listening to them, I found my center again. They brought me back to my body, my breath, and to the simple and quiet rhythms that lived on this island. The sea softened me so I could feel my grief and gratitude. To hear life carrying on like that gave me a way to carry on too.

Then, between two barnacle-speckled rocks, I laid down the leaves, shells, or pine cones I had collected, and put them into a shape or pattern—some semblance of order to remind me that there was such a thing. Even though I have been making impermanent altars out of nature for so many decades of my life and have even built a name and career from it, something I've come to call Morning Altars, this year in particular most of my creations weren't artistic as much as they were necessities. Every little altar put down became a grounding rhythm and rod.

This ritual also midwifed this book. It carried me through every day of writing and offered continuity every time my doubt surfaced, my fear took hold, or the ground under me dissolved.

Whether I like it, hate it, invite it, or refuse it, life is forever changing. Especially this past year, ritual has always given me a place to temporarily stand on, to understand from, to make meaning with, to slow down and bear witness to. Rituals are ways that I can recognize the reality of where and when I am—which as I write this still happens to be in Canada during a pandemic—and lets me locate my whole self again in this unfolding story.

Tomorrow, this ritual ends for now. Tomorrow, I move out of this tiny home and leave my daily visits to Seabright. I'm heartbroken to say goodbye to this everyday companion and friend—leaving behind the steadiness and continuity it gifted me this year. But before I put the last few boxes in the car and drive away, I will mark this threshold by saying goodbye in the same way I have said hello each and every morning. Tomorrow at dawn, I will head to Seabright one last time, to mark the end of this remarkable chapter—putting down an altar to all that's been lost and all that's come into being since arriving to these Salish shores.

As the world yearns to open again, as life tries to return back to its normal rhythms, I want to linger at this edge between coming and going—not yet ready to come out but not completely capable of staying in. This threshold moment is stretching me, tenderizing my heart to the point of breaking because I am once again remembering that my grief is really love and this ending is also a beginning. To let both be simultaneously is the truest way I can understand this time and, really, my life.

As I head out tomorrow on the road and return to my home country, facing a new variant of the virus and more uncertainty, I carry with me the reminder of what Antonio Machado said of this long and winding road: "Traveler, there is no path. The path is made by walking. Traveler, the path is your tracks. And nothing more. Traveler, there is no path. The path is made by walking. By walking you make a path. And turning, you look back. At a way you will never tread again. Traveler, there is no road. Only wakes in the sea."

—Day Schildkret
W̱ENÁ,NEȻ, Salt Spring Island, Canada
June 2021

Introduction

The times are urgent; let us slow down.

—Báyò Akómoláfé

Yesterday she forgot my name. A name she gave me. A name she's been calling me since I was born. She forgot it so easily—"What's your name again?"—as if it were nothing, as if I was an acquaintance meeting her in line at the grocery store. Even though I had dreaded this moment coming, it had finally arrived. And it defeated me as much as you'd think it would. For years now, my mother's memory has been in steep decline. At the beginning, we could just sense it coming, like whisperings about an inevitable and unwanted guest. At first, simple things went missing: keys, phone, her pocketbook. But this year was an avalanche of amnesia. This year, the year of the pandemic and the separation and isolation it brought to so many and especially people like my mother, accelerated what was already becoming undone.

And now my name. What can be done after a moment like this? How to pivot, as I usually do, to a sweet song or a funny voice or a benign "What did you have for lunch?" This time on Facetime, I had nothing in my pockets. And so there was only space between us. Just silence that felt endless which I'm sure lasted only a moment or two. Then, like two strangers, I reminded her of my name, to which she replied, "I know," and the conversation petered out as quickly as she forgot she was even on the phone at all.

Today, she didn't remember that moment. But I did. That moment meant something to me. It was another cairn on the long road of losing her. Another way to mark this ambiguous loss, this time of her being here and not here. Of her slowly fading away. To others, this grief would be more recognizable if she had died and I was mourning her. "How's your mom?" is a question my friends sometimes ask me, which sounds exactly the same as if she was in full health. For there isn't much in our collective arsenal of meaning to mark these small monumental moments. There isn't a guidebook that tells you what to do when your mom forgets your name, and so that day I just tried to carry on as usual. There was work to do; there were emails to answer, dishes to wash, calls to make. And as much as this moment pierced me to the bone, what else could I do?

This book is about what I did in that moment. And other moments, big and small, that plead for a ceasing of our regularly scheduled program. A way to ward off the spell of normalcy by recognizing that something has happened. The path we've been treading is winding in another direction. The highway we've been coasting on is merging into another. All the signs say: "Pay attention. Slow down. Be prepared to stop." But it's not that easy. If it were, we'd all be doing it. Most likely, if you're reading this, you too live in a modern culture that doesn't value slowing down. Actually, it's more pernicious than that. Our modern culture resists it, even fights it. Our culture is competency-addicted and aggressively compelled toward speed and mastery. Our collective mantras are "carry on," "chin up," "keep going," "just do it." Then these moments of change and uncertainty become diminished as things to overcome or sidestep in order to get back in the game. Or worse, these remarkable moments are treated like a spectator sport, something we watch but aren't impacted by. And the consequence is our days carry no evidence that anything even really happened.

I sat at the crossroads of that possibility after this video call with my mom. It might have been just like any call we'd ever had. But it wasn't. That moment marked me. It left a fresh wound on my flesh. And it sat there waiting for me. It wanted something from me too. An equal marking. It was looking for me to make it into something. It was available for that, like wet clay ready to be molded and shaped. It wanted my hands to do something. My mouth to say something. It longed for this sorrow to be made into beauty. To call together all of those who mattered and gather them around this time. It wanted teary-eyed songs that could be sung and heart-aching poems that could imagine what forgetting felt like. This moment needed something to crack open, like my heart was doing, or something to tear, in the same way our connection was being ripped in half. Anything symbolic would have sufficed so I could physically bear witness to my own loss and recognize it as real.

And that almost didn't happen. The insurance guy called. My neighbor came asking me to help jump his car. My calendar had a meeting scheduled at 3 p.m. Life did not care about my name. No one had time to notice me losing my mother in a new, distinct way. And even when I called a friend and got the earnest "I'm so sorry" in return, it paled in comparison to the utter wreckage that was my heart. I just couldn't carry on with my day as if nothing had happened. And, thankfully, I do have a little experience in refusing to go on while still going on, to paraphrase Samuel Beckett. And so I did just that. I set a limit on this incessant and relentless river of time. I stopped. I felt. I noticed: Something had happened. Something was different. And this gut-wrenching moment was asking more from me. It needed me to create a distinction in the everydayness of life so that I could really see what I was in the presence of. So I could remember what needed to be remembered.

Creating distinctions is a skill that's been hammered into me since childhood. Judaism has been my cranky old teacher, my companion, my guide to better understand how to mark "this from that." For instance, it says, these are the weekdays for work, and that is our holy day for rest. Or this is regular bread to eat and that is our sacred bread to remember. As our days progress, it instructs: Say these prayers, or light this candle, or shake this thing, or break this glass to make this special moment recognizable, to see it as purposeful and something worth remembering.

When I turned twelve years old, I came even closer to Judaism than my family ever would. I chose to wear our ancestral sacred garments every day—a head covering, or *kippah*; prayer fringes, or *tzitzit*—and became *shomer mitzvot*, or a practitioner of our commandments. For a decade, I immersed myself in the learning, customs, laws, and traditions of my people and had some excellent schooling in the acts of sanctification, or ways to make something distinguished and sacred. In fact, Judaism does this best with time. In my forty-something years, it has not only taught me the old ways to make time holy, but *why* it is necessary to do so. For without discerning and marking time, you forget where you are inside of it. And then you are lost.

After the call with my mom, I groped for something, anything. I could feel the grief rising up in me like a storm brewing and couldn't ignore it. Over the years, and especially since my father's death ten years ago, I have been practicing grief and grieving as a skill and capacity, a way of being with the way things are despite my preferences for how I want them to be. A way of being in the world that understands life as something bigger than my life. Rather than being afflicted with grief and hating on it as the thing that interrupts and messes with my day, I've come to see it as another way of loving—a way to love what is leaving or has left entirely. That heartbreaking love of life keeps stretching me open, especially now, witnessing another step of my mother's departure. And this welling up of grief and love and tenderness toward what was leaving needed more space to live in my day. This grief needed to be seen, to be welcomed in as a Gift Bringer, a Life Teacher, a Great Rememberer of the way things are. I needed to offer it the same kind of hospitality I would give any beloved guest; otherwise it would become a Grendel-like monster, clawing at the door and forcing itself inside my day anyway.

While I am known as someone who builds altars, in this moment all I could think to do was open the drawer and pull out two beeswax candles. I was rightfully undone, but I could at least do that. Lighting candles is a go-to meaning-maker for us Jews. We light candles to begin Shabbat and we light candles to end it. We light candles to remember our old stories and we light candles to remember our dead. And, while it wasn't a Jewish custom, I knew I needed to light these candles to mark this moment and make it different. I needed to see those little flames flickering as evidence of how tenuous, how beautiful and fleeting this day, my mother's days, our days truly are. And so I employed the same rhythmic ancestral memory used to distinguish "this from that." But now I was to distinguish those days past when my name easily rolled off my mom's lips from these new, uncertain days when that name was nowhere to be found. My, how things had changed.

My candlesticks are already covered in wax. Layers of it. Most recently, I lit candles alongside many others for an online baby shower. We sang songs, told stories, and offered prayers of health, happiness, and wholeness to our dear pregnant friend, on the verge of birthing a new one into this world. Below that was wax from the winter solstice and the candles I lit to mark the darkest day in the year and the much-needed return of the sun, especially for those of us in the Pacific Northwest. Under that were drips from the beautiful celebration of my best friend's summertime pandemic wedding, and peeking out from under that drops from when my dear friend began her journey into chemotherapy and her battle against breast cancer. The wax was like strata of stone, layered bands of storied moments and meaning made manifest from the year; joyful ones sitting on top of sorrowful ones sitting on top of grateful ones sitting on and on and on.

One of the deeper beds of wax was from the vigil I held this past summer when my ninety-four-year-old grandmother got diagnosed with COVID-19 at a rehab center in Florida. Those were dark days, indeed, but I kept those candles burning the entire time she was sick. Before one went out, another was lit. The candles delineated the time, marking a departure from the assumption of safety and health into the wild and viral waters we found ourselves in. Granny sat at the edge for more than two weeks, and the whole thing was honestly beyond me. Except lighting the candles. That I could do. It housed my fears, my prayers, my love, and gave them somewhere to live. It provided a solid place to stand on when everything seemed to be falling apart. Even though I was thousands of miles away, tending to these candles let me, in a way, tend to her.

These days, it seems like I am watching life happen from a distance. My mother's decline, my grandmother's sickness and recovery, my friends' wedding vows, and baby shower and birthday parties and divorce happening with us all apart. This pandemic kept us from coming together, isolating moments meant to gather us in, but also revealing how much we truly do need one another, especially now. You see, there are certain moments that can't be taken in by only ourselves. Or shouldn't be. Sometimes you just need to see it in another's eyes. Sometimes you just need someone else to hold your hand and affirm, "Yes, this is really happening. Yes, I am here with you. Please don't try to hold this yourself. The only way is for us to hold it together." Times of wonder are like that. Grief too. They displace us from the lonely perch of autonomy and certainty, and humble us to the point where we need one another in order to steady ourselves again.

The pandemic also caused us to stop taking "getting together" for granted. Places of worship were shuttered, concerts and festivals postponed, and even the smallest gatherings, like birthday parties and Christmas dinners, let alone funerals, were canceled. As we waded in the wake of so much loss and uncertainty, there also surfaced a real urgency to find a way to bring the brokenness in our lives back into some kind of wholeness. Yes, there is a plague but there is also life happening. Yes, there are restrictions, but people are still dying, marrying, graduating, birthing. And so what do we do when the familiar ways of gathering to mark, celebrate, welcome, mourn are not accessible to us? How do we make sense of our lives in a time that is beyond our control? We must be in deep waters if a mainstream newspaper like the *New York Times* puts out a headline pleading "We Need More Rituals," or the *Harvard Review* reminds us of "The Restorative Power of Rituals." Even NPR, Al Jazeera, the *Wall Street Journal*, and the BBC keep telling stories of how people are forced to reimagine rituals that can tend to life and death, alone but still together. Loss is an interesting beast. It wreaks havoc on our hearts but also can bring us face-to-face with a willingness to remember what we still have and force us to love it even more so. Maybe these newspapers and radio shows calling for new rituals are onto something. Maybe we do need new ways to hold both the grief of what is gone while praising all that still remains.

This book hinges on moments of endings and beginnings. Just when you figure out how to walk upright in the world, just when you've gotten used to and comfortable with things as they are, cocky even, you find yourself once again knocked over, tossed aside, scattered about, turned around by the Fates, like Odysseus at one of life's many thresholds: You leave your job. Your kid goes off to college. You miscarry. You receive a diagnosis. You move. You turn fifty. You come out of the closet. You survive a global pandemic perhaps. In these moments, the well-trodden path of your days turns, bends, crooks, or dips, and you find yourself in a totally different and unfamiliar territory. If you're reading this, maybe you're there now. And maybe those basic questions that were once so firmly in your hands, things you assumed you knew the answers to, reemerge unanswered: "Where am I?" "Who am I?" "Who are you?" "What do I do now?" What was isn't any longer. Someone left. Someone arrived. Something broke. Something was repaired. Life changed. Now what can you do to mark this moment and find yourself again, to recognize that this is no longer that?

I finally lit the candle. The little dancing light cast shadows around the room. I wished I was surrounded by my people, not alone. I wished my mother was surrounded by her people and not alone. I wished we were acknowledging this moment together, not pretending, from a distance, that everything was okay and nothing unusual had happened. I wondered if I wasn't the only one. Maybe she'd forgotten her friends' names too. Or her sisters'. And if so, had it wrecked them as much as it had me, or did they see it as just unfortunate and to be expected? Did they miss the woman we'd all known, and did they feel as alone in this as I did? That one candle suddenly seemed insufficient. I needed more. I needed a candle for every person that should have been there with me, with her, and wasn't. In the dark descent that is dementia, I needed more light. And so I lit more. Each one I named. Every candle was lit for another friend or family member that I wanted to be in this with me, so that I would not feel so alone. I even lit some for our ancestors: her mother, her father, her aunt, her grandparents, all gone but needed now again. Ten, fifteen, twenty candles, burning until my little room was dancing in light and in shadow. And though there was still loss and absence and grief, my teary eyes looked around and could now see beauty too. For turning grief into beauty is how ritual renews the world again.

And so I sat quietly watching those candles burn down until each one, slowly, softly, faded away.

WHAT THEY LEFT BEHIND

While I'm quite familiar with individual memory loss, there is such a thing as a culture losing its memory. What does this have to do with a book on rituals? Everything.

Some of us in North America live every day of our lives in a collective amnesia that began when our ancestors arrived to this sweet land of liberty, forgetting the places, languages, names, and customs they came from in order to be folded into this great melting pot. Yet most of them didn't casually choose to come; more so, they were running away from something, enslaved or forced out. My own family ran. Life for Jews in the Pale of Settlement at the end of the nineteenth century was brutal. Double taxation, merciless restrictions to owning property, and forced conversions plagued them, and after the assassination of Tsar Alexander II, which was falsely blamed on the Jews, it got even worse. Waves of bloody pogroms spread throughout the Pale, forcing a tidal wave of Jewish refugees to get to anywhere but where they were. To this day, I hear stories of my grandfather's father, who was imprisoned by the Russian tsar for being a troublemaker, or *vildechaya*, but more probably the real crime was being a Jew.

So, the story goes, my great-grandmother visited him in prison every day, rolling him cigarettes and slipping them through the barred windows, and though the whys and wherefores get quite blurry, when he got out of prison, he fled to New York, leaving behind pretty much everything. After settling in Williamsburg, Brooklyn, in an apartment right above a paint shop, he sent letters for his wife to join him, and began to make a new life in the new world. This also meant to actively and purposefully forget the old ways: English was now their language, and Yiddish, the language my family had spoken for hundreds of years, was relegated to the home. Their Jewish-sounding last name was Americanized, and the Jewish rituals that had been woven into the fabric of my family's everyday life for hundreds of years began to badly fray.

My grandmother, who has told me this story countless times, also reminds me that when she was a young girl, she never even thought to look back, to ask about the names of her grandparents, to wonder what rural village her parents were born in, to consider where all her relatives' bones lay, even what everyday life was like back in the old country, a life her family had lived for centuries. Instead, Granny tells me that she only wanted to look forward, to be modern, to be American. Forward-looking is often a code word for forgetting.

The reason I bring this up is because *if* none of our families had fled or were forced to leave; *if* we all lived as they lived, in the same village as our ancestors, having grown up on the same stories that happened in that very place, surrounded by elders, grandparents, aunts, uncles, cousins, and neighbors who had known us since birth and were committed to our lives and well-being; and *if* we had been raised on the foods, the clothing, the crafts, and the traditions of that particular place, continued for generations, then the book you hold in your hands would not be necessary.

These pages are not a product of things working out here in the West but rather a response to things having gone astray.

Our orphaned culture is ritually bereft. We have far too few ways of remembering where we came from, who we belong to, how we got here, what we have, what was lost along the way, and in the face of that, what it all means. Ours is an amnestic culture, often turning from the past and away from death and our dead, toward the new, the next, the easier, the faster, the better, the more. This impulse to relentlessly move forward is a traumatized response to the enormous loss of all that once held so many generations together—the land, the language, the food, the village-mindedness, and especially the ritualized and ceremonial way of living life together. To write a book on rituals is to first and foremost acknowledge our modern culture's bankruptcy, a word whose Latin root, *rumpere*, doesn't just speak to an inability to repay debts but more so, a rupture, a fractioning of what was once whole and together.

One of the greatest losses that this book swims in the wake of is the relationship between the places that many of our ancestors left behind and the rituals that connected the people to those places, and therefore, to their ancestry and living memory.

Without this relationship to the place itself—to the cycle of the seasons, to when the rains would come and not come, to the forest's gift of bark and berry, to what animals arrived in the spring but left for the winter, to the moon's fullness or thinness and what harvest that spoke to, or to the jagged contours of the nearby mountain range and the myths remembered there—without living in the presence of all of that, a people can easily forget their ways of remembering.

So many of my own traditional Jewish rituals make little sense when taken out of their place-based understanding. For instance, we have a holiday called Sukkot, for which we build little impermanent huts and shake a bundle of branches made of three tree species from our ancestral homeland (willow, palm, myrtle) called in Hebrew a *lulav*, while holding a particular citrus fruit called an *etrog*, all of which, when shaken in the seven directions, attempt to compel the rains to fall. While I love the earthiness of this holiday, it makes little sense when detached from the place where these plants grew and where these rains might relieve a thirsty people and a parched ground. Yet we still do this ritual, thousands of years later, all over the world, because its memory continues to carry the imprint of its original purpose, a reminder that we too, like our ancestors before us, find ourselves wandering in the wilderness and similarly humbled and in awe of life's impermanence.

Without this fundamental relationship to place that grounds our rituals, many in our modern culture look to other cultures and people who still have some semblance of intactness and memory to their place-based traditions. There is something so profoundly nourishing to be in the presence of a people who remember their old ways, old stories, and old ceremonies. I've been hungry for that myself, having attended through the years sacred circle dances hosted by Shoshone elders, prayerful pipe ceremonies passed down by a Cherokee woman, and *inipi*, sweat lodges, held in a traditional Lakota way. But what begins as hunger can easily reveal itself as starvation. A teacher of mine, Stephen Jenkinson, once said, "Food makes hunger," which I understood to mean that it's not the absence of something that manifests the desire for it but rather it's the presence of it. When what appears before you is the richness of a ritual that has been carried, continued, and cared for by many generations, it is appetizing to want to be a part of it, to take from it, and maybe even to inadvertently borrow or steal it. What many refer to as cultural appropriation is a real possible threat in any book that aligns itself with rituals, this one included. Therefore, I want to caution you, my reader, to proceed with discernment and curiosity, as I have while writing this book, and that even the scent of a ritual might awaken the devastation brought on by your own cultural displacement and may compel you, consciously or unconsciously, to take from another culture's traditions. While that is understandable and lamentable, it is unacceptable. This book does not traffic in or promote cultural appropriation. Hard stop.

So then what? In the face of all the rituals that my, and perhaps your, people have lost and forgotten from their displacement, *what role should ritual now play in our modern lives?* If we can't remember the rituals of our ancestors and ancestral homeland, do we dare not touch them at all? Should we only be doing rituals that were passed down to us by our religion and culture, or can we partake in another people's rituals? Can rituals be an invented thing, made up in the moment without ties to any heritage?

This book attempts to be a gathering place for these questions, by both deeply respecting the traditions and cultures that have inspired some of the rituals found here, many of them from my own Jewish culture, while simultaneously courting something redemptive, and possibly even creative, that reclaims our capacities to make meaning with our days, even and especially when we don't know what to do.

A RITUAL RECOLLECTS

What does a ritual do, and how do you create one? I absolutely love what the author Michael Meade said about this in an interview with the *Sun* magazine: "Rituals, traditionally, are made from what's at hand. They are partly remembered and partly made up on the spot."*

To me, it doesn't seem so different from cooking: Maybe you have a recipe that's been passed down through the generations, like my mom's delicious *mandelbrot*, or mandel bread (almond bread in German), or maybe you experiment with the ingredients you already have in your kitchen to make something completely new. Cooking is a way to remember and experiment. When I make mandel bread these days, I use a recipe that my mother received from her mother, handed down through the generations from Eastern Europe (and before that, possibly Italy), but because I now live in California, I use California almonds—so the dessert becomes both the continuation of an ancestral food, coming from another time and place, and something else that fits my new circumstances.

Rituals, like recipes, have an adaptive ability. They can be both traditional and reimagined, remembered and renewed. But rituals also serve up another kind of nourishment: food for memory. We need them to remember *where* and *who* we came from, but we also need them to remember *who* and *where* we are now. And even though many cultures and religions have frozen and fenced in their rituals to preserve them from the very real threat of being lost or stolen through appropriation, assimilation, or eradication, the basic function of crafting a ritual, like crafting a meal, doesn't belong to any single people or person. Each one of us can and must learn how to cook up small ways to feed this greater remembering, for that is how rituals adapt and evolve.

Why do we need ritual? Simply put, we forget all the time and need to remember. But forgetting isn't wrong; it's human. Forgetting is what actually gives a ritual its purpose, which is to recollect our memories. Robin Wall Kimmerer puts it perfectly in her book *Braiding Sweetgrass*: "Our elders say that ceremony is the way we can remember to remember." What that means is that when forgetting inevitably occurs, we need ritualistic and ceremonial ways to come together and remember again, which is why

---

* Sy Safransky, "By Fire and Water: An Interview with Michael Meade," *Sun*, January 1994, https://www.thesunmagazine.org/issues/217/by-fire-and-water.

so many rituals are repetitive. *But remember what?* What it means to be human, which includes temporarily forgetting what it is to be one. Rituals are a way to keep taking our frayed and tattered memory and make it whole again.

How do you do ritual? Rituals can't be thought; they must be done. With your whole body—your hands, your feet, your mouth, your belly. With fire, earth, wind, or water. Alone or with witnesses. Doing them is the only way to keep them alive. Especially during threshold moments, a ritual can slow us down and gather us in to all that has been scattered by the speed and busyness of our days, re-collecting that time into some semblance of understanding and meaning. When the season shifts, a ritual can align us with the greater cycles, marking and remembering what it is we're leaving behind and where we're arriving. When a death anniversary comes, a ritual can remember our beloved dead and allow the grief and love that connects us to them to resurface. Or if we survive a traumatic experience, a ritual can call us back from that frightening edge and remind us of what a profound gift it is to receive our life back, the same but different.

Any culture worth a dime understands that memory, both personal and collective, is not static but alive and changing, and therefore must be maintained and tended to, like a living garden. Rituals are ways we can replant the seeds of our memory in the ground of our everyday life, our waking, our eating, our sleeping, and, especially, our losses and celebrations so that our memory might flower again. No matter the culture employing a ritual, it carries a similar cadence, a willingness to remember together again and again, season after season, year after year, and, especially, as my people say, *l'dor v'dor*, from generation to generation. This is how we can be responsible descendants—by keeping our collective memory alive.

IDENTIFYING THRESHOLDS

The rituals in this book stand in the doorway between endings and beginnings, otherwise known as threshold moments. I keep mentioning thresholds, but what are they and why is this book devoted to them? It's a pretty commonplace understanding to interpret threshold moments as passages or doorway moments, leading us from what is known and familiar to the frontier of what is unknown. Sometimes we choose to cross a threshold, and other times we're pushed, cajoled, or shoved over it, landing with our face planted in a new reality. As we stride or stumble, these moments often require us to leave something behind in order to receive something new; whether that's an identity, a commitment, a relationship, a home, a hard lesson, or another level of consciousness. For instance, a threshold moment can be the end of your single life and the beginning of a partnership or marriage. Or it could be coming out of the closet—the transition from a false sexual or gender identity into a genuine one. This book, as its title suggests, is devoted to moments of coming and going, entering or exiting, those times of change when something or someone arrives and/or something or someone departs.

But threshold is a funny word, as it doesn't actually refer to a doorway at all. While the folk etymology of the Old English word *prescold* is sometimes misinterpreted as that, its history is quite ambiguous. What stands clear is that the root of the word refers to the action of threshing. To thresh is to sift, beat, and trample grain, sometimes by hand, foot, or flail, sieving and separating the edible parts from the inedible straw. When you're rhythmically beating the straw, it can sound like hitting a drum, often accompanied by a threshing song to keep focused and stay energized. This is important to the thrust of this book because threshold moments are rhythmic moments when we can and must remember the underlying rhythm of our lives. And they ask for something more from us than just simply crossing over them. They are times when we must practice a certain kind of alert discernment so that we can distinguish the difference between what was and what is now.

Discernment is tough. Sometimes we might be living a new life but still think we're in our old one, like being newly retired but still waking up every day at 6:00 a.m. as we did when we were working. One of the key functions of ritual is that it can externalize what is happening so you can both bear witness to a threshold and be witnessed in it.

Each ritual in this book is accompanied by fundamental questions to help make these distinctions digestible, but the *doing* of each ritual is how the distinguishing happens. Every ritual included here is based in symbolic action, often paired with an element like fire, water, air, or earth. Symbolic action is doing something tangible to represent the deepest feelings that accompany beginning or ending whatever it is you are going through. Instead of just engaging your intellectual self, symbolic action lets you engage your emotional and sensual body too, and access all the hidden layers that live subterraneously. It's often done by burning, submerging, cleansing, washing, tossing, binding, ringing, breaking, lighting, shaking, and/or burying something. The power in doing that symbolic action is that it empowers us, not as a victim but as a participant, to make sense of what's changing and make those changes feel more tangible and real. It gives our body and soul a way to bridge and orient between two distinct worlds.

A RITUAL COOKBOOK

Let's talk about how to use this book.

Since I've been talking so much about food, consider treating this book more like a cookbook, meaning it's not meant to be read once and done. Rather, it's designed to be used—a faithful companion for when life expectedly or suddenly changes and you need some meaning to stand on. A good sign of this book's usefulness will be if it becomes dog-eared, dented, and dirty from years of not just your use, but others' too—filled with fingerprints from the many hands that you passed it to.

This book consists of thirty-six different life or daily thresholds. Each chapter is broken down into two sections: The first section is "the what": an investigation into that particular threshold—historically, culturally, anthropologically, etymologically, mythopoetically. I strongly believe that to reimagine a ritual, it should be informed by and be a response to the culture and time they come from. That way the ritual can be, as author Starhawk suggests, "A symbolic act of activism that shifts consciousness."*

The second section is "the how": a tangible ritual recipe that you can easily cook up or use as fodder to create your own. And as with any cookbook, you can just skip to the recipe, because sometimes you just need to make food and eat.

This book is designed so you can easily and readily reach for a tangible way to make meaning when you need it most. If the recipe has ingredients you're allergic to, substitute them. For instance, if you don't resonate with my suggestion to burn something and instead want to bury it, go with your gut. The material is symbolic, the meaning is yours to make.

The heart of all rituals is relationships. But not just between people. Each thing you use in your ritual has the potential to be deepened in the ways you relate to it. Just like eating. You can get takeout and eat dinner immediately, or you can buy the ingredients from a grocery store and make dinner yourself, which requires more planning and takes a longer time. Or you can buy produce from a local farmer or plant seeds in a garden and grow food yourself. Ritual is very similar. Each object you use can be a doorway to endless relationships. For instance, in the chapter on death anniversaries, I ask you to use candles. You can absolutely buy these candles and I do all the time. But

---

* "Homebound: The Roots and Shoots of Earth-based Community with Starhawk," May 15, 2020, in *For the Wild*, podcast, 28:45, https://forthewild.world/listen/homebound-the-roots -and-shoots-of-earth-based-community-with-starhawk-182?rq=182.

you can also make them. You can procure beeswax from a beekeeper, learn about bees, and even attempt to keep a hive of your own, eventually making candles from your own beeswax. How remarkable would that be? There is an endless web of relationship potential, which leads us deeper and deeper into remembering.

But baby steps please. Maybe just start with buying a candle from a store. This is a practice in leaning into the edge of your capacity but not over it. As with any relationship, there is no getting "there"—it's all about the "here." The health of any relationship is maintained by the degree you take care of it, here and now. But in doing so, maybe you'll notice that bit by bit, these ritual-meals can start to resemble beautiful feasts.

MANY VOICES

This book is not an aria. I haven't lived all possible lives; I am a queer, Jewish cis man, and can speak only from my own experience. So I put out a call to which two hundred people answered, each willing to participate in an hour-long conversation with me about a moment in their life, large or small, that forever changed them. Some of those I spoke to recounted miraculous stories that clearly became the centerpiece of their lives and identities, like Jeanie, who at three years old was mistakenly run over by her father, an accident that cracked her pelvis and permanently transformed the way she could be in her body for the rest of her life (Jeanie is now a pelvis specialist). Others I spoke to shared silent moments, significant to them but invisible to everyone else, like Carl, who was born with cerebral palsy but was forced to grapple with his own mortality and frailty only after contracting a chronic illness. I interviewed a husband who longed to finally open up about his wife's many miscarriages and how they impacted him. And I listened to a mother speak about her own evolution witnessing her son transition into her daughter. Each conversation was profound, intimate, moving, and tender as these individuals shared how this threshold fundamentally altered their lives.

Ritual is a complicated topic, and I never assumed that we were on the same page when talking about it, and so each interview contained the question "How do you define ritual?" Just asking that question gave most people pause and produced incredible insight that went on to inform the very architecture of this book. Here are some of their responses to the question of what ritual is:

"It's a language for meaning-making."

"Something you do to mark occasions, out of traditions."

"A meeting place where the spiritual meets the physical. The unseen meets the seen. The formless meets the form, concretizing the sacred."

"I see ritual as a cue or road sign, to point me in the right direction."

"Ritual is a mini-journey. You start somewhere, sometimes you have a destination that you seek in the ritual and sometimes not."

"Slowing things down so that something can happen, so that something can appear."

"A way to ask for support, to offer gratitude or express awe at the wonder of the world."

"A way to get out of my mind and into my animal body and listen to what's around me."

"Ordering, removing stuff, reordering."

"Ritual brings change with it while acknowledging that change has happened."

"A ritual says I am, or we are, here."

I love all of these. To me, a ritual midwifes us through transition, helping us acknowledge the change and transform us from who we were to who we are now.

RITUAL, NOT ROUTINE

Let's talk about routine for a moment. Routines are not rituals. Even though many people confuse them, they are distinct and one does not mean the other. The etymology can help us distinguish them. The word "routine" comes from the French word *route*, which means a beaten path or a way. Routine describes the trodden course in which we can get from Point A to Point B. We do routines every day. They are repetitive actions that bring continuity and order. Whether your bedtime routine is to brush and floss, wash the dishes, put your kids' toys away, or draw the curtains, these actions are inherently goal-oriented, meaning that you're doing them to end the day and get your butt to bed.

Rituals have a totally different purpose. Sometimes they can look just like a routine, but the distinction is that they're imbued with meaning and purpose. For instance, before you go to bed, a ritual can simply be to light a candle and wonder about the day ending: Who did you meet? What did you learn? Do you have any regrets? What did you fail at? What were the small wins? What are you grateful you still have?

Ritual is a way to turn toward the big and small beginnings and endings in our life. Whether we're completing a job, starting a relationship, ending a big trip, beginning a new year, or simply waking up in the morning, rituals create "outlook moments" that let us reflect and find stability and calm in the midst of change. Sure, a routine can also provide stability, but a ritual can help us approach these times with curiosity and wonder. For instance, if, gods forbid, you receive a diagnosis, ritualizing that moment can give you a way to ask: *Why did this happen? Why me? Why am I still alive? What now?*—without the demand for an answer. To put it another way, the psychologist Esther Perel suggests, "Routines get us through the day. Rituals guide us through life."

I want to add something important here: Maybe performing a ritual seems easy and doable. If that's you, great; skip ahead. However, there's a real possibility that a ritual may seem totally foreign to you and, at times, just not possible. Perhaps the first thought that comes to mind is *I just couldn't* or *I don't have time* or *I've never done it before*, and that's totally fine. But what distinguishes a ritual from a routine is that it does indeed ask something more from you that you might not be accustomed to. It might feel like a stretch or a hurdle, but doing it anyway is actually what gives the ritual its prominence. So don't worry if this feels a bit strange to you, that's actually expected. But do ask yourself this: Can you do it anyway? Can you rise to the occasion and not shy away from it? If you can try something a bit unusual, you might find that it also brings unusual value to you or your family during those transitional times.

BEARING *and* BEING WITNESS

While some of these chapters are written for you, others are written for those who love and need you.

So many of our Western cultural values center on self-efficiency and mastery, and you'll be tempted with a heroic mindset that sounds like "I can do it myself," but sometimes you actually can't or shouldn't. For instance, while writing the chapter on rituals for aging childlessly, I spoke to a middle-aged woman who had never thought about doing a ritual to mark this time because, she said, "I could never do it myself. Even talking about it now, my throat gets tight. My heart starts pumping. I get scared thinking I need to mark this alone. I just can't be in charge of this and could never design it myself. I need others. And the only way would be if someone else, someone I trusted, could guide me into this."

There are many moments like this throughout the book when I will strongly encourage you to quietly hand it over to a friend and say, "I need you. Would you help me?" These times when you can't continue alone are not less than, but actually are how rituals bind people together. Some thresholds are too big to cross by yourself.

There are times when you may need to consider who to invite for a ritual. Creating a guest list for a ritual has two significant purposes. First, it gives you an opportunity to participate in a reflective process—reviewing who at this life stage matters to you and to renew those bonds. Second, it gives you a chance to exclude those who don't. *Exclude? Excuse me?* Yes, to limit your guest list to a small number and intentionally choose to not invite everyone. There is wisdom to this. In her book *The Art of Gathering*, author Priya Parker asks essential questions when creating a guest list: "Who not only fits but also helps fulfill the gathering's purpose? Who threatens the purpose? Who, despite being irrelevant to the purpose, do you feel obliged to invite?"

Excluding skillfully can help you create a guest list of people who can help hold the ritual's purpose. Here are my own questions to ask yourself when considering who should be there:

1. Is this person committed to my well-being?
2. Can I share vulnerably with this person?
3. Would they show up for me when I needed them?
4. Would I show up for them if they needed me?
5. Are they willing to look at things more deeply?
6. Can they listen well?

Lastly, many of the rituals in this book ask these guests to become witnesses. Witnessing is not watching. Witnessing, or "with-nessing" as the author Báyò Akómoláfé calls it, is an act of staying with what is happening in the ritual no matter what feelings, questions, or uncertainties arise. It's not about giving opinions or trying to fix anything, but rather, witnessing is a profound and generous act of listening and presence. Endings and beginnings can be disorienting, overwhelming, and vulnerable, and having a witness to steady you, remind you, encourage you, and deeply listen to you can be a stabilizing and affirming force when crossing that threshold.

PREPARING RITUAL TIME *and* SPACE

Ritual is a funny thing to a modern mind. We're so used to things happening when we press a button, like watching a movie or starting a car. But ritual isn't like that. Rituals are vessels that invite in something vulnerable, healing, and alive. Therefore, ritual spaces need to be approached like a courtship. The space needs to be prepared well. The objects need to be laid out beautifully. Think of it like setting up a stage for something special to occur. Setting the space beforehand can let the spirit of the ritual enter.

Like a play, all rituals have a beginning, a middle, and an end, so while they are happening, they require a held container and a similar courtesy to being at the theatre: make sure your cell phones are turned off, all distractions are eliminated, and you are fully present, being attentive to what's unfolding before you.

Also, be mindful about how you enter and exit a ritual. I've been a part of more than enough failed rituals to advise you: Don't just jump into it. Take time to have small talk, to set the altar, to admire the place itself, to nosh on a little food. Don't underestimate the power of arriving and settling down.

As much as you might think getting to the meat and potatoes of the ritual is the priority, it actually isn't. Rituals rise and fall depending on *how* they are approached, as the way you come to them impacts what comes *from* them. For instance, many rituals in the book begin and end by lighting or extinguishing a candle, singing songs, or with silence. These transitional moments help us settle in and be less driven to get the finished product, "the healing," or whatever your desired outcome is. The more you can give yourself and everyone else the spaciousness to slow down and show up, the more that can show up within the ritual.

Lastly, let's talk location, location, location. Wherever you choose the ritual to be, prioritize privacy. Ritual needs intimacy—a willingness for all gathered to come closer to something and to let it reveal itself. Whether that's anger, grief, or love, privacy provides a container for these expressions to come on their own without the fear of being self-conscious that someone else might be nosing around. Find a place where you are not going to have to contend with other people coming and going. For instance, in the chapter on divorce, the ritual asks you to approach your grievance and grief with a felt sense of safety. You need to be in a judgment-free space where the alchemy of the ritual can bubble and boil from your attentiveness. It needs a steady flame of focus where you can eventually feel safe enough to let the rage and sobs take you in order to pass through them.

A random passer-by can actually disrupt and undo the ritual's rhythm because they immediately bring to the participants a sense of self-consciousness. As with falling asleep, if you're too aware of yourself and what you are trying to do, it doesn't happen. So find a place where you don't have to worry about strangers prodding. Plus, in the case of an earnest, nosy voyeur wondering "What are you doing?" your witness/guardian can head them off so that you can remain in the ritual container. Keeping the container whole is essential to staying in the ritual.

IN CONCLUSION

Ritual is always our most trusted guide during times of change. When everything is unsettled, ungrounded, and unpredictable, ritual can refocus us back to what matters. When things seem so fast and wild, ritual can slow us down and remind us what we are missing. And when fear and doubt pervade our waking moments, ritual can help us let go of what we're grasping onto and reconnect us to courage and resilience. When people die, jobs are lost, babies are born, relationships end or begin, the world panics—ritual is there for us as a pathfinder through change. The more we can learn how to be in relationship with change itself as it happens—which is the very function of ritual—the more we can gracefully change too.

One of the interviews in this book was with a mother whose two-year-old daughter had been diagnosed with leukemia. After two and a half years of chemotherapy, the last day of treatment was, as you can imagine, poignant and quite special. Her daughter had the privilege of ringing the hospital's survivor bell three times to mark the end of her chemo. The sound, Karin said, was visceral and "filled me with full joy but also sorrow for those who didn't get to this point."

Ringing the bell three times was not only a symbolic action to distinguish the end of her daughter's treatment but a way to recognize how miraculous it was to arrive at that moment with sorrow and joy. A ritual's motivation is to compel us to "pivot toward the sacred," a phrase coined by French anthropologist Arnold van Gennep. Pivoting to the sacred is a ritual's way to turn us toward and not away from the Great Mystery, the Great Uncertainty of our lives, which is always changing. It is a way to make these moments of hello and goodbye holy and beautiful.

And so, with that in mind, I invite you to enter into this book accompanied by a 1,500-year-old Jewish prayer called the *shehecheyanu* that my people say to welcome all of these threshold moments, remembering once again the amazing grace it took to arrive right here, right now, and distinguish it as holy:

Blessed are you, Eternal One, Spirit of the World,
who has granted us life, sustained us,
and brought us to reach this time.

RITUALS
for EVERY DAY

Morning Time

This is a wonderful day. I've never seen this one before.

—Maya Angelou

Maybe it comes in gently on its own. The soft light peeking through the darkness. The heavy rise and fall of your eyelids, a blinking tug-of-war between more sleep and daybreak. Perhaps the alarm clock brings it in. The incessant bells and whistles faithfully hammering you to get up and at 'em, soldier. Or it comes with the baby's crying, pulling you from the depths of your dreams back into the grind of parental obligation. However it is that you wake up from sleep, do you just jump into your day? When your eyes open, do you immediately go for your phone? When you get out of bed, are you already onto what needs to get done? Or have you skipped over that most subtle but monumental moment: You woke up this morning.

When I was very little, I was taught to wake up whispering. That the first words off my lips in the morning should be the *Modeh Ani*, a six-hundred-year-old Hebrew song of praise and awe. For so long, I didn't understand why. "Just do it," my cranky Jewish teacher, Mrs. Siegel, told me. "Do it the moment you open your eyes, before a thought sneaks into your mind, before the day carries you away. Do it to say thank-you to God." As a five-year-old I had no idea what God even meant (still don't), but she didn't care. She just wanted me to learn the mechanism—wake and thank. I've wrestled with the obligation to do this, but the older I get, the more I understand why she was so adamant. Waking up is a privilege. No matter how many ways you slice it, that's the truth of it. And it's never a given, so when it does arrive, my practice is to remember that—to remember I'm on the receiving end of a gift, the gift of another day to love this life. I've actually sung the *Modeh Ani* every morning since then, and by doing so, I've come to realize that it's actually an act of hospitality—a way to welcome and be welcomed into the good graces of more life.

I say I've wrestled because, frankly, I'm increasingly distracted when I wake up. Against all common sense, I keep my phone next to my bed. Foolishly, I use it as an alarm clock, and once it's in my hands, I'm a goner. Like many of us, I get easily seduced into the information trap, lying in bed and pulling a slot machine of news, text messages, Instagram scrolls, scheduling alerts. There are so many days where I realize *Fuck, where did half an hour just go?* as the morning reliably gets three steps ahead of me. The phone isn't the culprit though—it's the accomplice. The real thief that steals this moment of praise and thanks is an underlying belief that the moment doesn't matter. That whether or not I pause to recognize this holy gem of my life carries no consequence in my life. That thing I said before about being welcomed into the "good graces of more life," that sounds nice and all but rather esoteric, and more realistically I'd say that the moment I open my eyes, my attention is pulled in thirteen thousand different directions. Maybe you too? In a way, pausing in the morning seems antithetic to the morning itself. My excuse is: "I just don't have time." I too often witness the morning's urgency checkmate any attempt at a real lunge toward gratitude.

But here's the thing: Certain routines in the morning are nonnegotiable. Brushing, flossing, showering always happen no matter how rushed I am, because caring for my body is sacrosanct. I would never use the excuse "I have too much to do" as a way of shirking my responsibility to brush my teeth. Yet somehow tending to my spirit is the first thing to be sacrificed on the altar of no time.

In addition to bodily hygiene, we need soulful hygiene every morning, a way to cleanse the gunk that builds up over our energy, vision, and purpose and reconnect us back to a deeper remembering of life's basic hospitality. Especially on those mornings where the anxiety, futility, and hopelessness hang heavy and thick, where all we can see is ourselves and our woes, we need to open a small window of time for soul maintenance—time to put our bodies on the earth, or our hands in some water, or our face toward the sun, and reorient ourselves toward all the relationships that comprise our lives.

My friend Lauren does this every morning—she rises before the sun, and no matter how much her mind resists it, she heads outside. As the night sky fades and the light swells, she looks up and greets the morning star, breathing deeply. There is nothing fancy in this. She breathes and listens as the dawn chorus of birds wake and sing their melodies to the rising sun. Then Lauren adds her own voice to the mix, offering songs that greet the light and remind her that she belongs to it all. Sometimes it's whatever earworm is on repeat, like the Beatles' "Here Comes the Sun," and other days it's songs she wrote or made up on the spot. But all of them are songs of praise—simple and profound ways she greets the new light.

She then turns her attention, quite naturally, to notice everything else around her—the towering, proud redwood trees, the quick purple finches flitting through the lichen-encrusted branches, the sweet, damp morning air, the wisp of feathery cirrus clouds slowly moving right overhead. It sounds so basic, like how I would approach a neighbor that I would see on the street: "Hi, how are you? Good to see you. How is your family? Enjoy the day." Her greetings sound similar. They are one of acknowledgment—a way of saying: "I see you, I am here with you, how blessed we are to be alive together today, how many ways that almost didn't happen and yet here we are again." The more she greets all those around her, the more animate the world around her becomes.

There's a clue to how this happens disguised in the etymology of the word "greet"— the original sense of the word coming from the Proto-Indo-European word *gher*, meaning "to resound." In other words, when we offer a greeting, it reverberates and swells, like an echo, bouncing from you out into the world and back to you again. To greet is an incredibly simple act of participating in the resounding renewal of the world, and the world's renewal of you.

Renewal is needed because every one of us forgets ten thousand times a day. We forget the little and the big. We forget what's really valuable and what matters. We forget to say thank-you and to ask permission. We forget to wonder where things come from and how they miraculously landed in our hands. We forget to marvel at our health and the health of those around us until it's gone. We forget to appreciate the clean water we drink, the clean air we breathe, and everything our ancestors gave and gave up for our lives to be what they are. But forgetting isn't wrong. Actually, it's part and parcel of being human, which is why we have ritual. Ritual is a kind of choreography for remembering what we've forgotten and seeing again what's gone invisible. It doesn't shame forgetting, it recognizes it as part of the whole dance.

Most days waking up is anything but inspiring. Most mornings it's "Mom, I peed in my bed," or "Shit, I overslept," or, "Ugh, I hate my job." The grind of life is all we can see, and just getting through the morning is all we can do, and doing anything more meaningful is a pipe dream. But that's why the heart of ritual is repetition. It's not a one-and-done thing—it's something we must return to every morning because every morning needs us to refresh our vision and see the world anew. Establishing a morning-time ritual is a way to court life, to call it closer to you so that you can once again be enamored with it, listen to it, fall in love with it again and see it as if it were the first or the last time you ever have or will. It's no coincidence that the original sense of the word "greet" can also mean to "cry" or "weep" in Old English—remembering how the impermanence of it all can turn a simple greeting into an outpouring of love because who knows when it will happen again.

Greeting doesn't have to be fancy or complicated. It doesn't always need to end dramatically or in catharsis. It is, simply, *intimacy in action*. It is a willingness to know that what you love is here as temporarily as you are, and through your wondering eyes, beautiful words, or kind actions you can recognize each other on this long, long road. And in your greeting, you can actually nourish what nourishes you or what author Martín Prechtel calls, "an honest attempt to give life to what gives us life."[*]

THE RENEWAL RITUAL

Today, I woke up parched. My mouth was arid and dry, eager to be wet again. My tongue was beached like a dried-up fish, and my lips were cracked like the clay ground after a season of drought. But thirst isn't necessarily bad. It reminds me to begin the day empty and receiving. Thirst tethers me to this Earth, whispering that I am no more than a small body of living waters, needing to return again and again to the source. And it is through thirst that I can feel the depth of my longing for water, and the water's longing for me. Waking up thirsty is to remember my relationship with life. To remember that water is life.

But this morning I woke up with another kind of thirst—anxiety. At first, I didn't know what to do with it or how to soothe it. I tried to ignore it, to keep up with my morning routines—stretching, showering, coffee, emails—to stay on track, but the thirst followed me. No matter what I did, it became impossible to do anything, let alone be comfortable in my own body. This overwhelming worry, which my father had and his father before him, rides on the coattails of isolation and scarcity, a troubling belief that says: "You don't have enough" or "You are not enough." This spell of insufficiency convinces me that no matter how much I have, no matter how much I've done, or how much I've given, I need to do, earn, be, take more. As much as I consume, I find

---

[*] Martín Prechtel, *The Smell of Rain on Dust: Grief and Praise* (Berkeley, CA: North Atlantic Books, 2015), 165–66.

there is little fulfillment from this incessant thirst. And what I constantly interpret as "my anxiety" is actually rooted in an impoverished culture that convinces me to never be satisfied, to forget that the real treasures are in plain sight here and now.

But this isn't true for all cultures. Robin Wall Kimmerer, the author of *Braiding Sweetgrass*, speaks about indigenous cultures all over the world being rooted in gratitude. She tells of a school near her farm in upstate New York, the ancestral homeland of the Onondaga Nation, part of the Haudenosaunee Confederacy, where the children don't pledge their allegiance to the flag every morning, but instead recite the Thanksgiving Address, an ancient pledge of gratitude, called *Ohén:ton Karihwatéhkwen*, which translates to mean "What we say before we do anything important." This morning ritual greets all the relationships that connect the people— to Mother Earth, to the waters, to the food plants, to the medicine herbs; to the families of trees, birds, winds, directions; to the sun, the moon, the stars, and all the gifts of creation—and reminds the children that there is a protocol in placing gratitude. As Kimmerer puts it, "You can't listen to the Thanksgiving Address without feeling wealthy. And, while expressing gratitude seems innocent enough, it is a revolutionary idea. In a consumer society, contentment is a radical proposition. Recognizing abundance rather than scarcity undermines an economy that thrives by creating unmet desires. . . . The Thanksgiving Address reminds you that you already have everything you need."[*]

This Renewal Ritual surfs on the same current of gratitude. It is a way for your rising body to greet the waters, to do this before you do anything important, because water is life. This is a moment of gratitude but not just of being grateful. This is way to bring your longing and worry, your overwhelm and underwhelm, your forgetfulness and doubts, to the waters. To give over the burden of scarcity and be filled up and enlivened again. As you feel the waters cleanse your hands, wet your lips, awaken your face, this ritual can bring you closer to water, which might help you remember the precious and abundant gift that you are made of—a gift that animates this world.

Prepare

Intentions

May I wake up thankful. May I be in a daily relationship to water. May I practice reorienting from scarcity to abundance. May I connect to

---

[*] Robin Wall Kimmerer, *Braiding Sweetgrass: Indigenous Wisdom, Scientific Knowledge, and the Teachings of Plants* (Minneapolis: Milkweed Editions, 2013).

water before technology. May I tangibly feel life on my hands, lips, mouth, face, and feet.

You Will Need
- A pitcher and basin of water
- A glass
- A small towel

When
Within my Jewish tradition, we have a ritual to wash our hands right upon waking up called *Negel Vasser* in Yiddish. While the custom is focused on purification, there is also a hidden thread of wisdom that says: Don't do anything before letting water touch your hands and mouth—first, renew yourself.

I've tried this ritual long after I am out of bed, but I don't recommend it. By the time you get to the bathroom, you might already be distracted. Bring a pitcher and basin of water to your nightstand. Preparing this could also be a beautiful ritual at night and a gift to your morning.

Begin
There are four rounds to this ritual. This might be the ideal assembly of steps for you, or if you're like me and constantly need to do it your own way, reorder them, eliminate a couple, or add your own. There is no orthodoxy in this, just encouragement to let yourself meet the waters every morning with an open heart.

First: Hands
Slowly pour the water on your hands or even on the little tips of your fingers. Feel the coolness of the water running down your skin. Listen to the drops of water running from your hands into the bowl. Sense how alive the water is. Since you are just waking up, and you're already moving slowly, take your time with this.

As you pour the water, ask yourself: *What am I holding that the water can cleanse?*

Dry your hands.

HELLO, GOODBYE

Second: Eyes

Pour water on your hands and gently bring them to your face and your eyes. Take a few moments as you feel the fresh dampness cleanse and awaken you.

As you feel the water wash over your face, ask yourself: *What am I not seeing that the water can remind me to look toward?*

Dry your face.

Third: Feet

Over the bowl, pour a little water on your feet and toes, welcoming your return from the dream journeys. Give your sole a kind rub, then cleanse your feet over the bowl as the water runs over them.

As you cleanse your feet, ask yourself: *Where haven't I gone that the water is reminding me to go?*

Dry your feet.

Fourth: Mouth

Lastly, pour a glass and put it to your lips. Don't immediately drink it. First feel the longing—the desire to put the water in your mouth, perhaps witnessing your saliva rising up to meet it—water rushing to meet water. Let the water slowly cross your lips and run into your mouth, like a stream meeting the ocean.

As you drink, ask yourself: *What haven't I said that the water is reminding me to say?*

Dry your mouth.

Conclude

As you come to the end of the water ritual, consider lingering just a little longer and take inspiration from the Thanksgiving Address by directing your thoughts toward greeting and praising more life. Call to mind other elements—the light, the air, the earth, the directions, the plants, the trees, the birds etc.—and acknowledge all the abundance and messages they bring, while offering gratitude for being on the receiving end of their gifts.

Questions for Further Reflection

- How does this ritual reorient me from a "not enough" mindset toward being grateful for what I have?
- How does this ritual change my speed, mindset, focus in the morning?
- How does my relationship to water change?
- What is nourished through this ritual?

THE BEAUTY *in the* BASIC RITUAL

I have a dear friend who is struggling in her marriage. For her, waking up every day is like scaling a mountain—dancing around the tension with her partner, preparing her kids for school and herself for work. The last thing she is thinking about is gratitude, because frankly, she isn't feeling it. She is feeling stress, anger, regret, uncertainty. She called the other day, and as we spoke, she told me that she didn't really need to talk. She just needed to hear my voice, to know that someone out there cared for her and could, in a small way, remind her of the simple joys and basic goodness that she is having trouble seeing in this moment.

After a pause, I reminded her that I loved her, that I know how hard this must be. Because she's been my friend forever, I made a request. I asked her to take a moment out of her morning and sit with something simple, small, and familiar. Maybe that is a fresh cup of coffee or that maple tree she loves so much in front of her porch or that soft wool blanket that her grandmother made. I asked her to just sit with it for a couple of minutes and see it again. She asked me what I meant by *again*. I told her that by *again* I meant as if it was the first or the last time she was seeing it. In other words, I asked her to renew her relationship to one thing she had and loved. Something small, something doable. And by doing that, she could practice renewing her capacity to see not just the *basic goodness*—a term coined by Tibetan spiritual teacher Chögyam Trungpa Rinpoche*—of the thing she loved but that that goodness might also be echoed back to her, reminding her of her own *basic goodness*. With all the fighting and emotional turmoil, all the craziness of her days, I thought she needed to feel the beauty in something simple.

---

* "Basic Goodness," Wikipedia, https://en.wikipedia.org/wiki/Basic_goodness.

HELLO, GOODBYE

The purpose of this Beauty in the Basic Ritual is to practice renewing our relationship to something already in our morning as a way of renewing ourselves. The greatest challenge to this ritual even getting off the ground is our willingness to see beauty as something as quotidian and necessary as breakfast. Both are nourishment for our day.

This ritual centers on doing something ordinary but doing it in a new way. Whether that is by making it more beautifully, doing it more carefully, or admiring it more closely, the point is to give our complete attention to the little things we love and, by doing so, to see them again with new eyes, which might renew how we see our own life.

Prepare

Intentions

May I practice a moment to wonder or praise something basic and ordinary. May I renew my relationship to these overlooked or familiar things as a way to return to life's basic goodness.

Begin

Step 1

Choose one action you already do every morning, like making coffee, washing dishes, slicing bread, or taking a shower. The more ordinary the better.

Step 2

Right before you do it, ask yourself this one question: *If this was the first or last time I was doing this, how would I do it differently?*

Step 3

Do it. Don't overthink it, but let that question adjust the way you do the thing you normally do on autopilot. What changes? What do you notice that you had stopped seeing? How does that impact the way you hold your mug or wash your dishes or lotion your body? Can you find the edge between getting it done and making it beautiful?

Conclude

Offer some praise to the very basic thing you just did, either out loud, in a journal, or to a friend or partner. For instance, "I love my morning coffee. I love holding the warm mug in my hands, smelling its delicious aroma, and the comfort that it brings to my day." See if you can continue to uplift this morning routine with your words. Can your words continue to make this doing even more beautiful?

Questions for Further Reflection
- What am I able to see again that I didn't see before?
- What did I remember about my own basic goodness?
- How did this ritual impact the rest of my day? Did it help me appreciate anything else?

Bedtime

So long, farewell, auf Wiedersehen, good night.
I hate to go and leave this pretty sight.

—Oscar Hammerstein II, *The Sound of Music*

The day is winding down and those familiar signals are calling you to sleep: The book slips as your eyes doze. The credits unexpectedly roll, marking the end of the movie. Your alarm gently reminds you it's time to retire. And with that, the nighttime choreography commences—the dance of brushing, washing up, closing, plugging in, quieting, and crawling under. Yet, aside from the functional routines that prepare our homes and our bodies for rest, what do we do to meaningfully mark the day's end? Is it enough to just call it a day and head to bed, or is this actually a moment lost in transition? If so, what would it take to slow down and do something to remember that, against all odds, you lived to see the end of another day?

Bedtime doesn't seem to be a big deal. We do it every night. We go through the same routines and end up in the same place. It's a very familiar daily transition, but because it's so routine, we can lose sight of it meaning anything at all. In fact, when we treat it this way, bedtime becomes a means to an end, meaning that its purpose is to just get to sleep. Believe me, I'm 100 percent guilty of this. At the end of a long day of work, after an hour of zoning out on a new Netflix series, there is nothing I want more than to be horizontal and drifting. And yet, in all the ways I turn toward bed, I'm actually turning away from something else quite meaningful.

Our greatest daily fantasy is to believe our lives will continue on indefinitely tomorrow. Because of that we can end our day without fanfare, without gratitude, and without an open heart. Just like in the movie *Groundhog Day*, there is a belief, if only an unconscious one, that waking up again is inevitable. But plenty of people don't. I'm not saying this as a downer but rather as a great reminder that every night we have an opportunity to not take our lives for granted. Every night we get a chance to look at all we lost and all we still have and be thankful we still do. Every night, we can awaken from the trance of inevitability and remember again that today wasn't guaranteed, yet we were granted the gift of it. And we may be granted the same gift again tomorrow. The more we can ritualize the ending of our day and bring some semblance of praise and thanks before we hit the hay, the more we might wake up the next day capable of choosing life again.

These bedtime rituals are ways to bring more meaning and reflection to the last moments of your day. Two are for you, and one is intended for those of you with children. Like all rituals, they ask you to slow down and practice renewing your willingness to wonder again. To wonder at how much you've been on the receiving end of life and to gather that in, as Kahlil Gibran says in *The Prophet*, to "sleep with a prayer for the beloved in your heart and song of praise upon your lips."

THE ANOINT *and* ACCOUNT RITUAL

A lot happened today. Some things took off and other things crash-landed. There were moments when you felt heard and others when you were misunderstood. You ran here and there, and there were times when things seemed smooth and to be going according to plan and others when you had to roll with the unpredictable. So much happens in one day but ask yourself: When do you take account of it all? When do you look around and take stock of all you gave, all you lost, and all that you still have? Every day we achieve, we fail, we figure out, we learn, we feel, we connect, and more often than not, we just go to bed and start all over again.

This ritual is meant to be done in collaboration with your nighttime routine. Specifically, it is inspired by my own bedtime ritual of lotioning my body. After a long day, I don't want to give anymore. I'm gived out, and I want to receive touch. My body is sore and exhausted, and rubbing my hands and feet, my temples and shoulders with oils and lotion feels soothing and caring to myself. I also get the sense that I am anointing my body each night as an act of hospitality, just like they used to in ancient Egypt, Greece, and Israel, welcoming this body back home. In a way, it's a quiet time to receive myself as an honored guest. During this quiet time, I reflect upon the past twenty-four hours as a way to process and metabolize those hours so that I don't have to carry the day's stresses to bed. The purpose of this ritual is to take account at the day's end by receiving your body and yourself with kindness and consideration.

Prepare

Intentions

May I honor my body and all it gave today. May I reflect on the highs and lows of the day so that it can settle in my system. May I not take today for granted.

You Will Need

- Lotion, essential oil, or body butter
- A candle
- A soft place to sit
- A journal
- Silence or gentle music

When

Let this be one of the last things you do for the night. Make sure all your responsibilities are taken care of so that you can return to your body and let the day settle.

Where

You can do this either in the bathroom, your bedroom, or anywhere where you have the space and safety to sit comfortably naked.

Ways to Reflect

Sometimes I like to speak out loud and hear myself process what's on my mind and heart. Other times, I like to journal. Choose what best suits your style of reflecting.

Begin

Candle

In a dark room, light the candle. Let your eyes adjust, and allow a minute or two to simply sit there silently—don't let this be another thing that you need to get done so that you can get to bed. Let this be a time to consecrate yourself and slow down with ease and grace.

Anoint

After each "taking account" question, gently rub and massage a different part of your body. If you want to do this another way, like responding to the questions first and then lotioning your body, please do. However you do it, let your touch carry care.

Taking Account

Do this your way. If you'd like to only explore one question, do so. These are simply prompts to inspire reflection. There is no right way to do this:

Today, I gave myself to _____.
Today, I was given _____.
Today, I succeeded at _____.
Today, I fell short at _____.
Today I learned _____.
Today I trusted _____.
Today I doubted _____.
Tonight, I am thankful for _____.
Tonight, I don't need to carry _____.
Tonight, I wish that _____.
Tonight, I don't take for granted _____.

Conclude

Feel yourself having been gathered in. Notice your breathing, how your skin and muscles feel, and especially, the state of your mind. Let yourself linger a bit longer in this quiet, dark space before extinguishing the candle.

Nighttime Gifts *for the* Morning

Who doesn't like receiving a little gift out of the blue? I love arriving to a dear friend's home, and because they know me well, they already have my favorite potato chips out. Or those sweet drawings that my seven-year-old neighbor colors for me and leaves at my door to find when I come home from the grocery store. It feels good to be remembered.

But is it possible to remember yourself too? For instance, in the locker room at the local pool, I would imagine how tired I might be after my swim. As a little gift to my future self, I would meticulously fold my towel and change of clothing so that when I came out of the pool, everything was already laid out nicely. It always felt so nice to come back to that. It's one of the reasons I make my bed every morning—so that after a long day of work, my nighttime self feels looked after and has a nicely made bed to crawl into.

I started doing this at night too. I wanted to give a gift to my morning self. So I've taken to writing an affirmative reminder in pencil on my morning coffee filter. Something that says, "you're needed," or "keep going," or "stay curious today." Just a little something that might be exactly what I need to hear the next morning.

You can do this little ritual for yourself or for another. When you do it, ask yourself: *What is a beautiful message or gift I could leave the night before? What do I or another need to hear in the morning?* Whomever it's for, consider it as a way of saying: "You are looked after and remembered."

The Worry Box

Recently a friend texted me and asked if there was a ritual to do before bed that could take his mind off his worries. His sleep was becoming more and more interrupted by nighttime angst because his mind was processing the worries from the day. The consequence was that he would wake up exhausted in the morning.

You can keep a little worry box next to your bed with a stack of paper and a pen. The purpose of this is to externalize your worries by writing them down and putting them in the box. As you do, you can even say out loud: "I am putting these worries in the box to hold so my mind doesn't have to."

When the worry box is full, you can burn or bury the papers as a way of continuing to ritually metabolize and process those worries.

THE BEDTIME RITUAL:
For Parents and Kids

Out of the many parents I interviewed for this chapter, the most common, most time-tested, most easily available and requested bedtime ritual was, no surprise, reading their child a book (or ten). There is something so calming and comforting for a child to hear stories at night. Yet what happens after the stories are read and it's time for sleep? You guessed it: Nothing is calm. Parents report their children fighting this transition tooth and nail—wanting to read more books, wanting more stimulation, or more attention. Depending on the age, bedtime can provoke a child's real resistance to so much of what nighttime requires: being alone, calming down, letting go. To a child those things can be really scary to do by themselves. And so, a bargaining commences: "I'll give you one more story or I'll stay a little longer *if* you go to sleep." To a parent engaged in this dance, it becomes a negotiation, a trade of anything for sleep and the avoidance of the tantrums that can accompany this time.

But what if the bargaining around bedtime was actually choreographed? Instead of it being a last-ditch effort to prevent a fight, what if the give-and-take was intentional? What if you could do something with your child that both helped ease them into this time of sleep and was also reflective, participatory, and tangible?

This ritual is inspired by the reciprocal nature of story-sharing. Its simplest purpose is for you and your child to reflect and share (in rounds) about different things that happened during the day. What you felt, what you saw, whom you met. The end of each share triggers a tangible "turning on" or "turning off" moment. For instance, after the child shares, the night-light is put on. Then, after the parent shares, the blinds get drawn. After the child shares again, the sound machine goes on. The sharing goes back and forth, over and over, until the ritual is complete.

The deeper layers of this ritual teach the child that this time is a sacred time to reflect and remember—a time you can linger in without resistance and even grow to love. But the power and effectiveness of a ritual is found in its repetitiveness, so the most important thing here is to keep doing it every night. As you and your child find your own rhythm, this transitional time can become one of the most precious in your day.

Prepare

Intentions

May I have a meaningful moment with my child before they sleep. May I help them reflect and remember about the day together. May I let our bedtime routines become ritualized and intentional. May my child go to bed peacefully.

When

This is intended to happen after reading your child books and before they go to sleep. Of course, choose whichever time works for you, but know that this ritual was created to be done during those last moments.

Begin

The Rounds

This ritual happens in rounds. The examples below are just jumping-off points and you can choose however many work for you based on your child's bedtime routine.

Round 1:

> **Question:** *Who is someone you met today and what did you do?*
>
> **Action:** Put on the night-light.

Round 2:

> **Question:** *Where is somewhere you went today? Tell a story of what happened.*
>
> **Action:** Close the blinds or curtains.

Round 3:

> **Question:** *Tell the story of something that sur-prised you. What happened?*
>
> **Action:** Put on the sound machine or sing a lullaby.

Round 4:

> **Question:** *What is a strong feeling you had today? And why?*
>
> **Action:** Tuck your child in under the blankets.

Round 5:

> **Question:** *What is something you learned today?*
>
> **Action:** Dim or turn off the lights.

Round 6:

> **Question:** *Remember someone you love and say why you love them.*
>
> **Action:** Kiss them on the cheek.

Round 7:

      Question: *What is something you are grateful for today? Why?*

      Action: Answer this question from the door. The last action is to shut the door.

Questions for Further Reflection

- What is the difference between only doing bedtime routines and doing a bedtime ritual?
- How does this ritual impact my relationship with my child?
- How does bringing more reflection to this time alter our bedtime experience?

RITUALS
for the YEAR

Seasons

The sun is golden light, transformative light, if we let it be.
Just like the dark, it affects how we see what we see.[*]

—Chani Nicholas

Winter arrives and we descend into those long, dark nights. Spring awakens and we can sense the sweetness of new beginnings. Summer lingers and we bask in those days that seem to last forever. Autumn returns and with it we witness that beautiful golden light fade away. Our days are an ever-changing give-and-take between cold and hot, long and short, deep and shallow. For thousands of years, humans have marked the solstice and equinox, celebrating the turning of the seasons; yet in our busy, modern lives, we barely notice these seasonal shifts. But these are momentous opportunities to synchronize the turning of our own lives with the turning of the Earth.

In the fall of 2006, I packed my bags and headed on a solo journey to Machu Picchu. Because of my experience with altar-making, I really wanted to see the Intihuatana, a huge stone that was part-altar and part-astronomical device. I flew into Cuzco, journeyed to the Urubamba River, and, with the help of a guide, climbed the mountain ridge to the fifteenth-century Incan citadel, coming face-to-face with this amazing stone. I remember the guide kindly laughing at me as questions stumbled out of my mouth: "Did this stone exist before Machu Picchu was built?" "How could it be

---

[*] Moi Garcia, ed., "Summer Solstice: A Testimony of Light," Chani, chaninicholas.com/summer
-solstice-testimony-light/.

so perfectly placed with each corner sitting at the four directions?" "What was its real purpose?"

My guide hinted that the clue was in the name, *Intihuatana*, which comes from the local Quechua language. He said *inti* meant "sun," and *wata* meant "to tie or hitch up," because at midday on the equinoxes, the sun stands right above the stone's pillar, looking as if the stone is hitching the sun. The stone functions like a super-sundial: The sun actually casts no shadow at all on the equinoxes, while on the winter and summer solstices, the sun casts its shortest and longest shadows, respectively. Long before any clock, telescope, weather app, or GPS device was invented, these stone technologies signaled to millions of people in the Incan Empire when the rains would come, when to harvest, store, or plant crops, and when to ritually celebrate the turning of time. The Quechuan people used their phenomenal engineering skills and expert star-tracking to keep their culture in rhythm with the Universe's greater tempo.

This love affair with the heavens isn't unique to the Inca. The ancient Celts, the Mayans, the ancient Greeks, the ancient Egyptians, and the ancient Indians in the Indus Valley all looked to the sky as a map to track the trail of patterns happening above them. The stars' movements, the moon's waxing and waning, and the sun's path offered a mirror to listen carefully to what they should be doing in the new season. "As above, so below," as the saying goes, and they tied their movements with the movement of everything above and around them.

Just down the street from where I'm writing is the entrance to the Tsawout First Nation's Reserve, the ancestral home of a Coastal Salish people who are one of the original inhabitants of this land. At the entrance of the trail is a beautifully painted circular chart filled with shells, feathers, starfish, moons, and berries. While it may at first seem purely decorative, it is actually a calendrical wheel. Each slice of the pie is devoted to a different moon phase, and within each moon is housed different relationships that are alive that time of the year. For instance, within the month of September and the *Ćenqolew moon*, or "the moon of the Chum salmon," live the Stinging Nettle, the Blacktail Deer, and the Seastar; within the month of December and the *Sis,et moon*, or "the moon of the elders," live the Licorice Fern, the Douglas Fir, and the Raven; and within the month of May and the *Penáwen moon*, or "the moon of the Camas," live the Mussel Shell, the Garry Oak, and the Thimbleberry.

By marking each moon cycle, these Saanich people also remember the songs, stories, and rituals that keep them in a rhythmic relationship with the place. Each moon alerts the people to logistical matters such as when to set up winter villages or spring camps, when to harvest, to gather, to store, to weave, to hunt, to build, to fish, or to teach. Rather than just randomly deciding when to do this or that, this thirteen-moon calendar is a map that navigates the people through time and place together.

Every day as I head out for my afternoon walk in the lush, mossy forest near my tiny home, I pass by this calendar and reflect upon how deeply rooted our Gregorian calendar is in Christianity and ancient Rome and how rooted this thirteen-moon calendar is in the place itself—keeping the rhythms of the moon and the rhythms of these Saanich people as one.

Counting is necessary for rhythm keeping. The ancient Chinese tracked the sun's journey in twenty-four solar terms, or *jie qi*. Zhou Gong of the Zhou Dynasty started it all by counting the Winter Solstice, or *Dōngzhì*, around 1030 BCE. He measured the breadth of the sun's shadow and began dividing it into the four terms, two for the solstices and two for the equinoxes. Later on, these were eventually broken down into eight and then again into twenty-four terms. These twenty-four terms reflect not just the changes in the seasons (Beginning of Spring, Spring Equinox, Beginning of Summer, Summer Solstice, and so on), but also the changes in temperature (Lesser Heat, Greater Heat, End of Heat, Lesser Cold, Greater Cold), changes in weather phenomena (Rain Water, Grain Rain, White Dew, Cold Dew, First Frost, Light Snow, Heavy Snow), and changes in phenological phenomena (Insects Awaken, Freshgreen, Lesser Fullness, and Grain of Ear). The twenty-four solar terms, which some call the fifth Great Invention of China (next to papermaking, printing, gunpowder, and the compass), gave the people a way to acknowledge the changes happening in that particular time and place. They informed them not only when to adjust their farming practices, what rituals to do, and what foods to make, but when and how to change their own focus, conduct, and daily routines. Think about it like this: Rather than the people wandering aimlessly without a compass, this incredibly detailed calendar gave the people a basic choreography so that their lives could flow in harmony with everything above and around them.

While my own Jewish culture's calendar is also faithful to the lunar rhythms, we track the solar cycles as well. Our ancestors called these times *tekufot*, meaning, "turns," points in the spiraling year to honor and celebrate the first days of spring, summer, winter, and fall. Our major festivals tend to fall around the equinoxes and solstices, times when the change in light also reminds us where to turn our *kavanah*, or "intention." For instance, two of our most important New Year holidays, Rosh Hashanah and Yom Kippur, fall around the time of the fall equinox, so as the sun's light fades, it becomes a time for us to look within ourselves, to reflect upon the past year, to take account of our behaviors and actions, to ask forgiveness to all we have harmed, and to reconsider the ways we conduct ourselves for the next year. The change in the season marks a time for us to reevaluate and change our own ways.

The thresholds of the equinox and solstice offer themselves as auspicious moments to lift up our eyes and look beyond the everyday routines of our lives. Routines can become ruts when we keep repeating them over and over again.

Yet these seasonal shifts are actually opportunities to snap us out of autopilot and wake us up from what has become too familiar and stagnant. In these moments we can look up and ask: "What is happening now?"—both in the world and in our own lives. Often, the very thing we need to be reminded of or the shift we've been seeking is actually happening in the natural world around us. When we can witness the trees, the moon, the rains, the sun distinctively changing, we can better tether our lives to a greater movement and guidance.

The spring equinox, for instance, when the Northern Hemisphere is budding and bursting from the confinement of winter, can become a time to look at our own journey from constriction and limitation into expansive freedom. Or at the seat of the winter solstice, when we're blanketed in darkness and cold with the promise of a return to more light, we might take time to reflect upon which relationships, projects, and responsibilities need rekindling. Marking these moments with ritual brings us to the living frontier of what's changing, a place where we can reclaim some humility and remember that we belong to this endless cycle of loss and gain, of death and birth—a cycle that existed before us and will continue after us. Recognizing the seasonal shift returns and reorients us to our own changing reality, and in doing so, we can ask: *What is this particular time for and how can this inspire me to change now?*

These four solstice and equinox rituals invite you to look around and notice the time and place you are living within and to do something to place yourself within it. The culture that so many of us were born into sees itself as uninfluenced by or even superior to the natural world, which leaves many of us feeling a deep-seated sense of disconnection and isolation. Yet these seasonal doorways are opportunities to remember how it could be otherwise—tangible ways we can refuse to see ourselves as separate from or untouched by change, and instead realign our lives with the unique qualities, gifts, challenges, and colors that the seasons bring, and by extension, touch those elements within ourselves.

AUTUMN EQUINOX

The closer you get to the light,
the closer you also get to the darkness.

—Parker Palmer

There's a shift. You can feel it in the air. You can sense it in the light. You can see it in the leaves. Here in the Northern Hemisphere, all that was bright is quickly fading, as the time teeters on the edge between dark and light. Everything must eventually change, and so the autumn equinox is a time to reassess—to come back, look around, and take stock of how things are, of what you have, of what you've lost, of all the success and the mistakes you've made along the way—and by doing so to renew yourself and your purpose at this turning of the year.

The Old English word for "autumn" was actually *harvest* until about the sixteenth century. Not only is this a time of gathering, plucking, and reaping crops, but also a time of reckoning with all that life has given us and how we have shown up to receive it. Have our hands been grabby, clingy, or possessive? Have we hoarded our harvests and kept our gifts to ourselves? Have we taken more when we've already been full? Or maybe we find that our thoughts are only focusing on scarcity when life is trying to show us its abundance? This time of harvest is asking us to not only reap the gifts of this season but also wonder about *how* we are taking them.

One way to distinguish between taking more and receiving more is by stopping to remember what we already have. The fall equinox asks us to sit at the edge of enoughness. It marks a time to reflect on our home, our friendships, the food in our fridge, the money in our bank, the health in our bodies, the togetherness of our family or community, the courage it took just to wake up this morning—and to consider letting that be enough. Autumn marks the seasonal end of growth and has a way of shaking us free from the daydream of always needing more, bringing us back down to the humble ground of gratitude. The nature of autumn is a time to hollow ourselves out, to remove so much of the excess that comes with the hunger of never being satisfied, of never having enough, of always needing more, so that we can really receive and be grateful for how much life is giving us.

Gratitude is a trending word these days, and as it gains in popularity, it seems to diminish in value and meaning, like a child who quickly says thank you before eating. But gratitude isn't just courtesy, it's courtship. It's a way of drawing closer by giving, not by taking. Gratitude refuses more because at the heart of it, it's like a full cup that spills over saying, "This is enough for now." Offering genuine gratitude comes from a willingness to take account for all you have been given and to understand that none of it was guaranteed. Through that lens, gratitude becomes a kind of praise that remembers and includes impermanence as a way to renew your relationship to all of life.

This autumn equinox ritual is a way to inventory our lives. First and foremost, it asks us to have a hard look at our "never enough" mindset and all the ways we deny, doubt, hide, or refuse to see all we've been given. This ritual presents us with an opportunity to shake this up and let it loose. Then it invites us to listen more closely—receiving the moment with wonder. It's a moment to sense the fragility and ephemerality of—like everything around us—being alive. This is a small way we can return to receiving what is here right now and to let that be more than enough.

THE SHAKE *and* HARVEST RITUAL

Prepare

Intentions

May I acknowledge the end of the season of growth and the transition into the season of gratitude. May I bring attention to the parts of myself that make me believe I don't have enough and ritually release them. May I practice listening. May I be grateful for all the abundance that is here right now.

You Will Need

- A large branch filled with many leaves
- Something comfortable to sit on the ground
- Optional: A journal and pen
- Optional: Autumn fruits and vegetables like apples, pears, squash, corn, pumpkins, etc.

Solo or with Others?

If you are solo, consider journaling about each question before you do the ritual shaking. If you are with others, bear witness to their vulnerabilities in the same way you want them to bear witness to yours. The heart of this ritual is found in our capacity to listen, to ourselves, to one another, and to our living world.

Where and When

There is magic percolating at sunset hour. Try to time this ritual just as the sun dips and the sky mirrors the colors of the leaves. You can do this in your backyard, in a park, at the beach, or on a hilltop. Most important, put your butt on the earth.

Begin

Silence

Before doing anything, just sit and take in the day ending. What is happening around you? Observe the light diminishing. Notice the shifting temperature. What are the birds doing? Bear witness to this everyday moment.

Go slower than you normally would. No matter how much you achieved today or didn't, how many places you went, how many errands you ran, who and what you cared for, all the stresses and worries and hustling of the day, let this time settle you back down to your breath and to the earth. Syncing yourself with the end of the day is another way to return to the rhythm of the season.

Part 1: Shaking

It's not comfortable to see the parts of ourselves that are greedy, disbelieving, doubtful, and dissatisfied. Actually, it's countercultural to have a willingness to turn toward our vulnerabilities and not abandon ourselves to them as we typically do. Autumn being a time of reflection and impermanence asks us to take account of our lives, but to do so we need to first see where we turn away from all we have. Part 1 asks us to confront these stories and, by doing so, shake ourselves free of them.

There are four rounds to this first part of the ritual, organized around four questions. In each round, ask yourself the question and speak the answer aloud or journal it and then shake the branch. You'll need to give it a really good shake—your goal is to have the leaves fall off.

Round 1:
What parts of my life do I believe are lacking and scarce?
Shake that branch.

Round 2:
When do I over-take and never feel satisfied?
Shake that branch.

Round 3:
When have I turned away from my gifts this year?
Shake that branch.

Round 4:
When have I turned away from receiving another's gifts this year?
Shake that branch.

If you have more questions to ask of yourself, add more rounds as needed.

Part 2: Sitting

When you have finished the four rounds, gently bring your body down to the earth. If you sit right on top of the leaves, even better. Shaking that branch was like a big storm coming through. In its aftermath, try to let things settle.

Bring your attention to your body. Listen to the way it sounds, to how it feels, to where the energy is now moving. Feel gravity grounding and rooting you back to stillness. Then bring your attention to your surroundings. Listen to the animal, plant, or human sounds. Sense the light changing. Feel your body sitting in this place.

Let your mind settle on one simple thing happening right now and let this be enough. You can even say out loud: "This is exactly as it should be."

Conclude

Gather for the Altar

Gather up the leaves that fell during the shaking ritual, to use them for a home autumn altar. These leaves can become a symbol of transforming your "not enoughness" into a harvest.

Whether you choose to place this altar outside or indoors, use the leaves as the base of the altar and fill it with the fruits and vegetables of the season—pumpkins and apples, corn and squash, each symbolizing the bounty of your life and this world we live in. Come back to your altar throughout the season as a reminder to slow down, listen, and receive the fullness that is found in every day of your life.

Questions for Further Reflection

- Why is the autumn equinox a time to reflect and take inventory?
- What is the difference between taking and receiving?
- What does the term "more than enough" mean to me? How do I practice that?

WINTER SOLSTICE

I have faith in the night.

—Rainer Maria Rilke

Oh, those brief days and ever silent nights. The year finally has descended into the womb of winter solstice. Deep in the forest where I live, all that is alive has turned inward. The maples are bare and sleeping while the plump and bright red madrone berries hang like Christmas ornaments. Being so far north in the Northern Hemisphere, dark comes early and swallows us whole. It feels like I haven't seen the sun in ages. But as this winter threshold arrives, a time of family and feasts, whether we know it or not, we mark the almost imperceptible return of that warm and wonderful light.

The winter solstice lies opposite to the summer solstice, and while summertime is the swelling of the external—the ripening of fruit, of travel plans, of visions, of love affairs—wintertime is the replenishing of the internal. It's the time when the trees' roots drink in the nourishment from the soil's depth, from the unseen, before it rises up and out into the world again. Similarly, wintertime asks us to plug ourselves back into the deep, dark source of life.

This dark time of the year is an invitation to be with the dark. It invites us to go within and put down our compulsion to keep doing more, to traveling more, to accomplishing more, and instead to do less and rest. It's not a time of self-striving but of deep reception, like being a baby gestating in the womb. To receive that deeply requires a willingness to surrender our need for achievement, for certainty, for control, and instead to renew our sense of awe and amazement at how much more mysterious life is than we thought it was.

And from that rich, still place of wonder germinates the seed of renewed light and life. The return of the sun and of longer days is gradual, like the faintest hint of the night's sky turning. So many world traditions understand this time mythically as gods or goddesses being reborn, a similar journey to the light. The winter solstice has us gather around this baby light and welcome its arrival.

The Winter Bundle Ritual orients you to the questions that sit at the heart of this dark, mysterious season, both in your life and in the world: What needs rest? What needs replenishment? What needs time to germinate? And how can you practice cultivating a robust trust in the unknown? This is a moment to honor the internal, dark womb of winter by planting visions and dreams within that which may grow again with the return of light's vitality.

THE WINTER BUNDLE RITUAL

Prepare

Intentions

May I enter gracefully into the wintertime. May the dark be a place of replenishment and renewal. May I celebrate the return of the light and the spark of life.

You Will Need

- A small cloth or sack
- Dried or fresh herbs, oils, or anything beautiful that smells good
- A tiny little piece of paper (and pen)
- A candlestick (and match)

When

Begin this ritual the night before the solstice. Ideally, you do this right before bed or even at midnight. This ritual honors the quiet and stillness of the dark. See if you can do the first part of this ritual without any electric lights on, and preferably without lighting a candle. Trust that you can do this.

Creating the Sack

Lay out the fabric and gently cover it with the dried herbs, evergreen needles, dried flower petals, or anything else you want to include. Think of it like a winter nest. Don't tie it up just yet.

The Vision

On that piece of paper, write down one word that represents something that needs to be replenished within you, within your family or within the world. Whatever you choose, it should be something that needs to rest and be deeply cared for. Don't worry about whether the writing is legible—if you can't properly see the paper because it's too dark, that is exactly as it needs to be.

Place the paper on the dried herbs and flowers, gather the bundle together, and tie it up.

Place this winter bundle under your pillow at night while you sleep.

Morning Time

If possible, rise before dawn, when it's still dark out. This time of the day is an auspicious time to welcome solstice—right as the light returns.

Remove the winter bundle from under your pillow and hold it in your hands. Remember what you wrote. Breathe with the first glimmers of new light. Feel your heartbeat. Feel your chest gently rise and fall. Feel yourself surrounded by something more vast than you.

Before lighting the candle, consider saying something simple, like "I trust" or "I receive."

When you are ready, light the candle and welcome the return of the little light on this holy day.

Conclude

Place that winter bundle somewhere safe and protected during the wintertime. You can keep it under your pillow or on an altar in your home. Let it be a reminder of your capacity to trust in the life's renewal.

On the spring equinox, open the bundle and let that sleeping vision out into the world.

Questions for Further Reflection
- What is my relationship to the dark?
- What does the winter solstice teach me about uncertainty and trust?

- Why is it important to let things (including you) rest?
- How can this ritual let me mark the dark beauty and the return to the light?

New Year's

For a decade of my life, I lived in the hustle and bustle of Times Square in New York City, which meant that for ten years I had the pleasure (and annoyance) of experiencing the chaotic, drunken, crowded celebration that comes with the iconic midnight ball-drop on New Year's Eve. Tens of thousands of people flooded the streets wearing numbered paraphernalia to welcome in the new year. There was so much built-up anticipation for this night of auld lang syne, but for what? The Gregorian calendar's New Year's is most certainly a threshold, but what does it mean to leave behind the old year and cross into the new one?

New Year's celebrations are markers, personally and collectively. They let us distinguish between what was and what will be. As arbitrary as it might feel, New Year's gives us an opportunity to reflect on how we've shown up the past year and to confront the parts of ourselves that we might not be open to facing, in order to change them: *How have I been treating my partner? How have I been talking to my kids? Am I doing the work I want to be doing? Have I been taking care of my body?* This annual threshold gives us a chance to pause at the end of the year and take account of our actions, patterns, and behaviors so we can change them. And it also provides a moment to set intentions and course correct for the new year.

This is a little New Year's ritual meant to change the way we use the booze we may already be drinking. Ritualizing this moment gives us the opportunity to practice the art of crossing thresholds, which always ask us: What are we leaving behind and what are we entering into? Thresholds are transformative, and crossing into this new year is a chance to harness the cultural energy of change and carry it into your life.

You Will Need

- Your libation of choice (can be alcoholic or not—whatever you're celebrating with)

Before Midnight

Raise a glass four times to the year passing, one every fifteen minutes. Each time you lift up the glass, pour out a little liquid (either on a plate, on the ground, or just take a drop on your finger) to honor the wins, the losses, the struggles, and miracles that happened that year.

1. Raise a glass to something that was realized that past year.
2. Raise a glass to something that never came to pass.
3. Raise a glass to a new or renewed relationship that happened that year.
4. Raise a glass to something you're not willing to carry into the new year.

After Midnight

After midnight, raise four more toasts, one every fifteen minutes. Each time you lift up the glass, top someone else's glass and let them top yours. Recharging the glasses is a symbolic way to lift up your new intentions, vows, and renewed commitments for the new year.

1. Raise a glass to something you are intending for the new year.
2. Raise a glass to something new that needs your attention and care.

> 3. Raise a glass to something you intend to change or make better.
> 4. Raise a glass to a relationship you want to commit to in the new year.

SPRING EQUINOX

You can cut all the flowers
but you cannot keep Spring from coming.

—Pablo Neruda

'Tis the season of the hidden and revealed. After the long haul of those dark and cold winter months, we are now arriving back to the season where light and warmth reign. So much life that's been in incubation is now popping out its cute little head, ready to live in the world. The camellia buds right outside my front door are swollen and bursting to the point of neon explosion. All the life that's been growing in the dark wants out! Now! It's exactly as Anaïs Nin prophesizes: "And the day came when the risk to remain tight in a bud was more painful than the risk it took to blossom."

While spring craves release, it's also escorted by a robust vulnerability. Release is terribly risky. There was safety and containment in the dark, still womb of winter. The wildness of spring, however, is the loss of that control and wherewithal. Spring certainly brings sweetness, newness, and vitality, but it also breaks things and births uncertainty. As new life is pushed forward, it is exposed to the wild and unpredictable. Suddenly, what was hidden is visible, what was slowly gathering is quickly escaping, what was manageable is chaotic, and what was familiar is now uncertain. The solid ground of winter breaks open and reveals the volatility of a blossoming spring.

And because of that, the spring equinox's axis revolves around death and rebirth, coupling, and the joy of new life along with the grief of losing what was comfortable and familiar. It is a time that asks us to both reflect on the patterns, narratives, relationships, and behaviors that have kept us safe but stuck, and to break loose from them. Every year at this time, my fellow Jews gather around dining room tables everywhere to reenact our Passover story, which tells of our ancestors who were once slaves in Egypt and then became free people. It's the same springtime motif: breaking free from the bonds that once held us down. At this ritual feast, the foods we eat, the wine we drink, the songs we sing, the praise we shout, and the stories we tell all revolve around the movement from slavery to freedom, then and now.

With so much budding, sprouting, and releasing, it's important to make room for it all—hence the ubiquitous spring cleaning. Spring needs space, and therefore it is a time to clean out the clutter, the blockages, the gunk and junk, so that there's more than enough room for all the new that wants to come in. The Iranian/Persian New Year's, or Nowruz, is celebrated at the threshold of the spring equinox, and to prepare for this holy day, the Persian people busy themselves with a major spring cleaning called *khāne-takānī*, or "shaking the house," which signals to their ancestors that they are invited into the home to nourish the *sabzeh*, sprouted wheat, a symbol of rejuvenation and new life.

The Release Ritual is a double whammy. It rides on the flow of the season, encouraging you to shake off winter's slumber while awakening to spring's growth. There are two steps to this ritual: the night before the spring equinox and the morning of. The first ritual is inspired by the traditional pre-Passover cleansing and tasks you to acknowledge four different ways your behaviors, patterns, routines, or self-talk have become inflated, self-serving, lazy, or aimless, and to ritually release them. The second part encourages you to renew your commitment to nurture the new, sweet, and tender growth happening in your life—whether that's taking care of your body, your home, your relationships, your community, or the larger world.

THE RELEASE RITUAL

Prepare
Intentions
May I break through the stagnancy of winter and make space to come into spring. May I inventory the behaviors, patterns, and mindset that need decluttering. May I ritually release them in order to make room

for what's new. And from that space, may I make new commitments to visions, projects, and relationships and support their growth.

You Will Need
- Four or more small pieces of paper and a pen
- A small ceramic bowl
- A candle
- A lighter or match
- Four seeds
- A pitcher of water

Inspirations
This ritual is inspired by Bedikat Chametz, my tradition's pre-Passover/springtime cleansing ritual in which we take a wooden spoon and a feather and by candlelight search for bread, or *chametz*, around our home. On Passover we don't eat leavened bread, which is symbolic of the aspects of our egos that are puffed up, selfish, inflated, and arrogant, and instead we eat a flat, unleavened bread called matzah, which one of our Chasidic sages calls the bread of humility. The powerful moment of this ritual is when, the next morning, we burn the leavened bread as a way to cleanse and prepare our home and our self for this holiday and this new season.

Begin
On the Eve
Start on the evening of the spring equinox. Shut off all the lights in your home and light one candle. Reorient to the dark, to the stillness. Let your eyes rest on the candle and take a moment to consider what needs to be cleaned out from the past three months of winter.

Next, take out those small scraps of paper and a pen. Four is a good complete number, but if you want to do more, who am I to stop you? On each piece of paper, write a word or sentence that represents some aspect of yourself that needs cleansing and renewal.

You might want to consider questions like:
- What is a way you are unnecessarily limiting yourself?
- What is a way you are not taking care of your gifts?

- What is a way you have gotten lazy?
- What is one stagnant behavior you keep seeing in yourself, your community, your country, or the world?

There are parts of yourself that you most certainly miss or can't even see, but they exist. Consider adding one more category that says something like "For all that I've missed."

Now hide these papers. Put them between books or high up on a shelf or even outside under rocks. It might sound odd since you will know where they are, but there is something symbolic and significant about this, based on how these sticky traits often hide in the cracks of our lives and seem to become hard to see.

On the Morning Of

Try to wake up early on the spring equinox. If you have kids or work, rise before them so you have enough time to do this yourself. The early morning hours are so precious.

Begin the morning by lighting a candle, and if you can, go outside and take in the light of the morning and the world waking. Spring is here, a new dawning and a new day.

Taking the candle with you, search for the papers from the night before and gather them in the ceramic bowl. After you've collected them, sit before the candle and take in a breath.

Burn each paper in the ceramic bowl, keeping the ashes.

The Seeds

In this second part of the ritual, you are going to place seeds into the ash to symbolize new life and new intentions emerging from the space you cleared. Think of a phoenix rising.

Each seed represents a new commitment that needs your attention, your care, or your energy in order to grow. It doesn't matter if you don't know what it will grow into, what's most important is that you recognize that there is something beginning and those little beginnings need your tender vigilance.

If you are outside, take the ash from the bowl and put it directly on the earth. If you are inside, leave the ashes in the bowl.

As you place each seed, consider these four questions:

1. What is a new way I can commit to taking care of myself/my body?
2. What is a new way I can commit to taking care of my home?
3. What is a new way I can commit to taking care of my relationships?
4. What is a new way I can commit to taking care of my community, country, or the planet?

Conclude

Ideally, these seeds find their way back into the ground to germinate and grow, but if you live in a city or for whatever reason can't get them back into the earth, consider placing them on an altar in your home.

Finish the ritual by washing your hands with the pitcher of water. Let the coolness of the water run over your hands, refreshing your body and these new springtime commitments.

Questions for Further Reflection

- What relationships, patterns and traits need regeneration?
- What dormant aspects of my life am I willing to shake out?
- What are new commitments I am willing to make this season?
- How does ritualizing the spring equinox help to align me with the season?

SUMMER SOLSTICE

We don't source power, we invite it.

—Caroline Casey

Overhead, the sun seems to linger at its zenith forever and ever. On this day of days, the Northern Hemisphere's summer solstice is the culmination of light. Up here in British Columbia, where the Earth's tilt is even more pronounced, the evening summer sky still glitters hues of blue from the day that just won't end. My own skin radiates warmth from lying like a lizard on the beach's hot rocks, and even at ten at night, everyone is still wide awake—the neighborhood kids refuse to go inside. As much as the summer solstice is the height of light, it is also paradoxically about the waning of that light and the beginning of the return to darkness.

Summer solstice is all about fullness. After the dark and subtle tones of winter and the fresh ripening of spring, midsummer calls for completion. Yet with completion comes decline. And just as we're getting used to devouring the plump joys of summer, the solstice reminds us that joy always teeters on the edge of sorrow. And all of that fullness will soon lessen and deepen, just like grapes do when giving way to wine.

For many traditions, including my own, summer solstice carries the scent of grief as the season turns. The Jewish summer solstice comes during the tenth month of Tammuz in our Hebrew calendar, a name that remembers an even older Sumerian god, Dumuzi, or Tammuz, and the story of his descent into the underworld. As the rains ceased and the ground cracked open, the ancient Sumerian women would wail and mourn Tammuz's death during midsummer and the beginning of the darkness returning. Tammuz's mythopoeic descent is also the journey of the grain being cut down at this time of the year in order to feed the people and grow once again. Everything growing is part of a cycle, and that cycle eventually reaches its peak, which is the spirit of this solstice.

Summertime brings things into the light so we can really see them as they are. But the bittersweetness of that is that life's ephemerality becomes clear. Suddenly, we glimpse the limit of the limitless. We can sense that what was so full of potential has or hasn't been realized. While the spirit of summer longs for celebration and fruition, it also wants us to live it, to paraphrase Albert Camus, to the point of tears. Being human is to continue to recognize that what was once in our grasp must leave us, and to love it even more so because of that. The richness of the long days of midsummer is found by remembering their imminent departure.

Similar to the way you might pause to take in the view at the top of a mountain, the summer solstice asks you to slow down at the height of the year so you can take it all in: *What happened in the past six months? What winter dreams fruited? Which seeds never even took root? What grew so much that it needs harvesting? What hard work can you celebrate? What now needs to transform?* Summer solstice is another moment in the year to return yourself to the Greater Rhythms and access their peaking brilliance. But as the ritualist Starhawk says: "We turn the Wheel, for we have planted the seeds of our own changes and to grow we must accept even the passing of the sun."

THE BEARING FRUIT RITUAL

Prepare

Intentions
May I acknowledge the beginning of summer and take stock of my successes and failures since wintertime. May I celebrate the fullness in this time of the year and also grieve the end of that full expression and the beginning of going within.

You Will Need
- One unripe fruit
- One perfectly ripe fruit
- One overripe fruit
- A large serving plate

Who
Ideally, you don't do this ritual alone but share it with at least one other person. If you want to do this with a larger gathering at a picnic in the park, at a dinner party, or even within your office, it's totally doable.

Beforehand

Sure, you can come to this ritual spontaneously and respond to the prompts below off the cuff, but I encourage you to take time beforehand to really consider them. Maybe this looks like journaling and letting your mind wander on the page, or perhaps it's a late-night conversation with a good friend, unpacking the questions together. This ritual asks you to raise up things you really care for, so they deserve taking some time to wonder about.

The Fruit

Each fruit represents a personal or cultural success, failure, or that gray area where you can't tell which it is yet. They symbolize the achievements and efforts, the messes and mistakes, the relationships and endeavors that have been growing or not growing since winter. Bringing attention to them externally helps to feed the ones that need your beautiful attention and release the ones that didn't make it. As you consider the questions, let them spark memories, musings, or steps forward.

One fruit will be taken home, one fruit will be eaten, and one fruit will be returned to the earth.

Where

It's summertime! Go outside. It's as simple as that.

Begin

The Unripe Fruit

Start with the unripe fruit: Hold it up and consider your past six months. This fruit symbolizes the "almost but not yet." These are places where patience and perseverance are needed.

- What ideas almost materialized but didn't?
- What relationships seemed promising and then fizzled?
- What projects are you still holding out hope for but are looking less and less likely?

- What change looked promising in yourself, your community, your country, or the world and turned out to be premature?

Afterward, wrap this fruit up and take it home and let it ripen in the sun in your kitchen.

The Ripe Fruit

Next, hold up the ripe fruit and consider your past six months. This fruit symbolizes all that has ripened well. These questions are to acknowledge all that is plump, full, and ready to be devoured.

- What did you achieve since winter?
- What relationships are thriving right now?
- What are your successes lately?
- What efforts and progress in yourself, your community, your country, or the world can you celebrate?

After answering the questions, eat that yummy fruit and enjoy that delicious juice running down your chin.

The Overripe Fruit

This fruit symbolizes the mess, the decay, the disappointments that need you to let it go so it can return back to the earth. As with the other fruits, hold it up and reflect on the last six months.

- What has come into your life and what has left?
- What old relationships need to be released?
- Where have you made a mess?
- Where does your heart break when you look at yourself, your community, your country, or the world?

After answering the questions, dig a hole to bury it or leave this fruit under a tree to be consumed by the bugs and birds. If you are in a public park or a place where you can't leave or bury the fruit, wrap it up and bring it to a compost bin rather than a garbage can, because all that compost will become soil once again, where new seeds can be planted.

Conclude

Complete this ritual with some praise and gratitude, especially for all those unseen and unknowable forces that guided and granted you all that you received and didn't receive since the winter solstice.

And of course, the last bit of thanks goes to the sun. Soak up that heat knowing that it will continue to fade.

Questions for Further Reflection

- What can I honor that is coming into its fullness?
- How do I discern between what needs to be let go and what needs my persistence?
- What needs witnessing in order to further its growth?
- Why would there be grief and sorrow during such a joyful season?

Birthday

To acknowledge our ancestors means we are aware
that we did not make ourselves, that the line stretches
all the way back, perhaps to God; or to Gods.

—Alice Walker

Round and round the Earth goes, circling the sun like a cosmic spiral dance. Three hundred sixty-five steps she takes to complete her annual hoop, and on one of those turns, however many years ago—you arrived here. Naked, bloody, and goopy-eyed, your beginning began on this precious, living planet. Stamped with a whirling thumbprint mirroring the swirl of the galaxy, your birth was indeed a miracle, and each year, as the Earth returns to the same spot in her orbit around the sun, you return to count how many years it's been since that wondrous day. Birthday cake, candles, parties, cards, and gifts mark the special day, but it's incomplete. If your birthday is a celebration of you and your life, who do you need to celebrate for helping to make it so?

While humans have been tracking the sky, especially the lunar cycles, since as early as twenty-five thousand years ago, birthdays are relatively new on the scene. The Torah mentions a pharaoh's birthday in Genesis, yet some Egyptologists believe this didn't correspond to the day he was born but rather to the year he was coronated. The people of late republican Rome also celebrated *dies natales*, the day of the birth. They not only celebrated an individual's birthday but also commemorated the *natales* of temples, cities, and, especially, a person's genius or Juno, a guardian deity or spirit who guided and governed them throughout their life's journey.

If you had been an ancient Roman, it would have been impossible for you to individuate yourself from your genius, and so your birth was their birthday too. Which means that rather than celebrating your own birthday, like we do in our modern society, Roman men and women were obligated to create feasts, bake cakes, pour libations, burn incense, and renew their annual *vota*, or "vows," as offerings to their genius on their birthday. The hope of these gifts and promises was that they "would be renewed the following year should the protection of the deity continue."* That is to say that birthdays were a time when one would look around and recognize all the relationships that comprised one's life, from parents and patrons to the city, the emperor, and especially one's genius, and re-up those relationships through ritual.

When I was growing up in the 1980s, my birthday parties were all about me. Whether it was at Chuck E. Cheese or the local roller rink, I got gifts, cards, money, and cake, and was expected to give nothing in return. For that one day, I got to be treated like a prince. But the day lacked any real reflection. Never once did any adult remind me to not take my life for granted. While my life and birth were celebrated, no one named the real heartbreaking miracle—that I had survived another year. For only just a few generations before that, many babies didn't live past a year old, and marking another birthday would have been considered a real accomplishment—a victory over death. It was only after a near-death experience of my own at nineteen years old, that I began to understand the preciousness of life and my life in particular and how not guaranteed another birthday is.

Life is a web woven by many hands. Many labored to bring you into the world and many continue to labor on your behalf to sustain your presence here. This web is made up of all the seen and unseen relationships that connect and tether us to this world. Yes, of course, our friends and family, but what about all that we can't see or properly acknowledge: the humans, plants, animals, places, both now and before now, that put food on our plates, a roof over our head, money in our bank, and air in our lungs? All of those that built the roads we drive on, who made the technology we employ, who passed down the languages we speak, who fought and died so that we could live? If our birthdays mark our first moment of life on this planet, why isn't that day used to raise up and renew everything that gives us our life?

The rituals below are created to break the birthday spell of "it's only about me." While of course your birthday is for you, that doesn't mean that on that day nothing is

---

* Kathryn Argetsinger, "Birthday Rituals: Friends and Patrons in Roman Poetry and Cult," *Classical Antiquity* 11, no. 2 (October 1992): 175–93, doi: 10.2307/25010971.

asked of you. Actually, this day you are sorely needed. For what better time to reflect upon all the ways your life is held, protected, encouraged, uplifted, fed, looked after, and loved up by everyone and everything around you? It's a day to remember your relationships with your ancestors, the Earth, and the place you call home. Somedays it might not feel like that, but perhaps it's because we stopped seeing all that we're on the receiving end of and forgot to reciprocate within these relationships.

You'll find in the following pages two rituals: One for a gathering of friends and one just for yourself. Both are ways to presence and honor the infinite number of reasons you are still here and to literally spill some gratitude in their direction. Just like the Roman tradition of reaffirming a *vota*, these birthday rituals are bond-strengtheners, renewing the networks that make up your life and, by doing that, re-inforcing your connection to it all—giving a mighty gift on your birthday to all who continue to gift you.

THE LIBATION RITUAL: *With Friends*

Whether it's to the gods, our muse or genius, our ancestors and family, or to all those whose names we will never know and faces we will never see but whose labor im-pacted our lives, a libation is an act of remembering and including. In its most literal sense, a libation is a pouring out to honor a god or deity, like your genius. Its root comes from the Proto-Indo-European word *lei*, meaning "to flow or pour," like a river does right after it swells from the rains. Yet the flowing isn't just a reference to *what* you pour but to your *willingness* to pour. As modern people, we have a tendency to "dam the flow" by taking or hoarding for ourselves. Instead, the pouring out of a liba-tion is an outpouring for someone else. In the African American tradition of Kwanzaa, libations from a community cup are poured onto plants or the ground to thank God for those ancestors that came before and to include them once again in this ongoing circle of life. By pouring this ancestral libation, participants are fulfilling the African saying "I am We" or "I am because We are."

The heart of this ritual is to create a birthday feast to share, inviting your friends over to celebrate your birthday with you. While a birthday dinner is pretty common, the actual "doing" of this ritual is found in taking away or lessening. Each course will offer another round of subtracting food and drink from each person's plate or cup and placing it on an empty plate or cup as an offering. Why? The purpose is twofold: The first is to break the "more for me" spell, especially on your birthday, by taking food off your plate, and liquid out of your cup, like a libation. The second, and more important, purpose is that the food and liquid removed are *for* someone or something else besides you. Below I created seven rounds of "others" to acknowledge on your special day, but if there are more to mention, keep going.

Prepare

Intentions

May my birthday ritual be a meaningful way to remember and acknowledge the web of connections I'm a part of. May this ritual help me practice reciprocating the gift of my life on my birthday.

You Will Need

- One or more friends to share the meal with
- A meal with at least a few courses and at least one drink
- One empty plate and empty cup

Inviting

Keep in mind that ritualizing any moment might be new for some of your guests. Here are some pointers to hit in your invitation that might give them some context before they arrive.

- Name the ritual: Let your friends know that this is not just any dinner. You are ritualizing your birthday meal. Giving your guests context beforehand lets them understand the importance of what you are doing.
- Invite their participation: You can share the rounds in advance or not, but consider welcoming their participation. This is a part of the spirit of "I am because We are."
- Share why you're inviting them: Those invited are a part of who you are uplifting on your birthday. Let them know that you are using your birthday to raise them and their lives up as well.

The Empty Place

Be sure to leave one seat and one place setting empty. This is for all the "others" that you will be acknowledging and feeding. In a way, this will become an altar at your table. You could just begin with an empty plate and cup, or if you want to add additional beauty and consideration, adorn the place setting in advance. If you have fancy plates or silverware, this is the time to use them. Consider surrounding the plate with photos of those you are feeding. Add flowers, candles, or beautiful objects you might have, like shells from the beach. Turn this seat into a throne, uplifting all that lifts you up.

Begin

The Rhythm

This is up to you. You can do the libations all at once at the beginning of the meal, or you can do it throughout the meal as you serve a new course. Just remember, the whole meal is the ritual. Don't do it to get it over with. By filling the empty plate and cup from everyone's plate, you are inviting all those you are honoring to the meal. Proceed as if they are sitting at the table with you. Let the gratitude pour from you throughout the meal.

Invite Participation

While you are honoring all those known and unknown who uplift, protect, nourish, and sustain your life, this isn't just about you. Invite your gathered guests to participate by taking food off their plates to recognize and honor all that underwrites their own lives. Let this ritual be an outpouring for all those gathered. By doing that, you are employing your birthday to inspire others to give back and honor their lives, which include yours.

The Rounds

These rounds are meant to inspire you to speak out loud and be witnessed in your veneration. Who are you honoring? Why are you honoring them? What have they granted you? How are you grateful?

Don't just make this into a one-sentence answer. Speak as if you are inviting those you are addressing to join you at the table. It's okay to fumble, to be tongue-tied, to not know how to do this, to feel silly or unsure. As modern people, we aren't used to speaking in this way, especially in front of other people. But you can redeem your eloquence. See if you can even try to speak beautifully *to* those you are addressing and not about them.

Round 1: Ancestors
A pouring-out for your ancestors, those remembered and forgotten. *Name those you can remember and acknowledge those you can't.*

Round 2: Community
A pouring-out for your circles of community, family, and friends and all of their beloveds. Name all those you love and try to include names of those that may be forgotten and sit on the community's periphery. *What are you renewing in this relationship?*

Round 3: The Earth
A pouring-out for the Earth, her many rivers, grasses, oceans, creatures, forests, mountains, and, especially and specifically, the actual place you live. Name the details of what you love about these places. *What are you recommitting to within these relationships?*

Round 4: Strangers
A pouring-out for those many hands that made your things, harvested your food, delivered your goods, fixed your machines, and worked on your behalf. *What are you acknowledging in these relationships?*

Round 5: Food
A pouring-out for all the food, especially all the plants and animals you have eaten. Name the food you are presently eating and see if you can name everything on your plate, including the oils and spices, and possibly where it came from. *What are you promising to do on behalf of these relationships?*

Round 6: Teachers

A pouring-out for all those that have inspired you, taught you, motivated you, past or present. *How are you inspired to keep this wisdom alive?*

Round 7: The Unknown

A pouring-out for all that is unknown and yet to come. *What are you doing to be in better relationship to the mysteries?*

Conclude
What to Do Afterward

By the last round, the empty plate and cup you began with should now be full. But what do you do with it after the meal is over? There are no real rules, but no matter what, do not toss it in the garbage. Throwing it away erases the power and meaning of the ritual. Ideally, after your guests have left, bring the food and drink outside and pour the cup directly on the earth and leave the food under a tree. Let this be consumed by other animals or bugs, which are the Earth's great metabolizers. As you do that, say thank you again for your birth, your life, and all that underwrites it. Say it twelve more times. Pour it out.

If you live in a city and can't do that right outside your home, wrap the food and drink up in a to-go container and bring it somewhere you can leave it—maybe to a community compost. If this is just not possible, try to bring it to a tree, to a shoreline, or bury it in the earth. While this might take some more effort, these libations are sacred offerings given back, so go the small distance and finish the ritual in a good way.

Questions for Further Reflection

- Why is my birthday more than just a celebration of me?
- Why do commitments and vows require renewing?
- Why is it important to have at least one witness at this ritual?
- What am I aware of when I acknowledge everything that grants me my life?

THE RINGS RITUAL: *Solo*

The rings of a tree mark the passage of time. Rippling out from its center, each growth ring measures a tree's birthday. But the shape, color, thickness, or absence of a ring tells a completely different story. Those concentric rings are a chronology of not just the tree's life but everything that happened to the tree during its life. From a long hard winter or a terrible drought, to seasons of pestilence or fires, the concentric rings tell a tale of the ecology of the tree's relationships to everything around it. In a way, the growth rings of a tree are a map of its connections and persistence through time.

We are no different. Every year we circle back to our birth date, we mark another year and are marked by it as well. Whether its new gray hairs or growth spurts, money gained or lost, friendships forged or forgotten, illnesses defeated or acquired, our birthdays are another annual opportunity to pause on this life-in-motion and take account of what has changed and what has remained within the ecology of our relationships. Whether these are to our bodies, our partners, our jobs, our musical instruments, our routines, or even our governments, all of our relationships weather over time, and to keep them healthy and alive we must continue to return to and renew our commitment to them.

But here's the thing. Commitments are not one and done. Even though we might give our word and pledge ourselves to something, that doesn't mean that that bond remains strong indefinitely. Relationships change, as do our commitments to them. Sometimes they need our attention and determination, while other times they need us to step away and let go of control. This is especially true with the parents of teenagers, who have to find a way to stay devoted to their child while also adjusting within the relationship as it changes. Attuning to our relationships is a practice of knowing how much give-and-take our commitments require. Even the etymology of the word "commit" speaks of this pendulation: The Latin word *com* translates to "with/together," while the word *miterre* means "to leave or release." In other words, sometimes our commitments need us to come toward them, and other times they need us to step away from them so we can find our way back again, renewed.

This birthday ritual asks you to circle back to your relationships before you move forward. Like tree rings, your life is impacted by everything around you, and these relationships require your maintenance and upkeep. Which need more focus and which need more space? Which do you want to recommit to, and which do you want to compost? This is a chance to take an inventory before you start your next go-round of the sun.

This ritual is inspired by the shape of a tree's rings. You will create nine concentric circles to represent nine different categories of relationships in your life. Each circle will be made from a variety of materials that will serve as an offering to that particular relationship. In the end, this altar's purpose is to be consumed, either by fire, earth, wind, or water, as an offering to all the relationships you want to keep alive and well.

Note on the Practice

When making altars, it's important—as a way to show respect and appreciation and not exploitation—to acknowledge, honor, and remember other traditions in which this has been practiced for hundreds of years.

For instance, within Tibetan Buddhism there is a tradition that involves the creation and destruction of a mandala made from colored sand. It is common for these mandalas to be labored on for weeks by Tibetan monks, and some, like the Kalachakra Mandala, are said to contain as many as 722 deities living within the mandala itself. The destruction of the mandala is ritualized as the sand is swept together into a "prayer pile," collected into a jar wrapped in silk, and brought to a flowing body of water to release the altar and prayers back into the world.

There is also a South American ceremony called *despacho*, which originated among the indigenous Quechua-speaking peoples of the Peruvian, Ecuadorian, and Bolivian Andes. These altars, which are made from leaves, flowers, seeds, beans, etc., are burned for a variety of occasions such as births, deaths, healings, restoring balance, or feeding the ancestral dead. The *despachos* are ritualized beauty offered to tend, pray for, and feed both seen and unseen relationships.

Learning about and lifting up other traditions is how we can honor and not appropriate them.

Prepare

Intentions

May I make an altar that recognizes, honors, praises, and blesses the relationships that make up my life. May I reflect on the past year and acknowledge when I've tended these relationships well and when I've dropped them. May I recommit to these relationships for the next year.

Outside vs. Inside

Depending on what's available to you, you can perform this ritual either in your home or outside in nature. Both are totally acceptable.

You Will Need

If you are doing this ritual indoors, you need:
- A large piece of poster board paper
- A marker
- String and a pair of scissors

If you are doing this ritual outdoors, you need:
- A small trowel
- A large piece of fabric
- String and a pair of scissors

Here's a list of what you need whether you are indoors or outdoors. Please get enough of the material that you can make a large circle on the paper/fabric with it.

HELLO, GOODBYE

- A handful of earth
- A small glass of water
- A handful or spoonful of something sweet
- Cut-up root vegetables like carrots or potatoes
- A handful of salt
- Flower petals and/or leaves
- A handful of coins or paper money
- A handful of seeds

Please note: These materials and their associations are simply suggestions. If you want to mix and match or completely shift this recipe around, go for it. What works for me might not work for you. Make it your own.

Begin

With that said, gather everything carefully. Be mindful of where you gather them from, your mindset as you gather them, and even how you hold or store them. These materials are offerings for your life. If you can make or grow some of the material yourself, even better.

The Nine Rings

If you are indoors, begin by drawing nine concentric circles on your paper. Make sure the paper is large enough to hold all of your material. Follow the directions below by putting that material over the drawn circles on your paper. You can answer the prompts out loud or in a journal.

If you are outdoors, you can do this directly on the earth.

1. The Body: Earth
Begin by making one small circle out of earth in the center to represent your relationship to your own body. *How have you treated your body this past year? How have you tended it well and where have you dropped the ball? What are you willing to recommit to for this next year?*

2. Healing: Water

Make your next ring by pouring water as an offering to your relationship to healing. *Have there been any illnesses this past year for yourself, your family or friends? Animals? The Earth? Has there been any healing or recovery? What are you willing to recommit to for this next year?*

3. Ancestors: Sweets

Make your next ring by placing the sweets as an offering to your ancestors. *Who are you able to remember and say the names of? Who can't be remembered but can still be included? Did you remember your ancestors at all this year? How so? How are you willing to recommit to this relationship this year?*

4. Home: Root Vegetables

Make your next ring by placing the roots as an offering to your home and the place you live. *How have you tended your home this past year? What has gone left untended? What is your relationship like with your neighbors? With the local waterways, forests, parks? How are you willing to recommit to this relationship this year?*

5. Food: Salt

Make your next ring by pouring the salt as an offering to all the food that has granted you your life. *What foods are you eating? Plants? Animals? Processed foods? Organic? Where do you source your food from? Do you care? Do you want to care more? Have you been saying a thank-you or grace before or after eating? How are you willing to recommit to your relationship to food this year?*

6. Family and Community: Flowers

Make your next ring by placing the flowers as an offering to all your friends and family and all of their families. *How have you shown up within your family this year? To your wider community? What relationships feel strong at this moment? What relationships are you currently in conflict with? Which relationships need more of your attention? How are you willing to recommit to your relationship to your family and friends this year?*

7. Workers: Coins

Make your next ring by placing the coins as an offering to all those whose names you don't know and whose stories you'll never hear but who built your technology, harvested your food, delivered your packages, assisted you on the phone, cleaned your hotel room, and picked up your garbage. *How have you been in relationship to these people? Do you ignore them or take them for granted? Do you approach them with kindness and courtesy? How are you willing to recommit to these relationships this year?*

8. Wisdom: Seeds

Make your next ring by spreading the seeds as an offering to all those who taught you this year, to all the learning and to the hard-earned wisdom you have acquired from your experience. *What were some of the lessons from this past year? Who taught them to you? Who have you taught this year? How are you willing to recommit to your relationship to learning this coming year?*

9. The Unknown: Breath

Make your next ring with your breath, literally blowing on this circle-within-circle altar. Your breath is an offering to the Great Mystery of life, to everything you don't know, to all that is yet to come, to the unpredictability of your days, and to Spirit or God or the Universe or however you want to call it. *How have you been in relationship with uncertainty this year? How do you deal with impermanence? How are you willing to recommit to your relationship to the unknown this coming year?*

Conclude

Once you have created these nine concentric circles, pause and take some time to witness the altar you've made. Not only have you renewed your commitments to these relationships, but you made libations and offerings to feed them as well. Now it's time to let them go.

Indoors: If you created these rings on paper, it's time to fold the paper up into a bundle. Grab the four corners of the paper and fold them toward the center. Fold again toward the center as necessary until the material is securely bundled inside. Take the string and tie the bundle tightly, like you are gift-wrapping a present.

Outdoors: Unless you are leaving your altar to the wind, you can collect your altar into a pile and gather it together in a piece of fabric. Place the gathered material in the center and lift the four corners of the fabric until you have a small bundle.

Now that you have a bundle, there are four ways you can let your offering go:

1. Wind. You can leave your altar outside to be scattered by the wind. This might be the simplest option as you can just leave what you made.
2. Fire. You can take your bundled altar to a firepit or fireplace and burn it.
3. Earth. You can dig a small hole with your trowel and bury the bundle. This becomes even more meaningful if you are in relationship to the place you buried it.
4. Water. You can release the material in a flowing body of water, like a river or stream, or at the edge of the ocean, letting the material be carried away.

Note: If there are things on your altar, like the money, that you don't want to burn, take them off the altar and donate or bury them.

As you release your birthday bundle to one of the elements, speak aloud your gratitude to these relationships. Praise them for they all tether you to your life.

After burning, burying, releasing, or letting go, spend some time sitting in silence. Let the power of these doings resonate.

Questions for Further Reflection
- What are my most important relationships?
- What are my most forgotten relationships?
- What has this ritual helped me appreciate and remember?
- How does this ritual help me enter into the next year of my life?

Turning a New Decade

If reaching another birthday is an accomplishment, hitting a new decade seems especially so. Turning thirty, fifty, or ninety, like my grandmother did, truly marks a beginning and an ending. It is the completion of one chapter of life and the initiation into a new one. We often refer to a decade of our lives as if it represents a certain kind of behavior, specific priorities, mistakes, accomplishments, and focus. For instance, my twenties were filled with exploration, experimentation, travel, many jobs, and many, many roommates. My thirties were devoted to community, career, and family.

Marking a new decade can feel like climbing to the top of a small mound of experiences from the past ten years and looking out from that vantage point and reflecting on all you see—the regrets, the successes, the losses, the growth, the journey. Ritualizing this moment can also serve to establish a boundary on all that you are ready or willing to be complete, like outdated mindsets, behaviors, careers, and dreams, so that new ones have space to emerge.

You can refine the questions within this chapter's rituals to speak specifically to crossing into a new decade. What are the commitments you are completing from the past decade? What are the relationships you are honoring from this time? What have you learned from living through those ten years? You can also adjust the rituals to make them reflect the number ten or the number of the age you are turning—if you're hitting fifty, for example, you can work with the number five.

What is most important is that as you cross into this new chapter, you make offerings and libations for your life, its longevity, and all that underwrites it.

Survival Anniversary

When a person is in great danger one day and is saved miraculously, s/he is obligated to make what is known as a *seudas hoda'ah,* a party of thanks.

—Rebbe Menachem Mendel Schneerson

I heard it called "bonus time" or "my new life" or "this precious gift." Each conversation I had with more than twenty-five survivors of drug overdoses, wildfires, diseases, car accidents, and bus bombings contained profound wonderings and struggles about what it meant to receive a second act in life. Questions surfaced in the wake of recovering from these life-threatening experiences, such as: "Why am I still alive?" "How do I want this to define me?" "Am I a victim or a survivor?" "What purpose does my life now serve?"

This was the case with Tad. After being rushed to the hospital for a crystal meth overdose, Tad, a cis man in his thirties, asked to keep his phone so he could record his last will and testament. For the first twenty-four hours, Tad was convinced he was going to die. His whole chest went ice cold, his heart was racing at two hundred beats per minute, and all he could think about was *This could be it. This could lights out and then nothing.* But he didn't die. When he got discharged from the hospital, he remembers looking outside and just being in awe that he got to see the world again. Even the anxiety attack he had later that day made him realize, *I get to have this anxiety attack. I'm alive. It's a miracle.* Every year since, on the anniversary of his overdose, he has written in his calendar in big bold letters, "Your new life begins again today," reassuring the parts of him that were still stuck in the traumatic memory and offering himself relief and remembrance.

When I asked Elena, a survivor of four near-death experiences, to name one word that would describe the biggest challenge she faced after each one, she immediately replied: "Choice." By recognizing these accidents as crucial thresholds where, against all odds, she received her life back, Elena realized that it came down to needing to choose between defining herself as a victim or a victor. Even though the aftermath of each trauma resulted in pretty severe limitations, the choice of seeing herself as a survivor instilled in her spirit "a will to live and a sense of courage to face hardship."

Surviving a life-threatening experience is a staggering and overwhelming thing to go through. It undoes you and undermines your stability in the world. The aftermath can bring isolation, shame, and, especially, an uneasy vulnerability. Just because you survived doesn't guarantee a full recovery, and often the biggest struggle to supporting that long road of recovery is being able to ask for help and to receive many reminders that you're not alone. Too often we can hear the internal shame and self-blame message—"I did something wrong"—which is why it's so healing to have others show up for support or to check in and say, "Your life matters. We need you here with us." Being acknowledged like this can help make sense of what may seem senseless and remember how valuable our life is and how needed we are in the world. Being received this way can plant us firmly in our lives again.

Michelle called her near-death experience "a highly disguised blessing." In the spring of 2009, Michelle was hit by her own truck, which had been parked at the top of a hill and came barreling down at her due to an emergency-brake malfunction. As the helicopter rushed her to the ICU, she heard a clear voice in her head that said: *It's not your time. You didn't die. Life wants you to grab onto it with both hands. This is your parachute now.* In the months and years that it took Michelle to even walk again, she came to understand the privilege of having been given her life back. She referred to it as "her biggest wake-up call," making her aware of all the things she previously took for granted—her body, her health, her relationships. "People were bending over backwards for me and my life," she said, referring to both the physical and financial support from her community as well as from strangers she had never met before. "I was so broken, and people kept on showing up to take care of me. They saved my life again and again and again." As reciprocity, Michelle organized a ritual feast where she fed and thanked her entire community, preparing for them an enormous meal with gifts, prayers, and thanks as an attempt to give back even a fraction of all she had received.

This ritual is inspired by her story and is a way to annually remember the privilege of getting your life back and the sacredness that it is. Your life is yours again, but it's certainly not yours. It's been gifted back to you, and rather than just taking it, the question is: *How do you give back and to whom?* Offering a ritual feast to feed all those that helped you, seen and unseen, known and unknown, human and beyond, is a way to give yourself as an offering of love.

Rebirth Day

On the anniversary of surviving your accident or illness, make sure to mark the date on your calendar just like you would a birthday. Except this is your *rebirth day*. Consider inviting your close friends to mark their calendars too, because this is the date they didn't lose you. As time passes and life gets busy, forgetting happens, and by marking this date, you remember to do the Feast of Thanks Ritual and continue to make offerings to the gift that is your life.

THE FEAST *of* THANKS RITUAL

The purpose of this ritual is to create an opportunity to honor the anniversary of your accident by gathering together your friends and family for a thanksgiving meal. The meal itself is also a gift that you are offering in reciprocity for being granted your life again. As author Lewis Hyde reflects in his book *The Gift*, one of the most important principles of any gift is to keep it moving by accepting it and then giving it to someone else, creating an experience of communion between the givers and receivers. This ritual feast first and foremost asks you to acknowledge what you received, while also placing you in the role of giver too, feeding those that love you, those that helped you, those ancestors you come from, and those unseen forces that you will never meet but that continue to make this life possible.

Prepare

Intentions

May I give back with gratitude for the gift of being here. May I give offerings and thanks to my community and to the Spirit for my survival. May I consider all this accident has taught me and continue to choose more life.

You Will Need

- A candle
- An empty plate
- A three-course meal

The Spirit Plate

While everyone at the meal gets a plate to eat from, this particular plate is special. It is not for a specific person but rather for all those who couldn't fit around the table but somehow are a part of your story of survival—the doctors who performed your surgery, the people in your AA group who had your back during your lowest moments, or all those people who donated to help you pay your hospital bills. While the plate *starts off empty*, you will fill this Spirit Plate throughout the meal, symbolically offering little bits of each of the courses until the plate is quite full. At the end of the meal, you are encouraged to take the plate outside and leave the food as an offering to something much greater than you, whether you call it Spirit, God, Goddess, Creator, Earth Mother, or any of the other ten thousand ways to acknowledge that which is Mysterious.

Meal Prep

This is one of those rare times where I am advising you to go *big*. Cook up a storm, prepare a feast, and make food like your life depends on it, because it does. Create at least three separate dishes for the meal but feel free to make more. What they are is completely up to you, but what is most important is that they are served consecutively and not all at once. If you want to go the distance, use recipes that are meaningful, like your grandmother's soup or maybe the favorite dish of each of your guests. Remember, treat this meal like a precious gift you are giving; therefore, the more you give your heart to it, the more it will be received in that way.

A Note on the Intention

Whenever there is ritual, there is always the danger of trying too hard to make it meaningful. Especially when the gathering has to do with something serious, like surviving an accident, the tone of the evening can veer toward a therapy session. Try to avoid that. This feast isn't intended to help you process unresolved emotion, even though it may surface. Remember that the meal's intention is to acknowledge the blessing of having been granted your life again and to feed and thank all that made that so. When push comes to shove, keep it simple and stay focused on passing the gift forward.

Begin

Don't underestimate the power of a warm welcome. Those gathering are the people who love you, care about you, and were devastated to consider living in this world without you. Let them know how much it means to you that they continue to show up for you. Thank them for being here.

Once everyone has settled in, light a candle to signal the shift into ritual, and state the purpose of the meal by explaining the mechanics of the evening: First and foremost, you are feeding your guests and are about to make their bellies happy. But, because this is a ritual, the meal is also meaning-infused.

Start by holding up the empty Spirit Plate to introduce its purpose.

Each dish that you bring to the table has a theme to it, and corresponding prompts to inspire storytelling. You don't have to answer all of them. They are there to simply spark a story as you eat and share. And while many stories will come from you, invite your guests to participate by sharing their stories, thanks, and blessings. The purpose of the courses' themes is to recognize the concentric circles of support and gifts that surrounded you as you healed from this accident. You did not do this alone and in isolation. The themes are devoted to honoring the interdependence of all your relationships.

The First Course: Appreciating

- What did you once take for granted?
- What do you appreciate now?
- Whom do you appreciate now?
- What are you grateful for?

Tell stories of big and little appreciations. Put a little pinch of food onto the Spirit Plate.

The Second Course: Helping

- Who were your major helpers?
- Who were your minor helpers?
- Who showed up when you least expected it?
- What are ways you still need support?

Tell stories of those who supported and helped you. Put a little pinch of food onto the Spirit Plate.

The Third Course: Recommitting

- What's become important to you now?
- How has your life's purpose changed?
- What purpose does your life serve?
- What are ways you want to give back?

Speak to how the accident has impacted your purpose. Put a little pinch of food onto the Spirit Plate.

Offering the Spirit Plate

While your plates are empty, the spirit plate should now be full. As the meal concludes, take the spirit plate outside to be left under a tree or wherever else it's appropriate to leave food. This is the most important part of the ritual as you are acknowledging the Unseen/Spirit in your survival and healing story.

As you place the plate, consider pausing with these considerations:

I acknowledge that there were unknown forces that helped me survive this accident.

Take a breath.

I recognize that a miracle occurred that aided in my survival and/or recovery.

Take a breath.

I honor, thank, and give back to the Great Mystery that is my life.

Take a breath.

Put the food down and give yourself space to be quiet as you offer the plate. Don't rush this moment. Instead, listen and consider how incredibly vast and wondrous life is and how precious your life is too.

Questions for Further Reflection

- How has being a survivor altered my relationship with life?
- How has this ritual helped transform my perspective?
- Why is it important to remember or mark the anniversary of my survival?
- What have I learned about humility and asking for support?

Death Anniversary

Our willingness to remember turns out to be
a kind of banquet . . . and the remembering is the food.

—Stephen Jenkinson

Here, again. So much has changed and yet their absence remains. For the
first time or the thirtieth, a year has passed that marks their departure.
At first, perhaps it was too much to bear living in this world without
them. Yet, as time proceeded, it got easier. Sometimes too easy. The grief subsided,
but in a strange way it also bound you to your beloved. It let you feel your love for
them in the world, maybe even feeling them still here with you. For better or worse,
time dilutes the potency of grief as it enhances the fog of forgetting. The longer they
are gone, the more their memory fades away. Yet time gracefully moves in a spiral,
circling back onto itself so that, if you choose, there are moments to remember and
renew that memory again. Anniversaries mark a return, and a death anniversary
returns you to your love and that original grief. But what's to be done with the day
as it arrives?

I know many people who want to forget that day. It was too painful, too uncomfortable, filled with too much grief. They tell me that they just want to remember the happy times and leave that death day in the dust. I understand this. The
day my dad died was painful too. Witnessing his breath fade away put me right
up against a loss I had never experienced before. The year that followed his passing was like emerging from another world, and when the first anniversary of the
day he died approached, I considered ignoring it and treating it like any other. Yet

something within me wondered what the consequences would be if I let this day pass unacknowledged. What would become of his memory if I didn't remember him well and consistently?

Memory needs maintenance. Just like a car, it needs to be brought in now and again, hood popped, and tuned up. Servicing memory requires that we return to it with full, careful attention. Time wears at memory like the road wears on tires. Because of that, memory needs to be tended to, checked out, dusted off, and put back together again. Stories need to be told, photos taken out, recipes cooked, songs played. That way memory stays functional, dynamic, and able to live again through you. In a way, memory requires you to revisit it often in order to keep it healthy and alive. And, consequently, what you remember might stay alive as well.

My father's death date is February 28, or the 24th of Adar in our Hebrew calendar. In my tradition we call that his *yahrtzeit*, which is Yiddish for "death anniversary." Every year on this date, our family lights a candle and chants a Hebrew prayer of mourning: a small way we acknowledge the big hole he left in our lives. Our little ritual is meant to stir up the forgotten grief once again so that the love can rise to the top too. The act of remembering is an important commandment in my tradition because we're taught how easy it is to forget. Life is like that. Full-on schedules, workloads, child care, cleaning, cooking, washing, schlepping, resting, and repeat. My ancestors understood that getting caught up in the everydayness of our lives can steal away our memory. And the consequence of not maintaining it is loss. We can and do actively lose our dead.

In modern English, loss and death have become twin words, one often confused for the other. But loss isn't synonymous with death. I've often heard my teacher, Stephen Jenkinson, speak about this, and it got me thinking: While it's a euphemism to say "I lost my dad," it's not entirely true. Yes, my father died, but using the word "lost" describes more what I might do *with* his memory if I don't maintain it. Losing my dad is actually a consequence of not tending to his memory.

The idea that we can lose our dead is such an odd consideration for the modern mind. Instead, we chisel stone, mountain, and metal to secure memory forever. We build monuments, plaques, memorials, and tombs to freeze memory in place so that it is unchanging, what French historian Pierre Nora calls "illusions of eternity." These permanent structures hold the remembering, so we don't have to. We break rock so our hearts don't have to always be broken. But then what? Could it be that in securing memory, we also solidify our hearts.

Tending to memory is the key. It suggests that we must reach beyond ourselves and consider that perhaps someone is reaching for us as well. Even the etymology of the verb "to tend" conjures up an image of extending one's hand, as its roots lie in the Proto-Indo-European word *ten*, meaning "to stretch." Tending to memory lets it extend and continue over time, like the weft being drawn by a weaver over and under the warp on a loom. Rituals that remember can guide our hands back to the frayed threads of our dead and loop them back into the fabric of our living memory. They can remind us, the living, that we have a responsibility, not just to our lives but to our dead as well. Our health and their health are intertwined.

Memory is promiscuous. Fluid, changing, alive, sometimes lasting and sometimes fleeting, memory is shapable like clay. Our hands, our thoughts, our songs, our food, our broken hearts can shape and reshape it. Molding memory keeps it pliant and alive. Yet, just like clay, if you leave it too long, it becomes brittle and crumbly. So we must wet that memory-clay with our tears, rebreaking our hearts again and again. Our responsibility is to remember our dead by keeping both our memory and our hearts supple.

Many cultures around the world understand this symbiotic relationship of remembering their dead, both their recently deceased and their long line of ancestors. The Mexican tradition of *Dia de los Muertos*, Day of the Dead, is celebrated on November 1 and 2. On these days, family and friends come together to make altars, *ofrendas*, filled with marigold flowers, photos, and the favorites foods of the deceased. Pillows and blankets are provided so that the ancestors can rest after their journey.[*] Similar to Day of the Dead, Japanese families make altars in their homes filled with food, flowers, and incense for the Obon festival, when the spirits are said to return to visit their descendants. Traditionally, families hang paper lanterns outside their homes to light the way for the dead returning to the world, and at the end of the festival a guiding fire, or *okuribi*, is built to help the spirits return safely to the realm of the ancestors.[†] In Vietnam, a death anniversary is called *giỗ* or *ngày giỗ*, and it is a special day when extended family gathers for a ritual and feast. The specifics of this ritual depend on how recent the death, but with each *giỗ* there is incense and joss paper burned, prayers at the altar, and a massive meal made specifically for this day. It is a feast for the living and the dead where all who gather can renew their relationships. In any culture's death

---

* John D. Morgan and Pittu Laungani, eds., *Death and Bereavement Around the World: Major Religious Traditions*, vol. 1 (Amityville, NY: Baywood Publishing, 2002).

† "Death Around the World: Obon Festival, Japan," Funeral Guide, September 2, 2016, https://www.funeralguide.co.uk/blog/death-around-world-obon-festival-japan.

RITUALS *for the* YEAR   95

anniversary rituals, there is a bittersweet understanding that one day, you too will become an ancestor. Therefore, the way you remember your dead is most likely the way you also will be remembered.

I want to acknowledge that all of this might feel incredibly intimidating, overwhelming, or even confusing at first. You might be asking yourself, "What does this even mean?" or "How do I go about doing this all alone?" especially if you don't have a living culture to ground and guide you in its ancestral traditions. Here's my advice: Go slow. Do less. Expect less. Listen and see. Let the "I don't knows" and the "what do I dos" be included in the ritual—doing so is where the success is born, and letting yourself make plenty of mistakes is what allows the ritual's success to even be possible.

With that said, the rituals below are simple choreographies to move your hands and words toward some tending. You can simplify them, make them elaborate, or just use them as inspiration, but what's most important is to do something. Rituals can't be done internally. They are done through what we make, cut, break, bake, sing, dance, burn, clean, and eat. They are how we mark time and how we attempt to tend to all that could be forgotten, yet might not be. This creative ritual's mission is to tenderize your heart a little bit more, and as it softens, the remembering can happen again.

THE MEMORY CANDLE RITUAL

This ritual is a bread crumb. It is a temporary marker that could be a part of a long line of "doings," weaving you back into relationship with your dead. It is a bread crumb because if you just do it once, it isn't very much. The real potential of this ritual is found in your willingness to return to it year after year or even more often, treating it as a trail that leads you back to this relationship. Like all relationships, the more often you tend to your relationship with your dead, the stronger you are bound to them and they to you.

The heart of this ritual is centered around a candle. In my tradition, lighting a candle has always served as a marker that reminds us to remember. We light candles at the beginning and end of our holidays to distinguish them and make them special—two for Shabbat and our festivals, eight for Chanukah and one large candle with three wicks for Havdallah, the ritual that ends Shabbat and starts the workweek. To remember our dead we also light a *yahrzeit* candle—a vigil candle that burns for twenty-four hours. But why a candle? Why use such a little light to mark these special moments? It seems to me that the candlelight's fleetingness and vulnerability is a part of its purpose. The light is temporary. So, while the candle helps us to distinguish sacred time from everyday time, it also reminds us how limited and precious that time truly is. For a brief moment, that flickering light is our cue to slow down our pace and soften our gaze so that we might see more clearly what would have been otherwise forgotten.

There's a childhood story told by Bella Chagall, the painter Marc Chagall's wife, in her book *Burning Lights*, in which she remembers making candles with her mother in Russia every *Kol Nidre*, the sacred evening of Yom Kippur, considered perhaps the holiest day of the Jewish calendar. The story begins with her holding the skeins of thread as her mother weaves and dips the wicks in wax, praying for the living and the dead. Every dip, she says a prayer for those that are still alive: "May all of us live long." Every weave of the string, she says the name of another who had died. Her son. Her aunt. Her father. Tears mingle with the wax, over and over again until, by the end of the story, the making of the candles and the prayers for her family have become one. Then what's even more heartrendingly beautiful is that her mother's memory candles are taken to the synagogue to be lit side by side with everyone else's candles made from their own tears and memories. On that holy night, the room is ablaze with the flickering glow of the village's candles, all remembering together.

That story comes from a time that my people barely remember. Nowadays, we don't make our candles, we buy them. Sometimes while I was growing up, we used an electric *yahrzeit* candle that we plugged into the wall, a fake red flame that required so little effort from us. Our modern culture enthrones convenience and immediacy over the slow, meandering path that remembering takes. So often a ritual's purpose arrives through the slowing down to make or follow that very thing. For instance, in the story above, each twisting of the twine and dipping of the wick gave space for the hidden to reveal itself. Without the intensity that comes with getting an immediate result, there is enough space and time for the real remembering to arise, for the stories to be told and the tears to come again on their own.

This ritual is inspired by Bella's story and a phone tree. It imagines that you aren't the only one who might want to remember your dearly departed. The heart of this ritual is for a small circle of friends and family to light a candle at the same time, all over the world. When you invite other people to partake in the ritual and know there are others lighting and remembering simultaneously, it becomes a way to bring many into one mind and one love.

If you want to start by doing this ritual just with yourself, go for it. Sometimes we need to feel it out for ourselves before inviting others to participate. Again, there is no ritual reward for the person who achieves the most. Small done well is better than big done poorly. With that said, this ritual is intended to be done with others, the friends and family who knew and loved this ancestor. They do not need to be living in the same place, for the reality these days is that most do not. Instead, this ritual will utilize the good, old-fashioned mail system.

I realize that this is a big ask. People are busy, disconnected, distracted, and asking a random relative to participate in a ritual might leave you empty-handed. But maybe not. And, what if just one person was willing? Could that be enough? This isn't a contest for profundity or the "more you do, the better," but rather it's about how you bring yourself to what you do. Think quality not quantity.

A Note on Timing

While this chapter is devoted to death anniversaries, this can also be done on birthdays. Or Father's or Mother's Days. Or any holiday of significance and remembering, like Halloween or Memorial Day.

Prepare

Intentions

May I remember my beloved deceased with other family who loved them too. May I slow down to remember. May our love and memory become one.

You Will Need

- A small list of friends/family
- One candle
- A match or lighter
- An envelope and stamps
- A photo or note

The Invitation

First things first, create an invitation that shares about the upcoming death anniversary and that you are inviting others to participate in this ritual. You'll want to send the invitation at least two weeks before the anniversary so that the people involved have ample time to buy and/or send a candle.

The invitation can work in two ways depending on your preference:

Option 1: You invite everyone to send *you* a candle in the mail. The candles themselves don't have to be large—a tealight is more than sufficient. Within the invitation, you can ask everyone to write a short note of a memory they might have to share of this person, or a photograph. Sometimes prompts are helpful. For instance, you can say, "Please fill in the blank: 'I will never forget the time with _____ when he did/she said _____.'" In the end, you are the one receiving all the candles to light on the death anniversary.

Option 2: You can create a candle mail tree. Just like a phone tree, everyone on the list is paired with another person to send their candle to. It works in a similar way to the first example, but everyone sends one candle and story in the mail and receives one in turn. The special part about this option is that it invites everyone to participate in the lighting and the ritual of remembering.

Placing the Candle

When your candle arrives, put it somewhere that you consider special. Maybe that's on the fireplace mantel, the kitchen table, or a nightstand. Or maybe that's under your favorite tree in your backyard. This becomes an altar for your deceased. You can adorn that altar with the candle(s), photos of the deceased person, flowers, or special objects that this person loved, to make the place even more beautiful. Beauty courts memory.

Begin

On the day and time chosen, prepare to light the candle by creating a sacred container for the lighting ceremony. The fewer distractions, the better. If you are gathering—whether in person or virtually—allow the natural conversation to ebb, and call the group to attention as you begin the ritual.

1. Light the candle and pause. The flickering light is enough at first. Consider seeing it as a memory rekindled. For now, just watch the light dance, like a meditation. Slow down your breathing with the candle. You don't need to say anything or do anything more.

2. Say this person's full name. Pause. Breathe. If they have other names, like "Dad," or "Aunty," you can say them here too. Let their name linger like you are addressing them and awaiting their response. Pause again.

3. Read the story that accompanied your candle. If you just received a photograph, let yourself gaze at it and remember that face and/or show it to the group. Allow whatever feelings to arise. Again, take your time—less is more. Pause. Take an inhale. Then exhale.

Conclude

Complete the ritual by offering two blessings.

The first one goes to the person you are remembering. It doesn't have to be elaborate or fancy. It could be enough to simply say, "May I never forget you." But because rituals always ask a little more from us than we are used to giving, try to speak a little more than you might want. You may be surprised at what comes from your heart straight out of your mouth.

The second blessing is for the living person (or people) who sent you the candle. Bless their life and health too.

Linger in this space a bit, witnessing the candle burn. Waiting and observing is as important in ritual space as doing the lighting itself. Sometimes when we give the space to not do anything, something else can occur.

If it is safe to do so, let the candle burn until it extinguishes itself.

Afterward

You can either clear away the altar after this ritual or you can keep it and add to it. In my home, I built an entire wall of ancestor photos around this candle ritual. I continue to replace the candle and add photos to the wall. Tending to their memory has transformed from a once-a-year ritual to an everyday candle-lighting ritual. Lighting that candle in the evening reminds me every day that my entire life is underwritten by their lives.

Questions for Further Reflection

- Why include the family or friends in this ritual? What does that do?
- How does preparing for the ritual impact it?
- What was strengthened through this ritual?
- Am I willing to continue next year? Why or why not?

RITUALS
for LETTING GO

Weaning

Note: This chapter and its rituals were inspired by conversations with more than twenty-five mothers and birthing parents. The term "birthing parent" is used to include and honor transgender and nonbinary parents.

A newborn has only three demands. They are warmth in the arms of its mother, food from her breasts, and security in the knowledge of her presence. Breastfeeding satisfies all three.

—World Health Organization

Another umbilical cord is being cut. Another tangible, instinctual, and profoundly mammalian way that your body gives nourishment to your baby's body is ending, along with all the comfort, mess, pain, relief, and deep connection that it entails. Maybe in the beginning it was awful. No latching; up every hour; the leaking; the horrible, endless pumping. And also, beautiful. Those quiet, sacred, bonding moments together when their little fingers wrapped around yours. Their weight and warmth resting and receiving your sustenance. The pleasure in pure giving. This ancient feeding rite that women and babies have undergone since time immemorial. But now, as one mother put it to her child, "no more momma milk." Now your body begins another round of returning to you. Your baby begins another step away from you, needing you less, needing the world more. So, as one door opens and another closes, what to make of this moment? Is it as simple as "it's over, what next?" Or can this time be properly honored, grieved, celebrated, and marked as the threshold it truly is?

Gwen, my oldest friend, posted online her last photo of her baby's nursing moment with the subtitle, "Bittersweet." In the midst of what she would call a "total mind fuck" of questions and doubts—*Is this the right time? Should I be nursing longer? What do the experts say?*—she realized that she was ready and not ready.

She had read all the research that told her that after twelve months the nutritional value of the breast milk goes down, and she understood that she was doing it now mostly for the connection and healing it brought them both. And that was important enough. Gwen's son's birth story was, in fact, traumatic—she suffered a placental abruption that caused the baby to be without oxygen while still in the womb. After an emergency C-section, he was immediately rushed to the NICU at a separate hospital, and Gwen didn't even have a moment to see or hold him. He had suffered irreversible brain damage.

Those first few weeks in the hospital were times of intense uncertainty, with a constant rush of doctors, ventilators, bad hospital lighting, and grief. The one lifeline she and her baby had was her breast milk. Multiple times a day, her husband would transport it to the NICU, where the nurses who would dip their fingers in it and line the newborn's mouth so he could taste the mother that he had yet to meet. On day 6, they let her hold him for the first time. She was warned that due to his brain damage, he might not know how to latch, or suck, or swallow, or even digest the milk. And yet, against all odds, he did, which was the first time she sensed this was going to be okay. At that moment, she said to herself, *I'm gonna nurse this damn baby until he's a teenager!* To her, nursing became a way not just to feed her baby but to heal the separation and trauma from his birth. While Gwen ended up nursing her baby until about fourteen months and not fourteen years, each mother and birthing parent I interviewed for this chapter told their own unique weaning story of "ready, not ready."

Mothers and birthing parents are faced with impossible mountains to climb in our modern culture, which directly impacts how long they nurse or if they nurse at all. In the many interviews I conducted, I heard stories about domineering and bossy mothers-in-law ("The baby's too old. You don't have to do that anymore"), embarrassment stories ("Excuse me, ma'am, you're making our customers uncomfortable. Would you mind using the restroom to breastfeed?"), sexualizing stories ("I'm trying to feed my baby and that perv is staring at my breasts"), formula pressure stories ("The nurse just kept on pushing the formula, so that's what I ended up doing"), self-doubt stories ("I felt selfish that I was putting my needs before my baby's"), and especially, employment stories ("I needed to go back to work after my baby was only six weeks old. I'm scared my baby will bond with someone else, but what can I do?"). Actually, the pressure to return to work has one of the most severe impacts on how long a woman nurses.

Let's do some math: There's a study from the *Surgeon General's Call to Action to Support Breastfeeding*, published in 2011, which concludes that women who intend to return to work are less likely to breastfeed than part-time or unemployed moms.* Add that to a study† that found women who breastfed for at least six months had their earnings decrease more than moms who breastfed for shorter times or not at all. Add that to only 25 percent of companies making any special effort to allow for breastfeeding, inflexible work hours, lack of privacy at work, lack of child care options, and limited maternity leave (here's looking at you, USA, with zero guaranteed weeks), and you have a very understandable but wildly poignant statistic: Fewer than 14 percent of moms in the United States are still nursing at eighteen months, which is dramatically different from the nonindustrialized world's average, which almost three years old.

My mom did not breastfeed me at all, and this is true for many of my peers' mothers and grandmothers. Many of us born in North America in the 1970s were formula babies as "breastfeeding reached its nadir in 1972, when only 22% of women breastfed [at all]."‡ While it's impossible to know the cause of why the latter part of the twentieth century saw a sharp decline in women breastfeeding, there are many culprits, especially the canoodling of scientific medicine, industry, and consumer culture. People wanted or were told to want things faster, easier, and more convenient. And breastfeeding was considered burdensome, old-fashioned, or even "a little disgusting,"§ according to letters and editorials in a popular 1950s women's magazine. Safe alternatives to breastmilk, like Carnation, inundated new mothers with advertisements of plump, rosy-cheeked babies clearly preferring instant milk instead, while at the same time, hospitals, rather than homes, became an affordable and preferable place to give birth. In the book *The One Best Way?: Breastfeeding History, Politics and Policy in Canada*, authors Tasnim Nathoo and Aleck Ostry assert that hospitalized birth "deterred the involvement of grandmothers, mothers, and other women who might possess practical breastfeeding knowledge."§ So, by the 1960s, the bottle was king and breastfeeding was becoming an almost forgotten lifeline.

---

* "The Surgeon General's Call to Action to Support Breastfeeding," Centers for Disease Control and Prevention, May 11, 2021, https://www.cdc.gov/breastfeeding/resources/calltoaction.htm.

† Phyllis L. F. Rippeyoung and Mary C. Noonan, "Is Breastfeeding Truly Cost Free? Income Consequences of Breastfeeding for Women," *American Sociological Review* 77, no. 2 (April 1, 2012):244–67.

‡ Daniel W. Sellen, "Comparison of Infant Feeding Patterns Reported for Nonindustrial Populations with Current Recommendations," *Journal of Nutrition* 131, no. 10 (October 2001): 2707–15.

§ Tasnim Nathoo and Aleck Ostry, *The One Best Way? Breastfeeding History, Politics, and Policy in Canada* (Waterloo, Ontario: Wilfrid Laurier University Press, 2009).

¶ Ibid.

Much has changed since then, with more women than ever breastfeeding—89 percent in Canada* and 74 percent in the US†—but women are still reclaiming their bodies from a male-dominated society that projects shame, judgment, control, objectification, and perfectionism onto breastfeeding, and, by extension, onto weaning. "This goes back to the idea of what belongs to me," one mother told me. "When I began breastfeeding, I saw it as me choosing to reclaim my breasts from a patriarchal culture, from greedy corporations, and even from other family members trying to tell me what to do with my body and my baby. But now that I am weaning, I'm in the process of reclaiming my body from my child for myself."

Reclaiming is an act of returning to wholeness, but that can sometimes feel confusing when there are contradictory feelings. The journey of weaning carries both a return to freedom and a loss of connection—the bittersweet taste of endings and beginnings, of gaining back and letting go, simultaneously. To author Rachel Naomi Remen reclaiming means "coming to recognize and accept that we have in us both sides of everything. We are capable of fear and courage, generosity and selfishness, vulnerability and strength. These things do not cancel each other out but offer us a full range of power and response to life."

For instance, many moms triumphantly shared with me all they got back after weaning their babies: "I got my body back," "I finally got sleep," "I'm able to wear whatever bra I want," "I can exercise," "No more leaking!" "I could finally have a drink!"

Freedom was a huge thread woven into every mother's story. Jordanna, a mother who recently weaned her three-year-old, said, "As a mom, you're totally tethered to your child. So leaving any more than two hours has been impossible. Weaning to me meant liberation—a sense that the kitchen doors can actually close rather than remain open all day, all night, whenever and however." But, often in the same sentence, the same breath even, these women tearfully lamented about what they were letting go of. Jocelyn, a mother of two, said, "I built this baby inside me and now I've been building him outside of me. And when he stopped nursing, on one hand, it was really exciting that he could explore all of these new foods, but on the other hand, there is a bond that was severed." This feeling of a cord being cut or severed is probably why the Old French word *sevrer* literally means "to wean."

---

* Linda Gionet, "Breastfeeding Trends in Canada," Statistics Canada, November 27, 2015, https://www150.statcan.gc.ca/n1/pub/82-624-x/2013001/article/11879-eng.htm.

† Yekaterina Chzhen, Anna Gromada, and Gwyther Rees, "Are the World's Richest Countries Family Friendly?" UNICEF Office of Research–Innocenti, June 2019, https://www.unicef-irc.org/family-friendly.

The first stage of your baby's life depended on you completely. You were the sustenance, the nourishment, the life-giving force. Weaning now marks the end of that time, the completion of you being that sole lifeline for your baby. Now comes the unavoidable heartbreak of recognizing that you can't be "the only" anymore. Your child needs the world more, which might feel like they need you less. Grief and relief mingle together amid this loss. And so, as it goes, you are being asked to relinquish your grasp on how things have been so that you can make space for what wants to be.

A mother I spoke to started out our interview confessing, "I can understand women that grieved this, but I didn't," yet as the interview proceeded and we looked back at the time when she was so closely bonded to her baby, the tears inevitably came. Marking this moment by ritualizing it is a way of making it meaningful. It's a way of stopping at that door before it swings open and before it closes, and remembering: *This mattered to me, this changed my life, I will never get this back, I am willing to let go, but damn, am I grateful. Ready, not ready.*

THE SUSTENANCE RITUAL:
For the Mother or Birthing Parent

There is a very old prayer in my Jewish tradition that we say whenever we experience something new or enter into a new time. While I've never heard anyone say this, I suspect that this prayer can also be whispered when we encounter the last time of something. In Hebrew, the prayer is called the *shehecheyanu*, which translates to "who has given us life." It's a short, eleven-word prayer that is packed with an understanding that, even though we could, we are not going to take this moment for granted. Actually, even more so, we say these words to acknowledge that in order for us even to have gotten to this moment, many forces must have conspired. We were sustained by so many others, granted life by so many others, and enabled and supported by so many others. While the prayer names God as the one who was responsible for all this, I am going to put my foot down and advocate for another that doesn't get named but should: our Earth. For without all the ways she nourishes and sustains us, we would not be here.

Weaning is a profound moment of grief and joy where you must let the larger world in. No longer are you, the mother, the exclusive source of life—now the child will, as one mom told me, "belong to the world and the world will now provide for this child." Weaning is the beginning of acknowledging our indebtedness to the world, for your child is no longer sustained solely by you, but instead by the plants, by the bees, the fruits, the roots, the minerals, and animals of our world. Now others will feed your child as they have fed you.

The purpose of this ritual is to both honor your body as a giving source of life while also honoring the Earth body as a forever generous source of life too. By offering your breast milk back to the Earth, you are both letting go of this chapter of bonding with your child as their sole lifeline of nourishment and giving back to our living planet that has sustained the generations that have come before you and that may sustain the generations that come after you. This ritual is a way of redirecting this nourishment back to the source and making a tangible offering to all that holds you and your baby in this threshold.

Prepare

Intentions

May I honor the sacred bond I have with my child. May I mark another layer of separation and create a place for my grief. May I celebrate the return of my body and freedom. May I remember all that sustains me and my baby.

You Will Need

- Bowl (preferably clay or earthen)
- Breast milk
- Wineglass
- Wine, alcohol, or your favorite mocktail
- Water pitcher
- Something sweet, like honey or chocolate
- Items for an altar

Who

This can be done solo, but consider being witnessed in this ritual. Many cis women I spoke to suggested doing this in a circle surrounded by other mothers and grandmothers—an intergenerational circle, even if that is only three or four others. By inviting these witnesses to see you through this threshold, you are being seen by others who have crossed it before and can hold you tenderly, strongly, clearly as you cross it yourself.

Also, this ritual is for you. The second ritual offered in this chapter is for you and your baby. Consider giving yourself this time as a way of coming back to nourishing yourself.

Where

This ritual is meant to be done outside on the earth. Find a backyard, a forest, a beach, or a garden and make sure it's private. You don't need any randos wondering what you're doing.

Setting an Altar

While it's completely fine to do this without any preparation, I am always an advocate for putting down an altar first. This can be as simple as making an altar out of items from nature or placing flowers and photos of you and your baby or significant objects from nursing on a table. Having something meaningful and beautiful helps to direct focus during the ritual, as well as adding symbolism.

You can also place the vessels and liquids for this ritual on the altar.

Begin

Song

Begin the ritual in song. You can assign this before the ritual begins or be spontaneous and ask if anyone has a song to start. Extra points for a song that acknowledges the bittersweet nature of this moment (I have a forever weak spot for "Sunrise, Sunset" from *Fiddler on the Roof*).

Rounds

The purpose of each round is to redirect the nourishment you've been giving your baby to either yourself or the earth.

Each round has a prompt question. You can answer it as many times as you need. And don't just answer it—let the prompt be an opportunity to reflect, to share stories, and let your heart be broken open by the joy and grief that this transition is asking of you.

Round 1: The Water

This round is devoted to honoring and closing this chapter of you and your baby's nursing time. Give the water pitcher to the circle of witnesses surrounding you.

Never again will I . . .

Let this prompt inspire you to name the parts of the journey of breastfeeding that you will be leaving behind.

Name all the beautiful, painful, delicious, frustrating, nourishing, and depleting aspects of nursing your baby—all experiences you are completing.

At the end of each response, let each witness wash your hands, your feet, or your head. Keep passing the pitcher around until you are done.

Round 2: The Wine

This round is devoted to reclaiming the parts of your body, of your freedom, of your lifestyle that you had to give up while you were nursing this little one.

Fill up the glass with wine (or a mocktail, if you don't drink).

I am ready to reclaim . . .

Speak to all that which you are excited about returning to— all the foods you can now eat, the sex you might want to have, the alcohol you can now drink, the places you can go, the sleep you can catch up on.

At the end of each response, either take a sip of the wine or pour a little on the earth.

Round 3: The Breastmilk

This round is devoted to honoring the nourishment that came from your body and that comes from the earth. This is a way to presence all that nourished you so you could nourish your baby, and all that will continue to feed you both.

Fill up the clay bowl with breastmilk.

I am indebted to . . .

Speak to all the people that are holding you in this process. Speak to your lineage and ancestry that you and your baby are a part of. Speak to the vegetables, the minerals, the animals, the water, and the earth that sustain you and your baby.

Keeping speaking and spilling a little milk on the earth until the bowl is completely empty.

Conclude

At the conclusion of the rounds, invite the surrounding circle of intergenerational witnesses to speak and share their own beautiful and messy stories of nursing and weaning. Be sure to ask the elders of your circle to speak first, as a sign of respect. In doing so, you are presencing your experience among others, being included within a larger circle of all those who have passed through this ancient passage.

Oh, and be sure to have something sweet to pass around, like chocolate or honey and dates, as others are sharing. Remember, this is a bitter and *sweet* time.

Be sure to conclude the ritual by thanking all that gathered around this ritual, seen and unseen, all that are showing up to support you in this transition. You can do so in either silence, song, or dance.

Questions for Further Reflection

- How does it feel to mark the ending and beginning in this moment?
- Am I scared of letting go of anything? If so, consider what.
- Am I excited for what comes next? If so, consider what.
- As I wean my baby, what do I need to be reminded of?

The Feasting Ritual: For Your Child

Let's not forget your little one here. They also need to be seen, as this is a significant passage for them too. Whether they are conscious of it or not, there is uncertainty and accomplishment for them in this transition, and as their parent, you can make it known. My question to you is: What needs to be said to them to recall that the bond between you is unbreakable? How do you convey that in this transition to the kitchen table, they will continue to be nourished by the world? And, of course, can you share with them that they can always find comfort, safety, connection, and love in your arms, just not from your breasts.

Ritualizing this moment lubricates this transition. Rather than expecting them to cope, forget it, or get over it quickly, you can hold it up and teach them that this is a time of achievement for both you and for them. And this moment can be made into something beautiful through your words and gifts.

One way that many traditions welcome transitions is through feasts. In my own tradition, there is a quote from the early stories in our Torah, when Sarah weaned Isaac, that says, "The child grew up and was weaned, and Abraham held a great feast on the day that Isaac was weaned." A feast is not only an act of celebration but also a way to invite the family to witness the child's growth and to continue to invite the child to the feasting table. It is a way of saying: "We see you changing. We see this stage ending. We celebrate this. And welcome to our table."

Reva, a friend of mine, shared that when she finally weaned her child, they filled a kiddie pool with milk and surrounded it with ice cream, cheese, and other delicious dairy delights. She said she wanted it to be a celebratory experience, something that would help her son understand he was "a big kid now." Rachel, another mother I interviewed, gifted her daughter her first necklace, a symbol of comfort so that she could always feel her mother near her heart. Gifting this allowed her to say: "We will always be connected. My love for you will never be less because we're not nursing anymore. Actually my love for you will grow as you become who you are becoming."

So what if you held a feast for your child sometime soon after the weaning is complete? What if that meal contained some foods that your child had never had before and they got a chance to try them for the first time? What if at this feast, you gifted your child their own special cup or plate that was specifically made or decorated for them? What if, at this celebratory feast, you reflected to your child the significance of this moment and reminded them of your love and connection and also of their growth? And what if you also took a moment and gave thanks for the food on that table that would, from now on, be the source of nourishment for your child?

Losing a Tooth

Listen to the wisdom of the toothless ones.

—Fijian proverb

T he wiggling has begun. Little by little, the baby tooth loosens its grasp on your child's mouth, making way for their adult teeth. Maybe they've been anxiously awaiting this moment because their friends proudly wear big toothless grins in school. Or perhaps they're scared of this happening, unsure if it will hurt, if there will be blood, and of what comes after. But losing a tooth isn't just a threshold for your child. It's also evidence that the passage of time is having its way with you as well, loosening that which seemed so much in your grasp. The loss of the baby tooth foreshadows another loss—your baby isn't a baby anymore.

The tooth in hand and the hole in their smile is evidence that something has actually happened to your child, but what's to be done to meet this moment meaningfully and mark their change? Most likely, the character you're relying on to bring the myth and mystery to the scene is the good ol' Tooth Fairy. You know her magic act: The tooth goes under the pillow and *poof!* she has paid your child handsomely for this gift. But she's a relative newcomer on the scene of tooth rituals, and cultures all over the world have many other ways of marking this moment, perhaps with even more meaning. For instance, kids in Egypt, Jordan, and Iraq throw their teeth toward the sun as an offering to this solar deity to conjure more adult teeth. In Korea and Greece, the baby tooth is thrown on the roof in hopes that a blackbird will bring a new and strong smile. And, in many cultures, the key animal that trades in teeth is a mouse. France has the character *la petite souris* ("the little mouse") to represent this, but Belgium, Scotland, Peru, Chile, Italy, and Spain also have mouse myths because rodent teeth grow throughout their entire lives and are considered models for sturdy chompers.

What these rituals all have in common is that something is being done to the little tooth. There's an exchange, payment, or offering to someone or something other than the child. A mouse, a fairy, the sun, the river, or even a tooth troll takes this object of childhood as barter for something of more value—something connected to adulthood. The underlying cadence of all these rituals centers on an act of letting go. But here's the big question: Aside from the tooth, what is really being surrendered and what is really being given—both for you and your child?

When I was a child, losing a tooth meant getting cash. Yes, there was the story of the Tooth Fairy, which at the time I didn't believe, but more important, it was an opportunity to trade in something I didn't understand had value (the tooth) for something I thought did (the money). My parents did this ritual without any understanding of what it meant and why. And because of that, there was no deeper meaning for this experience—for them or for me.

Since then, I've wondered why our culture gives money for a tooth. Is it to instill value? Is it because cash is the easiest and quickest gift to give? When we take a threshold moment like losing baby teeth and reduce it down to something transactional, could we be inadvertently teaching our children that only money translates as value? Yet here's the thing: The value of this moment is sourced not by how much they get for their tooth but by acknowledging how much they are growing and changing.

What makes this little moment of losing a tiny tooth significant is that it's a very real and tangible lesson in impermanence and change. Your child is witnessing their body change, possibly for the first time. Yes, they've grown out of their little pajamas and their adorable shoes, but this is different. This is an indicator of a much bigger developmental shift that announces that they aren't a child anymore, yet they aren't an adult either. They are entering the in-between, a place more akin to "big kid-hood" or middle childhood. Before this stage, you were woven way more closely into everything your child did and the decisions they made. As they enter into this stage, they begin to develop their own preferences, create their own stories, and cultivate their own relationships independent of you. They now have their eyes set on more autonomy, the holy grail of childhood. For one of the first times, your child gets to contend with the fear, excitement, pain, and pride of their physical bodies maturing, and as their parent, you are wrestling with yet another milestone of letting them go.

Rituals have the capacity to slow time down, not forever, but long enough to properly witness what's changing before it actually does. By ritualizing this moment, you get to celebrate and honor this new chapter of your kid's growth while also letting in the bittersweetness that they are shedding more of what tethers them to their childhood.

THE DREAM SEED RITUAL

The ritual below is a simple, fun, and active way to shift this moment from a purely financial exchange to one that could provide more meaning. It is inspired by tooth rituals from all over the world where the choreography is to let the tooth go into something bigger than the child. Whether that's the earth, the sky, the water, or even a mythical creature, this can be a moment where your child can be witnessed in their growing-up-ness, undeniably a bittersweet journey.

While I've chosen to do this ritual with the element of air/space, you are welcome to collaborate with another element, like water or earth. For example, instead of burying the tooth, you can place it into water, as water can receive that which we no longer need. Or choose earth and bury the tooth in a garden or backyard. Just as in any cookbook, this is just one recipe. Choose what works depending on what is available to you and to your child in your area.

One last thing about the Tooth Fairy. Myths and stories are essential teaching vehicles for meaning and ritual. No matter how shallow some of our culture's myths are (here's looking at you, Santa) these are the tales we have to tell our children. For those of you who want to keep the Tooth Fairy employed, I will include some ways to expand upon that ritual and help that exchange become more meaningful. And for those of you who are gifted with the storytelling gene, I encourage you to craft new stories to tell your children so that these rituals are even more inventive and accessible.

Prepare
Intentions
May I witness my child changing, not just physically but developmentally. May I welcome their desire for more autonomy and grieve them growing up. May this ritual bring beauty, story, and/or magic to this moment.

What

This ritual is inspired by air and space, and the ritualized action is to launch this tooth into the air or, more dramatically, into space. By doing that, your child gets to send their dream of the big kid they want to become out into the atmosphere so that it comes true.

When

You can do this ritual after the first tooth falls out or have your child collect their teeth and do this after many have fallen out.

Step 1: Dream

When your child loses their first tooth, have them put it under their pillow, Tooth Fairy–style. Except instead of the fairy, you can tell them that now their teeth are "dream seeds" and their task is to dream into them. The dream to dream is: *Now that I'm not a small kid, who will I be as a big kid?* You can create your own magical story about how these seeds will actually help the child grow up into the big kid they want to be if they wish on them every night. Try letting your imagination run free in fantasy. By playing with story, you can ask your child, in a non-explicit way, to imagine what these teeth mean to them.

Step 2: Place

Because this ritual involves air/space, consider going to a hill, mountaintop, open field, or even your backyard. Bonus points for the parents who want to do this at night, under the stars! When I did this ritual recently, I created a story about how all the stars in the sky were millions of dream seeds that had been wished upon for thousands of years. As always, let your imagination weave into the ritual.

The purpose of this ritual is to launch those "dream seeds" into the air/space as a way to let your child wish for the big kid they are becoming.

Step 3: Wish

This ritual is inspired by a story I heard of a parent who had trouble getting their child weaned off a pacifier. No matter how many times they tried, he wouldn't let it go. The parent had an ingenious idea of tying the pacifier onto a balloon and letting the child launch it off into the air as a big send-off. This gave the child the autonomy to let it go himself and to see the spectacle of it flying away. But! Our environment doesn't need more plastic in the world, so use this story as inspiration for another kind of launch. That could be as simple as having your child launch their tooth into the sky using a slingshot, attaching it to a bow and arrow, putting it on a kite, etc.

Before your child launches the tooth into space, ask them to share their wishes for the big kid they want to become.

Here is a prompt that you can ask them:

"You have been sleeping with these dream seeds under your pillow. They now carry your dreams and wishes! Before you launch them into space, what is a wish you want to make for yourself as you grow up?"

If there is more than one tooth, let them make a wish on each one.

Step 4: Launch

Three . . . two . . . one . . . liftoff! Launch the dream seed into the air. While this moment of letting go is for your child, it is also a moment for you to let go as well. See if your child can take a few pauses after the big launch to close their eyes and imagine their big-kid dreams coming true. You close your eyes too, giving time and space to mark this bittersweet moment of your child growing up.

Before you end, reflect back to your child what you heard them say. Affirmation is an effective way to reinforce for your child what is important to them.

You can conclude this moment by blowing air into the sky giving the dream seed a little extra juice on its journey into space.

Bonus

Follow this up with a small treat or celebration. We have a custom in my tradition of giving a drop of honey on our finger when a child is learning something new, to sweeten the experience. Let this transition be sweet.

The Tooth Fairy Redux

Losing a tooth is a personal experience for your child, but it's a social one as well. Many of their friends and classmates are losing teeth at the same time, and they are all going through changes together. Therefore, maybe it's important for you and your child to tell the same story as their peers or classmates, which most probably is that of the Tooth Fairy. If this is the case, go for it but consider changing a few things.

Three Adjustments

1. Refer to the tooth as a dream seed. Advise your child to put the tooth under their pillow and, when they go to sleep, to make a wish for the big kid they want to become.

   Here is a prompt that you can ask them:

   "When you lose a tooth, it becomes a dream seed. That means it needs you to wish so your dream can grow. Before the Tooth Fairy collects it, what is one wish you want to make for yourself as you grow up?"

2. Let them speak their wish. It's important for your child's wish to be heard. Let them share this with you before the Tooth Fairy whisks the dream seed away.

3. Money. While you are still giving them money for the tooth, consider advising them to spend it in a purposeful way. This money can be called "big-kid money" and can only be used for something that is distinctly for a big kid. For example, it could be an object that they weren't allowed to have before this time. This could also be a good time to practice saving money—if you can, tie it back to the dream they planted.

Releasing the Tooth

So now *you* have the tooth! What do you do with it? You might consider performing the Dream Seed Ritual on pages 118–20 solo. This way you can release the tooth and also take a moment to presence all your feelings that emerge from your child changing. Don't underestimate the importance of marking this moment for you as the parent. Remember: Their desire for more autonomy is directly connected to your willingness to let go.

Questions for Further Reflection

- What change does losing a tooth mark for both me and my child?
- How do imagination and story help to support the purpose of this ritual?
- What does this moment teach my child about growing up?
- What does this moment remind me about letting go?

Child Leaving Home

I don't remember growing older. When did they?

—Sheldon Harnick, *Fiddler on the Roof*

The dreaded, anticipated, vulnerable, liberating moment that eventually comes to most parents and children—leaving home. The everyday ways of being together are ending, and once again, a new and different relationship is forming. What looks like freedom to some might also contain enormous heartbreak for others. So many questions accompany this time: *How did this moment arrive already? Can I let go of my baby? Will they keep in touch? Will my parents let me go? Will my child rely on the values I taught them? Who am I now with them out of the house?* Uncertainty and wonder flood this moment of change and separation, yet many families tend to focus on the logistics, which can stand in for a ritual, be it shopping for supplies, driving or flying to school, organizing the move-in weekend, or that final, awkward hug. But unless we imbue these moments with meaning, we flail in those times of change, feeling the intensity of the emotion but scared to let go into the unknown.

When I was eighteen years old and left home for college, I could tell my parents were struggling to slow down enough to really express their feelings about what was happening. I could sense it through the way my mom was hovering, or my dad's earnest requests to drive me to my dorm room. But it was only after years of coming back home for the holidays and witnessing my childhood bedroom untouched that I could really understand both their love for me being in their home and the heartbreak that my leaving had brought them. The theatre posters were still on the wall, the old familiar bedspread in its same place, and the desk still scattered with photos from my high school days—all of this a relic of a time past and my parents' unexpressed longing for my return. They wanted what was already gone. I still wonder if that would had been different had we marked that time with a ritual.

However long you and your child have been living under the same roof, the moment of their departure is significant, emotional, and time-bound. It asks for something from both of you, something found not in the everyday routines of your familiar roles, but in your capacity to make this time meaningful together. This is where the ritual comes in. It allows you to step out of the weeds of everyday life and to rise above and drop deep into this transition by doing something to recognize and reflect upon it. And with the ritual, you and your child have the opportunity to come closer together as you step further apart.

Before I explain what to do, it's important to acknowledge the obstacles time poses to ritual. With so much to do, there are always many excuses not to do it: "I have to work," or "it will take too much time," or "we're all too busy," or "we will get to it soon." This pretty much guarantees that the moment will come and go, as life has a way of moving forward with or without these rituals. Securing this time provides a pause in the relentless river of everyday life so that you can approach these transitional events with centeredness, meaning, and reverence.

THE PACKING RITUAL

This ritual is inspired by the packing of a suitcase. There is an inherently ritualistic aspect to packing and unpacking—the sifting through of all that's needed for the journey and all that should be left behind.

When I left for college, packing for the dorm was one of the collaborative activities that my family and I did together to prepare me for this next chapter. We shopped for large plastic containers to store under my bed, bought new clothing and linens, and acquired lots of school supplies. My mom took me shopping for new clothes, my aunt came over to help me label boxes, my dad helped move them from my bedroom to the car, and my brother picked fights with me, which was his way of saying, "Please don't go."

This is a creative ritual to help you do that same preparation for what comes next but through meaning and not function. Part gift-giving and part gratitude, this ritual will give both parents and child an opportunity to reaffirm what's important, to provide the child with symbolic gifts that remind them of the values they carry forward from their family, and to feel the significance of what's changing.

While this ritual can be done with just parents and children, it can also be opened to your broader family of aunts, uncles, grandparents, cousins or friends, and community. Maybe it's more your family's way to keep it small, but there is something incredibly special about inviting all those that care about your child to participate.

PART 1: THE GATHERING OF GIFTS

What are your family's values? When was the last time you sat down and reassessed the principles that are essential to your family? In all the years of raising your child, you tried to instill the best qualities into them—emotionally, mentally, spiritually—but at this moment of departure, which ones do you want to ensure continue?

This ritual is performed in three parts: (1) gathering of gifts, (2) packing of the suitcase, and (3) unpacking the suitcase. The first step will give you an opportunity to reflect and reaffirm the values of your family. After all the years of camping, did you want your child to experience a lasting connection to nature? Is that important to them? With all the theatre you attended, did you want your child to fall in love with the arts? Did they? Maybe volunteering in their community was encouraged because you wanted them to be raised with the ethics of service? Is that an important part of their life? Whatever your values are, departure is the right time for you to reaffirm them and for your child to assure you that they hold these values dear.

Prepare

Intentions

May we approach this time together with love, care, and meaning. May I affirm the values of our family as my child goes out into the world. May they reassure me that they carry these values. May I open to change and let my heart open to the bittersweetness of this time.

You Will Need

- A small (possibly vintage) suitcase
- Many meaningful gifts to fill the suitcase

The Gifts

The parent's or family's objective is to gather a bunch of gifts that are *vehicles of meaning*. These gifts can be newly bought, handmade, or even family heirlooms that are ready to be passed on. These should be gifts that convey something special, that carry meaning and reflect your family's values. Each gift will be embedded with a story which will remind your child of what you want them to carry on from your time together.

The child's objective is also to gather objects that carry meaning and reflect the family values. It's a similar instruction with one big difference: Your objects are meant to *reaffirm* the values you tried to instill, and their objects are meant to *assure* you (and them) of the values they believe in. What is exciting is that in section 2, you both get to hear the similarities and differences in your values.

The Suitcase

While you are gathering your gifts, also choose a small suitcase. Maybe it's an old battered suitcase that has seen much of the world, or a cute new one that you pick up at a store. Either way, this suitcase will be used to hold these ritual items and protect them as they travel with your child.

Identifying Your Values

If you or your child need more assistance identifying some of your core family values, create three concentric circles on a piece of paper, so they look like a bull's-eye. Choose words that are important to your family. The words that land on the outer rings are values that are important but not essential. The words that land closer into the center are definitely important, but the words that land inside the center circle are nonnegotiable values that lie at the heart of your family.

Collect the words that land in the first two inner rings, and pair some or all of those words with the gifts.

Pairing the Value and the Gift

Imagine what gifts you'll get by using that list of values. For example, if travel is important to your family, ask yourself: What can represent travel? Could it be an old passport or postcard, or something you acquired during a past trip? If cooking is important to your family and you've made countless stews, curries, and soups together, perhaps one of the gifts is a wooden spoon that conjures memories of making your favorite meals together. Or perhaps "self-love" was a quality you advocated for with your child, and the gift is a hand mirror that reminds them to love themselves when they look at their reflection.

Choose as many gifts as you want, as long as they help to illustrate your family's values.

The Stories

As you choose your gifts, also remember some stories you will share during the gift-giving. These stories will help give the gift some context and transfer the meaning into what it represents.

PART 2: THE PACKING OF THE SUITCASE

Consider this part a ritualized show-and-tell. You and your child (and other family members if you choose to include them) come together to give meaningful gifts meant to fill the suitcase. The point of this ritual is that while you and your child are sharing the gifts you gathered, you are recollecting memories from the past that are also infused with value. What this is doing is helping everyone reaffirm what's important by instilling those reminders into the objects that will accompany your child.

Begin

Start by lighting a candle. Candles give everyone a sense that something meaningful is happening. You can also begin in silence or start by reading a poem. Really, anything that helps distinguish this special time from an everyday moment is good.

As you begin, go back and forth between adult and child, or however it feels most organic to your family. It might be helpful to offer this prompt as a way to introduce your object:

I chose to include this object because it reminds me of memories of _____ *and our family value of* _____.

A prompt the child could use is:

I am grateful you taught me about _____, *and as I leave I want to continue doing this because of you. This object represents how important this is to me and how I don't want to ever forget that.*

As you and your child trade stories, the suitcase should be getting more and more full—a treasure chest of meaningful reminders as a gift for this significant transition. The gifts that fill your child's suitcase are intended to become an altar, a special place for your child to return to and be grounded in the values they came from.

Conclude

As you finish sharing stories and packing the suitcase, take a moment to ingest what just happened. Maybe this time feels emotional or reassuring or just makes you all feel a little bit closer together. Perhaps this is a moment to tell your child how proud you are of them. Or for your child to say what they're grateful for.

As you finish, take a moment of silence, blow out the candle, and close the suitcase. Let this moment linger, knowing that change is imminent.

PART 3:

THE UNPACKING OF THE SUITCASE

This moment is solely for your child. You gathered meaningful gifts, packed them with each other, and did your best to remember the values you instilled upon your child throughout your time under one roof. Now it's their turn to unpack those reminders and let them inform their lives. The intention of unpacking these objects is for your child not just to see them but to keep them near, to lean into in moments of uncertainty and doubt.

Objective

The difference between an object and a ritualized object is both the meaning they carry and how you treat them. Your child has the opportunity to make an altar out of these objects and give them a place to live in their bedroom that can inspire, remind, and ground them at any time. Especially when we're young adults, it's all too easy to forget what tethers us, what to trust, and where we belong. Altars can be a personal place for contemplation, centering, and remembering that we are a part of something much bigger than ourselves, which can bring peace and stability during challenging times.

The gifts in the suitcase can live inside it or can be removed and displayed in any way that inspires your child. The main goal here is for these riches to be a resource and an anchor wherever they go.

Let Go

It might be that your child takes this suitcase, unpacks it, and creates a beautiful altar of photos, objects, and gifts that reconnect them to the values and love of their family. It also might be that this suitcase is left in a closet in their dorm room and not unpacked at all. Maybe it remains shut for many years. And perhaps at the right time, your child rediscovers it and is reminded of these values when they need them most.

However your child relates to the suitcase, you must let go and trust in them, for that's what this time is asking of you. This ritual provided you with the opportunity to reaffirm your values to your child and for them to assure you that they carry them. To let go really means allowing the change to happen without trying to control it. One of the last things my dad said to my brother, Matthew, and me before his death was "Keep the faith." And that is what you must do as you let your child become an adult.

Questions for Further Reflection

- What are the values I hope my child remembers in moments of challenge, struggle, or insecurity? Or in moments of growth, exploration, and curiosity?

- What do I fear they will forget?
- Does this move change the way I trust my child? Does it strengthen that trust?
- Does this change the way my child feels about their family? Is there more gratitude for all I've given them?

Leaving a Job

Work is an identity project. It's a place where we go
to experience meaning, community, belonging,
purpose, money, and survival.

—Esther Perel

One of the most common questions we ask when we meet someone new is: "What do you do?" It's a deceptively simple question to sniff out how someone spends their time, what their values are, what they are committed to, and if they do anything important, intriguing, or valuable in the world. But this question is also another way to ask *Who are you?* as identity and work/productivity are so wrapped up and tied together in our dominant culture. The consequence of that is that our sense of dignity and worth is directly derived from our jobs.

Years after leaving her job with a government agency, Shuly kept on having dreams about it. While working, she tirelessly gave so much of herself to running the program and became so invested in its success that when she told her supervisor she was resigning, she cried. Actually, she told me that she'd cried at every job she left. Whatever her work, Shuly's heart—and, consequently, her sense of self—was always in it. These anxious dreams of owing her supervisor work or trying to get hired back were the ways her subconscious processed her departure. In looking back, she said there was something scary about leaving that went deeper than the job.

No matter if you work at your job for one year or thirty, it can become a shelter in the storm. It's where you spend your days. It can be where you project a sense of belonging, togetherness, security, and shared purpose. It can become very easy to grow comfortable and familiar with that, and especially to substantiate an identity around it. But jobs change. And the real kicker is that when they end, when you leave or get deselected or terminated or laid off, all that stability disappears and then what? What becomes of your sense of self when the thing you tied it to vanishes?

Prior to the Industrial Revolution, most workers in Europe didn't change jobs like we do today. Actually, they remained at their jobs until death. Almost everyone lived and worked in a small village, and work was passed down a family line or as an apprenticed skill or trade. At the time, most of the population were either subsistence farmers or artisans making handcrafted goods. Your identity and even your family's surname came from your job, like the names Smith, Cooper, and Fletcher.

This all dramatically changed with the onset of the Industrial Revolution in England. From then on, the eighteenth century witnessed a major population explosion which demanded more food, clothing, goods, and transportation to supply the masses, and so, in a short amount of time, what was once a slow, time-tested, handmade, very localized way of working gave way to a fast and furiously mass-produced industry. No longer did it matter if you were a cobbler intricately making individual shoes for your customers. Speed and assembly became the new gods of the workforce, and workers became more and more disposable and replicable by machines. What this meant is that the work you and your family had been doing your entire life began to disappear, and the identity that bound you to that work was destabilized.

This continues today with so many modern workers carrying a deep-seated fear of being made obsolete or unneeded. So many of our modern workplaces are run like machines, with companies valuing product over people and money over job satisfaction. For instance, the podcast *Today Explained** did an episode on Netflix and their hiring culture, which they summarized as "team not family," the company's way of saying that this relationship is about them, not you. According to the episode, Netflix also employs another radically destabilizing practice called "The Keeper's Test,"† which asks managers at the company to constantly scrutinize their coworkers and ask if they would fight to keep them there. This nerve-racking, company-endorsed behavior encourages employees to keep on proving that they deserve to belong, which intentionally never allows anyone to feel too comfortable or secure at work. So no matter how hard you work at your job, how many grueling hours or years you give, how devoted you are to producing an excellent product and being a faithful

---

* "Netflix Has No Chill," in *Today Explained*, podcast, July 6, 2020, 34:00.
† "Netflix Culture," Netflix.com, https://jobs.netflix.com/culture.

player on the team, in the end, there is really no loyalty and you are just as disposable as the next person.

The fundamental transgression here is the assumption that the relationship has been purely transactional; you gave your time, and you were paid for it. The end. But that model denies the real, human investment of giving our heart to the relationship we have with our work. For example, I worked for more than a decade as the principal of a supplemental Jewish high school in California. I was in deep with the families. I attended baby namings, bar and bat mitzvah ceremonies, and funerals. Parents would call me up late at night and ask my advice on how to relate to their teens, and teens would text me at the oddest hours and ask for my advice on how to deal with their parents. And then, one day, the parent board fired me. They thanked me for my service, gave me an anemic severance package, and that was that. I was just supposed to sever that decade of relationships without any closure or even a chance to say goodbye.

This unwillingness for a company or organization to properly mark an employee's ending is a by-product of our modern consumer and corporate culture that believes endings lack purpose and that therefore they should conclude quickly and quietly: "Thank you very much, you're not needed anymore." When we don't have closure on something that's been so central to our lives, like a job, it can feel like an assault to our identity, our sense of belonging, and our belief in being needed.

I interviewed many people for this chapter. One in particular was a woman named Wendy who had worked in corporate human resources for thirty-plus years. Toward the end of our conversation, I asked her if she could boil down to one or two words the way most people feel when they leave their jobs, what would those words be? She said: "Being canceled." Without meaning to, I gasped, as I felt the coldhearted truth of this statement. I followed up and asked a similar question, slightly different: "Boil it down again and tell me what people would *prefer* to feel when leaving." She then paused and said, "Being thanked." These two phrases spoke volumes in their differences. One conjured images of business deals and transactions, like hotel reservations, television series, and ATM withdrawals, and the other simply felt human. During a departure, we have a need to feel seen, thanked, and reminded that we contributed and made an impact, yet those are the things most often sacrificed for the sake of efficiency and business. If our employers can't give that to us when we're leaving, and most don't, we need to find a way to remember our own value and dignity.

There are ten thousand reasons to leave a job. Perhaps you have outgrown your position and your departure is long overdue. Or your boss is belittling, abusive, or too controlling and you just can't put up with it anymore. Maybe you didn't even choose to leave, but got laid off because of budget constraints, downsizing, or because they no longer saw this as a good match. However this departure came to be, it's time to say so long to this job and everything that came with it—the coworkers, the salary, the workload, the commute, the lessons, frustrations, relations, and the everyday consistencies. Yet fare-thee-well isn't how most people experience leaving their jobs. Rather, bad feelings, destabilizing thoughts, and underlying worries bubble to the surface: *Where do I belong? Who am I? What am I good at? What is my routine now? How do I pay my bills and put food on the table?* Uncertainty, urgency, and logistics are all bundled together with the loss of an overarching sense of identity, because we believe that somehow our work defines who we are and how we are needed. Yet this vulnerable transitional time actually needs a whole set of other skills: to slow down, to stay open, to get curious, and to realign yourself with what you are really here to do.

Ritualizing this transition doesn't guarantee a better job, more success, or becoming an expert "manifestor," but it can help you move through these uncertain seas with grace, wonder, and resilience. Ritual isn't about betterment, it's about wholeness. It's a way to mark this moment by including all its parts—a willingness to be with the messy feelings, the doubts, the wonderings, and the dreams. These rituals below let you properly say goodbye to the work you've been doing, who you've been doing it with, and the person you thought you were, so that you can explore anew who you are becoming. Rituals that support good closure let you head out into uncertain seas with courage, humility, and curiosity to explore, once again, the original questions of *What am I doing here?* and *Where am I needed next?*

THE LEAVING GENEROUSLY RITUAL:
The Last Days of Work

There could be tears. Or anxiety. Or even enormous relief. But however you slice it, leaving a job can feel like severing a relationship. The language we use to describe it can be severe, like "he got the axe" or "she was cut from the team," and even the word "sever," like in "severance package," is used to refer to the break that comes with separating.

Because of that, we might think these moments of departure require a tight heart and clenched fists—just hold it together, power through, and make it to the other side. But what lies underneath that constriction is fear. Fear that we're doing it wrong, fear that we're disappointing someone, fear that we're not going to make it through this safely, fear of what we don't know, fear that we're not getting enough. And with that fear we forget what Buddhist psychologist Tara Brach calls "our basic goodness,"[*] and therefore our basic kindness and courtesy, when departing. In other words, we leave with a stingy heart and hard feelings.

Endings can hurt. And as a result, we might think the best way to navigate them is to protect ourselves and what we deserve. We might harden our hearts, and try to speed through it, but there is a real cost—we don't get to fully express and feel what the whole experience meant to us.

As much as we think we're protecting ourselves by powering through transitions, there are consequences to doing that: We forget that this job once mattered and that we mattered at this job. We forget those relationships we engaged with daily and truly appreciated. We forget how we grew, changed, and evolved during our time there. Deep down, this hurt is informed by our greatest fears of not being respected, appreciated, or needed, and the big one—of being forgotten. And when we embody that fear, we can act in ways that deepen our separation.

So how do we interrupt that? How can we open our hearts in this moment of transition and slow it down long enough so we can bear witness to the change? What does it mean to leave generously and whole?

This ritual is intended for you to perform on the last day of your job. In a time that is so often marked by non-generosity, the simple act of giving a gift is a way to re-humanize the situation. A thoughtful gift, no matter how small, can revitalize a room and help everyone return to a sense of kindness and remember our basic goodness with one another.

The Leaving Generously Ritual allows you to practice valuing the relationships you made and show up genuinely and generously to them as you say goodbye. It's a way to leave with care, presence, and consideration, qualities truly needed during change.

Prepare

Intentions

May I bring a generous heart to my departure. May I accentuate and value my relationships from work and humanize this moment by offering them gifts. May I practice another opportunity to end well.

---

[*] Tara Brach, "Part 1: Trusting Your Basic Goodness," TaraBrach.com, January 11, 2012, https://www.tarabrach.com/part-1-trusting-your-basic-goodness-audio/.

You Will Need

- Anything that comprises many parts. For example:
  - Blended teas
  - Bouquets
  - A dessert
  - Bath salt blends

Why

The inspiration comes from how a team or community is made of individual parts coming together to make something whole. This gift isn't just something beautiful but is something that carries meaning too.

To Whom

This is up to you. You can make just one beautiful gift and give it to one person you really appreciated working with. Or you can make many gifts and give them to your whole team or office.

Three Questions

As you consider what gift to give, ask yourself these three questions:

1. What did I do that I'm proud of?
2. What do I hope to leave behind?
3. What or who am I grateful for?

Let each part of your gift symbolize a response to these questions. For example, I interviewed a woman who had her favorite poem printed and embossed, and she left that gift in many coworkers' inboxes before she walked out of the office for the last time. The poem she chose, the embossed printing, and the people she chose to give it to symbolically expressed her pride, hope, and gratitude all in one gift.

When

Gifting is a beautiful way to say goodbye. Give this gift when you leave. And, if you can, try to give this gift in person. There is something incredibly touching that happens when you look into someone's eyes when giving and receiving.

Questions for Further Reflection

- Why would I give if I'm feeling hurt?
- How does giving at a time of leaving make an impact?
- What does it take to make a meaningful gift?
- Does giving a gift orient me toward generosity? What else does it orient me toward?

THE STORYSHARING *and* STORYLISTENING RITUALS:

After Leaving

Leaving a job can be disorienting. For a time there was a rhythm—you knew the cadence of your commute, the regularity of your paycheck, the nature of your workflow, the consistency of your colleagues, and then one day all that changed. And life quickly moved on, as it does, and your attention, focus, and labors already had their sights on the next thing. But what happens when we only look forward without also looking back? What are the consequences of not reviewing, remembering, acknowledging, and honoring our past labors as we move onward? What gets left out and forgotten when there is no space or time to recognize all that was experienced and accomplished? Are we just left wondering, *Did all of this happen?*

The culture we live in is future oriented. It is always looking to the potential of someone or something, whether that's technology, a product, or a person. There is more value placed in what you can become rather than who you are today. For example, within the modern workforce, there is a need to be constantly learning new tech and new skills because what you currently possess isn't enough to keep up. The consequence of that is an underlying feeling of never being enough, a fear of being obsolete, and a relentless push for the next thing. This malaise especially drives us in our job transitions, always looking forward and rarely looking back.

When I left my position as a principal, it seemed like the reasonable thing to do was move on and figure out what came next. But I struggled to do that. I couldn't trust moving on to something else unless I could answer the question of whether my previous experience had mattered, because it would impact the next thing I gave myself to. Thankfully, a dear friend of mine was paying attention. She took it upon herself to organize an evening where I got to tell my story of working at that job over those past twelve years and be witnessed in that sharing. We lit a fire, and for about two hours I sat before about fifteen friends and told stories about some of my favorite students, some of my least favorite parents, the staff drama, the shit shows, the highs, the lows, and moments that still stayed with me. My friend understood my longing in this moment to see and be seen as someone of consequence, meaning that I needed to know that my work and time mattered. And since my old job wouldn't or couldn't offer that to me, my friends did.

The purpose of this ritual is to interrupt the pressure to move on by offering an experience of slowing down, looking back, and remembering. This is a way not to ghost your experience but to include it in this transitional time. This ritual focuses on storytelling and storylistening, either with friends or by yourself. This is an opportunity for you to bring forward the adventures and misadventures that were a part of your experience at this job. You are recovering your whole experience—the beginning, middle, and end—and by sharing the story of what happened, you can really take in that you contributed, you made an impact, you did things that were needed . . . you were needed.

THE STORYSHARING RITUAL:
With Others

Intentions
May I be witnessed while sharing my story. May I process and reflect upon all that happened at this job. May I mark this departure by recognizing my impact and transition more gracefully into the next chapter of my work.

For Whom
This is a gathering of your friends and family. Invite those who care about you, who want to know more about how you've spent your

days, the work you've accomplished, and who can hold you in this transitional time.

Sending the Invitation

Of course, if you want to send out the invitation yourself, go for it. But consider asking a friend to do this on your behalf. In that way, you are asking for support and allowing your friends to hold space for you and your process.

The Invitation

Whoever sends it out, it should hit these points:

1. *Name what is happening.* For instance, "Our friend Jenny is completing ten years of working as the Marketing Associate." Name the length of time worked and the fact that it is coming to a close.

2. *Acknowledge the need to mark the moment.* So much has happened throughout these years and before moving on, there needs to be a sharing of some of the highs and lows of this experience. Name this in the invitation as a way of valuing this person when maybe their ex-company or job couldn't do that.

3. *Claim the role and purpose of those gathering.* Invite these friends and family to participate by listening, witnessing, celebrating, and eventually reflecting this experience.

Storysharing Options

There are many settings to tell a story within, all of which impact how the story is told. Here are a few ideas to get your imagination churning. Choose the one that most excites you.

1. Fireside Storysharing: An age-old storytelling device— make a fire outside or indoors and gather your friends around the crackling of the wood, the smell of the smoke, and the glistening of the embers.

2. Slide-Show Storysharing: Create a photo journey and tell the story of your job by projecting images.

3. Feast Storysharing: Gather your friends around a table and devote a meal to telling your story.

Or whatever else feels inspiring to you.

Storysharing Guide

This next section consists of prompts. Use them to spark your memory and as a way to navigate your storytelling. But what's most important is to let the questions coax your heart into speaking and sharing.

Also, give yourself a certain amount of time to speak. During that time, ask your friends/family to listen or ask questions. But this is your time to tell your story.

1. Tell the story of how you got the job. What happened? How did you feel?
2. Name a relationship that you learned the most from and what you learned.
3. Name three accomplishments you are most proud of.
4. Name a time you were almost fired or got in trouble.
5. Tell a story from your commute.
6. Did any drama happen at work? Share a juicy story from that time.
7. What is one of your regrets from this job?
8. Who is a colleague you will miss? Why?
9. Tell the story of how you left. What happened? How did you feel?
10. What are you grateful to have learned from this job?
11. What are valuable qualities or skills that you want to carry forward from here?
12. What do you want to leave behind or compost from this job?

The Listeners

After you're done sharing, invite those gathered to offer their reflections and observations. In doing so, you are inviting the whole group to participate in your storysharing and giving your friends and family the opportunity to add to the story.

Conclude

Consider concluding your storysharing by speaking to where you may be needed next. You and your friends/family can do this together for you.

"I am ready to close this chapter of work. Thank you for all it gave and all it took to work there. I am ready to open to a new chapter of work. Where am I needed? Who am I needed by? What is the work that needs to be done? What is my life's greater purpose?"

THE STORYLISTENING RITUAL: *Solo*

Prepare

You Will Need

- A notebook
- A pen
- A camera
- Walking shoes

Where

This should be done somewhere with few to no people, whether that's a regional park, a beach, a mountain trail, or a creek bed. If you don't have access to this kind of space, do it in a neighborhood garden or city park. This ritual is about connecting to a particular place and having time to reflect.

What

This is a wandering ritual. The intention is to go out for a certain amount of time and to explore the place. In turn, you are to imagine that the place itself is telling you a story, specifically about your life. Everything you see, smell, hear, touch has the capacity to reflect information, spark memories, evoke feelings, and become meaningful. Your role is to pay attention and listen. Anything and everything is speaking.

Three Parts

Break the wander up into three parts. For instance, if you choose to do this for three hours, each section should have an hour. Consider setting a timer to keep you focused.

Part 1: What Happened?

The first part of your wander is devoted to all that happened while working at this job. This is a time to remember, reflect, and consider. As you explore, let your mind wonder about how you got hired, some big projects you worked on, the coworkers you labored with, the highs, lows, and everydayness of this job.

Here are some questions to wander and wonder with:

- What did I do?
- What did I accomplish?
- Who were my allies?
- What was my commute?
- What were things I struggled with?
- How did I grow?
- What did I regret?
- Where did I overcome?
- How did I depart?

Consider journaling about this as you walk or at the end of this section.

Part 2: Where Am I Now?

The second part of your wander is devoted to deeply listening about this transitional moment. As your life changes, what are you wanting to mark and acknowledge? Again, look to the place to guide you, remind you, inspire your response.

Here are some questions to wander and wonder with:

- What am I unsure about?
- What is changing?
- What can I rely on?

- Where do I have support?
- What can I let go of?
- What do I want to carry forward?
- How am I feeling?
- What am I remembering?

Consider journaling about this as you walk or at the end of this section.

Part 3: Where Am I Needed?

The third part of your wander is given to wondering about your next steps. Leaving a job marks an ending time where you labored and worked on behalf of something else. As you move forward, you can begin to wonder where you are needed next. This is a time to blow on the coals of your needed-ness and to let this place—the birds, the wind, the leaves, the rocks and clouds—remind you of that.

Here are some questions to wander and wonder with:

- What is calling me now?
- What excites me?
- Who am I needed by?
- What work is needing me to do it?
- What people are needing my support?
- What am I doing here?
- What impact do I want to make?
- Where do I belong?

Consider journaling about this as you walk or at the end of this part.

Conclude

At the end of your storylistening and wandering, say thank you to the place itself. This ritual is meant to engage in the living world as a collaborator, a guide, a teacher, a friend. Perhaps you remembered parts of yourself that you had forgotten. Maybe you found the scent of what comes next for your livelihood. Whatever came, it's courteous and hospitable to leave this place saying thank you.

Questions for Further Reflection

- Why does the story of my past job need to be told or heard?
- What did I remember about myself and my values by sharing and listening to my story?
- How did sharing or listening to my story help point me toward where I'm needed next?

Putting Down Your Own Business

Many of us, myself included, do not have a nine-to-five job but instead are our own bosses. We manage our own websites, we do our own sales, we hunt for our own clients, we do the big visioning, the nitty-gritty, and everything in between. And sometimes it becomes apparent that it's time to move on from this creation of ours that we have given our blood, sweat, and tears to. So how do we properly say goodbye to a business that has been entirely our own, and especially when we are the only witness to it ending?

I have a very dear friend who had been running her own organizing business for more than ten years. Throughout the past decade she helped hundreds of clients declutter their homes, offices, and online spaces. This business was her baby and an expression of her gifts in the world. And one recent morning I received a text message that said, "It's over. I am saying goodbye. I need a ritual," with a screen shot of her website server's page that stated in big bold letters: EXPIRED. In some way, the "expired" message was her only evidence that this business was over. She had already moved on to new endeavors but was left with the lingering feeling that she had not properly put down her old biz. In a way, the business was just lingering on the web, a ghost from a time past. What I heard in her desire for a ritual was a longing to finally release this ghost and put it to rest so she could honor what had been in order to truly move forward.

Eulogies are ways the living can acknowledge the life and death of a loved one. They employ our eloquence to raise up the accomplishments, the memories, the gift and value of a life well lived. Eulogies are ways our language can help us remember while also serving to aid us in letting go. The etymology of the word "eulogy" tells us it comes from the Greek word *eulogia*, meaning "fine speech," or in other words, "praise." Praise is a willingness to see the incredible value of what you are in the presence of and to let that awe be lifted in language. It is, as I wrote in my book, *Morning Altars*, "my humble and impossible attempt to remember where all of it came from and how insanely blessed I am to have been visited by it, even temporarily."

The business you are putting down deserves your praise. This ritual is a simple way to honor all the work you, and perhaps others, have done, the lives impacted, and the blessing it all was.

Here's how:

1. Write the eulogy: State when the business was born, what it accomplished, how it grew, who it helped, and when it died.
2. Publish the eulogy: Post this letter on social media or even send it as an email to your past clients, acknowledging that something has happened—that this business is ending.
3. Burn it: Make this more tangible. Handwrite the eulogy and then burn it to truly mark yourself letting go of the thing you created.

Sabbatical

To rest is not self-indulgent; to rest is to prepare to give
the best of ourselves, and to perhaps, most important,
arrive at a place where we are able to understand
what we have already been given.

—David Whyte

ausing work . . . what an unheard of thing in our society. We might take breaks here and there, around the holiday time or maybe a couple weeks of vacation in the summer, but what does it mean to cease working for an extended period of time—to lay off the list of to-dos, kick the caffeinated commute, and jump off the nine-to-five hamster wheel? What does it mean to take time to just stop and reassess?

Many of us believe sabbaticals are impossible daydreams left to tenured professors and the wealthy class with enough resources or job security to make the dream real. There's so much riding on our work—that's where we're told to find our purpose, security, routine, safety, and especially our value—so it seems even more impossible to walk away. More pragmatically, many of us are strapped by debt or beholden to paying bills that keep us spending, so we need to keep working. It's an endless cycle that makes a sabbatical seem insurmountable, like something we will do when we're old and retired. But what are the consequences of never taking a break from work or school? How do we know our own value if it is always bound to our capacity to be productive? What if a sabbatical can be a ritualized reset—a release from our busy and distracted lives that lets us pause and remember so much that we've forgotten in the relentless hustle of it all?

The word "sabbatical" finds it roots in the word "Sabbath," or in Hebrew *Shabbat*, the seventh day of rest. Yet actually, it goes even further than that. In my Jewish culture, we have what I would call a "rest technology," where we not only rest every seven days but according to our laws, the entire culture is meant to rest every seven years. Can you imagine? An entire people taking a break together—it's almost unfathomable. We call that seventh year *shmita*, literally meaning, "release," where the society as a whole puts down all the things that have built up over those six years of work and production. What that looks like during *shmita* is a big, wide letting go—all the cultivated lands go fallow, all the private lands go public, and all debts get canceled. This is a rest and release, not just for the people but for the land as well. Everything we thought was ours and held to tightly gets surrendered back into the great mysterious wild, the source where everything came from. This time-technology understands that while it's normal for a culture to grow and expand, endless growth and work are profoundly unhealthy and there must be a limit to that. *Shmita* serves as a cultural reset button that reminds us that life is so much more vast than what we can make of it and that even the act of creation must have boundaries.

I spoke to quite a few people about their sabbaticals, but one of the most interesting stories I heard was from an eighteen-year-old high school valedictorian and her gap year. Lily, a self-described go-getter, overachiever, fiercely competitive student, referred to school being like a religion of sorts, where if you do well enough, you can get into your Ivy League heaven. At first, Lily had it all figured out: Her plan was to get into her top school (check), intern at all the best government institutions (check, check), graduate magna cum laude (eventual check), and launch her power career. Her overachievement was her identity, and she held it high like a trophy for everyone around her to see.

But as the conveyor belt pushed Lily forward, she hesitated. Something inside her knew she needed a break. Like most of us, she'd been in school for most of her childhood and didn't know who she was outside of that structure. "I just didn't want to jump into more school and into a life that I didn't know if I wanted," she said. So she applied for a gap year, a year off to explore if there were other paths different than the single runway that she'd been readying for takeoff. To her disappointment, her university refused her deferral and she was left to choose between continuing on with her original plan or giving up her slot and letting go of everything she used to orient her young life, her ambitions, and her sense of self toward. Lily took the gamble, chose the gap year, and leaped into the unknown. She said the gap year felt like "running into the ocean under a full moon—no set path, just a wide, wide open expanse where only possibilities existed."

Speaking to Lily reminded me that when we're in transition, sometimes taking a break and seeing what arises can help inform what's wanted next. But boy, is that in stark contrast to what many of us are taught by the modern culture, which is to pay little attention to transitions and instead just power through them. We are told: You must keep going—graduate from high school and go to college, graduate from college and either go to graduate school or immediately to work. Don't stop. You have debt to pay. You might miss this big opportunity. This university might not let you in again. You need to make money. You need to career-climb. Ugh, how exhausting. And with such enormous pressure to keep moving forward, taking a break not only seems pointless and purposeless, but dangerous because it immediately confronts the cultural framework that our worth and value as individuals is directly connected to our productivity. In other words, *If I stop working, who am I? If I interrupt my habits and routines, what do my days look like? If I have the space to explore, where do I go?* Lily said her gap year taught her that "to always be doing is not always doing what needs to be done."

Another couple I spoke to, Keshira and Tim, referred to their sabbatical year as a rite of passage where after working their whole lives, they chose to lay it all down and take a significant break that ended up lasting for over a year. They didn't just leave their jobs but also a world of familiarity—their weekly paychecks, their apartment and living arrangements, their routines and creature comforts, their friends and family and long-term certainty. They left it all behind to travel with only one suitcase and without a plan, aiming to simply see the world from a totally different perspective than the one that they had grown accustomed to. But this sabbatical wasn't just about travel, it was really about giving themselves permission to slow down, reflect, and question everything they thought was "the way it is." And that required them to step out of the everyday grind of work, routine, and habit and be in something else, something different that let them remember, *Oh yeah, there is another rhythm and pace that is more human, more alive and faithful to life.*

Even reading a book felt different. Before, Keshira would never ever consider reading a book in the morning, she told me. That time was devoted to work. By 10 a.m., everyone she knew was working, and therefore she should be too. But on sabbatical she really got to question these cultural constructs that told her a book was not read on a weekday morning. Weekday mornings were for coffee, email, and screens. Yet she picked up the book and read and read, without stopping. She got to reflect on her assumptions of what she should be doing, and when and for how long she should be doing it. She got to unlearn what she thought was right, question what she thought was real, and for a year try something else on. She reflected, "When we get into a particular grind, we can mistake it for the very thing that's holding us together. On sabbatical, I recognized that I will not disintegrate, I will not die if I let go of all my routines." If anything, she remembered what really mattered.

If a sabbatical is a ritualized time away, it needs a beginning and an ending. Like all rites of passage, sabbatical time is temporary in nature—there is a departure, a journey or experience, and a return. The return is crucial to all rites of passages because in many ways living a life of untethered abandon is appealing and attractive. But a sabbatical isn't a lifestyle. It's a time away from schedules to pause and take stock. To remember what can't be remembered during the hustle, so we can then bring that remembering back to our everyday life. To riff off a thousand-year-old quote from the sage Rabbi Hillel, if our life is just devoted to work and routine, what's the point? And if our life is unaccountable and free, well, who is it in service to? And if not now, when?

In writing this chapter, I've come to realize that rest is revolutionary. It might be that your first instinct is to pull away and say, "Oh, I wish I could do that," or "I don't deserve this," but consider this: Who doesn't feel the endless grind of these modern times, the ceaseless push to keep working, keep earning, keep doing, and the consequential exhaustion that comes with that? And, maybe, just maybe, there is a part of you that exhales and mutters, "Yes, I need this"—a sane-making pause from it all that gives you permission to step out of the driver's seat for a bit to remember who is really driving the bus. A sabbatical is not a vacation, even if it might feel like that. Yes, it is a time to unwind and slow down, but it is also a bookended time to encounter another way of being that is constantly forced into full retreat in our work-obsessed culture. A sabbatical is one way that remembers another way—a simpler, more connected, and uniquely present way of being alive.

Whether you're a student taking a gap year or a worker taking some time off, the rituals below are meant to mark this break as bounded and sacred. And by naming and acknowledging the separation, they invite you to temporarily let go of a very familiar way of living your life—those daily routines, work habits, the standard grind—and to treat this time differently. Without demarcating it, there's a good chance you'll be on sabbatical and still be checking email or finding your mind pulling you back to work. One of the cherished gifts of ritual is that it teaches us a way to make distinctions—a way to say, this is different from that. And the rituals below employ two markers: one that says *I am leaving*, and another that says *I am returning*. The Departure Ritual will help you set down all that you've been so immersed in to the point where you confuse it for the way life is. And the Return Ritual will help you harvest all that you've learned, remembered, and want to bring back and integrate into your regular life. And by marking these bookends with a ritualized exit and a ritualized reentry, you can proceed bravely into the open space of your sabbatical and experience *how life could be otherwise.*

THE TAKING-*a*-BREAK RITUAL

Taking a break. Three magical words that pretty much always sound good. But what does it actually mean to "take a break"? Breaking usually refers to what happens to something that gets cracked or smashed, like that plate you dropped on the floor; something whole got broken in pieces. So if the expression is "take a break," ask yourself this: What actually needs to be broken up and made separate and distinct?

This ritual is a way to mark a break from the work world—symbolically separating yourself from the world of doing, working, accomplishing, fixing, and figuring out, and entering into this holy time and space of being, resting, allowing, and recharging. It takes place in three parts—one for the departure, one for the sabbatical, and one for the return. Together they form a boundary between you and the responsibilities you are relinquishing, the habits you are letting go of, and the roles you will no longer be holding.

Our habits and routines are so slippery, and if we don't set a boundary, we can find ourselves picking up our phones to just send one email or check in with the office ever so briefly. And before you know it, you're back to work. The boundaries of this container indicate that you are choosing to enter into a time of rest and recharging, for your body, mind, and soul, so that when you do return to the world of work, you can reassess if in fact you want to continue heading in the same direction or if you'd rather completely shift courses. Think of this ritual like a guardian to help you protect this holy rest time and distinguish it from your everyday life.

This ritual container is meant to hold all the feelings that accompany change. There might be some fear that arises; there might be some wonder that accompanies the ritual; and there definitely might be some relief and joy that want to join in on the fun. And more, lots more. Whatever shows up for you, and your friends who gather around you, creates a bigger container to invite it all—the serious, contemplative stuff, the heart-soaked grief, the irreverent and weird feelings, and, of course, the joy.

PART 1: THE DEPARTURE RITUAL

Prepare

Intentions

May I demarcate this sabbatical time from work time by claiming the work responsibilities I am breaking from. May I be witnessed in my send-off. May I have anchors to hold me when I'm off and welcome me when I return.

You Will Need

- String or rope
- Scissors

When

This ritual is best done around the time of departure, if not the day of. Think of it like a send-off. You are being released from all the burdens, obligations, and needs of your work and life into the sabbatical's expansive open space.

Who

Gather together a group of trusted friends or family. It doesn't have to be a stadium full of people—a handful will do. These are your anchors who are not just witnessing your release into the sabbatical, but also holding space for you while you are gone and committing to welcoming you back when you return. Without this piece of the ritual, you might go off and have a life-changing experience, but when you return you might still feel unseen, as if things hadn't really changed.

This might seem obvious, but choose friends who are in full support of your decision to take a break and who see it as necessary for your well-being.

Begin

Naming the Purpose

Everyone is gathered: Now what?

Think of how a Broadway show starts. They don't just immediately start the show. The house lights dim. The overture begins. You have time to settle in and unwrap that sucking candy.

Similarly, before you start the ritual, consider shifting the lights; maybe light a candle or start in song or silence. Don't just immediately jump into the ritual—ease into it.

After you feel like everyone's settled, name the purpose: What are you doing and why is everyone here? Choosing to take a sabbatical requires some courage and permission to do something so against the mainstream cultural grain. Clue the people gathered around as to why you decided to give yourself this unbounded gift of rest.

Consider speaking to:

- Why is this sabbatical needed?
- Why do you want to be witnessed?
- What does rest mean to you?
- What are your intentions for your time away?

The Binding

The purpose of the rope or string is first to bind you physically as a way to represent all the ways that your work, your habits, and your routines have bound you. Before your mind heads in the BDSM direction, please note that there are many traditions, my own included, that symbolically wrap, tie, knot, weave, wind, and bind as a way to recognize a tethering to our devotions and life.

In advance, you can choose to have your hands bound, your feet bound, your body bound, or if that just feels too weird, you can bind up the rope to itself. There are nine or more bindings, and with each wrap of the rope/string, you can use the prompts below to proclaim how you are tied up in your life. Also, these prompts are just suggestions. Use them, lose them, or make up your own. I want you to be inspired to name all your obligations.

First Binding

Name the work/school responsibilities that have bound you. Wrap the cord.

Second Binding:

Name the family obligations that have bound you. Wrap the cord.

Third Binding:

Name the tech habits that have bound you. Wrap the cord.

Fourth Binding:

Name the ways your schedule has bound you. Wrap the cord.

Fifth Binding:

Name the ways that your or others' expectations have bound you. Wrap the cord.

Sixth Binding:

Name the ways money has bound you. Wrap the cord.

Seventh Binding:

Name the ways your ambition and goals have bound you. Wrap the cord.

Eighth Binding:

Name the ways your beliefs have bound you. Wrap the cord.

Ninth Binding:

Name the ways your fears you have of leaving have bound you . . . Wrap the cord.

After you have wrapped yourself nice and tight, or one of the anchors has done it for you, pause and take a breath. Feel the tightness, the restriction and tethering of the rope, a symbol of all your responsibilities and obligations.

The Cutting

Let's get undone. The action that truly symbolizes a sabbatical is release. For a temporary amount of time you are cutting free, breaking from and relinquishing all the cords that bind you. This part of the ritual is an opportunity for you to claim what you are freeing yourself from while also having your sabbatical commitments witnessed.

Keep naming as you cut each strand of rope/string. Do these nine times or as many as you want:

First release:
"*I release myself from these responsibilities of work . . .* " Cut a cord.

Second release:
"*I release myself from these obligations to my family or friends . . .*" Cut a cord.

Third release:
"*I release myself from these tech/phone/internet habits . . .* " Cut a cord.

Fourth release:
"*I release myself of these routines . . .* " Cut a cord.

Fifth release:
"*I release myself of these expectations I have on myself or that others have placed on me . . .* " Cut a cord.

Sixth release:
"*I release myself of these responsibilities I have to money . . .* " Cut a cord.

Seventh release:
"*I release myself of these ambitions or goals I have pursued . . .* " Cut a cord.

Eighth release:
"I release myself of the beliefs that I . . . " Cut a cord.

Ninth release:
"I release myself of these fears of what will happen (to work, to my family, to my social life) if I step away . . . " Cut a cord.

The Reflection and Blessing
Hand the mic over and let your gathered friends reflect on what they heard you say and what they witnessed.

This is also a time for blessings and advice for you as they send you off. The floor is open. Let the serious and irreverent blessings flow.

The Cords
Hand out each cut piece of rope or string. This is each recipient's reminder of their anchor to you as you go off, and be sure to keep one for yourself. These are the physical reminders that, even though you are off on sabbatical, you are still connected and not forgotten.

The string is now a ritual object. It can be worn, hung up, or laid down on a personal altar. Remind each person to hold on to theirs as they will need these strings again when you return.

Conclude
Send-offs are celebratory. Think smashing a champagne bottle on the side of a boat. Don't be shy: Conclude the ritual with song, music, gratitude, and especially sweets. Let the joy carry you off into the great, peaceful abyss. Bon voyage!

PART 2: THE SABBATICAL RITUAL

Intentions
May I allow myself space to rest, wonder, adventure, explore, and be in the unplanned and unproductive. May I let any grief and fear arise. May I retrieve a sense of self-worth that is not connected to my work. May I reflect on what I've accomplished and reassess if the direction I'm heading is where I want to go.

A Note

I am keeping this section intentionally ritual-light because it's less about doing and more about pausing and listening.

Reflection

However your sabbatical looks, consider committing to some time in the morning and some time in the evening for reflection. You could do it through journaling, meditation, walking in nature, a check-in with a therapist or mentor, or through a creative and contemplative project, like making a nature altar. Because there is no work to do, you have this time open for everything you wanted to do but never had time to do.

The Talisman

During your sabbatical, place your cut cord someplace prominent, where you can see it every day. This is now your talisman and can serve as a tool to ground you and remind you to stay faithful to this sabbatical container. Even the etymology of the word "talisman" tells us it comes from the Greek *telos*, meaning "completion." In other words, this object is there to help you fulfill your commitment to keep this time different and special.

PART 3: THE RETURN RITUAL

Intentions

May I be received when I return. May I recognize in the presence of my friends that something substantial has happened and tell my story. May I begin the integration process and carry the gifts from sabbatical back into my life.

A Slow Return

Don't rush it. Returning from a big trip or experience can be quite vulnerable and overwhelming. I recently was on the road for three years, and when I came back home it was disorienting. Everything looked and felt the same, but I had changed so much. Even though I was back, I needed my friends to see me as different.

Rather than expecting yourself to just jump back into the swing of things, consider giving yourself time to slowly return. A slow return can mean not immediately going back to your job, or resisting the temptation to fill your schedule up, but also instead giving yourself lots of permission to go at a slow pace.

A Point Person

When it comes to completing this ritual, it might be too much for you to organize it yourself. Plus, it's a bit odd to organize a "welcome home" ritual for yourself. Consider giving this over to a close friend who was at your Departure Ritual, and let them not only send out an invitation but also be the emcee of the gathering.

Preparation

I like to think of this part as preparing for a ritualized show-and-tell. What that means is an opportunity to gather together and organize a slide show of your photos and videos, plus anything else you want to share from your sabbatical, like journal writings, quotes, things you collected, gifts, etc. You are giving a taste of what you've harvested from this time away as a gift to your community.

And there's actually a subsequent benefit to preparing this: It gives you a real opportunity to review, reflect, and remember your experience, which in turn helps you metabolize it and integrate it back into the non-sabbatical world. You get to have a two-for-one: remembering all of it with yourself first and then again with your people.

Also, don't forget the rope/string! Part of this ritual's preparation is to make sure that this piece is brought by you and everyone that comes together for the event.

Welcoming

Like all rites of passages, this "welcome back" moment is crucial. After a big journey away, the community has an obligation to receive those returning and to recognize all that has changed.

Begin by lighting a candle and starting with either a song or some silence to set the container. The emcee should then go around the circle and officially welcome you, their beloved friend, back. They should lay it on thick with the hugs and the "welcome homes," speaking aloud about what it was like to carry on without you and proceed in your absence. In a way, it is like they are helping you land by telling you how much you were missed.

Welcoming someone back after time away is like casting a spell of hospitality. It can help bring them back in, include and anchor them, and remind them that they weren't forgotten.

Ritual Show-and-Tell

Now it's time for your ritualized show-and-tell. Really, you can do this however you want, but be sure to use this time to weave those gathered into the magic and story of what happened. What did you learn, and what changed?

Retying the Cords

The other big moment: retying the cords. For each prompt, you are to retie each cut cord to another cut cord until they're tied together in one long, knotted cord again. This part of the ritual is meant to be a way to harvest all that you've learned, remembered, and received during your sabbatical, and to recommit to your obligations and responsibilities with a renewed sense of value, purpose, and meaning.

The prompts below are there only as guidance and structure. Be inspired or create your own:

First cord:
What did you learn about work during your sabbatical time? What renewed values and purpose do you want to recommit to?
Retie the cord.

Second cord:
What did you learn about your relationships with family and friends? Is there anything you want to change or recommit to?
Retie the cord.

Third cord:
What did you realize about your habits around technology? What new habits or structures do you want to integrate?
Retie the cord.

Fourth cord:
What did you realize about your relationship to time, to being busy, and your daily schedule? Are there new rhythms you want to commit to?
Retie the cord.

Fifth cord:
What did you notice when you didn't have the pressure of expectations weighing on you? What values do you want to integrate back into your life?
Retie the cord.

Sixth cord:
What did you learn about your relationship with money, spending, and saving while away? Are there new ways you want to commit yourself to?
Retie the cord.

Seventh cord:
How did your relationship with your life goals change? What are the goals you want to recommit to and new ambitions you want to pursue?
Retie the cord.

Eighth cord:
Did you reassess any beliefs while away? What are the beliefs you want to reaffirm and recommit to?
Retie the cord.

Ninth cord:

What did you learn about rest while on this sabbatical? Are there new commitments to integrate more rest and recharge into your everyday life?

Retie the cord.

Keep going until all the cords have been retied.

Conclude

At the end of the ritual, you should have a string/rope with many knots. These knots are comprised of what you've harvested from your sabbatical and all of these recommitments to your life. You can keep this new talisman hanging somewhere special where you can see it and be reminded of the sabbatical gift you gave yourself.

Remember to give thanks to everyone who sent you off, held you in their hearts while you were gone, and helped to receive you back.

Blow out the candle and finish this reunion with a feast, and lay it on heavy with the desserts.

Questions for Further Reflection

- What was the scariest thing to let go of during my sabbatical?
- What was the easiest thing to let go of?
- What did the sabbatical teach me about my relationship to work? To rest?
- Did I learn anything about resilience? If so, what?

Moving from a Home

There is no house like the house of belonging.

—David Whyte

On one hand it's just a house. A place that holds your stuff, that gets your mail, that sees you come and go. Leaving it might not be a big deal. There are tons of houses and you're just moving from one to another. On the other hand, it's a home, made so by the way you lived, loved, fought, and cried in it. It's been a shelter through those tough storms and a lazy resting place where the couch was the only spot you ever wanted to be. Friends have gathered here, maybe children were raised here, and at times you have felt far too alone within these walls. But it's been a place you belonged in. A place you recognized and saw yourself reflected in. Now the boxes and bubble wrap are evidence that the time has come to say goodbye to this family nest, this sanctuary or keeper of your memories. You are not just leaving a house, you are ending a chapter. So how do you say goodbye to this big old friend?

I recently did a lot of packing and moving. Within one year, I not only packed up my own home, but I also helped my mother and my brother, Matthew, pack up our family home of twenty-five years. To do this second task, I felt like I had to scale a mountain of memories: sorting through old shoeboxes filled with years and years of saved birthday and anniversary cards; rummaging through the back of our childhood closet to still find those *Archie* comics and old board games; and emptying out the garage, also known as a mini storage unit, cluttered with old sporting equipment, rusty tools, luggage, and who knows what else. As my brother and I sieved and sorted more than two decades into boxes, I realized how much this home had rooted our family throughout the years. This home held us through the most mundane and everyday activities like waking up, watching movies, and making dinners, but also witnessed us through some massive changes too. As we packed it up, I kept on asking myself: *How can we slow down inside of this tornado? How do we not abandon this house but properly mark our departure?*

Moving can be such a frantic experience that most of us focus our attention on the practical necessities because there's so much to get done. What seems urgent is to bubble wrap the wineglasses or donate the clothing, yet before you know it, the home is empty and the moving truck has arrived. But there's so much more than the practical that needs tending. When something is ending, it also needs witnessing. To witness is to testify that something happened here. It is to look directly at the evidence of change and not turn away. What may come are tears or thanks, which is proper when saying goodbye.

Sometimes, it's not enough to witness an ending all by ourselves. Even the etymology of the word "testify" tells us it comes from the Proto-Indo-European word *tris*, meaning "three." In other words, sometimes we need others to help us witness big changes because we can too easily get caught up inside of them. Sometimes we need the eyes of our family or friends to wonder with us "how could this be" or "what will become." In that way, they help us look at the transitional times of our lives with tenderness, care, and humility. Bearing witness is one of the greatest gifts we can give and receive in moments of change.

In this chapter, you will discover a ritual recipe to serve up during those days of moving homes, giving you a place to stand as the ground moves beneath you. This ritual is devoted to reflecting on and honoring the departure from your old home with your friends and neighbors to ease you through this transition.

THE MEMORY FEAST RITUAL

If you've ever been at a party and wondered where so-and-so went, it could be that they left without saying goodbye. This disappearing strategy goes by many names—"a French leave," "an Irish exit," or "leaving in the English way"—but what they all have in common is a silent departure. Maybe these people believe an unceremonial exit is easier, quicker, or less painful. Maybe they don't have a desire to interrupt or they fear that their presence wasn't really noticed at all. But these kinds of invisible departures leave me wondering not just what the person disappearing misses out on, but also what everyone else misses too.

Moving homes could also be a disappearing act. My family and I moved a bunch when I was a teenager, and I cannot remember saying goodbye to our neighbors or even my friends. In looking back, it seems like we just vanished and reappeared in another home in another part of the country, with the expectation of just carrying on.

During times of moving, often the best and most heartbreaking goodbyes speak out of two sides of the mouth. One side says, "I know you have to leave," and the other whispers, "I'd rather you stay." This bittersweet doublespeak expresses that, even though your house stays after you're gone, you do leave a "you-sized hole" in your friends' and neighbor's lives. Two years after moving out of my most recent home, my neighbors-turned-friends take walks on my old street with their four-year-old, who still proclaims, "That's Day's house!" What the little one realizes is that even though I'm not there anymore, parts of me still remain—I did in fact leave a mark.

The purpose of this ritual is first and foremost to give a proper farewell in the form of a feast shared with your friends and/or neighbors. But this is not just any meal—it's a storytelling meal. Everything on the table tells a tale of your time living in this home; the friendships that have come and gone, the successes and failures, parties and gatherings, and of course, the everyday routines. This feast is meant to stir up memories in the wake of your departure, acknowledging all the life lived under this one roof. Its goal is to interrupt the possibility that you might slip away unseen, and instead it makes a proper fuss at your departure. And as with all rituals that mark transitions, it asks you to lean into and not away from the ending, so that it too might be included in the whole story.

Before we proceed, I want to add something important here: Maybe this ritual seems easy and doable. If that's you, great; skip this part. However, there's a real possibility that this may seem totally foreign to you. Perhaps the first thought that come to mind is *I just couldn't* or *I've never done this before*, and that's totally fine. But what distinguishes a ritual from your average happening is that it does indeed ask something more from you than you might not be accustomed to giving. It might feel like a stretch or a hurdle, but doing it anyway is actually what gives the ritual its prominence. So don't worry if this feels a bit strange to you, that's actually expected. But do ask yourself this: *Can I do it anyway?* If you can try something a bit unusual, you might find that it also brings something of enormous value to you or your family during this transitional time.

Prepare
Intentions
May I gather my friends and/or neighbors for one last meal before I leave, so we can all tell stories of my time in this home and in this neighborhood. May this mark the ending of a chapter together.

Ask a Friend

Ask a friend or neighbor to help organize this by handing over this book and earmarking this chapter for them. Instead of helping you pack boxes, consider this as a way for them to gift you a goodbye.

Inviting

For many people, this might be their first time being asked to participate in a ritual. Here are some helpful points to hit when reaching out and inviting:

- Name what's happening: Someone is moving. Start off by acknowledging the change that is occurring.
- Recognize the relationship: The person you're inviting is an intricate part of this person's life and will probably miss them. Don't be shy—say it.
- Introduce the ritual: Why is doing a ritual important during times of change? What does it offer the person moving? What does it offer everyone gathering? Speak to that.
- First timers: It's also good to acknowledge that this may sound foreign. By doing that you are meeting people where they are at but also inviting them to participate without needing previous experience.

This may go without saying, but if you are a friend or neighbor organizing this, it might be a good idea to reserve this date well in advance with all guests, and especially with those moving. This can be a very stressful time, and having a date secured can help the people in the midst of packing be able to plan around it.

Introducing the Memory Feast

You are gathering people together for a Memory Feast, which means that each person is being asked to make a dish that tells a story or memory. It can be a recollection of time spent together, of how someone witnessed the person/family love their home, or even a story of the area itself. The dish is a jumping-off point for a conversation that shares how integral this person/family has been to their community while they've lived there. And, most important, turn off the pressure! There are no right ways to do this, so please allow each person to get as creative, imaginative, practical, or inventive as they want.

If needed, here are some examples that you can offer to inspire the folks attending:

- Favorite place inspiration: Maybe your families go for brunch at the local bagel joint every Sunday or you hit up your favorite coffee shop after dropping the kids off at school. Bring food that is a nod to these places.

- Garden inspiration: Maybe there's a garden next to the home or you know how much the people moving love to grow their own food. Make a dish that contains food grown from a garden.

- Ingredient inspiration: It could be that a specific ingredient can tell a story. For instance, pumpkin spice or seeds can easily translate to a story about that one Thanksgiving.

- Event inspiration: Maybe you want to tell the story of shared experiences. Hot dogs could be a great way to talk about a baseball game, or cake could speak to birthday parties.

- Place inspiration: Perhaps the place where you all live is known for its oysters or apples or salmon. You can bring food that tells the story of the place itself.

- Number inspiration: You can use numbers to tell a story too. For instance, if the people who are leaving have been in that home for twelve years, you can make a salad with twelve ingredients, or if the address of the home is 82 Park Place, you can use the numbers eight and two in your dish. No holds barred on your imagination.

The Feast

The day has finally come, everyone has arrived, and the feast is ready to begin. Here are some things to consider as the meal commences:

1. Welcome: Before the meal begins, set the tone. You can do this by reminding everyone that this is not just a farewell dinner but a ritual that reminds the person/family leaving how loved they are and how missed they will be.

2. Introduce: Have everyone introduce their dish at the beginning of the meal. Invite them to name not just the dish they made but what it represents.

3. Eating: Encourage a free-form sharing of memories while everyone eats. Or if you need more structure, give each person a certain amount of time during the meal when they can "have the floor" and share more intimately about their dish and their stories. You determine how you want the container to be, so that all the tears and laughter can flow.

4. Farewell Blessing: As the stories have been shared and the dirty dishes pile up, it's important to have a distinct conclusion to the feast. Encourage everyone to offer a farewell and blessing to those moving. And then, invite those moving to express gratitude for the time spent in this home, with this community, and to offer a farewell to the community gathered.

Questions for Further Reflection

- Why is it important to have a proper farewell before I move?
- What happens by sharing memories of my time in this place?
- What does marking my departure offer me? What does it offer my friends and neighbors?
- What did this ritual help me remember?

Retirement

Often when you think you're at the end of something,
you're at the beginning of something else.

—Fred Rogers

You stand at a threshold. Behind you are years and years of "what you did," a wide expanse of the careers and titles, meetings and schedules, colleagues and clients, accomplishments and failures, and so much that underwrote your daily sense of value and purpose. Before you is another great expanse called "what you will be doing," a foreign landscape populated with a lot more time, more freedom, a different daily rhythm, and a new way of locating your identity not sourced from your work. And this very place you stand now is a cairn of sorts, a major trail marker on your journey, and one that forks the road between "what you do" and "who you are." But is it enough to just pass over this crossroads quickly and quietly? How is your retirement impacted when this passage isn't made into the meaningful moment it truly is? Could it be that in hurrying forward you are forever looking behind you—wondering what happened, if it all mattered, and especially, was that the end of your usefulness? Instead, this threshold could be a moment of reckoning—a chance to take stock and be witnessed in all that you've done, all that's yet to be and all that's changing—a moment of reorientation and reimagining.

It was 5 a.m. and Linda woke up stressed and confused. Did she need to start her commute? Was there a proposal due? A meeting scheduled? Even a full year into her retirement, Linda still struggled to move past what she referred to as corporate PTSD. The stress of thirty-one years devoted to her insurance brokerage career still lingered, but she had finally made it to the finish line. Linda hadn't been built for the corporate world, being deeply sensitive and an artist at heart, but years ago she'd made a tough bargain. She would take on this "soul-sucking" job in order to have stability and savings and then eventually retire to do what she really wanted to do, which was write a novel. She told me, "It was like serving a sentence. Prison for years, always with an end goal in sight. I knew that if I could get through it, I would be released and have that freedom. Prison and then freedom. I hated it so much and yet was so grateful for it too. It was a constant struggle."

Linda actually downloaded an app on her phone that counted down exactly how many days she had until retirement. She started that countdown 1,095 days before she finally left her job. On the last day, when she got to zero, she turned everything in and imagined disappearing dramatically in a puff of smoke. But in reality, she walked out the door without looking back. There was great relief in this new freedom, but Linda discovered that the real work actually began after she left. For more than three decades she had taken on a false professional persona and lost sight of who she really was. The very first mission of her retirement was to shed that inauthentic skin and get herself back. Linda said, "When some people leave their job, it's like their life ended. Mine began after I retired."

The transition that comes with retirement is a relatively new concept. Pretty much up until the dawning of the Industrial Revolution, people worked until they died. Prior to the eighteenth century, most people lived agriculturally and the common life expectancy was a mere twenty-six to forty years old, so there wasn't really a need for retirement. But all that changed as people lived longer and moved from rural communities to the cities. With that, the need to provide financial security to the aged grew throughout Western societies and was severely tested with the onset of the Great Depression.

Here's the thing: In 1932, only 5 percent of elders got retirement benefits, which meant people really couldn't retire. When the Great Depression hit, poverty exploded, and by 1934 half of the elderly in the United States could not support themselves, which led to the introduction of Social Security in 1935, guaranteeing a social insurance to workers sixty-five years and older.

Perhaps because retirement is still a relatively new concept, we haven't yet figured out what this transition truly means or what it really asks of us. Instead, our modern culture sees it as a time of deserved selfishness and golf/mah-jongg dates mixed in with an underlying dread of purposelessness, redundancy, and a fear of aging. I found no better place to reinforce this perspective than my local drugstore's greeting card aisle. One card had a cartoon lady with an attitude, in a bathing suit, sipping a cocktail, and saying: "I'm retired: Do it yourself!" Another one had an image of a weekly retirement schedule checklist: "Monday (brush teeth), Tuesday (shave), Wednesday (shower), etc." There was even a *Far Side*–like cartoon card that had two identical men sitting bored on a couch with two women standing in the doorway saying to each other, "Bob retired from the cloning lab, and now he doesn't know what to do with himself." These cards laugh at common retirement issues, such as boredom, aimlessness, and loss of identity, but they also finger the wound of our culture's inability to provide ways to make this transition meaningful.

Retirement, like all threshold moments, requires us to ask big questions about our life as it changes: *How am I now valued? What are my routines without work? Who am I without my job title? Is it okay to not achieve as much?* These aren't questions that can be answered immediately but need to be considered over time. They evoke uncertainty, doubt, curiosity, and excitement, yet there is a cultural expectation that we can transition from work to retirement flawlessly. I mean, what's so hard about that? Isn't it just not working? Doesn't it just mean you now have time to do all the things you didn't have time to do? The problem with this expectation is that we can't know who we are when not working because we've never retired before.

To view retirement as a working person is entirely different than viewing retirement when you're actually retiring. To many retirees, coming off the momentum of decades of school and work can conjure feelings of disorientation and even a sense of being lost, because the rhythm of working is all that they've had for so long. And the consequences are unsettling: According to research from the Institute of Economic Affairs, "retirement increases the chances of suffering from clinical depression by around 40%, and of having at least one diagnosed physical illness by 60%."[*] It's not that retirement is inherently depressing or bad for your health, but these statistics pose a significant question: With all the freedom and flexibility that retirement brings, why are so many retirees depressed?

For the first year of Judy's retirement, she felt like a "rolling stone." She had worked for twenty-five years in the Catholic ministry and absolutely loved her job. It provided her focus, structure, community, and meaning, but it was only after retiring that she realized how strongly she had identified with her work and its mission. Without real-

---

* "Retirement Causes a Major Decline in Physical and Mental Health, New Research Finds," Institute of Economic Affairs, May 16, 2013, https://iea.org.uk/in-the-media/press-release /retirement-causes-a-major-decline-in-physical-and-mental-health-new-resea.

izing it, she kept catching herself bringing up her job, in almost every conversation. Judy was looking for opportunities to remember that she was needed. "Maybe it was to make sure people knew I was still worth something," she said.

Judy was searching for her value because she was untethered to a job and the purpose that it provided her. Now she was in a liminal time in her life—transitioning from decades not just of working but also of belonging to something bigger than herself, something she believed in. All life transitions include a liminal period—the time between who you were and who you may become, also called "betwixt and between," a term used by ethnographer Victor Turner. Liminality is inherently disorienting. Think of it like leaving home and heading out to sea. You're adrift—having left the solidity of land for the fluidity of water—and haven't arrived yet to the new shore. Similarly, with retirement, you are leaving behind the familiarity of work and all that comes with it—your identity, status, routines, and purpose—and have yet to reconstitute a new identity—and the uncertainty is pervasive. But that's not wrong. That's exactly what liminal time is about. It's mysterious.

When we are in a major life transition and aren't aware of that liminal interlude that calls us to wander and wonder, exploring new ways of being in our life, we can end up thinking that retirement is, à la *Seinfeld*, really about nothing, which can lead to feelings of confusion, aimlessness, and especially depression. Joel Savishinsky, in his book *Breaking the Watch: The Meanings of Retirement in America*, explains why: "People retire *from* work, which is an activity. They retire *to* bed or Florida, which are simply places. But there are still no prepositions or figures of speech to indicate what retirement is *for*. Older individuals do not retire to a purpose or function. What they *do* in the place they retire *to* is ill-defined and largely up to them."

The transition to retirement longs to be infused with purpose. Everyone comes into this world with a gift. Some people live their entire lives wondering what theirs is; others are lucky enough to count themselves among those whose career and life's purpose converge into one and the same. Retirement can throw it all into question again—riffing off the lyrics from the Broadway musical *A Chorus Line*: "Who am I anyway? Am I my résumé?" Yet retirement is not the conclusion of living with purpose—instead, it has the potential to be a transformation of living that reorients us toward something beyond a job—a purpose that contributes to the well-being of the world.

The key here is ritual. According to an Oxford study done with 832 retirees doing retirement rituals, marking the exit from a person's old status of working and their eventual entry into the new status of retirement can lead to what the researchers called "higher post-retirement satisfaction with life."[*] If we can employ ritual to give this time distinction, to set it apart and bookend it with a beginning and an end, then we can give this undefined time some ceremonial heft. We can cease resisting the uncertainty that comes with retirement and instead give ourselves the time and permission to ask those big life questions: *Who am I now? What should I be doing? What needs to change?* That way, we can practice strengthening our curiosity and wonder during times of change, and have a better chance of coming into this new chapter with a re-imagined sense of identity, belonging, and purpose.

In other words, ritually acknowledging an ending can give us the space to grieve, celebrate, commemorate, and separate while simultaneously being witnessed in a new beginning, and the birth of a new self and new chapter. Rituals are our midwives through transition. During times of change, they make the fluid seem solid. They help us ease into and return from liminal and transitional times. They give our colleagues and friends purposeful ways to gather and provide actual support. They offer ways to learn and listen to all that life is trying to teach us as we change. And they offer us new sacred gifts that we must give back to the world.

RENEWING YOUR PURPOSE RITUALS

We've all been to those halfhearted farewell gatherings: a bit of cake and a bunch of people surreptitiously drinking prosecco from paper cups in a conference room. For some I interviewed, like Barbara, their retirement party was a predictable affair. People said a few nice words, gave gifts, raised glasses, but for Barbara the spirit of the thing wasn't present. Many others I spoke to recounted similar experiences. After twenty-eight years of teaching, Sheila called her party "an empty ceremony" which felt formulaic and lifeless to her. These stories left me wondering what was actually missing from these rituals. What wasn't being acknowledged? What if we needed to view the retirement ritual through the lens of an actual initiation that had one clear aim: the discovery of a new purpose?

---

[*] L. V. D. Bogaard, "Leaving Quietly? A Quantitative Study of Retirement Rituals and How They Affect Life Satisfaction," *Work, Aging and Retirement* 3 (2017): 55–65, https://www.semantic scholar.org/paper/Leaving-Quietly-A-Quantitative-Study-of-Retirement-Bogaard/8ccd1ac09 4ec3da1d1869c98f2a8bb6bde2cb242?p2df.

Traditional Dagara shaman Malidoma Somé teaches that the purpose of under-going an initiation is to discover what our gifts are and how to live and share them with the world. While these indigenous African teachings focus on the initiation from adolescence to adulthood, the cadence can be pulled through into all life transitions, especially retirement: a stage of separation, an ordeal to discover a new gift/purpose, and then, a homecoming. The homecoming is a crucial step and is often the thing most jarringly absent from retirement rituals, which focus primarily on separation. Being welcomed and celebrated for this new gift/purpose is one of the most impor-tant functions of this ritual. Somé says: "A gift motivates the presence of community, because a gift goes to work when a gift is seen. A community's responsibility is to see the gifts carried by each initiate. Noticing the gift is a fertilizing of that gift—it brings it alive."* We need our elders to renew their purpose for the sake of all those younger than them; retirement can't simply be about withdrawing.

I designed these rituals with the structure of a rite of passage in mind and in an effort to give those retiring time and space to metabolize this significant change in their life and bring forward their new purpose. It's unrealistic to expect that someone retiring can immediately pivot masterfully from work to retirement. The journey of retirement, like aging, asks us to return once again to question what's important, why we are here, what we are here to do, and to whom our life is in service. These are not small wonderings, and yet by asking these questions, you might come to understand yourself not as needy, but instead as needed, for this next stage of your life.

PART 1: THE LEAVING

Prepare
Intentions
May I celebrate and commemorate all the years of work and reflect upon what this time means to me. May I be witnessed in my departure from work, acknowledge what is ending, and what I am letting go of. May I choose friends that can anchor me and hold me in this process.

---

* Leslee Goodman, "Between Two Worlds: Malidoma Somé on Rites of Passage," *Sun,* July 2010, https://www.thesunmagazine.org/issues/415/between-two-worlds.

You Will Need

- Wineglasses
- Each guest brings something to drink
- Index cards with questions

Hand It Off

I suggest handing this role off to a friend or family member who can hold the ritual reins. Sometimes we might know we need a ritual but deep down want others to recognize this need. We want others to say, "Hey, I know this is big and I want to support you through it." It could be as simple as handing this book to a close friend while saying, "Help me do this."

When

Don't wait. Do this right at the time of finishing work, as the freshness and newness of your departure matters. If you postpone this for too long, you will already be adjusting and acclimating into your retirement, which is actually an obstacle to the second step. Treat this ritual like it has an expiration date and do it within the first month or so of your separation from work.

Where

Sure, you can do this ritual in your home, but I want to encourage you to bring this gathering outside. More so, I want you to consider *where* outside. Different places and elements in nature can lend themselves toward moving different emotions and experiences. When choosing where, ask yourself what kind of space would serve the purpose of this ritual.

For instance, I've advised retirees who hated their jobs to have their retirement ritual outside around a crackling fire. That fire matched their anger as well as served as a place they could bring old files or paperwork to burn and release. Other retirement rituals I've designed needed big bodies of water, like at the seashore, because the retiree wanted to feel the soothing quality of the water and have something mirror the great expanse they were feeling around this time of their life.

If you do choose an outdoor setting, be sure it's somewhere private. Rituals need safety and, therefore, containment and boundaries. It gives those participating in the ritual permission to let down their guard and really show up for something special, to make room for the heart, the spirit, and the symbolic. Give this gathering the privacy it needs so that the vulnerability can be there.

Ultimately, wherever you choose, don't underestimate the power of the place.

Guest List

Creating a guest list for this ritual has two significant purposes. First, it gives you an opportunity to participate in a reflective process—reviewing who at this life stage matters to you and renewing those bonds. Second, it gives you a chance to exclude those who don't matter. So limit your guest list to a small number and intentionally choose to not invite everyone. Excluding skillfully can actually focus a ritual's purpose.

When considering who should be there, ask yourself:

1. Does this person care about my well-being?
2. Can I be vulnerable with this person?
3. When needed, would they show up for me?
4. When needed, would I show up for them?
5. Do they have the capacity for depth?

An ideal number for this gathering is around ten people, but if there are three good friends who you know would really help fulfill the purpose of this ritual, then that's enough.

The Invitation

When you decide who you are inviting to this ritual, it's important to send out an invitation that clearly states its purpose—you are retiring and are entering into a process of renewing your life's gifts. What that boils down to is that you're inviting them to be an anchor of support, akin to a participant in a support circle. But be clear: You are asking if they would be willing to commit to a process, not a party. The first part is to send you off, and then eventually, to welcome you back.

But during that liminal time, are they willing to hold a prayer for you and even be available to you for support? On the invitation indicate that this is a three-part process and offer dates for both the Departure Ritual and the Return Ritual.

Begin

Let the host welcome everyone and state the ritual's purpose: "We are here not just to celebrate the retirement of so-and-so but to hold them in a process of rediscovering their post-work purpose and identity." The host may want to acknowledge how hard this is to do alone—and how needed everyone there truly is.

Also remind them that this is part one of a three-part process and this group will gather again for the Return Ritual about six weeks later.

The Rounds

The way the ritual works is relatively simple. The choreography is that each round consists of two prompts given by the guests. One of them can be considered negative and the other positive. This gives a chance for the retiree to represent the full spectrum of their work experience. For each positive response, the retiree takes a sip from their glass. For each negative response, the retiree pours some of their glass on the earth or on a plate.

There are seven rounds of drinks. While you are more than welcome to make these drinks alcoholic, that is not essential. You can make different mocktails. What is most important is that there are seven distinct drinks, one poured for each round.

Each guest should be given one index card with one prompt written on it. While each round features only two prompts, the retiree can give as many responses as they like. And be sure to keep drinking and pouring for each response.

Round 1: Commemorate
A guest pours the first glass.
"*I remember when . . .* " and "*I want to forget when . . .* "
Start with your story. How did your years in the workforce begin? Who did you work with in those early days? What were

your responsibilities? Also, what experiences and jobs do you wish you'd never had? Are there any embarrassing stories or unfortunate events that need to be shared?

Round 2: Celebrate
A guest pours the second glass.
"I am celebrating my . . ." and *"I am regretting my . . ."*
Crow about your accomplishments! What did you do that you're most proud of? What did you build, write, invent, achieve? What do you regret not doing? Name the big wins and big losses during your career.

Round 3: Let Go
A guest pours the third glass.
"I am ready to let go of . . ." and *"I am struggling to let go of . . ."*
Closure time. What feels complete? What are you happy to never do again? What will you miss? Who are you excited to never have to speak to again? Who are the people you love and are not ready to leave? What aren't you ready to close?

Round 4: Reveal
A guest pours the fourth glass.
"I am excited to . . ." and *"I am scared that . . ."*
How do you feel about leaving your job? What feels good, inspiring, uplifting, replenishing? And what worries you? What do you fear you won't have? What do you think you'll be missing?

Round 5: Harvest
A guest pours the fifth glass.
"I learned that . . ." and *"I never learned to . . ."*
There was so much you learned during years of work—things you never knew before, skills you never had, mastery that took time to build. Acknowledge some of the hard-earned wisdom you cultivated during your career. What would you pass down to someone just starting? Recognize what you never figured out, what you longed to learn, and what still feels incomplete.

Round 6: Imagine

A guest pours the sixth glass.

"*I got my wish that . . .*" and "*I wish I could have . . .*"

Maybe you had never thought you'd get that raise, work for that expert, own your own business, or teach the subject you loved. Proclaim the fantasies that actually came true. Also, maybe you wish you could have cursed your boss out but you never did, had that other career but you never pursued it, or written that book but you never got around to it. Acknowledge those lost wishes and dreams.

Round 7: Grateful

A guest pours the seventh glass.

"*I am grateful for . . .*" and "*I forgive . . .*"

The last round is for thanks and forgiveness. Who do you want to thank for those years of work? Who opened that door or noticed your talent or gave you that chance? Who do you need to apologize to? Who did you never thank? Who did you take advantage of? Who needs your forgiveness?

The Roast and Reflection

By this time, the gathering is either well hydrated or plastered. Let the end of the ritual be a time for the guests to raise one more glass each to the retiree. Maybe it comes across as advice, a blessing for the retirement, or as some serious reflection that needs to be shared. And don't forget the roasting—raise a glass to the failures, the flops, the strikeouts, and hilariously embarrassing stories. These need to be included too!

Conclude

Conclude the ritual with more gratitude and also reminding everyone that there are two more ritual parts to this journey into retirement. And they are all invited back for the third part—the Return.

PART 2: BETWIXT AND BETWEEN

The most important purpose here is to give you time "away." What that means is completely up to you. Maybe you just need time being home in your pj's or maybe you take a big world tour with your spouse. However you do it, choose a set amount of time to be in a liminal period. What that means is that you are neither here nor there—you are not working and not yet retired. It's a purposefully ambiguous period. The rituals below can fit into however you design this time and ask you to specifically employ this time to reflect, process, wonder, remember, and discover.

Prepare

Intentions

May I let myself be "in limbo" and devote time each day to slow down, reflect, and wonder. May I come to understand my new purpose by listening deeply and journaling.

You Will Need

- A journal and pen

Time

First and foremost, choose a specific amount of time for this part. It could be a couple of weeks, a year, or more. Because liminal time is so expansive, it needs boundaries. Make sure you put the start and end date on your calendar.

  I am structuring the ritual below on a six-week reflection time. If you decide to do more or less, adjust the ritual accordingly by adding or subtracting from it.

Begin

The Ritual

Each week is devoted to a particular theme and paired with an element in nature. Your goal is to spend at least one hour a day sitting with that element—observing, listening—just watching what comes and goes and what changes. Afterward, spend at least thirty minutes journaling about the question in the prompt or inviting a friend to discuss this with you.

There is no right way to do this. Instead, see this time as exercising your capacity for curiosity, awe, and self-discovery.

Week 1: Water
Question: *Who have I been? And what have I done?*

Week 2: Fire
Question: *Who do I want to be? What do I want to do?*

Week 3: Earth
Question: *How did I value myself? How am I valuable now?*

Week 4: Air/Sky
Question: *What once inspired me? What inspires me now?*

Week 5: Space
Question: *Where has my journey taken me? Where am I going?*

Week 6: Moon
Question: *What have I feared? What can I imagine my life to be for?*

Conclude

At the end of the time that you devoted to this phase, consider marking it by either lighting a candle, raising a glass of wine, or my favorite, building an earth altar. It can be simple, but just do something that acknowledges that this liminal phase is concluded.

PART 3: THE RETURN

If you got to this section, you're almost there. You did Step 1—closed the chapter on your working life. You completed Step 2—spent time away and asked some big questions about life and your life in particular. And now you are entering into this next chapter of retirement with a renewed sense of purpose and needed-ness. But here's the thing—you can't do a homecoming alone. You need others to welcome you, witness you, and remind you that these new gifts are wanted. Malidoma Somé speaks about the need to be welcomed back from an initiation with open arms:

> It's not really viable to think of formal initiations without community support. Not a lot is required. All people need is to be held, to be told that they are safe now, that they have arrived home. . . . The psyche knows when a homecoming is genuine.[*]

So much of what makes a transition viable is to feel others welcoming us back home.

Who
In an ideal world, you gather back the same group that sent you off. But if that's not possible, it's actually okay. Continuity and quantity are not the objectives here. What matters is to not do this by yourself. Maybe you invite those friends that were really there for you during that liminal period. Or that one friend who has been tracking your journey into retirement. This ritual can be performed with one or many, as long as it's with someone other than you.

Prepare
Intentions
May I be honored and acknowledged for the completion of this passage. May all those gathering again celebrate my new gifts and purpose that I am now carrying. May this next chapter of my life begin!

You Will Need
- Water pitcher
- Hand towel
- Water source

---

* Goodman, "Between Two Worlds."

- Wine and wineglasses
- Food/dessert

Where

Sure, you can do this ritual in your home, but I want to encourage you to bring this gathering outside, preferably to a place with water. Why water? Water and journey go hand in hand. I don't know about you, but after arriving home from a long flight, the first thing I want to do is take a long hot bath or shower. In my Jewish tradition, our old stories from almost four thousand years ago remind us that our forefathers and foremothers would wash a traveler's hands and feet as the holy etiquette of hospitality. Water cleanses and welcomes.

Begin

Let the beginning of the ritual be a gathering in. Maybe invite everyone to take a breath together, light a candle, or read a brief poem or prayer. Don't just jump into the ritual. Let yourselves arrive and let the moment arrive too.

When you're ready, fill the pitcher up. If you are near a body of water, use the water from the lake, ocean, or stream. If you're inside, there is no shame in using tap water.

The Rounds

Each round is accompanied by a prompt. These are cues for you to share from all that is on your heart. Don't hold back. Let yourself be witnessed in the messy, emotional, beautiful, changing moment you're in. Gosh, the whole purpose of this ritual is to recognize what is changing and to be received as a different person, so give it over.

At the end of each round, one friend will take your hands and pour water over them, cleansing them. Maybe they'll even be inspired to say something to you that warmly welcomes you back, acknowledging how much you've changed or saying, "you're not alone." That kind of earnestness is something we might express quite effortlessly with children, but tend to withhold from each other as adults. This is a good opportunity to soften with each other and practice the fine art of welcoming and praising.

Here goes.

Round 1
Fill the pitcher.
"I realized that . . . "
What came of your time sitting with those questions in nature? What did you notice? What did it get you curious about? Speak to some of the realizations that the "limbo" time has given you.
A friend cleanses your hands with water.

Round 2
"I see myself changing . . . "
What changes have you been noticing? How are you different? How are things different? Has this time taught you anything that you didn't know before? What more must continue to change?
A friend cleanses your hands with water.

Round 3
"I'm choosing . . . "
Where do you feel needed? What direction are you inspired to go in? What are you recommitting to? What do you want to serve? What needs your attention and care? What are you giving yourself over to in the years to come?
A friend cleanses your hands with water.

Round 4
"I am a part of . . . "
Where do you feel you belong and who do you feel you belong to? Who and what in this world do you love? What are the biggest and smallest things you are thankful for?
A friend cleanses your hands with water.

Round 5+
If necessary, don't stop! Keep going if something more needs to be acknowledged.

HELLO, GOODBYE

Toast

Now it's the witnesses' turn to toast.

To the witnesses: Uncork that bottle of whatever and pour each other a tall glass. Let this moment of the ritual carry a scent of praise, the power of honoring and/or some playful mischief. All that matters here is that you recognize this person's differences and growth. They are not the same person who started this journey. Remember that, proclaim that! Raise those glasses up and toast or roast this new someone in your midst. Bless their life, bless their journey, bless their needed-ness. Praise is how we call forth the unseen within one another and let it be seen beautifully. This is how we encourage one another, meaning to arouse one another's stoutheartedness.

Conclude

One Last Thing

It might be fine to end the ritual in a crescendo of toasting, but consider one more thing. Give thanks to all that you could never name and never remember—the body of water at your feet, the endless list of hardworking people who helped you to get where you are, your unfathomable line of ancestors whose lives directly support yours. Consider pouring one more glass for the greater-than-you world that gave you work, fed you, housed you, nourished you, and to whom you are forever indebted. This is always a good way to close a ritual—humbly and in awe.

Questions for Further Reflection

- What has been the most challenging part of this transition?
- What has been the most easeful?
- What needs to be embraced or accepted?
- What do I need to remember long after this ritual is done?
- What has this ritual taught me about change?

RITUALS *for*
NEW BEGINNINGS

Becoming a
Mother or Birthing Parent

Note: This chapter and its rituals were inspired by conversations with more than twenty-five mothers and birthing parents. The term "birthing parent" is used to include and honor transgender and nonbinary parents.

Just keep swimming.

—Andrew Stanton, *Finding Nemo*

You're poised on the precipice of an indescribable change, one both mundane and miraculous. For some time, there's been a being growing inside of you. A new heart beating within your body. Some days, it's hard to believe you are now a home for two, your own flesh and blood building another. Your belly and energy have become full, ripened like a plump fruit hanging heavy on the limb. If this is your first, this third trimester is animated with anticipation and wonder: Who is this little one? When will it happen? What does life look like afterward? If you've been here before, for better or worse, you have a sense of what this threshold asks of you: *everything*.

Now more than ever before, you can feel their swelling presence, their little kicks and rhythms. This is the calm before the storm. Maybe you've been busy making plans, imagining how you want that birth time to be, but when it actually begins, those quixotic ideas often get left in the dust along with everything else. Now you're in the sway of something otherworldly—this passageway between life and death where there are no guarantees.

The intensity of labor tells you there's only one direction that this whole thing must move: through. Yes, there will be an end to this ordeal and, however it happens— ecstatically or wretchedly, at home or in hospital, naturally or with an epidural, C-section or vaginal—on the other side of this wild passage pulsing with emotion and hormones, stretched beyond pain, flooded with sheer uncertainty, there you are with a tiny human in your arms. They emerge from the watery world of your womb, their tiny lungs breathing in this world for the very first time. And you emerge on the other side of this birthing threshold, not as a pregnant person anymore but—as a parent, a life giver. No longer are you a *me*, now you're a *we*.

For some new parents, however, it's not that easy. Sara Beth tested positive for COVID-19 as she got checked into a New York City hospital at the onset of the pandemic. The nurses came in with hazmat suits and put a sign on the door that made Sara Beth feel like the room was radioactive. "Honestly, I don't know what a normal birth is like," she told me. In those early days of the pandemic everything was uncertain. They weren't sure if Jeff, her husband, would even be allowed in the hospital at all. As much as Sara Beth longed to hold her baby, the moment she was born, they took her away to be tested for the virus. In every way, her baby's birth story was interwoven with the story of the pandemic, so much so that for the first month, her baby never even saw her parents' faces because they were both masked all the time. When they did get to hold her, Sara Beth recounted, "In those first few moments it was this weird timeless time where nothing made sense. The sun was rising outside the hospital and Jeff was about to be forced to leave and I had the virus and yet, we're both sitting here with this entire new world in our arms. It was wild."

Jenessa was only able to hold and kiss her baby for twenty seconds before they took her away to the NICU for twelve hours, after a premature birth. Her partner, Jon, took a photo of the baby right after she was born, and during their time apart, Jenessa stared at the photo and sobbed. "I just longed to hold her, to touch her. I felt like there was this emptiness that had never been full." When she finally held her safe in her arms, Jenessa remembers her baby latching as the most exquisite feeling she had ever experienced in her life. "It was better than sex. It felt like my whole body was finally doing the thing it was meant to do."

In birth, you are reunited with a kind of carnal inheritance. A connection to an endless human line of bodies birthing bodies, of skin on skin, of mouth on nipple—a return to tactile relating as human animals. Life becomes primal again—tending to poop and pee and milk and tears. The sounds are purely primordial. A new mother I spoke to referred to her baby's guttural gurgling as "the cry of a wolf cub." The touch is warm, fleshy, and sensual. The scent, hormonal. These two animal bodies, yours and theirs, are separate but longing for that original closeness. And as the baby begins to inhabit their own body, you must return to yours—slowly coming back to yourself and closing all that's been stretched or cut open.

The journey from pregnancy to birth to postpartum is a process of coming in and coming out—of opening and then closing. Author Britta Bushnell, in her book *Transformed by Birth*, uses the labyrinth as a symbol of the mysterious winding and turning that leads to and from birth. The journey to the center of the labyrinth, which is the birth of your baby, has clear direction and purpose, but the path afterward is more ambiguous. "Without a clear destination or definitive direction, the postpartum journey can be cloaked in mystery, doubt, and a feeling of losing your way." This is especially true on a physical level, as the body heals from the wounding that birth brings. When I spoke to more than twenty-five mothers and birthing parents about their postpartum journey, many acknowledged that losing control of their body and its normal functioning was the hardest to return from: "I'm still in pain from the C-section." "I have a belly that won't go away." "My boobs are three times what they were." "Pooping is super weird." "My pelvic floor muscles are so weak." "I pee a drop every time I stand up." "My abs are stretched." "My body completely changed after my first baby and then again after my second." "Every time I coughed, I cried." Healing the body is not a linear journey; it takes time and needs containment.

In many traditions, there is a specific time container that a birthing person enters into immediately following a birth to recover from this physical and emotional ordeal. They are not allowed to leave, to do any housework, to make any meals, or to have sex. For instance, traditionally in Mexican culture, there is a custom called *la cuarentena*, where for forty days after giving birth, a mother or birthing parent's only job is to bond with and take care of their baby—and return to the physical boundaries of their own body. To integrate this, healing needs community support. This is the time when the grandmother's responsibility shifts into high gear as she makes daily visits to handle the chores, the shopping, the cleaning, and especially, holding the baby so the mother or birthing parent can finally fall down and rest. Similarly, in Malaysia, postpartum mothers or birthing parents traditionally enter into the *pantang*, which is a kind of confinement, for about six weeks with strict dos and don'ts, all in support of bonding with the baby and healing the body.

But here in the West, the slow, surrendered interdependency of postpartum is foreign and unsupported. Instead, what is valued is self-sufficiency and individualism, which result in many mothers, birthing parents, and nuclear families carrying the burdens of postpartum all alone. Beth Berry, author of *Motherwhelmed*, claims that so much of the unrecognized and impossible weight on modern mothers, birthing parents, and families originates from the loss of living together in a community or village: "The majority of our mental load and emotional labor as modern-day mothers comes from constantly and creatively trying to piece together some semblance of a village, stepping into roles meant to be filled by other village members, and unconsciously grieving this soul-crushing loss (which is hidden in plain sight.)"

A Mexican American woman I interviewed, living in the USA, lamented that unlike her grandmother, her mother worked a full-time job and just couldn't show up completely during the forty days of her *cuarentena*. So within the first few weeks, even though she was still bleeding and in pain, she was out grocery shopping because "someone needed to," and a couple of weeks after that, she was back at her job because her family "just couldn't afford it any other way." With zero weeks of national paid parental leave in the United States, compared with thirty to sixty weeks of compulsory leave in countries like Austria, Japan, and Chile, vulnerable American mothers and birthing parents are forced to make an impossible choice between the well-being of their baby and their recovering bodies and the need to pay their bills, keep their jobs, and put food on their tables.

Even if you have the privilege of a job that pays for parental leave, a supportive family, or an amazing partner, being a new parent can still feel like you've been tossed out to sea and are drowning. It is what one mother referred to as "the basic-fucking-training that never ends." If this is your first, maybe you thought you knew what you were getting into. You read all the books, listened to all the podcasts, got all the baby equipment, but once you're actually inside of it, it can feel like your entire world is flipped upside down. No longer is it about you at all—for now, nothing matters except giving this other human all your attention, your care, your body. Your days and nights orbit around their sleep, their feedings, their diapers, their crying, as your individuality is entirely consumed and swallowed alive.

This journey into postpartum can also feel overwhelmingly isolating. In our performative culture, always pressuring us to present our best and hide our worst, what we see on the public stage of social media are images of perfect babies and parents: adorably dressed newborns peacefully sleeping or moms out with their strollers and their bounced-back bodies. This often cloaks the shit show that's happening behind the scenes. Rarely do people post about how this time wrecked them. Rarely do we see what a new parent looks like days after not showering, after being terribly sleep-deprived, or when in intense pain. But why is this all kept private and hidden? Maybe there's a pridefulness to it or a feeling like no one would understand or it shouldn't be this way. Because so much of the mess is hidden, the confusion shut away, the loneliness and depression not often named, so much of the suffering is done alone.

In 2020, there was a postpartum recovery commercial[*] that got rejected from airing during the Academy Awards broadcast. It was an emotionally driven short story showing the life of a new mom in her fourth trimester. It's the middle of the night, her baby is crying, her husband is sleeping, and she has to get up and feed the baby. But as she stands, she is clearly in tremendous pain. She waddles over to the toilet to pee, is still wearing this awful hospital padded underwear, all while trying to take care of her body as the baby cries louder and louder. This arresting imagery illustrates the lonely passage that so many mothers and birthing parents experience right after giving birth—with their recovering bodies, within their relationships, and especially, within this culture that's built around the overwhelmed nuclear family. When the network had to explain the reason they rejected this commercial, they deemed it "too graphic"—but *why*? If this is an honest example of what being a new mom taking care of her body and baby looks like, what are the consequences for not showing the broader public how it really is right after giving birth and how intense it is to return from this ordeal? Even though this is a common experience, when stories like this and others are not shared, many naively arrive at their fourth trimester unprepared to be dropped into the deep end with all the emotion it brings.

Becoming a mom or birthing parent is to also become a caretaker, but the etymology of the word "care" speaks to something too often invisible and under the surface. The Old English word *cearu* actually means "sorrow" or "grief," and recognizes the weight of the enormous burden that being a caretaker entails. The burden of trying to caretake your newborn, your body, your family, your home, your finances, and your own self can feel disorienting and overwhelming. You are needed in ways you may have never been needed before, and most likely, you are not getting your own needs met. For Jocelyn, it wasn't until she had her second baby that she realized she had lost herself for a while. The demands of caretaking two were more intense than she had imagined: "I didn't know how to balance my life in the way I always knew how to." Similarly, Alexandra, a mother of two and soon-to-be three, shared: "I'm caring for the baby all the time and I haven't showered in three days. I can't even eat a good meal. I'm taking care of everyone and no one is taking care of me." The responsibility of taking care of yourself and your baby can be overwhelming. Zivar, a mother of two, shared with me that when she gave birth to her first baby, she ran

---

[*] "Oscars Ban Postpartum Commercial for Being 'Too Graphic,'" ET Canada YouTube channel, February 7, 2020, https://www.youtube.com/watch?v=1q9leHVgecw.

from what it was asking of her. She tried her best to avoid stepping into this new rhythm and role. She kept on clinging to her old life and her old ideas about her body. But with her second baby, she felt it necessary to choose another way. "It took me running from it the first time to actually be with it the second. Now I am choosing to slow down. I'm not rushing to try to get back to my old life or my pre-pregnant body. I've become more gentle with myself—more surrendered. Loving myself no matter what. Of course, there is a part of you that dies when something so huge comes into your life but I've come to learn that that's okay. The death of my old life gave birth to this new one—to becoming a mom."

The endings and beginnings, losses and gains, pain and beauty that birth brings are the territory of initiation. And as with any initiation, there is a harrowing descent and then an ascent, according to the rites-of-passage research of ethnographer Arnold van Gennep. With birth, you leave behind the life you knew as a nonparent and enter into this mysterious liminal phase of pregnancy. You undergo an immense physical and emotional ordeal that can bring you face-to-face with pain, shadow, and mortality, and then, after the birth, you reemerge into the world charged with new responsibilities, an impacted body, and a new identity.

During my interviews, many new mothers and birthing parents wondered about who they were: *What does being a good mother or birthing parent mean to me? Will I be like my mother, for better or worse?* They asked questions about their body and new boundaries: *Is my body mine or partially my partner's and/or my baby's? How do I feel about my breasts being used for nursing and also for sex?* Other questions were fueled by exhaustion and obligation: *How can I have sex with my partner when I'm "gived-out" from giving all the time?*

What makes this time even more confusing is the grief for losing past identities as well. It could be the loss of who you were in your career, who you were to your partner, or possibly even the way you understood yourself as young or attractive. The principal consequence of initiation is that it annihilates your innocence and short-circuits your childish sense of self, all so that you can step into serving something much bigger than you.

Coming to terms with these losses can reveal deep layers of grief, which is often pushed aside to protect the baby. But still the grief remains, in tandem with all the happiness and joy. Rachel, a mother of three, shared with me: "I'm watching my friends who don't have kids take trainings and grow their careers. I'm watching my husband be more and more established in his job. And suddenly, I'm this nameless person on the sidelines that no one is interested in. It feels like this invisiblizing that's happening."

So much of the success or failure of an initiation comes down to being seen on the other side, and when you have a baby, it can feel like no one looks at you anymore. For instance, many expecting mothers and birthing parents take photos of their pregnant bellies at different stages, but once the baby is born, the photos are now of the baby—tracking the months of their life and leaving the mom or birthing parent out of the picture. *Being seen* is the third step of an initiation, also called integration. What this stage requires is for others to see and witness you as someone who has survived an ordeal and has been profoundly changed by it—physically, emotionally, and spiritually. It's actually not enough to just welcome the baby into the world—the new mother or birthing parent also needs to be welcomed back by their larger community too.

The author and traditional Dagara shaman Malidoma Somé speaks about the responsibility of a community to gather around and receive a person returning from an initiation: "What people need is someone willing to create space for them in which they can be seen, honored, and praised for what they have been through."* The purpose is to integrate all the change. Birth can make a new parent feel riven and not whole. Having a space that's held by another to listen, touch, support, understand, and celebrate you for enduring this initiation can help bring stability during a destabilizing time and return you to your center when everything feels fluid and chaotic.

At their core, rituals are like a doula for transitions. They can help open or close what needs opening or closing, remind us of our core essence when everything is ungrounded, and connect us back into a deeper sense of belonging to a bigger story—a story that reminds us that we aren't alone. Let the ritual below demarcate another turn on this labyrinth's path so that you can continue to ground in your body and in the world again, changed and unchanged.

THE CARE *and* SHARE RITUAL

The fourth trimester or "the sacred window," as it's called in Ayurvedic Indian traditional medicine, is a time to ground, to heal, and especially to call back the lingering

---

* Goodman, "Between Two Worlds."

parts of yourself. At the conclusion of the fourth trimester, this sacred window of time closes, which is an opportunity to recollect those parts of yourself still scattered and exposed and to continue to slowly return them back to you—back to wholeness.

Since the birth, you've been giving nonstop, but what about receiving? This ritual is devoted to you receiving care, touch, listening, pampering, containment, much like a baby. "Everything a new baby needs, a new mother needs," Kimberly Ann Johnson, the author of *The Fourth Trimester*, told me during an interview. "Mothers need swaddling, warmth, constant nourishment, and loving touch, too."

This ritual is broken down into two parts. The first part takes place in a bath as a way to care for and cleanse your body, as well as a time to reflect on how much your life has changed since having your baby. While the bath is inspired by the *mikvah*, a Jewish ritual using a pool of water for submersion and purification, its purpose is reimagined to be an agent of rebirth, marking this moment to renew your body, mind, and spirit.

The second part, post-bath, is a small gathering to share your birth story—told in the way you want to tell it. Together, these rituals mark the conclusion of the fourth trimester by honoring your body and sharing in the joy and heartache that comes with being a new mother or birthing parent.

PART 1: THE RITUAL BATH

Prepare

Intentions

May I mark the sealing of the fourth trimester, "the sacred window," by allowing my body to be held, nourished, cherished, and taken care of. May I gather in all the parts of myself and my birth story that feel dispersed and share them in a safe, held container where deep listening is being practiced.

You Will Need

- Your preferred oils or scents
- Bouquets of flowers
- Hot tea
- Candles

- Bathrobe
- Body butter
- A journal and pen

When

You can do this ritual months or even a year after you give birth, gathering a small group of friends around you when you're ready to be gathered around. Do not rush into this ritual. You will know when the right time is to mark the closing of this sacred window of time.

Caring for Your Baby

Time alone also means time not with your baby, which can be difficult. While I was speaking to Amanda, a doula from the Bay Area, she shared with me: "I'm aware that when I'm holding a healing space for a new mother, they are hyperalert, especially if the baby is nearby." She suggests that someone else hold the baby in another room, or if need be, she puts the baby directly on the mother and offers the healing and touch this way. Obviously, do what works for you and your baby, but if possible, let someone else caretake your baby during your bath so you can give yourself the gift of this time alone.

Begin

The Bath

Setting up and drawing the bath can be done by a friend or a partner, or it can be something you give yourself; however, my suggestion is to give this task over to someone else because this ritual is all about you receiving (and not giving).

If you do ask a friend to give you this gift, make sure you invite them over a couple hours prior to the second part of this ritual (the birth story ritual), so that they have enough time to create the bath experience for you and you have enough time to indulge in it.

Whoever creates the space, the bathroom should turn into a luxurious environment. Transform the space and let it be filled with everything you need to relax: lit candles, favorite oils, relaxing music, nice fluffy (even warm) towels, flowers, and a little tray of snacks and tea. Everything in this space is meant to pamper you and your body. Even if you're thinking, *I don't deserve this kind of attention*, see if you can let yourself be treated like royalty just for today.

Before entering the bath, brush your hair to remove all the knots. Do this not only to take care of your body but also as a symbolic way to remove the obstacles and restrictions that keep you from entering into this ritual moment and proceeding into this next chapter of your life.

As you dip your body into the bath, breathe in and release. Let your breath deepen as you bring your attention to your body. Feel the water touching your skin. Feel it holding every limb, bringing buoyancy to every muscle. Feel the warmth unwinding you. Smell the scented oil in the water easing your tension or anxiety. Allow yourself to take this time to soften.

Three Rounds

Whenever you feel ready, begin the three rounds of acknowledgments and release. You can speak to these prompts out loud, or if that doesn't feel comfortable, grab a journal and write down your response.

Also, there are no right answers. These questions are meant to draw out what might be lingering beneath the surface. Let yourself explore and feel into what surfaces. When you feel complete after each round, submerge your entire body under the water, as if you are entering a womb and birthing yourself again.

Round 1: *"My body has changed . . ."*
Acknowledge the parts of your body that have been impacted and changed from birth. This is an opportunity to welcome and love everything your body has been through and to release

any shame that says, "it shouldn't be," or "it should be another way."

Submerge your body.

Round 2: *"My identity has changed . . ."*
Acknowledge the parts of *who you are* that have changed since giving birth to your baby. This is an opportunity to welcome the new roles and responsibilities as well as to grieve the losses that come with this new identity.

Submerge your body.

Round 3: *"My relationships have changed . . ."*
Acknowledge the ways your relationships have changed since birth. Whether it's with your baby, your partner, your friends, or even yourself, this is an opportunity to reflect on and identify your changing needs within your relationships and to recommit to the relationships you value.

Submerge your body.

Conclude

Linger in the bath as long as you need. After the bath, make sure you take your time coming out of this space. A slow integration is important.

PART 2: THE BIRTH STORY SHARE

Prepare

You Will Need

- Seven small candles
- A lighter or matches
- Objects for a small altar
- A warm blanket
- Hot tea
- Dessert

When

These two rituals can occur back-to-back on the same day, or on completely different days. Don't overwhelm yourself with doing too many rituals, and choose what works for you, your energy, and your family.

Who

There is a custom among many modern pregnant persons to receive a "Blessingway" before their birth. While the roots of this ritual originate in the Diné Navajo tradition, it has been Westernized and changed. The common thread is that it is a time for other mothers and birthing parents to gather around the mother/parent-to-be and offer blessings, reflections, and guidance from their own experience of having already traversed this threshold. If you had a Blessingway, consider inviting those same mothers and/or birthing parents to gather around you again, bookending this ritual. If you didn't, invite at least one other mother or birthing parent to honor and celebrate you and deeply listen to your birth story.

Their Role

Unlike the offerings of the Blessingway, the primary purpose of this ritual is for those gathering to *listen* and hold a safe space free of judgment, shame, commentary, and opinions. One of the best ways to support someone recounting and recollecting their birth story is through the practice of attunement. This is a therapeutic practice,[*] researched by clinical psychologist Richard Erskine, that is an emotional and kinesthetic sensing of another. In other words, it's a way of listening with your whole being that embodies empathy, mindfulness, presence, attentiveness, and deep care. It allows the one sharing to sense active listening.

As you invite a select group of people to hear your story, consider their capacity and skill in listening and refine your invitation through that lens.

---

[*] Richard G. Erskine and Rebecca L. Trautmann, "Methods of an Integrative Psychotherapy," Institute for Integrative Psychotherapy, https://www.integrativetherapy.com/en/articles.php?id=63.

The Altar and Candles

Set the altar in the middle of wherever you imagine the group sitting, whether that's on the floor or around a table. The altar can contain objects that are meaningful to you, your baby, your family, your ancestry. Around the altar create a circle of seven candles. Seven is a number that symbolizes completion, like seven days in a week, and the circle is a symbol of wholeness.

Begin

As with most rituals, it's important not just to begin but to slowly find your way toward beginning. In this case, start with a song as a simple way to set the ritual container.

Touch

If touch doesn't feel right for you, skip this part.

Invite everyone to gently place their hands on you. I have seen this be as simple as hands lightly touching different parts of the body—the soles of the feet, the top of the head, the shoulders, the belly, the hips. I have also experienced this become more like massage, gently rubbing and caressing the body.

One of the overarching purposes of this ritual is to offer you containment—for you to physically feel held, just like you would your baby. Beginning and ending this ritual with being touched or held is a deeply healing way to ground again in your body and gather the dispersed energy, pulling it back together.

Offer this for a set amount of time, maybe five to twenty minutes. Don't remove all the hands at once, but rather slowly, one at a time over the course of a minute or so, so that you feel supported and held even as the ritual transitions.

Your Story

Sharing your story is a sacred and generous act. It can be healing to express yourself in front of others, even if the story is difficult or emotional to recount. It can also help integrate fragmented memories, gathering them back together into a whole story.

If sharing your entire birth story feels too vulnerable or traumatic, consider sharing only one part of your story, maybe a single moment that stands out. Go slow. Rituals are never one size fits all, and you should always check in with yourself to determine if and when it's the right time.

As you share, you will be lighting the seven candles one at a time. Do not light them all at once but rather light a candle when you come to a meaningful moment in your story, something you want to mark and distinguish. Author Kimberly Ann Johnson calls this "mining your birth story," and she shared with me the importance of identifying turning point moments in the story—moments that need to be remembered. Lighting these candles can help you identify and pronounce these moments.

Here are some prompts that can help reveal some of these story gems. Take the ones that cause a story to stir and leave the ones that don't:

- What surprised you most about this experience?
- What do you know now that you didn't know before and couldn't have known any other way?
- What needs to be acknowledged that often gets left out or overlooked?
- What moments happened differently than you would have liked and how would you have preferred it?
- What parts of your story need your acceptance and forgiveness?
- What parts are you struggling to forgive and need more time?
- What truths or beliefs did the birth help you remember or teach you?
- What support did you receive that needs to be recognized?

By the end of the story sharing, all seven candles should be lit.

Conclude

Blessings and More Touch

Once more, invite those gathered to put their hands on your shoulders, feet, hands, belly, and anywhere else you want to feel touch.

With all the hands still holding you, go around and ask everyone to offer a one-sentence blessing for your life, your baby's, and your family's life, and the courage and healing it took to pass through this initiation.

When everyone is finished, take a deep breath together.

Slowly release the hands in the same way you did the first time. Be sure to end this ritual by wrapping yourself in a warm blanket and asking someone to pour you hot tea. After opening like this, self-care is an essential follow-up.

Conclude this ritual with lots of desserts to celebrate this sweet time of your family's life.

Questions for Further Reflection

- What is concluding as I complete my fourth trimester?
- What is beginning as I complete my fourth trimester?
- How have I changed over this time? My body? My relationships?
- What still needs more time to heal?
- What did this ritual help mark and recognize?

Becoming a
Father or Non-Birthing Parent

I look at the moon that looks like a boat.
My dad's arms are like a boat, too.

—Stein Erik Lunde

You are the anchor, the protector, the supporter. Despite what is happening for you, your greater purpose at this threshold is to learn and practice how to fully show up, to take care and be in service to your pregnant partner and, eventually, your baby. But because there is so much to tend to during this time, it might be that your own questions, fears, and prayers go untended. Moments like these are so profound that they need us to approach them differently—to stop the endless to-do lists and open our eyes wide to the enormity of this time—wondering how it could be that not only have we been brought into this world, but we are now poised at this miraculous doorway to bring in new life too.

When I interviewed a dozen fathers and non-birthing parents about what they needed before crossing this threshold, the most common response was: "To remember that I am not alone." While there are baby showers and Blessingways that gather friends and family around the soon-to-be mother or birthing parent, they acknowledged that there isn't much to honor and sanctify this rite of passage for a soon-to-be father or non-birthing parent.

Simon, a father of three, felt the lack of ritual and chose to create one for himself. He went out to the woods behind his home and sat with a fire all night. This gave him time not just to reflect on the significance of this moment before his child's birth but to wonder about the ways he wanted to show up as a father. Throughout the night he fed the fire and realized that the fire itself was a proxy to better understand the skills he needed to cultivate to become the parent he wanted to be: a capacity to stay put, to be patient and attentive, to tend to something other than himself, to be generous, and to sometimes do it all without sleeping. Connecting with the fire helped Simon mark his continual path into adulthood.

Simcha, a new father, also chose to do an overnight ritual outside. He spent the night alone with a fire and a journal, reflecting about the family he came from and the family he was creating: "I wondered about all the ways I wanted to and the ways I didn't want to emulate how I was parented." In the middle of that wondrous night, Simcha felt himself standing within his lineage, taking his new place in an endless line of fathers. What made this ritual especially poignant was being welcomed back the following morning by a circle of cis-male friends and fathers. At daybreak, they gathered him in, listened to his story from the night before, and witnessed him unpack all the insight he'd gleaned, while offering him reflection and blessings. Often in these monumental moments, it's too much to hold on our own—we need other hands and hearts to help us receive the vastness of our changing lives.

This Fathering a Fire Ritual follows a similar cadence to these stories: Time alone and time together. The time alone is an opportunity for you to be quiet, to listen, and to consider the big questions that this time is asking you. The time with your community is a chance for others to gather you in and witness you at this life-changing threshold.

THE FATHERING *a* FIRE RITUAL

PART 1: THE TIME ALONE

Prepare
Intentions
May I give myself time to reflect upon what it means to me to become a father or birthing parent. May I invite others to welcome and witness me in this rite of passage and new role.

You Will Need
- A journal and pen
- Material for a fire (matches, tinder, branches, wood)
- A small cloth pouch

When

Try to do this ritual a few weeks before the baby comes. If the mother or birthing parent has a baby shower or Blessingway, consider doing this in conjunction with that.

Where

Sitting out and watching the moon rise or the flickering flames of a fire is a way to reconnect with a sense of awe at our living world. If you have the space and capacity to do this outside all night around a fire, choose this option. If you don't, you can always go on a nighttime walk in your neighborhood, lie in a hammock in your backyard, or have a candlelit evening in your home. What is most important is that you do this first part when and wherever you can have the space to be alone.

Who

Invite friends to gather and receive you the next day. Priya Parker, in her book *The Art of Gathering*, suggests doing so by intentionally excluding certain people.[*] This can actually be a generous act that allows for a clearer purpose and more inclusion for those gathering. For instance, if you are a cis man who is becoming a father, you might want to only invite other cis-male fathers. Or if you are a gay cis man becoming a father, you might want to only invite other gay fathers. Choose what works best for you, but remember that thoughtful exclusion and inclusion provides a space for deeper connection with everyone gathered.

Begin

As you respond to the questions below, either wonder about them out loud or write your response in your journal.

---

[*] Parker, *The Art of Gathering*.

Round 1: The Dark

Before lighting the fire, pause and allow yourself to sit in the dark and to take in the night sky, the nighttime sounds, and this moment of solitude.

Ask yourself: *How is my life about to change? What am I scared of? What am I excited and joyful about? What is mysterious and unknown?*

Speak or journal your response.

Round 2: The Lighting

Light the fire and spend time tending to the baby flames. After the fire is established, take some time gazing at it, watching the flames dance.

Ask yourself: *How was I fathered? How was my father fathered? What values and behaviors do I hold dear that I want to pass on to my child and which am I choosing to let go of?*

Speak or journal your response.

Round 3: The Tending

Stay vigilant, feeding and tending the fire.

Ask yourself: *What am I going to do when I need support? Who has my back? Who are the people that can I call upon for help, advice, or a shoulder to cry on? What are the myths, practices, or traditions that guide me?*

Speak or journal your response.

Round 4: The Coals

As the fire dies down, observe the glow and crackling of the coals.

Ask yourself: *What is a blessing I can offer my partner? What is a blessing I can offer my child? What is a blessing I can offer my family and community? What is a blessing I can offer this moment in time?*

Speak or journal your response.

If you sat up all night with the fire, conclude this first part in silence and awe.

PART 2: THE TIME TOGETHER

The gathering should happen close to when the fire was extinguished, allowing your open, tender heart to be received by your friends and community. Alternatively, you can keep the fire going and have the gathering happen around it.

Begin by sharing about the gathering's purpose, in other words, answer this question: *Why are we here, and what do I want from the group?*

Round 1: Your Share

Tell the story of last night. What questions really touched your heart to consider? What realizations did you have? What felt challenging? What were the blessings you made for your family?

At the end of this share, the group should acknowledge you by saying something like "amen" or "I hear you" or "we love you."

Round 2: Their Share

Go around the circle and let everyone gathered speak directly to you. This is a time where each person can share their own experience about being a father and offer you guidance, reflection, or prayers for this auspicious moment.

Ask that each sharing be brief and no longer than a couple minutes.

Conclude

At the end of the sharing, take a pinch of ash from the fire and put it inside the cloth pouch that you brought. This sack can sit in a special place within your home, like upon an altar, and remind you of this moment of support and togetherness right before your child came into this world.

Questions for Further Reflection

- Why is taking time for myself important before my child is born?
- How does this ritual impact my capacity to trust myself?
- What does having my community gathering around me help me notice?
- How did this ritual change my perspective?

Becoming a Brother or Sister

Father, mother, sister, brother. You know we're gonna
need each other. You just can't make it by yourself.

—African American spiritual

When I was just over three years old, my mother gifted me a little shirt
that let me know someone new was going to be living with us and that
I was becoming a "big brother." I wore that shirt and title proudly. Even
though I was too young to recognize it, this was my very first shift in identity. I was no
longer an only child, and I had to learn how to share my family, and what being a big
brother actually meant.

While becoming a big brother or sister is a wonderful thing, the young child who
is assuming this new role needs support through the change. They need to be reassured
that they are loved and won't be abandoned, that they are an integral part of the process and that this time comes with special big-kid responsibilities. Ritualizing this moment can be one of the ways to help a young child adjust by giving them a special space
to express their emotions and ease their anxiety with all the changes in the home nest.

The Magical Doorway Ritual is a way for your child to tangibly pass through this
transition by literally passing through a decorated doorway. On one side, you'll give
them space to express their feelings about this moment. As they cross through to the
other side, they will be received and honored by friends and family in their new role
and purpose as a big brother or sister. Passing through this doorway celebrates the
change while reminding them that no matter what changes, you will love them no
differently.

THE MAGICAL DOORWAY RITUAL

Prepare

Intentions

May my child be loved, included, and uplifted as they become a big brother or sister. May they have the space to express their feelings and be reminded of my love for them. May my children love each other.

You Will Need

- Streamer, tinsel, colored paper, flowers, fairy lights, and/or anything else you want to decorate a door frame
- A crown (either made from flowers or paper)
- Treats
- Optional: blindfold

When

This ritual should be done before the baby is born to give your child a chance to assume this new role before there is an influx of change in the home.

The Door Frame

This is the fun part for you. You get to wildly, beautifully adorn a door frame in your home so that it feels like your child is passing through a magical portal or gateway. Don't under-do it—bring on color, flash, and beauty!

Inviting Others

Because your family is growing and you will be spending more time with your new baby, this can be an opportunity to invite aunties, uncles, friends, or neighbors into the moment. Even for a young child, being witnessed by many people who love them can give them a secure sense of being held and remembered. Additionally, it can give your community yet another opportunity to come closer to your family during these transitional moments. Of course, if it's just you or your partner, that is great too.

The Crown

Prepare a flower or paper crown for your child to receive on the other side of the doorway. It can be just a crown, or it can say "Big Brother" or "Big Sister" on it. Either way, it's a gift that they get for walking through the passageway and a sweet way to honor their new role.

Right Before

Ask an auntie, uncle, or friend to take your child out of the house so you can prepare the doorway. It's important that when they see the door frame for the first time, it surprises them and feels special.

Begin

Make this into a game.

You and your child should be on one side of the doorway and any other guests should be on the other side.

You can lead your child to the magical doorway with them wearing a blindfold or just by holding their hand and telling them that you have a surprise in store for them.

When they arrive at the magical doorway, introduce it. You can say something like "This is the magical doorway just for you. Right now you are our only child, but once you pass through the door, you will become a big brother/sister. We are so proud of you and we know how excited the baby is to have such a special big brother/sister."

Before Crossing

Before they walk through, ask them how they feel about becoming an older sibling. This part is intended to give them space to identify any fear, sadness, or concern they might have and, of course, their excitement too. Give them plenty of space to answer in their own way.

After they've had a chance to express their feelings, you can name your excitement too and what their crossing through this passage means to you. For instance, you can say, "Your little brother or sister is so lucky to have you give them [name a special quality they have]" or "Being a big brother or sister means that you are going to have an important job, to [name a responsibility they will get]." By doing this, you are celebrating this new role and honoring their experience.

After that, ask them: "Are you ready to walk through this magical doorway and become a big brother/sister?"

The Other Side

As the child walks through to the other side, encourage the aunties and uncles to sing, clap, and celebrate this passage. They can all gather around and hug or kiss the child too. What's most important is that other adults are on the other side receiving them with love.

Also gift your child with the flower or paper crown. Explain to them that the crown means that they have new responsibilities when the baby arrives: to care for them, to protect them, to be generous with them, to love them in a way that only a big brother or sister can.

Conclude

After the crossing and crowning of this new big brother or sister, conclude the ritual with treats and dessert. While this part may sound peripheral to the ritual, it isn't. Beginning and ending with treats is a way to surround transitions in sweetness.

Lastly, encourage your child to keep the crown and to wear it the first time they meet their new brother or sister. The crown is a special ritual object that can remind them of their new role and identity.

Questions for Further Reflection

- Why is it important to mark this moment for my child?
- How does this ritual give them reassurance?
- What qualities am I celebrating in my child?
- How does being witnessed and received help them through this transition?

Becoming a Grandparent

I remind the young ... that they are seed carriers—
human seeds—of future generations.

—Grandmother Flordemayo

This kind of news brings only elation. This kind of love is purely unconditional. The birth of a baby not only makes mothers and/or fathers but transforms parents into grandparents. If you've been here before, you already know the deep well of care, pride, and unique joy that this time brings. If you're newly a grandparent and are witnessing your own child step into parenthood for the first time, this transition doesn't just offer you a new title, or even a new name, but a new purpose within your family. You are becoming a sanctuary for the next generation, a place where they can always find safety and love.

Becoming a grandparent is also a departure from the everyday responsibilities and obligations of parenting. No longer are you the caretaker, the manager, or the disciplinarian. The dynamics aren't like a parent/child relationship. Instead, you are more like a refuge, a resource, a solid foundation that your children and grandchildren can return to anytime they need. One grandmother I spoke with says she sees the evolution of her role as becoming the go-to for confidentiality. "My grandchildren can tell me anything. From the moment they were born, I knew I needed to become someone that they could always trust." She told me that she saw her intention become manifest as her youngest grandchild now refers to her home as "my calm space."

Oftentimes this new role comes with a new name. Lela, a grandmother of three, became "Mima" with her first grandson. This name always made her smile and represented care, safety, wisdom, and being an ear for listening. Lela said that she constantly strives to embody what that name means in her relationships with her grandchildren. Recently, she worried if the name was too childish and asked her teenage grandson if he would start calling her something else someday. His response touched her deeply when he replied, "Absolutely not. You will always be Mima to me."

Becoming a grandparent is also a supporting role. Like the rings of a tree, you find yourself moving toward the outside and a less centered place within your family structure. Instead of sitting at the helm, your role as grandparent asks something else from you—to step back, to learn to be available when you're needed, and to receive with unconditional love. A grandfather I spoke to reflected, "My grandchildren taught me how to listen and what listening actually meant."

But in stepping back, you are also stepping into being a link between the past and future generations—connecting "those who have departed" and "those who are arriving." You can provide the family a sense of the continuity of spirit through time. I spoke with David, a grandfather of five, who shared with me the strong bond between his deceased mother, Sue, and his granddaughter, Aya. Apparently, they don't just look alike but have similar mannerisms—even the way his granddaughter squints and points at things reminds David of his mother. One day, his granddaughter came for a visit and noticed the oil painting of his mother as a young girl in Europe before she fled the war. Aya, looking just like the little girl in the painting, squinted and pointed just like David's mother would, and said, "That's me." In that moment, David felt time and spirit weaving together. He glimpsed life beyond his own life. He felt his mother in his granddaughter, and how life lives on through the lineage.

Collectively we lack new rituals that mark the arrival of the grandparent. Some grandparents told me it was enough to receive phone calls of congratulations, to hold the baby at the bris, or be honored at the baby naming. But for others I spoke with, there was a longing to be acknowledged by their community in this new milestone in their life and with their new purpose.

Jeanne Marie said she longed for her family to ritualize her transition of becoming a grandmother but knew they weren't in a place to do so at that time. So instead she organized four rituals for four friends as they became grandmothers, as her way of giving what she wanted to get. One of her friends was a beloved teacher in her church, and her new granddaughter would be a fifth-generation member, so Jeanne Marie had the children of the church write poems for this new grandmother to honor how much she had given over the years. During the ritual, the community also lit candles for her ancestors that had come and gone, inviting their presence in to witness the ritual too. Everyone gathered around to hear stories, see photos, and behold the invaluable wisdom and presence that this new grandmother carried.

Ritualizing a milestone moment can provide a sacred time and space to reflect upon your life, be affirmed in your new position, and be witnessed in what is changing, so that you can become more present with what's happening. The Bridge Ritual is a way for your friends and family to honor this meaningful moment as you become a grandparent, and also this new and important function within your family, which is to be a living bridge from the past to the future.

THE LIVING BRIDGE RITUAL

The heart of this ritual centers on two altars. One is devoted to your ancestors—to everyone that came before you and is not here anymore. The other altar is for the future generations—your grandchildren and all those that might come after. What makes this ritual potent is that you are serving as a "storied bridge" between those past and future generations. The meaningful action of this ritual is transferring the flame from one altar to the other, as you get to speak your hopes, dreams, and prayers for your grandchildren's life and the generations to come.

Prepare
Intentions
May my community of friends and family gather together to acknowledge this new role as grandparent. May I presence and transmit the spirit of our family's traditions and stories from the past to the future.

You Will Need
- Two candles
- Objects for two distinct altars (food, drink, photos, letters, handmade items, seeds, etc.)

Ask for Support

I suggest handing the organizational role over to a friend, perhaps another grandparent. Rather than organizing your own ritual, it is an act of generosity to let someone else honor you so that you can focus on preparing the altars and the stories. It could be as simple as handing this book to a close friend and saying, "Please help me do this."

Work with this friend to create an invite list, including family, friends, and your larger community to witness you in this ritual.

The Ancestor Altar

As you consider what to place on this altar, think about your family's recent past and the extended past. What stories do you want to tell, what people do you want to presence, what part of your culture do you want to share, what qualities of your family lineage do you want remembered? Whatever you place on the altar will serve as your cues for story-sharing. For instance, you could place a bottle of scotch on this altar because your father loved to drink it, but it also serves as a prompt to speak about your family's Scottish heritage. Choose objects that carry meaning and message.

The Future Generation Altar

For this altar, think about both your current grandchildren and all those who might come after them. Choose objects that represent your deepest prayers for their lives. For instance, you can write your grandchild's future self a letter and place it on the altar. Or place a handful of seeds on the altar because you deeply value the Earth and want the future generations to be good stewards of the planet too. Consider what you want for them, their lives, and the world they will inherit.

Begin

In the center of each altar, place a candle. Begin by lighting the Ancestor Altar's candle.

Pause and take in a breath.

Acknowledge the grandmothers and grandfathers who came before you. If you know some of their names, speak them out loud. You now stand with them in a long line of grandparents.

This is a time for you to tell stories of your family and what you value about them.

If you need help getting started, you can use these prompts:

"I remember when . . ."
"Our family values are . . . "
"We came from . . . "
"I inherited [this quality] . . . "
"I don't want to pass on . . . "

Go for as long as you'd like, and then when you're ready, carry the flame from the Ancestor Altar to the Future Generation Altar.

Take a pause and breathe. Transferring that flame represents the bridge from the past to the future.

Say the name of your new grandchild (or grandchildren.) Use this time to identify your new role in your family and what that means to you. Also, speak about what you placed on that altar and all you want to pass down to the next generations.

Here are some prompts you can use to speak from:

"I see my responsibility as a grandparent as . . . "
"I commit to helping my grandchildren to . . . "
"I want to support my family by . . . "
"I pray for this new generation that . . . "

When you are done speaking, take one more pause and breath together.

Conclude

Allow the candles to burn down on their own.

Finish the ritual with you and your community raising a glass (alcoholic beverage or not) to your new grandchild, to your family, and to your community for the continuity of spirit and the regeneration of the generations.

Questions for Further Reflection

- What is important for me to pass down to my grandchildren?
- What do I want my community to recognize in me?
- What does this time mean to me?
- Why is it important to connect the past with the future?

Baby Naming

"I have no name: I am but two days old." What shall I call thee?
"I happy am, Joy is my name." Sweet joy befall thee!

—William Blake

Naming a newborn is a difficult matter. Out of the infinite names you could call your child, you need only one. Dozens of best-selling books offer a deluge of names, like, *100,000+ Baby Names* and *The Name Book: Over 10,000 Names*, which could make the process all the more confusing. But however you settle on a name, or a name settles on you, this is one of the first human-making gifts you give your child—a gift that denotes or marks them. Whether it's derived from a beloved ancestor, is a symbol of something important to you, or is just new and popular, this name is a gift of your child's first identity, the first thing they can claim as their own.

These days, birth announcements are how everyone gets the news. Because many of us in the West don't live near our families, lots of new parents publicly welcome their newborn with a cute card or a social media post featuring the baby's photo, name, and something like "Look what the stork dropped off!" or "There's a new boy/ girl in town!" While most are fridge-worthy, baby announcement cards do what most new parents are too exhausted, too overwhelmed, or too immersed with their new-borns to do: announce their baby to the community. In speaking to dozens of mothers and fathers about those first few weeks after their babies were born, many expressed regret about not doing something more ceremonial when sharing their baby's name for the first time. Some of these parents wished they had known what to do or had a way that was passed down to them—a way to speak their baby's name out loud and have it be welcomed by all their friends and family gathered. But what I really heard was that they longed for the sharing of the name to be the first time their community claimed this brand-new child as their own.

In the Jewish tradition, we commonly practice two baby-naming rituals—the *brit milah* (circumcision and baby naming for the boy) and the *simchat bat* (baby naming for the girl, which is newer)—but there is another, almost forgotten baby naming ritual called *Hollekreisch*,* which began in the Middle Ages with bestowing a secular or cradle name upon the boy or girl, as we Jews in the diaspora give both a secular and a sacred or Hebrew name to our children. During the ritual, the children of the village gather around the baby's cradle, lift it up three times, and cry out: "*Hollekreisch! Hollekreisch!* What shall the child be called?" (In Yiddish: "*Wie solls pupele hasse?*") And the adults gathered in the house would answer back with the name of the child three times. The Hollekreisch ritual, connected to the Germanic divine feminine figure Frau Holle, is a way to both ask protection from and guard against the dangerous yet benevolent forces on Earth and, especially, to entrust the child's life to the care of the entire community.

Rituals that announce the new name of a child tether them to the people and places that came before them. They are a way of bestowing reminders of who they are, where they came from, and what is important, and renewing these bonds by giving them over to a new person to carry. For instance, Natasha, a mother I interviewed, shared with me that her son's name was the same name found in her Scottish lineage for four hundred years, and this was her way of reclaiming that lineage and laying claim to all those from way back. She said it was her way of saying, "I am one of you and my son now is one of yours." Reva, another mother I spoke to, shared about hearing the name of her son in the place she gave birth in. For many days after the birth, they just called him "Squeekers," but then she remembered a moment during her labor at home when she saw two male deer right outside her window. She just felt the strong, noble, and graceful qualities of the deer in her son, which informed and inspired the name she chose: Ayal, which is Hebrew for deer. However the name comes, a name tells the story of who your child is to their people.

---

* Jill Hammer, "Holle's Cry: Unearthing a Birth Goddess in a German Jewish Naming Ceremony," *Nashim: A Journal of Jewish Women's Studies & Gender Issues* 9 (2005): 62–87, doi: 10, 1353/nsh.2005.0003.

HELLO, GOODBYE

In many traditions, including the Tla-o-qui-aht First Nation's tradition, when someone is publicly recognized, they stand up and introduce themselves and say, "I am so-and-so, daughter of so-and-so, granddaughter of so-and-so." Their name is not just their name. Their name is in relationship to the culture, to their ancestors, to the land and their traditions. Babies born of the Kongo people living along the Atlantic coast of Central Africa believe that a baby is not considered to be truly a person until the baby is named. The name is part of a long developmental process that makes them human. A name also places them in the middle of a story that began long before their birth and will continue long after. And that name is a way for that story to continue through them.

While a name carries a story, it is hearing that story that binds us to that child. One mother shared that the babies she feels most connected or even responsible to are the ones that she attended baby naming ceremonies for. "I've been at those first few days of their life," she said, "and now I have an obligation to be in their life." Even the etymology of the word "obligate" gives us a clue as the very purpose of these rituals. The word comes from the Proto-Indo-European word *leig*, meaning to tie or bind, which can also be found in other words, like religion and ligament. These ritualized moments bind us to each other. Even though a name individuates us, a baby-naming ritual invites the community to include the name and baby back into the whole. It's like saying, "Yes, you're becoming a separate individual, but you are also a part of us."

The Cords of Connection Ritual is a small way to inspire you to gather your friends and family and ritually call your child by their name. Names have power, and there is something quite special and sacred about sharing this new name at the right time.

With that said, don't rush toward this ritual. Some parents don't choose the baby's name for many weeks after the baby is born, and that is perfectly fine. I strongly advise against performing this ritual sooner than eight days after you've brought the little one home. If a naming ritual feels like too much to plan in those early days and weeks after the birth, consider deputizing the new grandparents or dear friends to support you in planning and holding space for this moment.

Naming a baby is a sacred act, for you are giving your child their first gift. And also giving your community the gift of receiving the name and the child. In the back-and-forth of giving and receiving, you are tethering small but significant cords between your baby and your community, which is the ligament that holds them together.

THE CORDS *of* CONNECTION RITUAL

All our relationships are bound together by invisible cords. Some of them are razor-thin, as with a cabdriver or a cashier, those we meet once and never see again. Other relational cords are stronger, thicker, and are woven together over much time and can't be broken easily, like those friendships that have lasted for years and years, surviving lean times and then bouncing back stronger than ever. The way we show up, how often we show up, how reliable we are when we show up—all inform the strength and durability of these relational cords. And in times of need and change, these relationships are what tether us, hold us, and what we fall back on and lean into.

The purpose of this ritual is to externalize these cords around the newborn. Right after a birth, new parents are just establishing their cords of connection to their baby. But after some time, those cords need to extend to that family's community so that this baby can be included into their greater web of connections. Aunties, uncles, grandparents, friends, and neighbors all need to be called into this relationship. And the more formally they are called in, the better chance they have at maintaining it.

This ritual's intention is to make this first moment of sharing the newborn's name into an opportunity for the community to not just gather but respond with actual cords of connection. At the end of the ritual, the baby will be surrounded by a weblike structure so the parents and the entire community can clearly see how much support already surrounds this newly arrived one.

Prepare

Intentions

May my community of friends and family gather together to ritual-ize the naming of my baby. May we witness the cords of connection surrounding this newborn and bind this baby more closely to all that they belong to, both living and dead.

You Will Need

- A ball of string or yarn (any color)
- Scissors

Don't Share Just Yet

Within Jewish tradition, many of us are taught to withhold sharing the baby's name with anyone (besides the parents) until this ritual is done. I would encourage you to consider a similar withholding. Names have power, and there is something quite special about sharing this new name at the right time.

Emcee

Depending on your capacity and energy, it could be a good idea to hand off the role of emceeing to one of the deputized new grandparents or dear friends to help hold the space and keep the ritual moving along. See the sidebar on Honoring Roles for more on this.

Begin

As you gather your friends and family together, have them stand in a circle with the baby in the center, either in their cradle or held by a parent.

When you have assembled, let the emcee remind the community what they are here to do: to receive the name of the baby and, in doing so, to welcome the baby into the fabric of the community. It might be appropriate to go further and ask the individual members of this circle of friends/family to state their own personal intention and why they're here. Giving people an opportunity to name their purpose allows that purpose to become more tangible and real.

The String

The new parents should hold the ball of string first and, when ready, announce the full name of the child. They then should pass the ball of string to one person in the circle. It's proper to begin with the elders, so first pass the string to the grandparents, if they are present.

When receiving the ball, this person says the name of the baby again. This should happen over and over again, with the ball arriving to a new person and that person saying the baby's name and then passing on the string to another new person. By the end, there is a web of string surrounding this baby and the baby's name has been spoken many, many times.

The Cutting

The cutting can begin either in the center with the parents or with the last person who receives the ball of string.

The instructions are, before you cut the thread, to say out loud what you are committing to for this baby. Pass the scissors around the circle, hearing each person's commitment, until the web is all cut.

Conclude

Tying the String

Invite each person to tie their string to their wrist or somewhere else where they can see it. While the string won't last forever, it is a temporary reminder of each person's obligation to this child.

End in Sweetness

As with all good baby rituals, consider giving out sweet treats at this ritual's conclusion as another way of blessing this baby and this moment.

Questions for Further Reflection

- What does my child's name mean to me and to my family?
- Why is it important to establish a bond between my baby and my community?
- What does seeing all the cords of connection feel like?
- How do I continue to strengthen these cords of connection between my baby and my community?

THE BEHOLDING RITUAL

Babies let us see again. So much so that what we once took for granted or grew familiar with comes back into view through their eyes. Because they are still arriving to this world, being around them, holding them, gazing at them can remind us of what we've stopped truly seeing. They are messengers of wonder, and so being in their presence renews our capacity to recognize life's little miracles.

The purpose of this ritual is to welcome and name this newborn by beholding them. Beholding isn't seeing. When we simply see someone, we notice them but quickly move on. When we behold them, we don't just see them; instead, we slow down and our perception opens up as we regard all that they belong to, are connected with, come from. When beholding anything, and especially a newborn, you are getting into, as Dr. Martin Shaw says, "the many layers of relatedness." This baby is not just this baby. They are the culmination of infinite people, stories, names, and actions coming together through this child. The newborn is the continuation of the story. And all of this is impossible to see just with one set of eyes, so you must lift the baby up so that everyone can behold them and wonder together.

The ritualized action of lifting a baby up is not new. It's found in many old European customs where they would lay the newborn on the ground, in the earth of a garden or a hearth, and then lift them up into the air. This motion speaks of delivering the baby from the Earth Mother or Otherworld to the arms of the community. You can even see this lifting up in *The Lion King*, during that iconic moment when Rafiki stands at the edge of the mountain and raises newborn Simba before all the animal kingdom. This isn't just a moment of seeing but of claiming. The baby is being lifted up into all the arms of all those they now belong to.

The ritual below provides some simple choreography to attempt this. But please remember there is no right way to behold someone or something. Wondering is not answering. Rather, it calls forth other qualities like awe, attentiveness, curiosity, and remembering. Wondering is a way to be with something mysterious and miraculous without boxing it into an answer. This ritual of welcoming this new baby asks all those gathered to try to wonder toward how this miracle came to be, who this baby is connected to, and what may become of them. And by lifting them up with wonder, you are blessing their life.

Prepare

Intentions

May I gather my community of friends and family together to bless and claim this baby. May we share stories about this baby's name and their ancestors and heritage. May we bless their life.

Honoring Roles

In many different traditions around the world, there are other people, besides the parents, at the helm of the baby-naming ritual. In Maharashtra, Bengal, the paternal aunt has the honor of ceremonially naming the baby. In Turkish traditions, the paternal grandfather speaks the chosen name of the newborn baby three times.

If you are a new parent reading this, consider asking a close family member or beloved friend to facilitate this ritual and be the first to lift up the baby. Because the intention of the ritual is to welcome the baby into the arms of the community, it makes sense to offer this role over to someone who can be the bridge. Plus, by honoring this person, you are also recognizing their relationship to the baby and helping them step more into their new function within the community.

Placing the Baby

The first action of this ritual is to lift the baby up, but you'll also want to consider where the baby will be lifted up from and returned to. Obviously, choose some place safe, where the baby is comfortable. This can be the cradle, their car seat, a soft and fuzzy blanket on the floor, in a parent's arms, or however else you imagine.

Begin

As you gather your circle of friends and family around the baby, pause and take a moment. Slow this moment down either through a breath, a song, or in silence. This is a way to focus everyone's attention and create space for the ritual to find its way.

As you begin, speak toward an intention: *Who are the people gathered here? Why are these the people meant to gather around this baby? What does it mean to welcome this little one into this circle? Why is it special for all those gathered to be among the first to call this baby by their name?* Ask these questions to the group gathered and encourage some wondering.

Whispering the Name

Before lifting the baby, the parents can whisper the baby's name into the ear of the person honored to first lift the newborn. This is another action of transferring and entrusting the baby to the community.

Lifting the Baby

Here is the dramatic moment. As the baby is lifted up, reveal the baby's name for the first time publicly. If you like, invite the circle of friends and family to repeat the name, to cheer, to sing, or to do whatever the spirit moves them to do. What sweetness.

Let the name linger. There is a new human in your midst.

Storytelling About the Name

The parents should be invited to tell the story of the name. How did it come to them? Does it mean anything? Is the baby named after anyone? Does the name come from a particular language, myth, or tradition? By sharing the story of how they chose it, the parents bring the name to life.

Passing the Baby

Pass the baby around the circle and behold this new being. As each person receives the baby, they should take a moment to be with the new human.

Before each person passes the baby, invite them to whisper a blessing over this baby's head, their hands, their feet, their joints—blessing their entire body. Each blessing should begin or end with that child's new name.

Prompts that might help inspire blessings are:
- May you remember to . . .
- May you always have courage to . . .
- May you be surrounded by . . .

- May you be grateful for . . .
- May you feel loved by . . .
- May you always belong to . . .
- May you be comforted with . . .
- May you find the strength to . . .

Sweets, Gifts, and Responsibilities

As the baby is handed back to their parent/s, whoever is facilitating this ritual can remind the group of the responsibility they have to this new child. Let the ritual be closed as it began—either in song, a breath, or silence—and afterward give out treats and gifts, as it's proper to complete such an auspicious event sweetly.

Questions for Further Reflection

- What is the difference between seeing and beholding my baby?
- What do I feel when raising my baby up and revealing their name to my community?
- Who is my baby connected to in story, in name, in ancestry?
- How does this ritual empower my friends and family to be obligated to my child? Why is that necessary?

New First Name

He said, your name shall no longer be called Jacob,
but rather Yisrael, because you have wrestled
with God and men, and overcome.

—Genesis 32: 28

To be honest, I was hesitant to write this chapter and tried several times to exclude it from this book. While acquiring a new name is not a new custom, the way it is done in our modern culture is troubling. Too often, I've witnessed people discard their given name because they feel it doesn't suit them anymore. Perhaps it feels too old, too traditional, or tied to a completely different time of their life that they've outgrown, and so a new name is taken to represent something novel or more accurately faithful to the person they've become. I even did this myself years ago, shortening the given name I received (David) while taking on a more unique nickname (Day) that better fit the personality I had come into—though to this day, my mother, aunt, and grandmother struggle with this and always resort back to my given name.

Look, I don't want to judge when a new name is or is not appropriate. There are a million and one reasons that cause someone to adopt a new first name, but the trouble is when the naming is regulated to a self-determined and self-done thing, and especially when it is not tethered to a people or a significant event. For instance, in many traditional cultures, like Mahayana Buddhism, new names are bestowed, like gifts given, after an initiation ritual by someone official, like a monk. It's common for Buddhist teachers to have many new names that represent various stages of their careers, like the author Thich Nhat Hanh, whose given name at birth was Nguyễn Xuân Bảo. In this regard, the bestowal of a new name is less about the individual person's personality and more about placing that person inside of a tradition or lineage. The etymology of the word "bestow" is a great doorway to understanding this connection. Coming from early fourteenth-century Middle English, the word is made of *be* plus *stowen*, meaning "to put in a particular place." In other words, names are like plants whose roots need earth. When a name is bestowed upon someone by their people, community, or culture, it plants that person into the soil of a larger context and an older story of who came before them—a story which is always rooted in relationships.

In 1899, the *American Anthropologist* journal published a paper called "A Pawnee Ritual Used When Changing a Man's Name"[*] by Alice Fletcher, which speaks to the naming rituals used by the three divisions of the Pawnee, the Chai-I', Kit'-ka-hah-ki, and Pita-hau-I'-rat. While this article is a product of its time, ripe with colonialist-dominant language, it is also filled with hidden gems thanks in part to the cooperation of a Pawnee elder and priest, Mr. James Murie. While sharing about the Pawnee's sacred naming ritual, Murie explains that "a man's [or person's] life is an onward movement. If one has within him a determined purpose and seeks the favor of the Gods, his life will 'climb up.'" There might come a point where someone does something in response to the Gods giving them an opportunity to express a new "power in action," which marks that person's life and career, and as a result they are given a new name to indicate that they have *climbed up* from the level they were previously on. While Murie says that some people might only rise a little in their life, if someone wants a new name or to change their name, they must strive to overcome their normal walk and level-up.

Murie shares that the Pawnee have three essential customs when giving a new name: Firstly, a person is only able to take a new name after proving themselves by an act of great ability or character, exhibiting qualities such as courage, generosity, and prowess. Secondly, the name itself must be taken before the people or tribe who know of this great act. And thirdly, the name must be announced by a priest or elder in connection to the ritual and not by the person themselves. The customs of the Pawnee suggest that a new name has nothing to do with what you want to feel about yourself, but rather it is a reflection of how you've changed in the eyes of your people, a change granted by the gods.

Most of us in the West don't come from a living culture like the one James Murie

---

[*] Alice C. Fletcher, "A Pawnee Ritual Used When Changing a Man's Name," *American Anthropologist* 1, no. 1 (January 1899): 82–97, https://www.jstor.org/stable/pdf/658836.pdf.

came from. Most of us keep our given names for the whole of our lives because that's what you do. And even if we decide to change our name, our modern self-made culture doesn't understand the deeper purpose of doing it and how a person, a people, and Spirit are all necessary and interdependent actors in the drama of giving and receiving this new name. So then, where does that leave us?

If you are reading this chapter because you feel the deep, undeniable call to change your name, how do you attempt something that steers away from an exclusively self-proclaimed act into something more planted in a people and in Spirit? What would it look like to hand over something to your people that is so personal and precious—for they are the ones who will be calling you by this new name. While this is a far cry from how it might have been done in the past, perhaps even in your own ancestral lineage, could you consider this being a step or a stumble toward something redemptive? *What if your new name could root you in something beyond you?*

The ritual below is profoundly imperfect, which could be a recipe for a solid beginning. It asks you to consider doing something which is unusual and even unlikely—giving your name over to your community and letting them give it back to you, renewed. My hope is that this ritual offers a different approach to taking on a new name that deeply considers story, community, ancestry, and, especially, a power greater than you. And, lastly, this ritual will ask you to consider what you will do with your old name, perhaps the first gift ever given to you, long ago.

THE CLIMBED UP RITUAL

Prepare
Intentions
May I deeply consider what my new name is for and why now. May this ritual help me shed the old name with respect and tell the story of the new name. May I let my community play an important role in giving this name and connect it to a greater power.

You Will Need
- Three candles
- A lighter or matches

- Two pieces of paper and a pen
- Honey and a small spoon

Is a Ritual Necessary?

Maybe you're wondering: Is gathering my friends and family together so I can take on a new name self-indulgent or too self-centered? Is my new name worth everyone's time or attention for a ritual? Changing a name is easy, but changing your name in the presence of your community is more challenging. Consider this: It might be more self-indulgent to not ritualize the changing of your name, because if you don't do so, then it's just you. But when you gather your community together to mark this moment, you are including them, giving them context as to why, what happened, and why this name. And they are offering you accountability, questions, witness, and wonder as you put down an old name and pick up a new one. Even if it's just a couple of your good friends, consider not doing this alone.

Hand It Over

Because the crux of this ritual involves your community as the intermediary, if possible hand this over to someone else—someone you know, trust, and who understands the importance of this moment for you. Even better would be if this person was significantly older than you, as they might come with experience and wisdom that could ground this ritual.

Gathering

Invite your community to gather. Whoever sends out this invitation, its purpose is to call together a group of beloved friends and/or family to recognize what has changed with the person they are gathering around, by ritualizing their new name.

The invitation should include:

1. *Why?* What achievement or life change happened that is initiating this name change? Place this ritual in a time or a moment to give it context.
2. *Why everyone?* Why not just do this alone? Make an ask here that could sound like "your presence is needed" or "we can't do this without you."

3. *Name the purpose.* Speak a bit to the need to mark this moment, to lift up this person, and to tether this new name to new commitments, responsibilities, and life purpose.

The invitation should not mention the new name. Hold that closely until the ritual moment.

Begin

The ritual is broken down into three parts:
1. The Old Name
2. What Happened?
3. The New Name

Part 1: The Old Name

Light the first candle.

Your old name carries stories. Before shedding this name, this is a moment to lift this name up again, as it was once lifted up as a new name. First, write the name down on a piece of paper. You can either hold it, put it in the center of the circle, or pass it around.

1. Share the origin story: Why were you given this name? Is this name for anyone? Is it connected to a story, a myth, an ancestor?
2. Share about your experience carrying this name: When did you feel connected to it? When did you struggle with it? Let this moment be an opportunity to really speak to the life of this name.
3. Give thanks to this name: You have built a life and identity around this name for many years. Before putting it down, give it gratitude.

At the conclusion of this section, give your community a moment to speak to this name. Invite them to remember their experience with this name and share what it meant to them. Let them ask plenty of questions.

Either at this point or at the end of the ritual, burn the paper that has this old name written on it.

Part 2: What Happened?

Light the second candle.

Something happened that led to this moment. Perhaps you accomplished something significant, you survived a major accident or illness, you had a life-changing realization, or you moved through something monumental. Or maybe it's just that, over the course of time, you slowly changed and you are just coming to realize that your old name doesn't fit anymore. Whatever occurred, this is the moment in the ritual to tell the story of how you, as James Murie said, "climbed up."

1. *Share what happened:* Track back to when you started to notice yourself change.
2. *What did you confront?* If it was an event or accomplishment, what did you overcome? If it was about your identity changing, what were those outdated narratives you rewrote? If this is the outcome of a long-held prayer, share that journey.
3. *What did you learn?* Speak to the hard-fought understandings, learnings, realizations you now have about yourself or about life thanks to this up-leveling.

At the end of this sharing, the community can reflect upon what they heard, ask questions, and continue to bear witness.

Part 3: The New Name

Light the third candle.

It is time to reveal the new name. Take this moment and whisper this name to the person who is facilitating the ritual, and then they can announce the name to the community gathered.

Write that new name on a piece of paper and either pass it around, keep it in the center, or let the person acquiring that name hold it.

Introduce the new name:

1. *Share the origin story:* Where does this name come from? Is it tethered to an ancestor, to a myth, to a story, to a place,

or to a culture? What is the language and etymology of the name?

2. *Name the attributes:* There are qualities and virtues that this new name contains. Speak to them and why they are important to you. Invite the community to speak about how they see those virtues related to you.

3. *Make commitments:* Since this name is evidence of a leveling-up in your life, speak to what you are recommitting to, what you deeply value and are willing to sustain, and how you want to grow with this name. This part is the most important.

Invite the community to say the new name together.

Conclude

Blow the candles out and end the ritual in celebration and with sweet treats.

Afterward, put the paper with the name on your altar or in a special place in your home as a reminder of this moment.

Questions for Further Reflection

- Is this the right time for a new name? How do I know?
- Why is it important to be witnessed when taking on this new name?
- What is being asked of me with this new name? What new responsibilities or attributes am I now carrying with this new name?

New Last Name

Words are things.

—Maya Angelou

To keep it, change it, hyphenate 'em, smush 'em together, or create a totally new one—that is the question! I surveyed more than a hundred people who changed their last name, and as you can imagine, there were 101 different stories of how and why. Most involved marriage but some didn't. There were stories of people who couldn't wait to distance themselves from their family of origin, and others who were really excited to take on the name of their new family and mark a new beginning. I heard stories of people who married into names that carried hundreds of years of history, and others who invented a name because it sounded better phonetically. Children were also a key factor in changing a last name, as many parents wanted to share the same surname as their kids for the sake of convenience. And while I did hear a few experiences of cis-gendered men, an overwhelming majority of people who had stories to share of changing a last name were cis-gendered women, young and old. What I kept listening for was what changing their last name actually *meant* to them. I wanted to know if, besides all the legal paperwork, this was a significant moment worth marking. *Could changing a surname be a transformation, not just of legality, but of identity?*

Interestingly enough, surnames are a relatively new invention in the West. Most people in medieval Europe were known by only one name, often called their "Christian name" as it was given at baptism, and surnames were virtually unknown before the ninth century. After that, thanks in part to the establishment of a parish registry by King Henry VIII, all births, deaths, and marriages were recorded. And since it was impossible to keep accurate records when tracking all the "Johns" and "Jameses" and "Jeffreys," all family members had to adopt the same last name for this registry to make any sense. Surnames were a way not just to distinguish one family from another, but to proclaim these identities via the family head's occupation (Baker, Fisher, Weaver), their landholdings (Montgomery, Hamilton, Lincoln), their nationality (Walsh, Scott, Norman), or the unique qualities of the place they lived (Wood, Rivers, Bush, Fields, Meadows).

Eventually, these names, like most things in that time, became dominated by men. Women went from their father's surname to their husband's, which soon became English law in what was called "the doctrine of coverture," which basically states that the woman became "covered" by the man and had no right to own real estate, enter contracts, or even own personal property. In other words, the law saw a husband and wife becoming one single person, one flesh and blood, and that one was, you guessed it . . . the husband.

A lot has changed since then. Thanks in part to a feminist uprising in the USA during the mid-1800s and again in the 1960s and '70s, laws were passed that allowed women to gain individual legal status and retain their birth surname if desired. Even the honorific title "Ms.," which was adopted in the 1970s, continued to distinguish and separate a woman's identity from marriage. But the spirit of "coverture" lingered. I remember growing up in the 1980s and noticing wedding invitations addressed to "Mr. & Mrs. Michael Schildkret" and wondering why my mom went missing from the invite and if she even noticed.

Here's the thing: Even with all the progressive change giving women back their legal rights and individual identity, 70 percent[*] of American women still change their surnames when marrying. Why? When listening to all the stories of women (and others) sharing about their choices to take on a new last name, it struck me that while the practice looks the same, what has changed is that there are now stories of choice— choosing to keep or change an identity. One woman in her sixties shared what had felt like a binary choice when she got married: "It was very easy for me at the time. I was twenty-three and my surname was either identifying me as my father's daughter or as my husband's wife. I chose the latter." For other younger couples, the choice

---

[*] Maddy Savage, "Why Do Women Still Change Their Names?" BBC, September 23, 2020, https://www.bbc.com/worklife/article/20200921-why-do-women-still-change-their-names#:~:text=In%20the%20US%2C%20most%20women,they%20still%20follow%20the%20practice.

was playful and imaginative: "My husband's 'maiden' name was Cheresnick. Mine was Johnson. We married in 2010 and legally combined them to make, 'Cheresson.' We're the only two Cheressons in the whole world." Changing a last name might also have nothing to do with marriage at all but with reclaiming a new self after a significant transition. When *Wild* author Cheryl Strayed filed for divorce, she chose to legally rename herself, changing her former last name Nyland to Strayed, symbolic of her veering off path.

Deciding to change your last name can serve as both an expression of your freedom to choose and also a moment of choosing what you value. Part of that choice asks the question *Do I want this to be a reflection of my values or just go along with convention?* and another part might sound like *Is going along with convention a part of my values?* Some actually choose both. Quite a few women I spoke to moved their maiden names to their middle names because they wanted to be tied to both lineages. One woman shared: "I wanted to remain connected to my own history while also building a new history that felt whole for the family I was creating with my husband."

Last names carry power, story, history, and meaning, and changing them is a statement. While most of our attention and efforts around changing a surname involve government paperwork and social media feeds, this also might be a special moment worthy of ritual and acknowledgment. However you come to it and whatever name you choose, this transition can be an opportunity to reaffirm your values and honor both the lineage of the name you've been carrying since birth and the new name you're about to take on.

THE LINKING TOGETHER RITUAL

Prepare

Intentions

May I honor the name I've been carrying as I change it. May I share the intentions of what a new name means for me and my family.

You Will Need

- A roll of wide ribbon
- Scissors

- A Sharpie
- Needle and thread
- A tree near your home (if possible)

Who
Depending on the circumstances, this ritual can be performed solo, as a couple, or as a family. If it is done for just you, it is always best to do it in the presence of a friend or loved one who can witness you.

When
Rituals are most potent when they happen in sync to the moment they are marking. Whether you are changing your surname due to a marriage, a divorce, or a major life event, perform this ritual in the vicinity of that moment. Too often, changing a last name can be overwhelmed by legalities and paperwork. My suggestion is to do this ritual around the time you make the decision to change your last name.

Where
If your home has trees on the property, choose one that you can sit under and hang the ribbon. If you live in an apartment or don't have access to outside space, you can hang this ribbon indoors by the entrance to your home.

Begin
Invite everyone to take a breath together. Feel the ground under you and the tree overhead. If you are doing this with your partner or family, take a moment for everyone to get present together. Rituals need us to slow down in order to enter them.

The First Ribbon: The Old Name
This first part of the ritual is intended for you to speak to and honor this birth surname. Whether or not you love this name or hate it, this is a name that you've been carrying since you came into the world and a name that some of your ancestors have been carrying as well. Before changing your name, honor it.

Take out the ribbon, unroll enough space for you to write your given name on it, and cut it. After doing so, speak your given last name out loud.

1. *Share the history of the name:* Where does this name come from? What language is it? What does it mean? Who carried/carries this last name? Was it altered during a migration or because of an event?

2. *Share stories of what it was like to have this last name:* Are there memories of being teased for this name? Are there accomplishments associated with this last name? Do you have a reputation made with this name?

3. *Speak to what it feels like to change or alter this name:* Is there grief? Is there relief? Is it exciting?

Either place the ribbon on the ground or give it to your partner or family.

The Second Ribbon: The New Name

This second part of the ritual is intended to presence the new name you are taking on, and to hear its history and stories and origins. Depending on whose name it is, it can be appropriate to let the person who has been carrying the name speak here.

Take out the ribbon, unroll enough length for you to write the new surname on it, and cut it. Whether you are hyphenating two names, creating a new name, or taking on another's name, write that name on this second ribbon.

After doing so, have all gathered speak this new last name out loud.

1. *Speak to the history of the name:* Where does this name come from? What language is it? What does it mean? Who carried/carries this last name? Was it altered during a migration?

2. *Share personal memories of this name:* What does it mean to you? When is the first time you heard it? How do you feel about this name?

HELLO, GOODBYE

3. *Speak to the intentions and purpose for taking on this new name:* What kind of person or family do you want to become with it? What values does this new family name promote? What commitments are you willing to make for yourself or your family as you acquire this new name?

Place this ribbon next to the other ribbon.

Sewing Them Together

After everything has been spoken, take both of the ribbons and stitch their ends together with a needle and thread (don't worry if you're not an expert seamstress—this doesn't need to be perfect). Whether or not these last names will legally be your new name, these families, histories, and stories are now bound together.

Hanging the Ribbons

Once the ribbons are one, hang them either on a tree outside, by the entrance of your home, or you can even frame them and hang them on a wall. One couple I know actually made this new ribbon into an ornament on their Christmas tree.

Completing the Space

Before concluding this special moment together, have everyone take a breath. Let this moment of linking together lineages and families linger a bit longer.

Questions for Further Reflection

- What does my birth surname mean to me? What is its story?
- What does taking on a new surname mean to me and my family? What is its purpose?
- How did I feel while stitching the ribbons together?

Puberty

Your children are not your children.
They are the sons and daughters of Life's longing for itself.
They come through you but not from you,
And though they are with you yet they belong not to you.

—Kahlil Gibran

Changes, oh! Growing spurts. Budding breasts. Cracking voices. Hair down there. Sweat and smell and those erratic mood swings. The volcanic eruption of hormones and the relentless drive of biology fundamentally change this child, maybe your child, before your very eyes. But perhaps to you, yesterday still lingers with unripened innocence. Remember how easily they would lie in your lap? How uncensored their silliness and unburdened their curiosity? Annoying at times, yes, but so sweet, so earnest in their love for you and of this wide, wide world. Today, however, the home is too small, the family too constricting, the rules too suffocating. Today needs privacy. Today needs friendships. Today their body begs. Who they are becoming, both you and they, don't yet know. But one thing is clear—they are gawkily shedding their childish skin.

My parents could never really pivot, even though there were signs all around us: I required more time alone in my room with the door locked tight. Under my mattress, I stashed shoplifted *Playgirl* magazines, my pre-internet sexual lifeline. During these early days of puberty, my primary need was to be around my friends more and family less. I longed for the safety and status of a larger flock of teens who understood me. Because at home, I was still a child and too often treated like one. Maybe my parents weren't paying attention or were too embarrassed to name it or lacked the skill or the community support to acknowledge the real pubescent elephant in the room. And so, anger and aloofness became my strategies in our persistent battles over my need to be seen and treated not as a child, but as a young adult. And the line drawn in the sand that almost broke our relationship was their refusal or inability to end the childhood that persisted in their minds.

Rachel also lacked any parental guidance when hitting puberty. She was a late bloomer and, after waiting "forever," finally got her period at fifteen. She was so excited because all of her girlfriends had already got it and now she could, so she thought, become a woman. The day she started bleeding, she nervously, excitedly, embarrassingly revealed the news to her mom, who just casually pointed to the bathroom and said, "The pads are in there." That was it. As if she needed paper towels because there was a mess to clean up, nothing more. And so, the directions on the package became Rachel's first inductor into womanhood. Rachel recalled: "I was in this bathroom, all alone, feeling cold, and funny, and like something was really, really wrong."

She told her girlfriends from school, and the day after, her best friend gave her a colorful package filled with congratulatory notes, stickers, trinkets, and practical things like tampons, Midol, and chocolate. Rachel couldn't stop laughing and crying when she received it, and in looking back, she said that this gift actually did two things: It gave her the much needed external and social recognition that she was seen by her friends and wasn't alone in what was happening. In a very tangible way, it acknowledged her, welcomed her in, and let her know she belonged. But it also was juxtaposed against the absence of any real cultural or familial recognition—no honoring of or instruction in what it actually meant to become a woman. Her girlfriends filled the gap as best they could, but it paled in comparison to what, in retrospect, Rachel said she truly needed: aunties gathering around her, celebrating this time and teaching her about how her body was changing and how to care for it. She needed older women, well-practiced in womanhood, to help her weave the links between her own rhythms and cycles and the Greater Rhythms and Cycles above and around her. Without that, she felt, she was groping in the dark.

For both parent and child, puberty is, frankly, a mess. By its very nature it is utterly destabilizing. Before it begins, there are these beautiful, awkward cues of its imminence—maybe their arms get weirdly too long or their breasts begin to bud. And, before you realize it, they are popping out of this tender world of childhood, not only losing their wonderful innocence but also the stability that this world provided—that you provided. Adolescence itself is a liminal state, betwixt and between the child they were and the adult they will become. As is true with most liminal experiences, it's a time when nothing is predictable and everything is always in flux. Sure, this child is metamorphosing physiologically—like my friend's fourteen-year-old son's feet, which grew from a size 9 to a size 13 within a year—but what makes this time even more confusing is that their social reality is dramatically changing as well.

No longer is the family and home the central point of their lives. No longer are you, their parent, the sun they orbit around. They are turning away from their need of you and turning toward others. They are deeply concerned with how they look, where they fit in, if they are liked, when and why they are noticed, and what their status is among their peers and the greater-than-family world. They are publicly and privately struggling with the fluid question of *Who am I?*—an exploration of identity that they are trying to form independent of your influence. And while this might be brutal to watch because it's so often filled with failure and many crazy choices, it turns out to be the only way for them to come to understand themselves. The big question for you, the parent, during this time is: *What is my role and responsibility here?* For as your child turns away from you, if you are not able to clearly see what is actually happening, it can also be a time that destroys this relationship. But if you can see it and pivot, you can shift from the role of guide and guardian to that of a witness.

As much as you'd like to help, to fix it, make it easier on them, you just can't and shouldn't. You must step back and observe. What you are witnessing is, at times, a painful, heartrending, messy, emotional kind of separation and individuation. This is the time when you must begin to think of your child as an independent human who has their own unique story, gifts, and challenges that don't revolve around you, while simultaneously considering that your story cannot center around them. This time asks you to untangle from the child that you've been enmeshed with: a child that you once held in your arms and cuddled with on the couch—the same child who would come to you in the middle of the night because they were scared or lonely or just needed your undivided attention. And now they are becoming the adolescent who is constantly pushing or even shoving you away in order to come into their own life and into their own sense of self.

In the long and devastating list of all that you are losing, what might near the top is that loss of intimacy. You might even look back in sorrow and wonder: When *was* the last time? For nowadays, those shared moments are few and far between as you are no longer invited into the many aspects that your child is becoming. Your earnest questions are judged with folded arms or deflected with a gruff "fine" or "whatever" or

"I don't care." But this standoffishness isn't your fault; it's a consequence of what puberty fundamentally needs: separation, the first step in a three-step journey into what anthropologists call rites of passage.

The principal purpose of a rite of passage, a tradition found in almost every indigenous culture from the beginning of time, is to make humans. You see, from this perspective, humans aren't born, they must be made, and in order to do that, the child must at some point be killed off. Even though that might sound jarring to a modern ear—as it did for me the first time I heard my teacher Stephen Jenkinson use that language—this is the only way for the adult to stand a chance of emerging. An initiation's function is to make a hole in the child, sometimes literally punctured, as a way for their adult self to pass through. Like a harrow to the soil, traditional initiation disturbs the child's ground and removes them from the safety and sanctuary of their family and village. That's the first step, which is unsettling enough. But the second step, often referred to as transition, is when the child faces an ordeal or test where they must come face-to-face with the sheer uncertainty if they will succeed or even survive at all.

What this process mimics is a death and then a rebirth. The whole point is to introduce death to the child so that they can come up against and learn to respect their own limits and, especially, the limits of humanity. Depending on the culture, initiates might be buried, pierced, flogged, isolated, or even given hallucinogens, all to physically test and push them to the edge of their capacities. In the initiation ceremonies of the lower tribes of the Congo, as told through van Gennep's *Rites of Passage*,[*] the initiates are removed from their homes and considered dead to the village during this trial period, which could range from a few months to six years. During the ordeal, they are not just subjected to seclusion, lustration, and mutilation but must speak a special language, eat special food, wear special paint—all unique to this limbo phase. Upon reintegration, the last stage, the initiates "pretend not to know how to walk or eat and, in general, act as if they were newly born (resurrected) and must relearn all the gestures of ordinary life."[†] This is the second birth and their emergence into their new life of adulthood.

Maybe this all sounds quite foreign and terrifying to you, or maybe even a little bit exotic: How and why would anyone introduce death to their young people? Don't children grow up into adults without these initiation rites? Maybe our modern culture has evolved past those primitive ceremonies and we don't need them anymore?

---

[*] Arnold van Gennep, *The Rites of Passage* (Chicago: University of Chicago Press, 1960).
[†] Ibid., 81.

All valid questions, but here's the thing—because most of us had ancestors that left, ran from, or were stolen from their ancestral homelands and lost so much of their traditional culture in the passage over, we, their descendants, have consequently lost not only the memory that our ancestors had initiation ceremonies but more so the understanding of why they're even necessary in the first place. However, the longing for them still lingers within our youth.

I've taught hundreds of teenagers over twenty years and seen firsthand their craving for the structure, the edge, the intensity, the recognition and mentorship that a traditional initiation might have brought them. I noticed that so much of what they struggled with in their everyday lives—feeling unseen, unguided, wrong, or not enough, with low self-esteem, peer pressure, the need to be liked, the temptation to make risky decisions, and more—was a result of the culture itself not meeting them where they were during this time. Instead, life to a teenager looks pretty much the same as it did before puberty: They still live at home, still go to school; maybe they get some new privileges or responsibilities, but they're hungry for more—desperate even. They long to be felt in their pain, seen in their dreams, affirmed in their longings, empathized with in their confusion, unleashed in their sexuality.

We lack so many ways to infuse this transition with mentorship, guidance, and welcome into the adult community, and so teens attempt to initiate themselves anyway. Whether by exploring drugs or driving fast cars or cutting themselves, they are unconsciously seeking out the old bones of initiation as "an attempt to fill in the missing pieces of their education for being human."[*] They are playing with fire in order to explore the edges of life and death, but if they are not met and validated by the culture itself, they will inevitably, as the old African proverb warns, "burn down the village just to feel its warmth."[†] So nowadays, that's what we've got: a culture burning, evidenced by too many headlines of school shootings, too many instances of cyberbullying, too many desperate youth feeling profoundly unwelcome and unseen in their own communities. And that wildfire doesn't just burn down the culture, it burns our teens too,

---

[*] David Adam Lertzman, "Rediscovering Rites of Passage: Education, Transformation, and the Transition to Sustainability," *Conservation Ecology* 5, no. 2 (2002), https://www.ecologyand society.org/vol5/iss2/art30/.

[†] Michael Meade, *The Water of Life: Initiation and the Tempering of the Soul* (Seattle: Greenfire Press, 2006).

with a whopping 70 percent* admitting that mental health is a major struggle for them and their peers, a statistic that coincides with skyrocketing depression and suicide rates, all of which suggests that our youth are on the brink of a major mental health crisis.

But here's the thing about fire: Fire in excess is wildly destructive and fire that's deficient goes out too quickly, but when fire is balanced, it is profoundly life-giving. Our teens must learn the gifts and power inherent in their own fire so that they can renew and not destroy themselves and our culture. I once personally heard the author Michael Meade say, "It takes a village to raise a child, but once childhood is over, it takes a culture to bless the dream that is trying to awaken in the soul of each young person."†

That is exactly what originally called me to work with teens. I felt that I needed to give the youth in my community something more than what I had received when I was their age. I needed to offer them a way to learn about the fire of their life's purpose and how to tend to it and gift it back.

What came of that calling was a class I founded and taught for twelve years that came to be called "the Fire Circle." Basically, every Tuesday night I would take twenty-five teens out of the classroom to the forest behind the school so we could sit around a fire unpacking issues that they were struggling with but couldn't talk about at home or at school. We covered topics like *Why do I feel like I'm not in control?* and *How do I get liked by someone I like?* and *Is watching porn wrong?* and *How do I tell my parents that I'm trans?* and *Why are all my friends on so many meds?* and *Why am I so angry all the time?* In a way, the Fire Circle flickered back to life an unlived memory of how it might have been if we lived in a culture that understood the challenges our youth are facing and their need to explore those challenges within a group. Our Fire Circle provided them with what they called their "special space," something intensely private and contained where they could wrestle with the craziness of their lives in the presence of their peers and a mentor without judgment or shame. While it was certainly not an initiation rite, this Fire Circle became a weekly ritualized space for them to practice paddling out as an adult.

---

* Juliana Menasce Horowitz and Nikki Graf, "Most U.S. Teens See Anxiety and Depression as a Major Problem Among Their Peers," Pew Research Center, February 20, 2019, https://www.pewsocialtrends.org/2019/02/20/most-u-s-teens-see-anxiety-and-depression-as-a-major-problem-among-their-peers/.

† Michael Meade, "It Takes More Than a Village," Mosaic Voices, May 11, 2015, https://www.mosaicvoices.org/it-takes-more-than-a-village.

One of my tactics was to give over the responsibility of tending the fire to a different teen each week. By doing so, I also gave over the reins of providing some of the fundamental needs of the group, especially our source of heat and light. What became immediately clear was that tending a fire was an excellent teacher of consequence—if they used too much wood or too little, if they ignored the fire or got distracted, there was an immediately felt impact on the whole group. Each time a teen let the fire go out completely, it got cold quick, which was actual, hands-on, real-time learning. As they struggled to keep the fire alive, I would always repeat back the same mantra—"The way you tend the fire is the way you tend your life"— to help them find themselves in what they were doing. They got to practice relating to this living, dangerous, beautiful element that always required respect, vigilance, caretaking, practice, and a willingness to listen, not just for their sake but so that the whole group could benefit.

And with that, a major lesson would faithfully emerge, so big that it carried the scent of those old initiation rites: This life, your life, is much bigger than you. It has been and always will be. And the teens of my little fire circle got to witness this each time we gathered together, a small way to redirect their life's focus from "I" to "we." For a couple of hours in their week, they felt that human-making spell of awe. Above them was the vast array of stars and galaxies spinning. Before them was a living, breathing crackling fire that was their responsibility to tend and keep alive. Behind them were the mysterious sounds of the night forest, a reminder that we weren't the only ones out. And around them were the softly glowing faces of their peers and mentor within whom they got to see a reflection of themselves. My students kept on coming back year after year to our little enterprise because it kept meeting them at the razor-sharp edge of where they were and what they were facing, while faithfully reminding them: *You are not alone.*

The rituals below are profoundly flawed ways to both meet your young person where they are and to meet yourself there too. I say flawed because they are in no way attempting to replicate an intact culture's initiation ceremony, nor could they. The crater left by that absence is too daunting, and its repair must come from the roots of a culture and community, not a book. But I also believe that doing nothing while our youth struggle is entirely unacceptable, and they need help during this time. Even if our youth don't know how to ask for it, they need to be seen and honored as their bodies, identities, friend groups, and mindsets change. They need to be taken in by non-parental adults who love them, and brought to an edge so they can discover what they are capable of, instead of constantly needing to prove themselves. And you, their parent, also need something—a way to be witnessed as you step back and let go of your grasp on this child so that they can fly and fall on their own.

THE EDGE RITUAL:
For Teens and a Mentor

I started this chapter researching the wrong people: parents. After twenty different interviews with twenty different mothers and fathers, I kept on coming up against the same wall in every conversation—safety. Sure, each parent claimed that they wanted their child to experience freedom, to better understand themselves, to grow mentally, spiritually, physically, but when push came to shove, their uncompromising parent gene just fundamentally needed to keep their kid safe and alive. After each conversation, I left feeling like we never really touched on the thing that I kept trying to get at and that adolescents need more than anything: edge.

So I pivoted. I sought out non-parents, self-described mentors, guides, and role models—most interestingly, men and women in their twenties and thirties who professionally take all kinds of teens out into the wilderness to provide an experience for them to touch that edge. Some referred to themselves as links in a chain, having had mentors of their own when they were younger and now feeling compelled to pass on those gifts.

Part of the gift they gave was to help these youth *survey their lives* and develop a profound curiosity and appetite for it—a cultivated hunger within them for things that aren't immediately comfortable. You see, that pleasure-reward cycle is perfectly fine for children but turns out to be quite disastrous for a healthy adult human. So much of their efforts is to get these kids to shed layers and layers of their childhood skin, which doesn't want responsibility and has no interest doing anything uncomfortable or without immediate payoff. On these trips, these kids find themselves frequently at a crossroads where they are being asked to do something that doesn't feel good, like hiking in the cold while being rained on, all while still craving that immediate gratification. The goal is to compel these kids to do something for reasons other than just trying to get a reward from it.

Some of these trips orbit around a thirty-six-hour ceremony where the youth spend two nights out by themselves, fasting with just a little bit of water. Sometimes the mentors get strong pushback that sounds like: "Hell fucking no. You can't make me do that. My mom didn't tell me about this. No food? I'm going to die. Wild animals? Fuck that." But what they find is that after a while they actually don't need to tell anyone to do anything. There is an innate curiosity that takes hold within this social container, acting like positive peer pressure. One kids says to another: "Do you want to go out?" "Are you going to sit?" And that eventual willingness reveals itself removing another layer of childhood.

Eli, one of the mentors I spoke to, referred to his work as "profoundly provisional—an unlayering and relayering of these childhood patterns, taking them off and putting them back on again." What these mentors hope for is that this experience plants a seed in the psyche of these youth, giving some air to an aspect of themselves that needs their attention, longs to grow, that wants to face the edge in challenges.

This ritual is inspired by the spirit of this edge work: to offer your teen an opportunity to face such a challenge by being brought to a physical edge. Before you read further, you must hand over the responsibility for this ritual to an uncle or aunt, to neighbors or adult friends—any grown-up that you and your kid trust. The role of this mentor is to hold enough space for the adolescent to approach the edge on their own while not falling over it. So much the better if this experience is not centered on just one kid but is in collaboration with one or more teens their age, as so much learning and reflection happens for them in a social environment.

The ritual itself has three parts, inspired by a traditional rite of passage. It separates the teen from their family with a mentor to have an edge experience and then brings them back again, the same but different.

Parents, please bring humility to this whole endeavor. What you are able to give your child and what your child truly needs are sometimes miles apart. This ritual is an attempt to try to reveal certain capacities that your teen has never encountered within themselves before in the presence of someone they respect. And, in doing so, this could mark the beginning of a new chapter of strengthening these adult capacities by being more awake, curious, and attentive to the growing edge of their lives.

Prepare

Intentions

May this ritual forge a connection between my teen and a non-parent figure that they trust. May my teen grow their capacity for curiosity and resilience amid an uncomfortable experience. May they return from this experience with a better understanding of themselves and a new dynamic between us.

The Mentor

From here on out, I will direct my comments to you, the adult mentor, assuming that the parent of this child has handed over the book and the organizing role. Hello.

Ideally, you already have an established relationship with the teen(s) you are taking out to do this ritual, but it's not necessary. What is most important is that you are committed to the quality of this experience for them, holding a sound container that gives the adolescent enough space to approach that edge on their own while not falling over it.

The Three Stages

This ritual has three clearly defined stages, like traditional rites of passage:

1. Separation
2. Ordeal
3. Reuniting

Please try to distinguish these stages from one another, making them clearly defined and identifiable.

Designing the Ritual

Because I don't believe that one ordeal is better than another, I am providing you with a lot of space to design the ritual. But what that means is that you must prepare everything in advance. Sometimes this can take weeks or months to do. Keep that in mind.

Here are some questions to consider as you plan this:

- Will the child know in advance that this is happening, or will it be a surprise?
- To what degree will you be involving and looping in the parents?
- Who are the other kids and adults you are collaborating with?
- What supplies will this ordeal require?
- How much time will this ordeal take?

A great way to think about planning for this experience is as choreography or stage directions. The more dialed in the script, the easier it becomes to confidently lead the teens through this ritual's three stages.

While you are designing this part, please remember: Whatever you decide to do, it must involve something that is *physically challenging*—don't just talk about feelings or tell stories of adulthood. The special sauce is in the physical part. It needs to be what these youth mentors call "high challenge, low risk," meaning you don't want the teen to panic but you do want them to be stretched by their physical capacities, which might intentionally bring up some fear in the teenager. The teen might think to themselves, *Holy shit! I am doing the craziest thing right now*, but behind the scenes you the adult are keeping the risk relatively low. So, for instance, if you design an all-night solo fire, you (and maybe other adults) are nearby with water, first aid, and cell phones, just in case something goes awry.

Some ideas to get your design juices flowing are:

- An all-night hike
- Tending a fire from dusk to dawn
- Swimming across a large body of water
- A solo sit spot
- A challenging scavenger hunt
- A blindfolded nighttime walk
- Or think bigger, like a multiday experience.

Where

As you can probably tell, all of these involve the child engaging with the natural world, ideally the wild. Why is this important? One of the qualities you are trying to cultivate is humility, and learning how to be humble within the wild world is an excellent way to do that. Teaching a child how to be in relationship with fire, with water, with earth and air is an excellent way for them to practice being in relationship with themselves.

One Important Note

As you read in the introduction to this ritual, the child might likely protest. At first they might think it's cool or fun, but as they come to feel the burden of the challenge, they may try to abandon it, run from it, defuse it, plead with you to not do it. Expect this, while still encouraging them to proceed. Speak directly to the maturing part of them that you and they want to emerge in the world. This is the crucial moment when they need to encounter this aspect of themselves and to support it. No matter what, persist with the ordeal and do not succumb to their fear.

Begin

Separation

The separation part is the moment you come to remove or separate the teen from their parent and/or home. This step alone can be specifically marked and enhanced by encouraging the parents to actually say goodbye to their child and the child to say goodbye to their parents, as if this is the last time they are seeing each other. Conjuring a "last time" moment actually makes the impact of this ritual more recognizable.

Entering the Ordeal

Like any ritual in this book, this one's success rests on the way you approach it and the way you depart from it. Some of the most significant time you will have with the youth is how and when you get into and come out of the ordeal. You'll notice that in the example of the two-day ceremony that I mentioned earlier; some of the most vital moments for the children was when they hiked into and out of the ceremonial spot. During this time, the children eased into this experience, began to forget about the comforts of home and the distractions of technology, and approached the ceremony over many hours. Most important, it gave the mentors some time to pose questions and have conversations with the teens—*grown-ups asking grown-up questions.*

Here are some fundamental questions that you can pose to the child or children to get them to consider what this time is all about:

- What kind of adult do you want to be?
- What kind of adult do you not want to become?
- What are you going to miss about being a child?
- What are you not going to miss about childhood?

- What do you want your parents to know about you?
- What do you not want your parents to know about you?
- What freedoms would you like to have?
- What parts of adulthood are you scared about?
- What new responsibilities would you like honored and celebrated?

Exiting the Ordeal

After the ordeal is complete, feel into what is needed. Does the child need space and quiet? Do they need your presence and to be reassured that they are safe? There is no right recipe for this moment, but it does require from you a certain kind of vigilance and adroitness that you must trust within yourself and, consequently, bring to the youth.

As you come back together, go slow and create a space for recounting and reflection. Maybe you build a fire to sit around or you watch the sunrise together. But what is needed during this time is *their story*—a literal recollection of their experience. Ask them what they saw during the ordeal. What did they feel? What did they experience? Draw out the detail with your explicit curiosity. Don't assume they know how to do this. Many teens need real guidance to recognize what a transformative experience actually looks like. While asking them questions, be quite cognizant of not cajoling them into proclaiming this as a "monumental moment." This isn't about a catharsis but about what they actually experienced.

As their mentor, pay attention to a subtle distinction in this moment: How much meaning do you want to prescribe? How much do you let them create their own expression of significance? One of the risks here is that if you translate this experience into meaning something too quickly, the youth can lose the substance, texture, and story of the ordeal. Instead of focusing on meaning, keep pulling out the storied details from them with good questions like:

- Did you feel despair at any point?
- When did it feel like it dragged on forever and when did it go quickly?

- Were there moments when you wanted to give up?
- Did anything surprise you?
- Did any thoughts keep repeating themselves?
- What was it like when you knew you could complete it?

Reuniting

The homecoming might be the most important step. This is when the youth is seen, honored, and praised for what they have been through. It is the step that the parents and the greater community are needed for, and it really doesn't have to be anything elaborate—just a genuine space for public acknowledgment that the young people completed something important, as well as an opportunity for the community to be gathered in.

The other outcome of this third step is that it marks the beginning of a different relationship between the parent and child. They have been separated from each other for a little time, and now there's this sweet moment of being reunited, when the youth has something to share that is unknown to the parent. Dan, one of the mentors I interviewed for this chapter, advises the youth to not immediately jump into the arms of their parents. He says, "hold that," because this is a precious moment to create a new interaction between them. The teenager has a story to share of what it was like for them to complete this challenge, and the parent has an opportunity to step into their new role of witnessing, which this ritual is attempting to cultivate.

Hosting a homecoming should be simple. Sit outside around a fire or make a picnic out on a lawn. There are really no right ways to do it, but you might want to let this experience still have some formalities:

- There should be a time that lets the youth speak and tell their story.
- The parents might want to gift their child something to help mark this moment as special.
- You, the mentor, may want to create an opportunity for the parents or the community to speak and reflect back the qualities they see in this youth.

Questions for Further Reflection

- Why is encountering a physical edge so important for youth?
- Why can't the parents facilitate an ordeal?
- What qualities and skills does this ritual promote in the youth?
- What did I learn from this experience?
- What did I witness the teen(s) learn?

THE BIG TASK RITUAL:
For Teens and Community

What does your child maturing actually look like? Sure, they are physically changing, but how else can you identify that change? How is their mindset and behavior changing, evidenced within the family structure? Since they were a baby, there has been a basic pair of roles you and your child have played with each other: authority and dependance. As the parent, you (and if you're partnered, you both) have been the sole decision makers in the household, determining stuff like when bedtime is and what is being made for dinner. Even to this day, maybe that authority spills over as you still clean up after your teenager or continue to wash their dishes, but as they get older, there's a fundamental question that contends with these old roles: What would it look like for this young person, in their own unique way, to step into and occupy a different role within the family and even within their community—one of less dependance and more independence? What would it mean to and for them to actively participate in not just taking, but contributing something?

With children, it's expected that most tasks will only be done because you ask or demand it. How many times have you told them to get off the couch and do something that would be helpful? How often do you wish they would, just for once, notice what needs to get done and just do it? Maybe it sounds like his: "Stop playing that video game and help me shovel the driveway," or "Get off the phone and go finish your homework." As a parent of an adolescent, you are constantly trying to redirect their attention toward being curious about their life, but that kind of curiosity can't be enforced or demanded—it must in some way be tended to within them, by them.

When I was a teenager, my mom always did my laundry for me. Whenever a dirty pile of clothes would build up, she would immediately take it, clean it, fold it, and hand it back to me to put away. And while I'm sure she found herself useful in doing so, in retrospect she was also stealing away another opportunity for me to see what needed to get done and to do it myself, and if I didn't, to face the consequences that come with inaction—in this case, no clean clothes.

What is available to a young person in this time of life is to practice pivoting from dependent to independent—from thinking, *I'm only doing this because my mom told me to*, to *What do I need to do to make this feel or be different?* Each time a teenager can choose to do something of their own accord, they are also making sense of some more fundamental questions: *What would happen if I do this or don't do this? How will this help me become the person I want to be? If I do this for others, how will that impact my life and theirs?* What they begin to learn is that with independence also come responsibility and consequence.

For them to pivot to a new role in the family, a new method is also required for you, a shift from *Who do I want you to be?* to *Who are you meant to be?* Granted, this is a pretty steep learning curve, because they are changing so fast, but what is being asked of you is to loosen your grip in trying to shape them and to practice watching and witnessing the choices they make with a genuine curiosity. Practicing this offers them the freedom to make new choices, to make mistakes, to try again, to explore and discover their own identity and purpose that is independent of you and how you would have done it. And again, this is a two-way street, which means you can't expect them to change if you continue to treat them as if they haven't. You both are trying to find a new arrangement together, and by meeting your child with that genuine curiosity, you are actually making yourself more trustworthy to them.

The ritual below has two purposes: The first is that it sets up your adolescent to accomplish a big task: to make something substantial for a group larger than themselves. This task asks them to inhabit a different role, one of giving rather than receiving. Within this task, they will assume all of the responsibilities it takes to make it happen and all the lessons that come with fulfilling or not fulfilling it. While this big task can have many creative options, like a massive beach cleanup or serving a local homeless shelter, I chose to center this ritual around a simple, everyday one: making a meal for their family and/or larger community. Why a meal? Because it is an opportunity for them to now practice reciprocity, by feeding the family and/or community who have fed them their whole lives.

This ritual's second purpose is for the larger community of family and friends to affirm this young person's value within the community. Their challenge is to make a collective gift for the teenager—something that can be given in the spirit of fortifying them and seeing them through this transitional time. The purpose of this gift is to communicate, in a tangible way, the impact this young person has had on each person attending and to relay how much they truly matter to everyone gathered.

Prepare

Intentions

May my teen be challenged with the responsibilities of a big task and may it help them pivot from a taking to a giving role within the family and the community. May my teen be presented with a community gift that lets them feel how valuable they are and the influence they have had on each person gathered.

The Big Picture

Keep your eyes on the prize. Sure, the meal happening flawlessly would be great, but the learning is more important than the task itself. What you are communicating is that the preparation of this meal is another way for them to understand that they are becoming a full person with full autonomy. Instead of this being another thing that "my mom and dad want me to do," it can and must become something entirely their own, that carries their thumbprint, their style, their taste, and their own unique flavors—not yours! Celebrate all the ways they might invest themselves in this big task.

When

Every adolescent has a window for being influenced, especially by their family, that keeps getting narrower and narrower. What that means is there's such a thing as too late. Ask yourself: When is the right time to present this big task—not too soon and not too late but just right.

Making the Ask

Like with most requests of adolescents, it's best for this to not come from their parents. If that's not possible, it's perfectly fine, but ideally this is asked or encouraged by a non-parent (aunt, uncle, family friend) that this young person admires and respects.

However you present this to them, underscore the question *Why?* Don't assume that this young person will understand why doing a ritual to mark this time will be good for their life. Ask them honest questions that excavate the why: *Why now? Why you? Why this?* And, of course, listen curiously without leading them. The thing that is as important as the event itself is their ability to make sense of it.

Setting Parameters

When presenting the task, be sure to give a definable structure that they can operate inside of. Give them limits of money, of time, of number of guests, and consider presenting this as a challenge that they can accomplish. You'll be surprised at how their ingenuity thrives within limits.

Invites

While this is your child's big task, I would encourage you to work together to create an invite list. Explore with them who the people are that have been present and invested for their entire life. Who are the people that are currently significant? Space limitations usually provide a good parameter to discern who must really be there.

Also, remember: As you limit your guest list, those left out can still participate in the gift-giving part. That is an excellent way to still include a larger group of beloved family and friends while limiting the dinner to a doable number.

Community Gift

Your major job as the parent is to organize and prepare the community gift. Whatever it is, it should be made of many parts. For instance, a friend of mine asked all the adults in her son's life to create a collage book that they would gift him for his thirteenth birthday. Each adult was asked to create one page of the book made of cut-out magazine images and words describing the qualities they saw and admired in this young person. The book became a handmade, colorful reflection of the love and care so many felt for him, and he, in turn, treasured it as a big affirmation of the person he was becoming.

Your Child's Preparation

Some of you reading might think to yourself: *My kid has totally got this.* But others of you might begin to feel yourself doubting your child's capacity as it gets closer to the meal, and you might be tempted to help, remind, or even do it for them. That would go against the entire purpose of this ritual—so please, hands off. This thing sinks or swims by their labors.

The Meal

While preparing and eating the meal is the ritual, there are two places that require structure during the meal itself:

The first is a moment for your child to give thanks publicly. You might want to include this in their responsibilities when you tell them of the big task, so they can prepare, or not, depending on their preference.

The request is simple: "You will have less than ten minutes to give thanks at the beginning of this meal." You can let them figure out what that means to them, or if this is completely new territory, you can offer a structure that could help them break it down.

Here's an example:

- Offer gratitude for a quality that you received from your family.
- Offer gratitude for something your teachers have taught you.
- Offer gratitude for a way your friends have made you a better person.
- Offer gratitude for something challenging that you accomplished.
- Offer gratitude for something that is much bigger than you.
- Offer gratitude for something that you too often take for granted.

Ideally, they are just speaking from their heart and not reading from a script.

The second moment in the meal for structure is the giving of the community gift. Before you give it, acknowledge the big task that this young person accomplished: They fed their people. That is no small feat, and it's very important that you recognize that.

As you present the gift, be sure to frame it as marking this particular moment of stepping out of being a dependent child and stepping into becoming an independent adult. And, of course, express all the gushy pride your heart will overflow with. Also, be sure to offer this moment to allow all those gathered to let their hearts overflow too, giving this young person words of reflection, encouragement, fondness, courage, and blessings.

And, of course, enjoy the delicious feast.

Questions for Further Reflection

- How does this big task offer my child an opportunity to inhabit a new role in our family?
- What is the new dynamic emerging between me and my child?
- What qualities and skills do I notice this young person exercising?
- How can I support them in being the person they are becoming?

THE SIDE-*by*-SIDE RITUAL:
For Parents

Adolescence can be hard on a parent's self-esteem. So many methods of relating to your child are suddenly outdated and the relational learning curve is damn steep. One day you're keeping step, and the next, you're playing catch-up and have no idea why the old ways don't work anymore. Maybe you're left feeling a sense of incompetence, like you're doing it wrong or you're not doing enough—not asking the right questions or asking too many. No matter what you do, you're told it isn't right, and you aren't given many clues as to how to adjust. You might even ask a question and get the classic teenage eye roll that not-so-subtly lets you know you're pathetic. Not too long ago you were a major influencer to this kid, and now it's like you're not even on the B-list anymore—or as my friend Michael, a father of a preteen, says, "I suddenly went from hero to zero."

As they continue to individuate into their unique identity, and you continue to succumb to your ever-diminishing influence, many tugs-of-war ensue. As their parent, your gut reflex still tries to figure out how to pull and push them toward doing the right thing. Sometimes it sounds like "Get off the couch and go play outside" or "Put down your phone and finish your homework," but these moments are received less and less as authority and more as sheer annoyance. What your kid is usually aware of long before it dawns on you, if at all, is that what you thought was the best thing to do or the right course of action to take is actually you just trying to control the situation. This is a hard pill to swallow for any parent because not too long ago you did know what was best for your kid and they did the very thing you suggested. But now, in these power exchanges, you might find yourself among the hordes of parents repeatedly ignored, yes-ed, told to shut up, made fun of, and continuously faced with this brutal question: *Would you rather be right or be connected?* It's an impossible choice because you probably want both, but ask yourself: How much of your need to be right is directly tied to your identity as a "good parent," and is that an identity that must also undergo a change?

While I was writing this chapter, I spoke with a dad whose teen was into video games, but he wanted them to try out for sports. They found themselves in a tug-of-war, and when I asked why they kept pushing, he got angry. Even though he gave legitimate reasons, like "it's good for them" and "it will teach them about this and that" and "it's great exercise," underneath that, he disliked what his child loved to do and he was pushing his values on them. I asked him: "What are you unwilling to accept about who your kid is?" What I didn't expect was that this brought back memories of his own childhood and how his parents forced him to give up certain activities that he loved to do in order to please them. I followed this up with a doozy of a question: *What aspects of yourself haven't you yet accepted?* So much of the time, our adolescents expose parts of us that are unintegrated and unaccepted, and when we are confronted with those parts that now live in them, we can unconsciously take our discomfort with those parts of ourselves out on them too.

So many parents want to feel like they have everything handled and are doing all the right things all the time, but this mindset banishes the value in making mistakes and revealing your vulnerabilities, uncertainties, and humility in front of your child. Parenting an adolescent means being snapped out of the story you told yourself of what being a "good" parent meant and learning to love and care for your child while in the presence of your failures, your unmet expectations, and your brokenness, which are constantly reflected back to you. And what's even more defeating is that sometimes these patterns bubble up from things you heard from your own parent's mouth that you promised you would never say, or ways you dealt with your parents that your kid is now dishing back to you.

What you need isn't to regain control over your child. You need to cultivate compassion, to take things less personally, and to gain perspective about how old patterns from your own adolescence might be playing out. You must acknowledge the loss and grief that naturally exists during this time. In the blink of an eye, your little nugget became a gangly, annoyed teenager who will soon enough leave your home to go off into this sideways world.

The ritual below is not a cure-all. It doesn't promise to solve your guilt or overcome your failures as a parent. But it might be a way to mark what's changing by distinctly seeing how much has changed. The ritual itself centers around the creation of a Memory Book where you can juxtapose pictures of your child's childhood with photos from your *own* childhood. By putting them in proximity to one another, you will be able to reflect on the ways that you and your child are similar and the ways you are different. It might offer you the perspective you need to see your child where they are instead of where you think they should be and, just as important, hold space for you to bring understanding and attention to the parts of your younger self that still vie to be loved and accepted.

Prepare

Intentions

May I witness and be witnessed in my changing role as a parent. May I see my child's development and my own, side by side, making the distinction about what I need and what my child needs. May this Memory Book serve to help me process this change.

Witness

For this ritual, invite a handful of friends to join you, but if possible let it be other parents of adolescents who are going through something similar. If you do that, everyone can witness the others while also participating at the same time. Also, consider having at least one elder parent present, perhaps a person whose children are now parents, who could offer another kind of far-reaching perspective that might be valuable during this ritual.

You Will Need

Since this ritual centers around making a Memory Book, it will take a bit of advance preparation. The power of the ritual depends on the photos you can compile, so give yourself ample time to find and, if necessary, print any photographs you need. You'll want to feature photographs from a variety of life stages, from infancy to adolescence—do your best to find at least one or two images for each moment.

You will also need:

- A photo album or scrapbook to house the photographs
- Scissors and glue (if needed)

Begin

Lest this turn into a casual night of scrapbooking, remember to set the container for this ritual. It doesn't have to be fancy or complex; try lighting a candle, taking a moment of silence, or raising a glass of wine. Name why you are sitting down to this task: *Why this? Why now? Why you?*

When you are ready, sort your photos into the different age categories, and begin to organize the pages. On the left side should be photos of you from your childhood. On the right side should be photos of your child. Each spread (a left page and a right page together) will feature a different age of development, from infant to adolescence.

I recommend that you sort the photographs into the following six categories:

- Infant
- Toddler
- Early childhood
- Middle childhood
- Preteen
- Adolescence

If you want or need to simplify this list, you can refine it down to three categories: Infancy, Childhood, and Adolescence.

The Questions

As you work to glue or tape the photographs into the book, either reflect quietly or, if you've gathered with others, share aloud as you think about the following questions concerning your childhood and questions concerning your child's experience. There's no need to go in any particular order. If you can, pass the book around and let everyone pose a question to the group, and let the stories unfold.

Your Childhood

- If you could be a parent to yourself at that age, what would you give that you wanted but didn't get from your own parents?
- What do you think is the best thing your parents gifted to you?
- What do you think is the worst thing your parents cursed you with?
- What was one thing your parents never noticed about you as a teenager?
- Did your parents ever embarrass you? What happened?
- Tell a story of a time you exploded at your parents. What happened?
- What is something your parents said to you that you swore you would never say to your kid? Have you ever said it?
- How did you push your parents away when you were a teenager?
- When did you feel most connected to your parents as a child? As a teen?

Your Child

- In what ways is your child similar to you?
- What do you see in your child that is different from you?

- What ways do you see your kid exhibiting personality traits that are unfamiliar or challenging?
- What ways do you see your kid behaving that are challenging and familiar?
- Where do you feel ease in your relationship with your child?
- Where do you feel tension or stress in your relationship?
- What is something you always wanted to ask your teenager but haven't?
- What is something your teen doesn't want you to know about them, but you do?
- What kind of control over them are you willing to let go of?
- What kind of control are you unwilling to let go of?
- What qualities or actions do you need to see in your child that can assist you loosening that control?

Conclude

Passing the Books

As you complete your book, take time to pass each one around the group. These moments can be bittersweet—having others witness the waterfall of how quickly time has passed and how beautiful, challenging, and profound growing up and parenting a child have been.

When you are viewing another's book, speak up! Offer words that fill the pockets of that parent's heart with little bits of courage, kind reflections, blessings, or wonder.

End the Ritual

End as you began, either by blowing out the candle, raising a glass of wine, taking a moment of silence, or however else seems most genuine to everyone gathered.

Questions for Further Reflection

- How can I better relate to my child in our similarities and differences?

- How does recapitulating my own childhood inform how I treat my child?
- What unprocessed pain or challenge from my past am I realizing I'm projecting onto my child?
- How can I continue to support my child's differentiation and unique gifts and challenges?

Coming Out

Queer people don't grow up as ourselves, we grow up
playing a version of ourselves that sacrifices authenticity
to minimize humiliation and prejudice. The massive task
of our adult lives is to unpick which parts of ourselves are
truly us and which parts we've created to protect us.

—Alexander Leon

Coming out is a modern initiation. There's the death of an old identity and
the birth into a new one. The old skin was a survival skin, a way to navigate
safely through a world that wasn't ours. But there came a point where that
skin grew too tight, too suffocating, too untrue, and shedding it was the only way
out. We had to shed it without any guarantee of safety or belonging. Coming out is
nothing short of courage made manifest, proclaiming who we are before we really
even know what that means yet. And trusting that somehow there will be others
who recognize this courage and will catch us, greet us, and welcome us home to our
truer self.

Not all initiations succeed. That's what makes them transformative. They walk us
to the edge of what's familiar and known and require us to leap, which also means we
can fall. True initiations contain the risk of failure, and in the case of coming out, it can
look like more denial, total rejection, or self-harm. But if the initiation is successful,
someone new emerges from the other side. Uncertain and cautious, this new someone
tests the waters of their reception, which raises questions like *Who am I now? Can I*

love who I am? Will who I am be accepted? Who is there to welcome me? How does this change my life? So much of the experience of being closeted occurs in isolation, where we hide and contain the truth in order to feel protected and safe from a family or society that shames, threatens, or denies us. The real labor of coming out is exercising the trust that *all of you* is wanted, accepted, and worthy of celebration and belonging. This loving acceptance, however, must first be exercised from *within*—and only then can it be shared. I started this chapter with a quote from activist Alexander Leon that beautifully captures how coming out is not just proclaiming an identity but the life-long task of identifying *who we are* and *who we aren't*.

Growing up in the eighties, I didn't know coming out was even possible. I had never met an out queer man until I was in my twenties, and there were no queer stories on TV or in the movies, so I couldn't accurately see a reflection of myself in the broader culture. Unlike today, I knew no LGBTQ+ students in my high school and no queers orbited my parents' constellation of friends. I was completely isolated and the consequence of this was that I hid my attraction to men from everyone because it was also hidden from me.

Only at the end of my junior year of college did I actually discover another gay young man my age, who, rumor had it, had come out months before. Curiosity got the best of me, and one day I asked if he would take a long walk to share his story. As he shared, I let myself get vulnerable enough to give him the sense that I was willing to crack the door to my most deeply guarded secret. So when he asked me "Do you also like guys?" the word "yes" barely escaped my lips. I was actually trying to my best to say "no," but I just couldn't hold that yes in any longer. I remember my body trembled, my heart thumped hard, and I looked like a deer in headlights. In that moment, it had felt like I needed to let it out or I would die, which compelled my friend to take my hand, look into my eyes, and say: "You're safe. The most important thing is to tell the people you love."

I recently asked my friend Geo if he could go back and redesign his coming-out journey, what would he change? His immediate response was: "Intention." He said he would have created more structure and purpose during this very vulnerable moment, so that he could be reminded of the love and acceptance that actually surrounded him. That really resonated with me, as my own coming out experience felt so ungrounded and unheld—it was mostly just me stumbling over my tears and fears to tell my family and friends and them not really knowing how to speak to their own feelings, questions, and sympathy.

But even hearing the words "I'm gay" unlocked a door to see who I really was underneath all that denial and gave me an opportunity to accept myself. After years of locking that truer self away, this moment of emergence asked for an intimate presence and profound compassion from me and from those I was coming out to. Which is why even though coming out is a whole life project, for our purposes, this chapter will focus on this initial emersion.

The rhythm of hiding and revealing is found in many rituals, and coming out has its own particular cadence. While there are ten thousand ways to come out of the closet, it is overcoming the fear that is what binds them all together—the fear of not being accepted or loved, of being harmed or hurt, and of being abandoned when this emergence needs authentic welcoming. April, a trans woman, said, "I was so fearful the first time I said anything out loud. I was scared of the reaction I would get because it's been beaten into us that this is not okay." Of course, that fear varies dramatically depending on the culture, country, family, race, or religion we were born into, but every coming out story contains the same ritualized choreography—a movement from concealing to revealing.

Coming out is a returning to wholeness, what Carl Jung calls individuation—a winding road of confronting the many parts of ourselves that we abandoned—the beautiful and ugly, the light and shadow, the wounded and wise—and bringing them into a new, whole understanding of ourselves. Abandonment often occurs because we believe on some level that certain aspects of who we are won't be tolerated or welcomed. At the heart of the word "abandon" is the Proto-Germanic word *bannan*, which means "anything done by proclaiming it as so." In other words, our willingness to abandon parts of ourselves is connected to our unwillingness to say those parts out loud and claim them. Basically, if we can't acknowledge it, we can't be it. All that which is unspoken remains unclaimed. Unless a person coming out of the closet has the space to both speak and feel heard, there will always be parts of themselves that will remain left in the closet. This is why proclaiming who we are and who we aren't is a lifelong journey—for there are so many hidden shadows in the closet that continue to need our attention years later.

It's unrealistic to expect someone coming out to know the consequences of the closet on their life. Just announcing their queerness is more than enough. The most important thing is to hold a space of love and acceptance so that they can open up on their own terms whenever they feel compelled to do so. And while this is a sensitive and transformative time, it can be enormously healing if there is a space provided to receive the person and make this moment meaningful and sacred.

THE SIFTING RITUAL:
For Those Coming Out

Coming out is relational. We shed the thick armor that protects us, to reveal a soft and supple heart longing for connection. Our longing is to belong as we are, not as the person we think others want us to be. Even though the first step on this long road of acceptance is made when we proclaim to another person "I'm a lesbian" or "I'm trans," the real journey is when we befriend and forgive the relationship with our own self. To accept ourselves in the ways we want to be accepted, we must learn the skill of discernment and practice distinguishing who we are from who we are not. This isn't something we can do once and be done. This is an every-day practice to sift out the old protective layers that once shielded us from rejection, to reveal the realness of what lies underneath. And, as with any practice, we get better at it the more it's done.

The purpose of this ritual is to create a moment twice a day to pause, remember, and acknowledge what you are leaving and what you are becoming. At least in the initial time after coming out of the closet, it's challenging to understand how to operate as this new self. Sometimes we need to say things over and over again until they become real. These rituals can provide a solid ground for sanity and stability when everything seems unstable.

Prepare
Intentions
May I slow down when I'm feeling overwhelmed and take the space to come back to my body, to my breath, to myself. May I set aside brief moments in the day to remember and affirm who I am and distinguish it from who I am not.

You Will Need
- Something to write on (a journal, a phone, a mirror)
- A pen or erasable marker

How Long
You could do this for thirty days, six months, a year, or as long as you want! However long or short a period you choose, you must be deliberate

about your time commitment. Again, ritual needs a container, not just a beginning but also an end. You can, of course, recommit to more time if you want. But be clear about the stretch of time you are committing to.

PART 1: THE NIGHTTIME RITUAL

Begin

Before climbing into bed, ask yourself: "What part of my old identity am I letting go of?"

For example, this might sound like:

- "Tonight, I am letting go of fear."
- "Tonight, I am letting go of my shame and concern about what people will think if I share more of myself."
- "Tonight, I am letting go of my old name."
- "Tonight, I am letting go of an old pronoun."
- "Tonight, I am letting go of caring so much if I will be liked."
- "Tonight, I am letting go of thinking I'm doing it wrong."
- "Tonight, I am letting go of believing I am not enough."

Record this statement. You could write it on a piece of paper or on your bathroom mirror, or make a video of yourself on your phone.

Pause for a few moments to reread or relisten to what you're releasing. These old beliefs or patterns kept you safe for a time and that's why you believed in them. They served you then, but they no longer serve the person you are becoming. See if you can thank this old belief, this old name, or this old identity for protecting you for as long as it did. When you say, "I am letting go," it means that when this emotion or behavior or identity arises again to try to protect you, you're saying to it, "You are not mine anymore."

But with ritual, you can't just say it for it to be true. You must do something. That's why you made a record of it. You must actively, physically let go of what you wrote down or recorded. How you do this is up to you—tear it up, burn it, crumple it, erase it, delete it, or however else you can imagine eliminating the sentence you wrote or recorded. It doesn't matter how you do it but that you do it. The ritual's potency is that you start off seeing this old belief or behavior written down and then conclude the ritual by physically letting it go.

After doing this, pause again. Put your hands on your stomach, heart, or both and feel your body. The word "incorporation," which is the last step of an initiation, literally means "bringing it into the body," which is the path toward wholeness. So take a breath and imagine an old weight being lifted from your heart or an old skin being shed.

And, if a little "amen" or "mmhm" or "yassssss" escapes your lips after you do it, that couldn't hurt either. Letting go of old ways and identities sometimes needs an extra "thank you and see ya" as they walk out the door.

PART 2: THE MORNING RITUAL

Begin

When you wake up in the morning, before you make that first cup of coffee or check your social media feed, ask yourself: "What part of my new identity am I claiming today?" This might sound like:

- "Today, I am claiming courage."
- "Today, I am claiming my new name."
- "Today, I am claiming a new pronoun."
- "Today, I am claiming trust—I can trust that I am worthy and wanted."
- "Today, I am claiming that I am indeed enough"
- "Today, I am claiming my capacity to make great decisions for myself."
- "Today, I am claiming my body as sexy."

Just like with Part 1, write this statement down or record it somewhere. Whether that's in a journal, on your bedroom wall, on a mirror, on Instagram, or in an album on your phone—wherever you can, collect these daily statements that proclaim proudly who you are becoming.

After you write this statement down, pause and say it out loud three times. Why three? Because sometimes we need to hear it a few times before we start to believe it to be true. If you want to say it twenty times or a thousand times, be my guest, but just start with three.

As you collect these proclamations, place them somewhere where you can see them every day. Maybe you want to create an altar on your dresser where you can go to remember them, or perhaps you create an account on Instagram made up especially of these reminders. What's most important is that you can see them and affirm that this is actually the person you are transforming into.

After writing these proclamations down and saying each of them out loud at least three times, close your eyes and put your hands on your heart or belly or both and take a breath. Feel the gentle rising and falling of your body receiving this new way to understand yourself. Feel the love that you are proclaiming to yourself. Let these words settle in your system. Just like a good stew, give yourself plenty of time to let these statements cook inside of you.

Questions for Further Reflection

- How does acknowledging and letting go of old identities and patterns open me up to my new identity?
- How does it feel when I choose to let go and ritually release old ways of being?
- How do I feel when I choose to affirm and proclaim new ways of being?

THE AFFECTION RITUAL:
For Parents, Friends, and Family
of LGBTQI+ Children

Your child recently came out to you. In that moment when they courageously offered to show you who was behind the veil, perhaps you greeted them with love and support—but what do you do with the days or weeks following this big reveal? How do you continue to show you care without inundating them with questions, emotions, or too much attention? Is "acceptance" the only thing being asked of you or is there more you need to do?

So many parents want to convey a sense of "normalcy" when their child comes out. I often hear queer people say that their parents responded with good-hearted statements like "You are no different to me" or "I love you the same no matter what," all attempts to express a consistency of love. What they miss, however, is an acknowledgment or even an honoring of what has changed. Things actually *are* different, and to ignore that pushes your child back into the place they are trying so faithfully to come out of.

It seems to me that most families struggle with their role and purpose after their child comes out, especially the weeks immediately following. Becky, who is the mother of a trans daughter, said that when she told her she was transgender, she didn't know how to react. "I needed time to let this revelation sink in. What did this mean? What was I supposed to do? I didn't even know what cis-gendered meant at that point." Parents walk the delicate tightrope of figuring out how to support but not overwhelm their child—how to give them space but not too much. Oftentimes, parents need to come to terms with their own losses and grief so that they can fully show up to welcome and celebrate this newly transformed person.

One of the most misunderstood and most important aspects of an initiation ceremony is the return of the initiate to their society or community. This person has undergone a major ordeal, and the most important role a community can play is to welcome them back as a new person by acknowledging their different identity and stature within the community. In many traditional rites of passage ceremonies from around the world, the village calls them by a different name, offers them new opportunities they could not access before, like marriage, or literally approaches them as an entirely new human that was forged through the ordeal. These are essential functions of the village to help the initiates not feel like they are walking in two distinct worlds. The willingness or unwillingness of a community or society to welcome someone back from their ordeal can lead to the successful integration of their experiences and identity or to their isolation and unnecessary trauma.

Whatever the rite of passage is, the homecoming can make or break the experience. Even if your child never left home, their time in the closet was concealed and "away" and their coming out is a return, albeit with a new and different identity. So much depends on the family and/or broader community's capacity to see and celebrate this person's entire journey. Therefore, the family's purpose is to recognize all that this child has overcome in order to come out, by literally welcoming this new person in.

Becky shared with me that a year after their child came out as trans, she and her husband celebrated their daughter's "first birthday" just like they did when she was a baby. "We created a concrete stepping stone together, with her handprint and her new name, rather than a footprint when she was a baby. Her old stone was retired to the side yard and the new stone now sits near the gate to our garden. Our son's life ended and our daughter's began. This was our way of welcoming her into the world in a 'concrete' way and celebrating this transition by acknowledging the loss but also the birth, growth and change."

The purpose of the Affection Ritual is for your whole crew of family and friends to gather together around a common project: the creation of a deck of cards. These are not just any cards. Part cheerleader, part heart-soother, the Affection Deck is meant to inspire, affirm, love, and ground this queer person as they arrive to the world with their new, colorful queer wings. Receiving a deck like this will feel a little like receiving a stack of handmade birthday cards all at once, but these are celebrating the receiver's re-birthday.

A handmade gift can last a lifetime. It tethers us to all the hands that made it. The other day at a dinner party, someone asked at the table, "What is the best gift you've ever received?" Almost all the answers centered around a gift that was made specifically for that person or for a particular time. These cards have the potential to be a companion that accompanies and affirms your child as they continue to come into themselves.

Prepare

Intentions

May I offer my queer child a tangible gift that they can return to anytime on their long road of coming out. May this ritual give my community a hands-on way to positively support my queer child and their transformative coming out process.

You Will Need

- 5 x 8 index cards, one for each person
- Markers or crayons
- Crafting supplies like glitter or glue

Your Approach

The most challenging aspect of this ritual is how to navigate the landscape of looping everyone in. Coming out of the closet can be touchy, sensitive, slow, fast, not a big deal, or a very big deal. Most important, it should never be rushed or dominated by anyone else—especially the parents. You might already sense this, but it is worth repeating: It is not your role to share this information unless your child has given you their permission. Period.

With that said, there are a few ways to go about testing the waters. The first is to check in: Ask your child in advance if you can speak to Aunt Miriam or Cousin Adam. Giving them the power to control their coming out process shows them enormous respect and also establishes a clear yes or no so it's understood who you can and who you can't speak to. Let them know you would like to be able to acknowledge and celebrate this news with close friends and family. If they ask you to wait—wait. Going at your child's pace is how to navigate the process.

If your child is still in the process of coming out to other friends and family members, you might consider taking a broader approach to ask support from family and friends without revealing the reason. A simple statement like "My child needs some help remembering how much love and support surround them at this time" can rally the support of your community without betraying your child.

What to Say

Assuming you can speak freely about your child coming out, there are several way to broach this ask.

Perhaps you want to introduce this as a sacred moment: "Our child has been hiding their identity for so much of their life and we are so proud that they have gathered the courage to speak what's true for them to others. I/we feel like it's important to ritualize this moment and not let it slip away without acknowledging how much they have changed. We would love for your participation . . . "

Or maybe you want to bring it up as a creative idea: "You've known our child for so many years. This moment in their life is a big deal. We thought it would be incredibly helpful for them to feel how many people love and welcome them right now. We had an idea . . . "

The Affection Deck

It's time to get creative. Each person or family is being invited to create one card for the Affection Deck. Just like with a deck of cards or a tarot deck, each card will be unique and tell its own story. Each person should start with a blank 5 x 8 index card, on which they will write a word or expression that they believe is essential for your child to remember as they come out of shame and fear and into love. Give your extended community the freedom to decide what word or phrase they want to represent—but feel free to make suggestions. What is most important is that each card expresses an important value and reminder for your child to remember, embody, and receive.

My suggestion is to let one side of the card be the word or phrase while the other side of the card says something like Love, [Name]. That way your child can literally flip through this deck and see all the names of the people that care about their well-being and emergence.

If people need some inspiration, consider using a few as examples in your invitation or as suggestions:

- Celebrate!
- Remember who you are
- Forgiveness
- You belong to us
- We honor you
- Shine, baby, shine
- You are seen
- All of you is loved
- You are enough
- Bless your life
- Courage
- You are not alone

Once people have decided on a phrase, it's time to decorate the card. Encourage people not to be shy, to let their imagination—and their crafty side—shine. As I said in my book *Morning Altars*, "By marking time with beauty made from our hands and our words, we can slow down the moment so as to find our way back into it."

Begin
When
Once you have assembled the Affection Deck, it's time to give it. While this can be done whenever the deck is ready, consider an alternative route: Give the deck on a meaningful date, like on the anniversary of your child's coming out. By doing that, you are harnessing the power

of ritual, which lets us return to a moment and make it meaningful. In circling back in on the anniversary of this date you let your child know that their coming out wasn't forgotten. It is something that deserves to be continually honored. Honestly, it breaks my heart a little bit that so many of us don't honor this date as significant.

Giving the Deck

Whether you choose to gift the deck privately or as a group, I encourage you to not give it too casually. Start by establishing "time boundaries" by turning off your phones, clearing your schedules, and limiting distractions. Perhaps you ask for an hour, and for that time there is something different available: a space for reflection and speaking from the heart.

How you go about introducing this gift is up to you. Perhaps you want to reaffirm your love for this person or reflect on the time since they've come out or share how proud you are of their choices. If there are many people there, give everyone a minute or two to speak. If there aren't, maybe you want to read the names of the people who submitted each card and presence them in the space. Most important, convey that this moment is worthy of something, and that something is the giving of this gift made by many.

Conclude

Once you give the gift, don't rush through the moment. Give it space. You are shining quite a bit of love on this human and they may need time to let it seep in. Conclude the ritual simply and in love.

Questions for Further Reflection

- How does this ritual center my child's or friend's experience?
- What role does this ritual offer my family or community?
- In what ways does this gift express love and support?
- What happens when I celebrate and welcome my child or friend for their transformation?

A New Home

It may be our new house, but we are its newcomers. . . .
Yes, other families have settled here, other lives have been
played out here. But now it is our time. We renovate, renew
this structure, make changes. Slowly it is becoming ours.

—E. Goodman[*]

You've just arrived. You are greeted with bare floors, blank walls, an empty canvas. Keys in hand, you enter into your new dwelling, a place to settle and soon to call home. With each box unpacked, picture hung, and piece of furniture set, the space becomes more identifiable, almost familiar, as you begin to make your mark on it. Many memories will gather under this roof as it becomes a shelter for your troubles, a sanctuary for rest, an anchorage to return to time and time again. Yet this place is still very much a stranger. Like you, it comes with its own history and own stories, which you are now a part of as much as it is now a part of yours. So what can you do to greet this place meaningfully, like a new friend, as you begin to move in and make it yours?

Everything has a story. Everything comes from somewhere and travels to new places, even if that's just a beach stone that the waves move an inch or two every season. And along the way, everything has a resting place where it can lie down and dream. People, trees, objects, and yes, even homes are made of stories. Not too long

---

[*] E. Goodman, "On 'Second Time' Marriages and Houses," *Lawrence Daily Journal World*, November 23, 1982.

ago, and perhaps even in some places today, people knew the stories of the things they had and the places they lived in. For instance, a carpenter might have made a chair where they not only knew the story of the felling of the tree that gave them the wood but also the planting of the tree too. And because of that, the chair is so much more valuable. It is rich in story.

Sadly, in our modern world, many of us have forgotten that our things have a tale to tell. We buy plastic toys, synthetic clothing, and technology that too soon finds its home in a landfill. Our objects are orphans. We don't know where they were born, whose hands made them, or how they traveled. They just show up at a store and we adopt them for a while before giving them away again. Our stuff has become "destoried" and soon becomes disposable. But why? The etymology of the word "dispose" gives us a clue. The Latin word *disponere* is made of two words, *dis* and *ponere*, meaning "apart" and "to place." In other words, the disposability of something is a result of it being uprooted and away from its place. It has no history, no longevity, no belonging. In a way, it's homeless.

This sense of home and belonging is tethered to relationships, for that is where we are connected. And our relationships are maintained by stories. The more we understand the story of someone or something, the stronger that relationship becomes. The poet John O'Donohue puts it like this: "Where you are understood, you are at home. Understanding nourishes belonging."[*]

It might seem completely foreign to our modern minds, but this is not just true between people but of how we relate to our stuff as well. The more understanding we have with our belongings, the more they belong to us and us to them. For example, when I traveled to Morocco, I was dead set on buying a Moroccan rug. I originally thought I would go into a shop, find one I liked, and purchase it. Little did I know that isn't how it works. The process of rug shopping takes a willingness to slow down and, at first, to not shop. Instead of it being just a transactional encounter, the necessary ingredient was to come into relationship. Each shop I entered began with a long conversation with the owner over hot mint tea, sharing stories of where we came from and who our families were. But it was also important to each shop owner that I understood where the rugs came from and which families had made them. While sitting, sipping, and sharing, I learned that the patterns in the rugs also told the stories of the wool, the weavers, and the place the animals, plants, people, and their ancestors came from. Originally, I just wanted to buy a pretty rug, but this became a master class in understanding relationships.

---

[*] John O'Donohue, *Anam Cara: A Book of Celtic Wisdom* (New York: Cliff Street Books, 1997).

Moving into a new home is no different. Whether the home you are moving into is brand-new or a hundred years old, you are entering into a new relationship. And it has all the quirks that new ones have: a bit of awkwardness, attraction, curiosity, generosity, and a lot of forgiveness. You just don't know each other that well, and so the first meeting is somewhat of a clumsy dance of coming together. It may be strange to anthropomorphize a house like this, but actually this is how many cultures around the world understand homes. They don't see them as inanimate objects but as animate, living beings—as relationships that require the same maintenance that all relationships need. For instance, according to ethnographic literature about indigenous communities like the Pueblo villages of the Hopi and Zuni people, a home was understood as alive, a living thing "that comes from the earth and returns to the earth. They have a life cycle like any other living thing."* While most likely you are not inhabiting a pueblo, the common link here is that your home too is more alive than you think it is. It was made by many hands, with material that came from the earth, and possibly has had other people inhabiting it before you. Your home is filled with stories, just like you.

So what if you marked the first time in your new home like the beginning of a new relationship? What if you slowed down and approached this place with consideration and care—like you would when meeting a new friend? And what if the first thing you did in the home wasn't unpacking or organizing but instead looked a lot more like an introduction? In this way you would greet the home before moving into it. Meeting, introducing, listening, and sharing are all relational skills that establish deep and healthy roots of belonging. Actually, the etymology of the word "relate" is rooted in the Middle French word *relater*, meaning "recount or tell"—like, telling stories—the very thing you share in relationships. In this way, you can begin this next chapter by sharing the stories from the last one.

THE HELLO HOME RITUAL

The purpose of this ritual is for you to slow down amid all the change. Instead of moving in with stress, this is an opportunity to enter into this new home gradually, mindfully. This greeting ritual asks you to introduce yourself to this new neighborhood, this

---

* Catherine M. Cameron, *Hopi Dwellings: Architectural Change at Orayvi* (Tucson: University of Arizona Press, 1999).

new home, this next chapter, and to enter into this transition with more grace, ease, and curiosity.

Intentions
May I slow down and ground myself after the high-speed intensity that comes with packing, moving, and unpacking. May I approach my new home like a new relationship and connect the last chapter of my life to this new one.

When to Do It
Ideally, try to do this before the moving truck arrives, when the home is in its transitional state. It is empty, clean, and neutral. If you can't, do it before unpacking your boxes.

For How Long
This is akin to a meditation, so take as long as you want, go slow, and stay curious.

Begin

1. The Neighborhood
Start in the neighborhood, maybe just down the block. Approach the house or apartment slowly, only taking a few steps at a time. Take in the neighborhood. Who else lives on this street? What sounds do you hear? What's the weather like? What tree do you notice? Is anyone observing you?

Pause as you step onto the driveway or, if you live in an apartment, into the lobby. Ask yourself: *Who are my neighbors?*

2. The Entrance
As you approach the front door and reach for the doorknob, pause. You are opening the door to your new home, to this next chapter. Slowly open the door and linger at the threshold, letting your senses take in the space. From the doorway, see if you can allow yourself to notice the details of the home: the way the wood was cut, the trim on the walls, the shape of the glass, the scent of the place, the interplay between light and shadow. Go slow and curiously.

As you cross the threshold, ask yourself: *What is welcome here and what isn't?*

3. The Kitchen

Enter the kitchen and pause. This is where you and many others will be nourished and fed. Notice the oven, the stove, the refrigerator, the sink, perhaps a place that has already fed many people. Now, imagine the many more meals to be made here.

As you greet the kitchen, ask yourself: *Who will be nourished here?*

4. The Bedroom

Stand at the doorway of your bedroom. Envision yourself tucked into your bed after a long day. This is a room for resting, dreaming, making love, reading a book, sleeping.

As you greet this new bedroom, ask yourself: *Can I let myself rest here?*

Keep Going

Everyone's home is different. Maybe yours has many more rooms or only one, a backyard or a basement. Keep greeting your home and all of its many parts, taking in its personality and story, and imagining what kind of home you want it to be.

THE ALTAR *of* STORIES RITUAL

You Will Need

Start with an object from your last home or neighborhood. Maybe you lived near a beach, so it could be a shell you collected. Or a stone from the driveway or even the old key from your last apartment. It doesn't have to be monumental but just an object that carries a memory of where you've just come from.

What You Do with It

Find a central place in the home. This could be the mantel on the fireplace, a prominent windowsill, or on the ledge next to the stairs.

As you place the object there, it can become the cornerstone for your new home. However, before placing it, remember its story. *Why is this object important to you? Where did it come from? Why did you decide to keep it?* If you are alone and it feels strange to speak out loud, write these stories down. This object and its story will be the beginning of your home's first altar.

Afterward

Let this spot be a place that collects other important objects during your time in this new home. As you live there, this altar can be a gathering place for other precious possessions that you acquire, find, or are gifted while living here.

Since this is an altar of stories, your objective is to learn and remember all you can about what lives on this altar: *Where did it journey from, what is it made of, who made it?* This isn't just a place of things, it's a collection of living stories.

Story Time

As guests come over, you can introduce them to your altar of stories. Make tea, sit with them, and share or let them ask you questions about what lives on your altar. In this way, you have a place in your home where you can practice remembering and telling these stories.

THE LITTLE BIT *of* EARTH RITUAL

This ritual is a simple way to connect the two places you have called home by sharing the earth from one place to another. The purpose of this ritual is to remember where you came from and incorporate it into where you are now.

You Will Need
- A little pinch of earth from your last home
- If you have land, that should be simple to get. If you live in a city, take some earth from the landscaping near your building or the closest park.

What to Do

Find a place you are going to mingle the earths together. If you have a garden or yard, that could be perfect. If you don't, using an indoor clay pot is an excellent choice.

Hold the earth in your hand. Take a moment and/or breath. Maybe put the earth up to your nose and smell it. This is the earth from the place you recently lived.

If a story comes to mind from that place, tell it. *What did that place look like? Do you remember the foliage of that place? The weather? Were there any trees you loved? What was your favorite outdoor spot?* If you have a family or partner, give everyone a chance to remember together. You are introducing the place you departed to the new place you are arriving to.

Once you are complete, mix and mingle this earth with the new home's earth. Take a breath or a pause.

You can conclude this ritual with a blessing for your time in this new place. Here's an example: "We are brand-new here. We don't know the place, the land, our neighbors very well at all. May we love our new home by learning it well."

Bonus

An idea is to use the spot where the two soils mixed to plant something special. That plant can then grow in a place that tells the story of when you first arrived at this new home and where you came from.

Questions for Further Reflection

- Why do stories help create a sense of belonging?
- Why is it important to carry the story of our last home to our new home?
- What happens when I slow down and introduce myself to this new home? What gets included?

RITUALS *for* LOSS

Losing a Friendship

The loss of a friend is the greatest of losses.

—Publilius Syrus

There are some friendships you think will last forever. Endless memories shared. Countless photos taken. A kind of intimacy that comes over time when its longevity almost seems inevitable. A way of being with each other that is as dependable and reliable as a well-trodden path. And through the years, that long road of friendship has moved closer and further apart but never separated entirely. No matter how much time has come between you, it's as if no time at all has passed when you find your way back together again. And in that way, friendships move like seasons. Sometimes you might find yours in the heat of summer—playful, carefree, easy—while at other times it might feel quiet and internal, like winter. And friendships that survive many seasons of rain and drought, sun and storms, tend to be the ones you can count on when your own life teeters. They can be a sanctuary in a troubled time, a place to remember how to forgive, an honest mirror for reflection, a wild party for mischief, a wellspring of encouragement, a shoulder for grief, and an open door when loneliness threatens to haunt you.

They can also be like a garment, and as with anything well-worn, friendships fray. They can show signs of strain, of misuse, or abuse, of too much of you or not enough of them. Some friendships were forged when each of you was someone that you aren't anymore, and what still binds you together are remnants from a time past. Other friendships are wrecked by secrets or lies or too much truth. Judgments, assumptions, and expectations undermine what was once an easy generosity but now feels clouded with constraint and caution. Yet friendships have a capacity for renewal and revival. They can bounce back, like a fallen tree whose new shoots burst from old wood, reinventing themselves for a new time and a next chapter. But sometimes they don't. Sometimes friendships end and they simply fall and it's over. And then what?

In our modern culture, we have collective ways to speak to loss. The ending of a marriage is called a divorce. The ending of a life is called a death. The ending of a career is called a retirement. But what is the ending of a friendship called? How do we refer to the grief, or relief, or whatever messy, hard-to-describe feeling that comes with having to say goodbye to what was once a beloved friendship? And more so, even if there's been deep hurt or bitterness between you, how do you put the relationship down without resenting the other person for doing something wrong? Instead, what if you could see this resembling what everything else in nature is doing—changing? And whether this friendship ends abruptly or fades over time, slowly dying out like a wick without wax, it is asking you to bring yourself to accept and surrender to what is, with more beauty and grace.

Some of us are blessed by the kind of friendships that possess more intimacy, honesty, commitment, and love than a marriage ever would. And yet, when those end, when those huge trees fall, it might be that we carry on silently, unchanged, as if our lives don't need to skip a beat, as if that friend's absence is just like they were another stranger passing through. But what do we lose by ignoring the significance of this separation, and what gifts do we refuse when we choose to just turn away?

These two rituals sit at the crossroads of a friendship splitting. The first ritual is crafted for a friendship that is truly ending. Rather than walking away angry, with bitterness in your heart, this ritual offers a way to close the friendship's bundle with beauty. The second ritual is made specifically for friendships that need space and separation but also a framework to find their way back together again, changed and reconfigured. Both are tangible ways to mark the change that inevitably visits all relationships.

THE PUTTING IT DOWN RITUAL

Just like with a divorce, the ending of a friendship can carry pain and grievance that might outlive the friendship itself. Grievances are like ghosts, haunting the memory of the relationship, shrouded in the threadbare shawls of anger, resentment, or regret. "She did this" and "he said that" and "I'll never forgive" and "I'll never forget" are ways these ghosts still rap at the chamber door, feeding the phantom stories of what should have been or what you deserved or how wronged you actually were.

What lies beyond your resentment is the hard truths and consequences that can be found at the ending of things. And if you allow these endings to be, without fault or blame or finger-pointing, there's another thing that emerges that might not have any answers about the whys of what happened, but instead is a way to see what it hurts to see and a way to be with what you'd rather not be with.

Grief is a kind of heartbroken understanding. Not in order to find it and move on, but as a way of staying with the understanding—of standing in the wake of the way things are as it changes. A well-practiced grief is a way to love something even as it ends, even as it's over. It puts to rest those aggrieved ghosts of a time past and lets the love of what was stand beside the loss of what is. It doesn't attempt to bypass, ignore, or sugarcoat the pain, but instead includes it in the bigger story of the whole relationship.

This ritual is not a therapy session or an exercise in trying to iron things out and reconcile. Rather, this ritual is a way to honor and acknowledge the change that has visited your friendship and dissolved it. It holds up the change, not as something bad that happened, but just as a natural progression of the life of the friendship. The ritual can be done together or alone—either way, it is a real attempt to end the friendship beautifully, and with integrity and gratitude for the life-giving thing it was.

Prepare
Intentions
May I intentionally put down this friendship and practice grieving and not staying aggrieved. May I work with the natural elements to bring beauty to this loss and let go gracefully.

You Will Need
- A firepit or fireplace (or candles if that's not possible)
- Four sticks for the fire or four candles
- Four different colored strings
- A gift

Who
If it's feasible, do this together. If need be, invite a third friend to bear witness. While this option might appear uncomfortable or challenging, there's enormous value in putting the friendship down together

and witnessing each other's perspective and pain in the presence of a fire. If not, certainly do it anyway, as it's possible to honor and recognize the ending of this relationship on your own.

Why Fire?

Fire is first and foremost a mediator. Rather than being face-to-face with your friend in conflict, fire can sit between you, dispersing and metabolizing the energy. I've witnessed fire be the necessary element for arguing spouses, disagreeing neighbors, and warring parties to sit around and attempt to burn through their grievances. Years ago I attended an assemblage near Jerusalem called a *sulcha*, which is Arabic for "a gathering for reconciliation," where about one hundred Palestinians and one hundred Israelis came together to work with their anger and loss. The gathering compelled families on both sides who had lost children, fathers, mothers, sisters, and brothers to attacks, bombings, and incarceration to sit around a fire and cry, scream, be silent, listen, and sometimes come to a greater understanding that couldn't have happened in any other forum. Fire can be the intermediary, helping to process and burn up whatever you bring to it.

The Sticks or Candles

Collect four sticks that will be placed in the fire after each question. If you are doing this together, each person should gather their own bundle of four.

In preparation for the ritual, wrap each stick in a different color string or yarn to distinguish it. There is no predetermined pattern or design, but the more beautiful you can make each wrapping, the more you can honor the relationship you are letting go of.

If you are sitting with candles and not a fire, do the same thing but wrap the four candles in different color string or yarn.

Lighting the Fire

Whether separate or together, begin by lighting the fire/candles in silence. Witness the fire slowly take to kindling and smaller pieces of wood. The beginning of this ritual doesn't need anything fancy, but be sure to let the fire be the first to speak.

Time and Structure

The rounds are meant to give each person a way to speak to different aspects of the relationship and how it has changed. Most important: This is not a dialogue or a discussion. This is a time to speak and a time to listen. Therefore, it's helpful to have a timepiece to ensure that each person gets the same amount of time as the other.

Also, in these types of rituals it's sometimes difficult to understand when someone is done speaking, and it's best to be clear when you have said your peace. There should be no rush and no interruption. A good practice is to establish a simple call and response. One phrase announces that you are finished speaking and the other recognizes that you have heard the other person. For instance, "I'm complete" is a helpful way to punctuate the end of your turn and to help the other person know you're done. Similarly, "I hear you" is a good way to let the other person know that, whether or not you agree, you indeed heard them.

Another way is to pass an object back and forth—whoever holds it is empowered to speak.

Rounds

There are no rules for each round except to allow each person to respond to the question with no interruption or cross talk. Each person gets the predetermined amount of time for that round, say ten minutes each.

Remember, if there are two people, each person gets an equal amount of time to speak. After you have finished speaking, place one of your sticks in the fire, or blow out the candle.

> Round 1:
> *What are some of the memories and gifts that have come from this friendship?*

Round 2:
What realizations has this friendship brought to you?

Round 3:
How did I grow within this friendship? How did this friendship stop growing?

Round 4:
What is a blessing or kind words that you can offer the other person for their journey ahead?

Putting Out the Fire
After each of you has said your peace, stop feeding the fire and let it die down slowly. End as you began, in silence.

Gift-Giving
There's so much hurt at the end of a friendship, which is why it's good to conclude this ritual by gifting each other something sweet. This could be food, like chocolate, or something handmade and considered. Hard times like these need an infusion of something sweet to bring both people into balance again.

Questions for Further Reflection
- What is valuable about putting a friendship down and not ghosting it?
- What does this ritual let me say and hear?
- What does acknowledging the end of a friendship give space for?

THE MENDING *the* FRIENDSHIP RITUAL

This chapter almost didn't make it into the book. Actually, it wasn't even in my purview, but in the midst of writing, I had a major falling-out with one of my best friends. Without warning, something monumental shifted in the usual and familiar ways we had always related to each other and what emerged seemed threatening: unspoken and withheld judgments, deep-seated frustrations and mistrust in the basic architecture of the relationship. We both were hurt and licking our wounds. All we could agree upon was taking time away, and we didn't know for how long. But we agreed not forever.

During the separation, I had time to cool off and gain some perspective on what I wanted. I got the space to ask myself if, in the face of all that had changed between us, I even wanted to remain friends at all, which broke my heart to consider. The potential loss of this friendship felt overwhelming, as we had shared more than a decade together and had a close community as well. On some level, the potential split felt more akin to a divorce than anything else.

After four months, we circled back for a walk. There was still heat in the way we spoke to each other but way less hot. We were both trying to find common ground and mutual trust again. I could sense both her and me not wanting to give up on this thing we had once loved. Our friendship was still alive and breathing, albeit gasping and desperately needing repair. In that conversation, we both came to understand something: that there was one more necessary step before reviving the relationship. We needed something that could mark that difficult but important time away and our conscious decision to return to our friendship, changed and renewed. An idea we had was to hand-make each other a gift, something woven that could represent the mending that we were choosing to do together. I had no weaving experience, so this excited and intimidated me, but after consulting with another friend's seven-year-old daughter, I realized I could easily make a friendship bracelet. The seven-year-old approved, and even provided the string.

When my friend and I came back together to exchange these gifts, I understood how close we had been to losing our friendship and how this time away and the sweetness in the handmade thing helped us find new ways to approach each other and not take the friendship for granted. At the end of the gift-giving, my old new friend looked me in the eyes and said, "This needs to go in your book." And so here we are.

All relationships go through times of real closeness and times of hurt and distance. But that doesn't always lead to the friendship ending. Sometimes, like with my friend, there are reasons to step away and other reasons to come back together again. The ritual below was inspired by this uncertain dance.

Prepare

Intentions

May we consciously step away from our friendship that might not want to end but still needs space. During that time, may I reflect upon the relationship and what it means to me. May we make special gifts for each other and let that generosity help mend the frayed relationship.

You Will Need
Any materials you need to make your gift

No Guarantee
Let me start by relieving you of any guarantee that this ritual "will work." Just like with the story of my best friend and me, there is no way of knowing if a friendship will survive a separation. We needed the time away to determine if we were both still invested in each other and committed to the friendship's repair. But I've had many more friendships that didn't make it and just faded away without any acknowledgment or ritual. I'm sharing this with you not because I'm trying to sell you on ritual as a fix-it solution but because ritual is a way to recognize that you are in the fluid, changing waters, and it empowers you to slow down and reflect on where the current is taking you. And perhaps by doing so, you will see and know things that you couldn't have beforehand.

Begin
Step Away
The goal here is to pause the relationship and step away before it completely descends into an unredeemable place. If you can both agree that space apart would be valuable, it can provide you with a framework that acknowledges when to be apart and when to come back together. Before my friend and I realized we needed this, we found ourselves in a dynamic where she kept on approaching me for further connection because *she* was ready, and I kept stonewalling her attempts, as I am someone who needs a lot of time to process my feelings. Determining this as time away helped give me the space I needed and relieved her fear that I would ghost our friendship.

How Much Time
If you and your friend can agree on the value of taking time away, consider choosing a predetermined amount of time that has a start

and end date. Maybe you both decide you need a few weeks or a couple months, and while there is no right amount, there needs to be agreement on the same timeline of when to come back together, and you both need to stay committed to that.

Preparing the Gift

During this separated time, you both have one tangible objective: to hand-make something special for each other. As you consider what to make, it's a good opportunity to wonder about how well you know your friend. What do they like? What would make them feel good? How can you showcase your own gifts or talents and channel that into a handmade thing? For instance, if you are knitter, perhaps you knit something for them in their favorite colors, or if you are a baker, you bake something for them that they absolutely love. Maybe you're a poet and you write a poem that they might appreciate. Crafting something with your hands is both a way to work through your own feelings and to end up with a gift worthy of giving to your friend.

Conclude
The Return

Whenever it is you decide to come back together again, you are reconnecting through the gifts you both made and the love housed in those gifts. Consider each taking a certain amount of time to tell the story of the gift: *Why did you decide to make it? What about it brought to mind your friend? What realizations and experiences did you have while making it? How did this time away and crafting give you the proper space to reflect upon the relationship?* The gift is both an act of generosity as well as a physical marker of your friendship's revival.

Questions for Further Reflection
- What did taking time away provide me and my friend?
- What emotions or memories came up while making the handmade gift?
- How did it feel to come back together with gifts for each other?

Loss of a Pet

Someone asked me what the most difficult
part of having a dog was. I replied—the goodbye.

—Unknown

I f you've been down this path before, you know it's a rocky road. The bond that forms with an animal is unlike any with a human. It's a visceral kind of love. A love you seem to never get over. These little ones get past all your barriers, defy all your defenses, and burrow down into a supple tenderness you didn't even know your heart was capable of. While their lives are far too short, the space they occupy is enormous. Your pets are your home as much as your house, wife, husband, or children are. They welcome us no matter what and tether us to a simpler, happier way of being. A dog at your feet or a cat on your belly is, contrary to all the endless insanity of our world, evidence that life—for the moment—is just fine.

Those end days, however, just break your heart wide open. My dog Rudy was a miniature schnauzer, which is code for "I will do it my way, thank you very much." I grew up with Rudy, who was my father's dog originally, and when my father died, I took her under my wing and adopted her as my own. Maybe it was because "Ru" reminded me so much of my dad, or because I had no children of my own, but the bond that formed between us was particularly tight. We walked together, slept together, ate together—and since we both liked to be the stubborn queens of the castle, we even fought together. Rudy was nine when I adopted her and sixteen when she died. Those seven years were everything to me.

During the last six months of Rudy's life it was obvious that she wasn't going to last much longer. Every day was another day I held her closer knowing it wouldn't be long until I was going to have to let her go. Endings are so bittersweet, a place where love and grief mingle. The closer to the end, the greater the love, and the greater the love, the harder it is to end.

But what made Rudy's death and the days after manageable and even beautiful was all the ritual that surrounded and held them.

Having a dog has a built-in ritual to it already. Every morning and every evening, I'd grab the leash and poop bag and we'd be on our way. This daily responsibility gave my days structure and discipline. No matter what was going on, no matter how I was feeling, Rudy needed to be walked. But these walks weren't just for her—they were also where I could think, reflect, ground, and explore. That time of the day was sacred to me because it was consistent—I could rely on this ritual happening and it brought me stability and joy.

When Rudy died, this ritual also ended. Not only did I lose her companionship, I also lost our daily rhythms. Her death broke my heart and interrupted my days. Now what would I do in the mornings during our walk time? What would pull me outside on those days when I just wanted to stay in and be a hermit? The weeks following her death were a dramatic change that needed to be marked and acknowledged not ignored.

This chapter was inspired by the many rituals that surrounded Rudy's death and the days after. Ritual has the capacity to hold the pain and love simultaneously. It can help you pass through these transitions gracefully by giving you something to do to sanctify the moment. When I say sanctify, I'm not necessarily speaking religiously, but more so about an act to make the moment holy and whole. The wholeness of your pet's life *includes* their dying, and allows for you to have all the many feelings that this time provokes.

Ritualizing Rudy's death was so vastly different than how my family and I did it with our childhood dog, Snickers, a sweet-as-pie golden retriever who died with strangers in a vet office. After years of living with her, we put her down rather unceremoniously and did nothing to celebrate her life or properly grieve her death. We just tried to carry on with life as usual. In looking back, I see that the absence of ritual in this moment also meant the absence of meaning in the face of our loss. I regret not honoring my beloved childhood dog and wonder how ritualizing her life and death could have also brought my family together in our tenderness.

Life shouldn't just move on with a death. Our grief is evidence of that. Grief interrupts our lives and tells us that someone we love has left. But because we live in a grief-phobic culture, we don't know what to do with that grief. Instead, too many of us carry unexpressed grief too long, which quickly becomes depression. A ritual done during a grieving time lets us channel our grief into action. It gives our grief purpose and lets us express our hearts with beauty and meaning. Ritual is the place where we can let our broken hearts speak.

In this chapter, I offer you some creative rituals for both your animal's dying time and those weeks after when their absence is truly felt. Because this transition is so big for so many of us, the more ritual the better. Remember, ritual is rhythmic, meaning that the more you do it and sync up with that rhythm, the more you can stabilize yourself in the midst of change. Your pet's life was so meaningful to you, so let their death also carry the same meaning. In this way, you honor the wholeness of their life and what is changing within yours.

THE GOODBYE COMPANION RITUAL

A wise man once told me, "If you can say it, you can see it." Naming makes things tangible and real. Naming an imminent departure is no different—once you say it, you can see it happening. And that is the point of the ritual: To acknowledge what is happening allows you to be more present and grounded during this changing time.

In times of grief, the pain can be so severe that our only strategy is to not see what is happening and to turn toward ways that we can be in control. But that robs both you and your little one of your last moments together.

While it may at first sound strange to have a conversation with your pet, if you're like me, you speak to them all the time. When Rudy was alive, I was absolutely convinced that she could understand everything I said. But whether or not you believe that your pet can understand you, it's still important to name the change. Giving this moment words might lessen your anxiety, or help you come to more peace around what is happening.

This ritual is not meant for just you and your animal friend, but also to gather all those who love this creature and give them an opportunity to say their peace.

The ritual happens in two parts: The first part is to look your pet in their eyes and name what is happening. The second part is to read them notes written by everyone who loved this creature and would want to say goodbye to them. Consider asking another to help hold and witness you in this heartbreaking ritual—it's better to not grieve alone.

Prepare

Intentions

May I have the courage to acknowledge the ending that is happening with my beloved animal. May my heartbreak be a sign of my profound love for them. May I honor them by saying goodbye and letting them know how loved they are by so many.

You Will Need

- A candle and lighter
- The goodbye notes
- Tissues because the tears will flow

Gathering the Goodbyes

Make a list of all those who had a connection with your animal throughout their life. They don't have to live close by. The only prerequisite is that when your pet dies, they will be among those who miss them.

This can be done on the phone, in email, or, gasp, by written letter. Let your friends and family know that your animal is in their last days and that you are collecting notes that will be read to your animal the day of their departure. Ask them to, within their letter, say goodbye to the animal and maybe share a meaningful memory of their time with them.

Compile the collection of letters by printing them out or having them in a document on your phone.

When

Imagine you want to have a heart-to-heart talk with your spouse or your child about something important or emotional. Perhaps it's obvious when it is *not* a good time to have this talk: right before they go to school, while they are watching TV, or when they are in the middle of doing work. Maybe you even give them a heads-up that you want to have this conversation when the time is right.

With your pet, the right time is a quiet time. It could be on a walk or when you are lying down together. This time needs space for care and reflection.

Begin

If you are indoors, begin by lighting a candle and sitting on the floor with your animal friend. If you are on a walk, consider the moment you leave the home the beginning of the ritual.

Either way, you can enter the ritual in silence or by singing a song to them that is familiar. For instance, every time I gave Rudy a bath, which she absolutely hated, I would sing her "Edelweiss" from *The Sound of Music* to calm her down. This became our song, which I sang on her deathbed.

Whenever you feel ready, kneel, squat, or lie down with your animal friend so that you are face-to-face. However you do it, be sure to look them in the eyes.

Take your time getting there, but when you're ready, name what is happening. Perhaps you want to express to your animal your hesitation to say this or how much you can't imagine living without them. But eventually the words "You are dying" must be spoken. I like to imagine that the animal already knows this, and that these words are more for you to hear and feel their resonance.

Let the next words you say be "You are so loved." Take out the letters and read out loud all the love, blessings, and goodbyes that so many wrote to your animal friend.

Conclude

Conclude this ritual by expressing in your own words your love for your animal friend while petting or nestling them. Let your grief be met with touch, which can be a comfort to them and you.

If you decide to print the goodbye letters that were written to your animal, you can ritually release them. Burning them in a fireplace or with a candle is a good way to let them go. If you are burying your animal, you can bury them with all the letters. Or if you'd like to keep them, make a memorial scrapbook of all the goodbyes so that you can look back on them years later and remember how much love gathered around your friend in their departure.

Questions for Further Reflection

- Why is saying goodbye necessary?
- What happens when I acknowledge what is happening?
- How does "saying it out loud" impact my love for this animal?

- What gift does it give me, my animal friend, and my community to allow others to express their love and heartbreak?

For the Time After

Grieving your animal takes time. And the grief that comes with their death might look very different days after versus months or even years after. Grief is our capacity to express love in the presence of loss and is conveyed differently depending on how close we are to that loss. Let the time after be a time to slow down, do less, be supported more, and let your grief speak, for that is also the love for your animal friend speaking.

THE CUTTING *the* COLLAR RITUAL

One of the hardest realities while grieving is to be alone in it. Your entire life has changed, and yet, in some ways, you are expected to continue on with the everydayness of life as if nothing has changed. This is true even more so with the loss of an animal. If an American worker only gets three days off to mourn the death of a family member, how much time off do you think an employer would give to mourn the death of a worker's pet? When my dog died, I had a flight scheduled for the following day that needed to be canceled. I called the airline and spoke to a customer care representative who told me, "Unfortunately, refunds are subject only to the death of an immediate family member." "But," I said, "you don't understand. My dog *is* my immediate family member!" And so, this dichotomy reinforces a heartbreaking struggle to carry the burden of your grief amid a greater cultural narrative that tells you: It's only an animal—get over it.

What we need in these moments are tangible reminders that allow us to navigate our "normal lives" by helping us remember we are still grieving.

Rending clothing is an old custom that is instrumental in both expressing grief and helping us remember that we are grieving. For example, in Judaism there is a tradition called *keriah*, which is the ritualized tearing of clothing, inspired by stories in the Bible of people rending their garments upon hearing of the death of a beloved. In ancient Greek burial rites called *prothesis*, women would ritually tear at their hair and clothing to mark the vivid anguish and grief they felt when witnessing a death. This custom of tearing, ripping, and cutting clothing at the moment that one learns of a death is a way of outwardly expressing inner pain and symbolizes the unmendable tear that this loss has left in our hearts. As Menachem HaMeiri, the Provençal rabbi, says so profoundly: "When the garments are rent, the hearts will be rent."[*]

The tearing also serves as an outward acknowledgment of the emotional state of the bereaved. The torn garment can communicate to people that understand the meaning that this person is grieving. But it also serves as a conversation starter. When my father died, I tore his clothing (the cuffs from one of his suits) and wore the scrap on my jacket, like a ribbon over my heart. It often would pique the curiosity of people unfamiliar with this ritual, which led to sharing about my dad, and consequently, I got to remember him. Wearing a symbol that reminded me of my grief, as well, allowed others to acknowledge it and let me carry my broken heart while carrying on with my life.

There are few objects that connect us more literally to our animals than a leash or collar. Especially for those of us with dogs, the leash represents attachment and security, but even collars on cats are functional reminders of a sense of belonging. In the days after Rudy died, her leash just sat there, untouched. Something that was so integrated into my every day became so immediately irrelevant and reminded me how my daily routines had vastly changed. Rather than throwing out the leash, I had an idea to cut the cord as a ritual of letting go.

Prepare

Intentions

May this ritual acknowledge the end of this daily routine of caring for my animal friend. May I continue to hold them in my heart but also let them go. May the torn leash or collar become a symbol of my grief and love as I remember them in the days after they are gone.

---

[*] Samuel C. Heilman, *When a Jew Dies: The Ethnography of a Bereaved Son* (Berkeley: University of California Press, 2001).

You Will Need
- Your animal's leash or collar
- A pair of scissors
- A safety pin
- A box of tissues

This can be done alone or with others—whatever seems the most comforting to you.

Begin

Step 1: Remember
Hold the leash or collar to your heart, close your eyes, and take a breath.

Rub your fingers along the leash/collar and feel the wear and tear made on the material.

Quiet your mind and allow the memories of time with your animal to surface.

Share out loud some stories of times you felt connected to your animal.

Step 2: Cut
Hold the scissors.

Acknowledge what you are letting go of.

If you need a prompt, you can say: "I love you, _____. I miss our time together so much. This leash/collar has bound us together for many years. And while you will always be woven into my heart, our daily life and routines have ended. To symbolize this, I will cut your leash/collar."

Cut the leash/collar.

Step 3: Wear
Pause. Let this moment linger. Feel the severity and finality of it. Let whatever grief that arises be heard as your song of love for your companion.

If needed, cut the leash/collar again so that you have something the size of a two- to three-inch ribbon, preferably with the clip intact.

Clip or safety pin the leash/collar ribbon to your coat, jacket, or shirt—right over the heart.

Let this sacred accessory serve as a reminder to you and/or a conversation starter with others, to remember your companion as the days carry on.

Conclude

What was once an object that bound your animal to you now binds you to your animal. And as your grief changes or lessens, feel free to put on or take off this symbol of mourning. While I no longer wear my dog Rudy's cut leash, I do keep it on my home altar and adorn my jacket with it every year on the anniversary of her death.

Questions for Further Reflection

- How did I feel when I cut the leash or collar?
- How does this ritual presence my grief, both for myself and for others?
- What does wearing a reminder of the loss of my animal let me remember?

Miscarriage

There is no greater agony
than bearing an untold story inside you.

—Maya Angelou

The hope. The devastation. And perhaps the isolation. Miscarriage is a kind of loss shrouded in secrecy. Those precious and vulnerable early weeks of pregnancy begin so uncertainly—a mixture of excitement, caution, happiness, withholding. If this is your first, the dream of parenthood starts to become real, and as the weeks continue, you inch closer and closer to passing that twelve-week "safe zone." But then something happens. There's blood. There's cramping. There's a doctor's visit. For some, there's the intuition that the miscarriage is happening, and for others, perhaps a sonographer or doctor delivers the news: "I'm sorry. There's no heartbeat." And then comes the grief.

In our modern culture, a miscarriage isn't spoken of as a big loss. Actually, it's hardly spoken of at all. Life is just expected to carry on as usual. But the perceived shame and isolation, the loss that weighs on the heart, and the toll it takes on partnerships—all lead to unexpressed grief. But how to uncloak this grief and mark this moment with support, connection, and resilience? Could it be that there is something needed from you, whether you are the person who miscarried or the partner who bore witness, that expresses the deep and complex feelings that come with touching new life ever so slightly? What are ways to honor, acknowledge, and express the grief of, as a young woman remarked, "having lost something, or should I say someone, you never really knew."

Out of the many interviews I had with people who had miscarried, one in particular stood out. Even before I could ask my first question, Lilli jumped in with "Why do women keep this quiet?" I paused. I could sense there was something she wanted to say that had been simmering for some time. "Seriously, this befuddles me. Why do people obey this crazy rule that says 'keep it secret and safe' until after the first trimester? Why are we setting ourselves up to be alone if we miscarry?" She continued: "Ask yourself, after all the interviews you have done with people sharing about their miscarriages, have you ever once questioned this 'don't share until after the twelfth week' rule?"

She was right. I must have spoken to and listened to stories of at least thirty people who had "suffered" a miscarriage, and every one of them, whether they followed it or not, mentioned this "safe zone" rule, yet it never once crossed my mind to question it. But now it did. Lilli continued, "I had a miscarriage after my son was born. I was in my late thirties and I knew that a miscarriage was likely because the statistic is that one in four women have one. I thought: If I go through this, I want to be able to call my friends and family for support. I want to say to them: 'If I've been pregnant for twelve weeks, you've been pregnant with me for twelve weeks. And, if I have a miscarriage, you are going to feel the loss in the way I feel the loss.' Then, I don't have to carry my pain alone."

Our conversation left me wondering why the common advice trades in safety. While I understand that the statistics for miscarriage are greatly reduced after the first trimester, why is it advised to keep it quiet until "it's safe" and what does "safe" even mean? It seems to me that "safe" is another way of keeping the possibility of death quiet. This myth of safety within our dominant culture is death-phobia in action, which leaves us woefully unprepared for it when it does happen. And what is the consequence of keeping quiet due to fearing the worst? What I kept returning to after this one interview was how isolated everyone is in the face of life's uncertainties, especially in those early days of pregnancy and possible miscarriage. And how this modern culture subtly and not so subtly encourages us to keep our fear of death to ourselves and to suffer our losses and grief in isolation.

It wasn't always like this. Historically, death was very much a part of the experience of giving birth and raising children. In the last two millennia, on average a quarter of the world's newborns died in their first year of life and half died in their childhood,[*] an unsettling statistic that drastically lowered over the course of only the

---

* "Infant Mortality," Wikipedia, https://en.wikipedia.org/wiki/Infant_mortality.

last hundred years. But because so many families lost infants and children to diseases, there was reasonably less of a focus given to the loss of early pregnancies up until very recently. But all of that changed.

In the book *The Myth of the Perfect Pregnancy: A History of Miscarriage in America*, author Lara Freidenfelds questions something we assume is so normal: "How did early pregnancy loss become an experience that many women find devastating?"* Her research suggests that this is a rather new phenomenon. Due to modern technological and medical innovations, from birth control to infertility treatments and cesarean sections, parents have been provided with "an unrealistic expectation of near-perfect control of conception and pregnancy outcomes." In other words, new parents went from pregnancy and childbirth being completely out of their control—pregnancy was an act of providence and a baby surviving was most certainly not a guaranteed thing—to thinking that pregnancy and childbirth were fully in their control. If you only try hard enough, plan perfectly enough, buy the right products, eat the right foods, set the right intentions, and do all the right things, you can have a perfect pregnancy and baby. Miscarriage, then, is evidence of what lies outside of our control. and the cost of this kind of thinking can be feelings of failure.

Modern life is addicted to competency. There's a pervasive sense of always needing to be on, to get it right, to be satisfied and successful. Just look at social media, which is chock-full of examples of people who appear to constantly be winning at life. You would have to dig deep to find personal stories of the real messiness of loss, because we are told to value winners and demote losers, to praise success and to hide failures. So when we come up against life not working out the way we prefer and things being completely out of our control, there's enormous shame that accompanies this loss. Shame that says "You should have done better" or "You fucked it up" or "You waited too long"—in other words, it's your fault.

In the case of miscarriage, this shame-based thinking says that not only has the pregnancy gone bad but you yourself did something wrong—as if your own body failed you. One woman revealed: "I've lost faith in my body. It lied to me. I was almost out of the danger zone and it betrayed me." Another brave woman I interviewed spoke of her inner shame. "I felt like I was not fertile and there was something deeply wrong with me." Even the etymology of the word "miscarriage," dating as far back as the

---

* Lara Freidenfeld, *The Myth of the Perfect Pregnancy: A History of Miscarriage in America* (New York: Oxford University Press, 2020).

1580s, conjures images of mistakes, misbehaviors, and a perverse course of conduct that continues to spin a shameful tale that this is the woman's fault, her body's failure, or that it shouldn't have been this way.

The weight of "wrongness" can be a burden for the non-pregnant partners too. Many of the partners I spoke to struggled with their own feelings of uselessness and powerlessness. Their fear that they were overreacting or that their grief wasn't legitimate kept them suffering in silence. Graham, one of the cis men I interviewed, was on the verge of tears sharing his gratitude that his wife was well resourced and supported during her miscarriage, while also lamenting his own aloneness and invisibility during that time: "I felt a lot of shame and reluctance to talk about it, and [was] very lonely inside of this. I wanted this loss to feel real and valid. Especially as a man who didn't carry the child, it's easy to say I didn't lose anything. But I did lose something. Even though it's invisible, I lost the dream of what it means to be a dad."

A miscarriage can feel like an invisible loss—losing something so immensely present and simultaneously so unseen. A feeling of it being here but not here. The term for this, "ambiguous loss,"* was coined by Dr. Pauline Boss and refers to a kind of loss that lacks closure or logical understanding. So much loss has a tangible, knowable element to it. You can see it, feel it, and understand what's missing. But ambiguous loss is illogical, hard to grasp, and often difficult to even name. Miscarriage is an ambiguous loss because there is so little physical evidence of a pregnancy—maybe a sonogram or a pregnancy test—but psychologically, it's very present.

Most of us like things to have easily answerable questions, clear linear processes, and a defined resolution. This is true even for grief, where there are said to be steps and stages that end in acceptance and an eventual cessation of grieving, showcasing the underbelly of our culture's addiction to mastery and problem solving. But ambiguous loss is a complicated loss and a complicated grief. There is no straight-line, easy solution or perfect fix.

Ultimately, according to Boss, "the only way to live with ambiguous loss is to hold two opposing ideas in your mind at the same time."† For instance, "I lost the baby *and* the baby is still with me," or "The pregnancy wasn't viable *and* it was exactly what it

---

* Pauline Boss, *Ambiguous Loss: Learning to Live with Unresolved Grief* (Cambridge, MA: Harvard University Press, 1999).
† Krista Tippett, "Pauline Boss: Navigating Loss Without Closure," in *On Being with Krista Tippett*, podcast, June 23, 2016, https://onbeing.org/programs/pauline-boss-navigating-loss-without-closure/.

needed to be," or "This has been an incredibly painful experience *and* I/we have found resilience and depth within it." This is the skill of ambivalence born from ambiguity. And when practicing this skill, which resists either/or thinking and promotes both/ and thinking, we strengthen our capacity for resilience in the face of loss. Because ambiguity often feels purposeless, hopeless, and meaningless, creating meaning from these losses is what give us a sense of grounding and understanding when we feel there isn't any. Author Viktor Frankl puts it succinctly in *Man's Search for Meaning*: "If there is meaning in life at all, then there must be meaning in suffering."* In other words, this loss might make no sense and seem meaningless, but instead of trying to get over it or suppress it, what if we conjured the courage and resilience to make meaning from our grief—a way to transform the ambiguous pain and loss into beauty and understanding?

I interviewed Jodi, a cis woman in her early forties, who spoke about her second miscarriage as a "beautiful sorrow." She said there was so much grief and so much beauty in her experience. When she was bleeding and going through the pains of miscarriage, she went down to the creek near her home, held her partner's hand, and said, "This is what it's going to be like when I give birth." She was simultaneously holding the experience of both death *and* birth. Weeks later, Jodi turned to ritual as a way to access her grief and bring it forward instead of hiding in isolation and pretending she was okay. She invited two of her best friends to sit around a fire to witness her story, sing songs, and pray with her. Ritualizing this moment offered Jodi a way to be acknowledged in her grief, to metabolize her pain, to make sense of her suffering, and to orient toward a deeper wisdom.

Ritual can bring us back into connection with the Earth and life's ever-flowing movement between birth and death, over and over again. Ritualizing our losses lets us strengthen our capacity to simultaneously carry sorrow *and* gratitude, pain *and* beauty, power *and* powerlessness—to say hello *and* goodbye meaningfully. Ritual calls us back to our broken hearts, our community, the greater-than-human world, and our sense of belonging to something vast and utterly mysterious.

---

* Viktor E. Frankl, *Man's Search for Meaning: An Introduction to Logotherapy* (New York: Simon & Schuster, 1984).

THE BUNDLE RITUAL

The purpose of the Bundle Ritual is to both give your grief space to exist and be witnessed while also making this loss more tangible and meaningful. Bundles are often associated with pregnancies, like the myth of the stork carrying a baby bundle, and are also traditionally held within Indigenous and First Nations communities of North America as a collection of sacred items that have been gathered together or been given. When my ancestors were forced out of their homes in Eastern Europe, they also carried bundles of their treasured objects in order to start a new life in a new country.

The Bundle Ritual below asks you to create a bundle of material that symbolically represents all you loved and lost from this pregnancy and to bury it in the ground as a way of making meaning from what might appear meaningless.

The ritual is not a solution. It does not guarantee any kind of success, release, or reward. In fact, it is just a faint remembering of how else it could be. How a sorrowful experience could also be marked as a moment of slowing down, gathering support, being witnessed, opening up, remembering how precious life is, and how small your place is in the grand scheme of things. This ritual is there for you to use, to be inspired from, or to completely toss out and try something else. But it is pleading for you to not let this loss go unmarked, unrecognized, resisted, or disrespected. Rather, this ritual is a way to practice the braided skills of grief and love within our very human experience.

Prepare

Intentions

May I acknowledge what is and is not in my control. May I practice allowing contradictory truths to be true. May I tangibly mark this moment in order to build resiliency after this pregnancy loss.

You Will Need

- A two-foot by two-foot piece of fabric
- Ten feet of string to wrap the bundle
- One trowel
- A variety of objects (see below)
- A pitcher of water

A Note About Witnesses

This ritual should not be done alone. While it can be done between partners, I encourage you to have at least one or two trusted friends present. Having non-grieving witnesses allows you to be held, seen, and honored in your experience without having to tend to anyone else's grief. Plus, when we are witnessed in our grief and loss, it becomes more valid and real.

Where

Because this ritual involves a burial, consider doing it somewhere where you can dig into the earth that's also a place you can return to. Often with an ambiguous loss like this it is helpful to have a place that holds the loss, like a memorial or cemetery, where you can, for example, come back and touch base with the memory of this baby.

This ritual can be done in the absence of a body, as the bundle can represent the body itself. However, if you would like to incorporate the presence of the fetus or blood into the bundle, this ritual can allow for that.

The Gathered Material

The material for this bundle tells a story. Each item you choose for the bundle will be imbued with meaning and symbolism—objects that describe an experience or feeling. The categories below are points of reflection and inspiration—feel free to collect all or some of them, or even make up new ones. Since you will be burying the bundle, consider choosing material that is biodegradable. For example, when searching for "something that symbolizes your ability to recover and be resilient," you could choose a leaf from a succulent plant, like aloe vera, as these plants thrive in difficult situations, especially when there is a lack of water.

There is no right way to do this. Employ your imagination and creativity!

Item 1:
Something to symbolize the journey to become pregnant.

Item 2:
Something to symbolize the feeling when you found out you were pregnant.

Item 3:
Something to symbolize what this pregnancy meant to you.

Item 4:
Something to symbolize what this miscarriage meant to you.

Item 5:
Something to symbolize all the unanswered questions.

Item 6:
Something to symbolize what you have learned or discovered.

Item 7:
Something to symbolize courage in the face of suffering.

Item 8:
Something to symbolize how your relationship has changed.

Item 9:
Something to symbolize your relationship with uncertainty.

Item 10:
Something to symbolize your ability to recover and be resilient.

Begin

Don't rush into this. Let everyone arrive and let small talk bubble up, like soda bubbles releasing. Eventually, the mood will change on its own.

First things first: Ritual loves a beautiful and slow transition. Either through silence, song, or poetry, shift into the ritual intentionally. Even a simple and collective breath will do.

Then speak the intention. Name why everyone is here. What are you here to do? Try to give clear words to your purpose. Proclaiming the intention can help sanctify the moment and distinguish it.

Laying Out the Bundle

Lay down the fabric cloth. You will be placing the material on top of it, either on its own or surrounding the body. Again, there is no right way to do this, but consider arranging the material beautifully. How you place the material informs the ritual as much as what you place.

Go through each item, one by one, using it as a prompt to tell your story. Each of these items might conjure feelings, hopes, dreams, loss, memory, and longing. But speaking about these things out loud, in the presence of others, you are telling the story that needs to be told. You are, to paraphrase Maya Angelou, telling the untold story within you.

A Full Bundle

Once you have gone through and laid out each item, spoken your story, and said all that needs to be said, it is time to wrap the bundle.

Each corner of the fabric can represent one of the four directions—north, east, south, and west—as a way to center you and this bundle. As you bring those directions to the center of the fabric, you can see this as a symbolic way of returning to your center, amid the uncertainty and loss.

Continue to fold the bundle until it's tightly bound, small enough to be buried, and wrap the bundle with the string.

With each wrap of the string around the bundle, say goodbye. There might be many, many goodbyes here. If there is a partner, do this together.

The Hole

Take the trowel and dig a small hole.

Take a breath. Don't put the bundle in the hole just yet. Witness the absence of things within the hole and don't rush to cover it up so quickly.

Then place the bundle within the hole. Consider saying one last goodbye before filling it.

As you cover the bundle, you can do so in silence or in song.

And, of course, wet the earth with tears if they come.

Conclude

Washing

Within my Jewish tradition, it is proper to wash your hands after a burial and/or leaving a cemetery, to repel bad spirits, purify the body, and remember the soothing, healing power of water.

The witnesses can take the pitcher of water and pour it over your hands, letting the water bring renewal, comfort, and healing.

Conclude with either a breath, a song, or simply with gratitude.

Optional: Months Later

Living with grief is consuming at first—the oscillation of ups and downs. But as time goes on, the ebb and flow of our grief might lessen and we can begin to turn our attention to healing, hope, and peace. Sometimes this asks us to transform our old dreams of how we wanted things to be into new dreams, deeply informed by our journey with uncertainty, loss, and resilience.

After some time, whenever feels right for you (and your partner, if there is one involved), gather together materials for a second smaller bundle. This will be your New Dream bundle. This bundle will live in your home, on your altar, or wherever you keep your special, sacred things.

This is similar to the first bundle, but fill this one with material that symbolizes new questions, new dreams, and new realities.

Here are some ideas to inspire material:

1. Something that symbolizes your renewed vision for family
2. Something that symbolizes what you've learned from this journey
3. Something that symbolizes how your relationship with yourself or your partner has changed
4. Something that symbolizes what you are recommitting to
5. Something that symbolizes gratitude

Wrap this bundle up while saying hello to this new vision for family, and for your longing and continued resilience.

Questions for Further Reflection

- What does this loss mean to me?
- How does it feel to be acknowledged for my loss and grief?
- What is my experience with holding two contradictory realities at once? Loss and love? Pain and gratitude?
- How does ritualizing this loss help to bring understanding?
- What have I come to learn from this journey through miscarriage?

Aging Childless

Every great loss demands that we choose life again.
We need to grieve in order to do this. The pain we have not
grieved over will always stand between us and life.

—Rachel Naomi Remen

It's ending. The window is closing or, in fact, has shut. The idea of becoming a parent is being put to rest. Whether by choice or circumstance, willfully or unwillfully, you are coming to terms with the idea that you will never become a mother or father in this lifetime. Maybe for some this decision came easily and with relief. You never wanted children in the first place and might even feel joyful and grateful for the opportunity to age childless. It means more time to pursue your career, to travel—to say yes to everything you've wanted to say yes to. But for those women and men who have longed for children, have felt their hearts tug at the idea of becoming a parent, and have watched the years pass without them, this realization can be laden with a feeling of loss—an ambiguous kind of loss. Not just the loss of a dream that never materialized but also the loss of an imagined identity. And because there is no evidence that something is missing, no date that announces "this isn't happening," it could be that this time is accompanied by a disenfranchised grief that isn't validated or considered worthy by our friends or family. So then, what would it look like to bring attention to this threshold? To acknowledge that, in fact, "this is happening." And through the grief, to reclaim our own worth and wholeness from a culture that places enormous value on the family.

"I'm old goods." This is how Jessica, one of the cis women I interviewed, considered herself after turning thirty-five years old. She was in a partnership at the time with a man who came from a big family—five siblings and about twenty nieces and nephews. The father of his family encouraged all his children to have children, even tempting them with a "baby bonus" bribe to have many. Because she was someone who had never spent much time around young kids, this impressed Jessica. She was enchanted by the huge holidays, with tons of kids running around, and saw how much joy was built into the fabric of having a big family.

When she turned thirty-five years old, her partner revealed to her that he hadn't realized how old she was. It turned out that as a man, he wasn't concerned with his own biological clock, but he wanted many kids and an older partner just didn't fit into his vision of having a big family. "That devastated me. I never felt so judged by my age before and my ability to procreate."

This idea of having children is deeply ingrained in our culture and deeply informed by the time and place we live in. For example, during the Great Depression of the 1930s, money was a big reason not to have children. Almost 25 percent of women were childless at the time as families were penny-pinching and the lack of resources was enough reason not to have a baby. Of course, all of that changed in the USA after World War II and the advent of the Baby Boom as jobs, growth, patriotism, and family flooded the cultural consciousness, and "in an attempt to create jobs for returning soldiers, the US government urged women to go back to their previous roles of housewives."[*]

For women, having a baby wasn't just a personal choice, but a decision pressured by parents, expected by the culture, and rewarded by the government. And that changed again between the 1960s and 1980s, when the childless population skyrocketed to 25 percent, as women's (and LGBTQ) rights interrupted that *Leave It to Beaver* mindset and pioneered alternative lifestyles for people that were not centered on the idea of having a traditional family. Nowadays, in many parts of the world, young people are delaying their decision to marry and have kids, which results in a whopping one in four women who now age without children.[†] Even more

---

[*] Kyung Hee Lee, "Journey to Remain Childless: A Grounded Theory of the Decision-Making Process among Voluntarily Childless Couples," dissertation, August 2011, https://ttu-ir.tdl.org/bitstream/handle/2346/ETD-TTU-2011-08-1872/Lee_kyunghee_DissREVIEWED.pdf?sequence=3.

[†] "Statistics," Ageing Without Children, https://www.awwoc.org/statistics.

telling, there's now a growing contingent of people who feel a deep uncertainty and irresponsibility to bring a child into a world ever more impacted by climate change.

Bearing children is valued in our Western culture, where being childless comes with both an externally projected and internally possessed feeling of worthlessness. Barb, a cis woman in her late sixties, remembers her thirties, when she figured out that she didn't want children and also realized that she was not able to bear them. When she told her mother of the decision and circumstances, her mom cried and lamented that she had failed her daughter and that it was all her fault. Other childless cis women I interviewed were deemed less valuable by their families, written out of wills, and refused family heirlooms for not having achieved the role of mother. "My grandmother was a genealogist and among the rewards reserved only for wives and mothers was a copy of all the stories and records of my family. The insult of nonexistence unless married or with child goes so much deeper for those acculturated as women and I have a particular flavor of it being raised Mormon," said Kait.

Our sense of value is woven with the threads of how others see us and how we see ourselves. In the many interviews I had with childless cis women and cis men, questioning their identity was talked about as part and parcel of their struggle on this journey: *Without kids, what does it mean to be a woman? What does femininity look like when it's not informed by fertility and childbearing? What does it mean to be a man? What is expected of us as a couple? What does being "productive" or "fulfilled" actually mean?* When he was young, Barb's nephew asked her why she didn't have kids, and even though she explained to him that it "wasn't in the cards" and "I can't physically have them," she admitted to feeling like she was disappointing him by not fulfilling her function in the family and by not providing other nieces and nephews for him to play with. Years later at a wedding, while speaking to a friend about her decision to not have children, he surprisingly whispered, "While you never had any kids, you're a mother to many." Even after years of doubt, it soothed her heart to be seen as valuable and needed.

One of the most difficult and triggering moments I've had to encounter in many phone calls with my mother is when she asks, "When are you going to make me a grandmother?" This comment is a minefield of guilt, hope, pressure, identity, and longing, which is even more complicated by being a queer man not currently in a life partnership. While I have yet to "make the decision" to fulfill this lifelong dream, I can feel the under-acknowledged grief that I carry, built up over years of avoiding the choice, not fulfilling what's expected of me, feeling left out as my friends have kids, and, just as painful, not living up to what my culture believes to be my fullest potential. Many friends still try to include me in the club by refocusing my attention

on the future and saying things like "it'll happen" or "you're going to be the best dad."
But, because families and babies are prioritized, there isn't much attention given to
being presently childless. Actually, there is an invisiblizing of this which leaves many
of us with a disconnected intimacy toward our own grief—a grief that is hidden, unexpressed, and often felt as, both internally and externally, invalid.

It is easy to find meaning when there is something to point to and clearly see its
absence. To paraphrase ambiguous loss expert Dr. Pauline Boss, even death carries a
sense of certainty which allows opportunities for grief, mourning, and comfort.[*] But
being childless is ambiguous because it is loss without a face, without a story or moment that defines it. Instead, there is a coexistence of something absent with something very much present. In our modern culture that constantly demands evidence
for something to be real and worthy, the grief that may come with being childless
is a homeless grief, wandering in search of a place to be seen, to be heard, and to be
recognized as real.

When we can properly make a place for this grief to exist by acknowledging that
this transition is happening—that something monumental is ending while something
else is beginning—we can properly walk across this threshold, renewing our sense of
purpose and identity for what comes next.

Rebecca, who is in her late forties, said that while she doesn't necessarily have
grief about not having children, the deep grief she had faced was the realization that
"some things are just not going to happen." Having always been rather ambivalent
about having her own children, the choice was made for her when she went through
early menopause at age thirty-seven. "From then on I realized, I am no longer a child
and some things are not going to last forever. So I must make choices with what I want
the rest of my life to look like." In a way, the ending of her ambivalence brought her
closer to understanding the preciousness of her life and the need to be clear about
what she wanted her life force to be committed to from then on.

This is ritual's terrain. Ritual draws a line and demarcates an ending in order to
make it visible. It helps us come closer to the grief that may accompany the ambiguous
loss of being childless while also providing space to renew and recenter ourselves in a
reimagined identity. In a culture that demands either/or thinking, ritual allows both to
happen simultaneously: "I grieve that this isn't happening *and* I am still alive, creative,
and needed." And as our lives change, as certain dreams and choices that were once
available to us are no longer an option, marking these moments can allow us to relin-

---

[*] Boss, *Ambiguous Loss*.

quish who we thought we were or what we thought would be in order to step more clearly into who we are becoming.

And, most important, ritualizing this moment doesn't mean everything is going to be okay from now on. For many of us, it takes years to move through this loss, if at all. Ritual simply acknowledges an ending and a beginning at the same time. Just like a marriage doesn't end with a wedding, but rather begins with it, the ritual below is a way for you, and perhaps your community, to help bring this chapter and identity into being—reminding you and them that you are a beautiful, needed, and valuable childless human.

THE REFLECTION RITUAL

When there is a loss that is unclear, unseen, and has no resolution, the grief and need for understanding can find other ways to pop up and come out. When I interviewed Jessica, she spoke about still having dreams of being pregnant or having a daughter, years after she made the decision to remain childless. She said that she felt like her subconscious was creating stories in order to place the grief. "My mind is trying to create a person or a face that I can miss." She would wake up and think, *Wow, I had a daughter*, and then, she thought, *I guess this makes it a bit easier to grieve that loss*.

This ritual does not attempt to erase the ambiguous loss but rather offers a way to make meaning with its complexity. You are childless *and* needed. You are aging *and* beautiful. You have grief for what has not happened *and* have curiosity about what might transpire. Rather than denying the grief or coming to a premature closure that only focuses on what's next, this ritual makes room for both to occur. Its purpose is to make the ending seen, so that your grief can find its place, as well as making the beginning visible.

I once heard someone say to me that their idea of family is love multiplied. But "love multiplied" doesn't have to just translate to children. Walking the path of childless aging is to both acknowledge what didn't happen, while also acknowledging what is happening—to find and recognize the other outlets where you are called to direct that procreative life force. Beth, whom I quoted earlier, felt like she needed to both come to terms with life without children and also not take the rest of her life for granted. Her grief was accompanied by a fierce curiosity as to what else she wanted to do with her time: "That creative energy didn't leave me, it just didn't go into having children."

The Reflection Ritual has two stages: undressing and redressing. Each bit of clothing being taken off represents the loss of a dream and the stripping down of an identity associated with children and, if you're a cis woman or trans man, your childbearing years. And each bit of clothing or makeup put on represents a renewal of what a meaningful life means. The ritual concludes with a mirrored reflection that affirms your value, your purpose, your ambitions, and, especially, your attractiveness and beauty.

Having children is a very real way of leaving a legacy that may transcend your lifetime. When that door closes, there is still a purpose calling you forward that needs you to live for something beyond yourself and to recenter yourself within your life's legacy—a legacy of love. This ritual is devoted to supporting all the needed gifts you are birthing into the world.

Prepare

Intentions

May I acknowledge the end of one identity and the beginning of another. May I create a place for my grief to be witnessed without judgment. May I reaffirm and renew my purpose and path. May I witness my value, attractiveness, and needed-ness reflected back to me.

You Will Need

- Two sets of clothing and accessories
- Whatever you use to beautify yourself (makeup, oils, perfumes)
- A hand mirror
- A candle and lighter/matches
- Something sweet, like chocolate

Who

This ritual needs at least one other witness. What's most important is choosing one or more friends whom you trust, who can hold space for this ritual, and who can receive your vulnerability.

Also, as you consider choosing to mark this moment, there might be grief, hesitation, doubt, and fear that arises. One woman I spoke to said, "I can't be in charge of this. I need someone else to guide me to this moment." This is reasonable, and I advise asking a trusted friend to take the reins of organizing the ritual. While our modern culture relentlessly promotes competency and self-mastery, sometimes we just need someone else to take our hand and help us get over these difficult thresholds.

Beforehand

Because this ritual is about undressing and redressing, you should begin already dressed in one set of clothing. Consider wearing enough layers or accessories so that one can accompany each prompt below.

Also, this ritual does *not* require you to get naked. (Although, if that's in your comfort wheelhouse, go for it!) But as the ritual progresses, undress enough that you can access a physical vulnerability. By doing so, you are symbolically representing what this loss may feel like to you and letting it be witnessed by those gathered.

An Altar

Set up your materials beautifully—the clothing, the oils, the makeup, the water pitcher. By doing so, you are creating an altar and acknowledging the materials as ritualized and not everyday items.

This can be as simple as putting them with a candle on a piece of fabric on a table or floor. Or you can make something more elaborate with flowers or other natural material, photographs, or even beautiful notes.

Four Rounds

This ritual has four rounds:
1. The Undressing
2. The Cleansing
3. The Dressing
4. The Reflection

Rounds 1 and 3 are for you to do. Rounds 2 and 4 are for the witnesses to do.

Round 1: The Undressing

With each round, take as much time telling your stories as you need. Sometimes getting at the emotions within a story is like wringing out water from a wet cloth. We have to keep speaking to unearth the feelings underneath.

Each of the prompts below is just a jumping-off point to presence your story, your longing and grief. And each prompt ends with the removal of a different article of clothing. Use these prompts or make up your own.

Question 1: Begin by remembering this imagined identity.
What can you recall about your dream of becoming a parent. What were your hopes and longings? What excited you about the potential of having a baby? Tell these stories.
Remove something.

Question 2: Reflect on what changed.
When/how did you come to being childless? What happened? Was there a moment you realized this was happening? How did you feel? Tell these stories.
Remove something.

Question 3: Acknowledge your experience of not having children.
Did you feel any pressure to have kids? Any shame for not having them? Any regret? Jealously? Relief? Tell these stories.
Remove something.

Question 4: Speak to the loss and let the grief speak.
What do you feel you are letting go of? What are you saying goodbye to? What are you acknowledging isn't going to happen? Tell these stories.
Remove something.

Question 5: Name the fear, if there is any.
What does being childless leave you unsure of? What feels unknown and scary? Do you fear being forgotten or unneeded? Tell these stories.
Remove something.
If there are more stories, feelings, longings to speak to, keep going.

Round 2: The Cleansing

The witnesses take the water pitcher and gently wash the hands and feet of the person grieving. This can be done in silence, in song, or with simple words that acknowledge "I hear you," "I understand," or "I'm sorry." Most important is that this is a physical act that expresses care, cleansing, and renewal.

Round 3: The Dressing

This round is devoted to proclaiming the alternative route you are taking and that you are needed and beautiful.

Each of the prompts below has you beautifying yourself with a different article of clothing, oil, or makeup. You can dress yourself, or if you want to really be pampered, allow another to dress you.

Question 1: Begin with forgiveness.
You didn't do anything wrong. What needs to be forgiven? What parts of yourself or others need your compassion and kindness? What bits of you need some extra TLC? Name this.
Put something on.

Question 2: Acknowledge where you need support.
None of us can do this alone. Where do you need help? How can others show up in service to your life? Name this.
Put something on.

Question 3: Next, speak the gifts you've been tending.
What have you given birth to? What are you tending in your life? What do you feel responsible for or accomplished in? This can either be people or projects. Name this.
Put something on.

Question 4: Reaffirm your commitments.
Where are you needed in your community? In the world? To what are you devoting yourself? What are you saying yes to? Make some vows toward what needs you next. Name this.
Put something on.

Question 5: Reclaim pleasure and beauty.

Can you acknowledge your beauty? What is a new identity you are proclaiming? What are you celebrating? What do you value about your body? About your life? Name this.

Put something on.

Again, if there are more stories, moments of gratitude, or love to share, you keep going!

Round 4: The Reflection

Have a witness take the mirror off the altar and hold it up to you.

The witness should ask you the question: "What do you see?" You can speak to reflections, affirmations, reminders of how needed you are.

If there is more than one witness, pass the mirror around and repeat.

Let yourself surrender and receive the reflections of how you are seen as whole, valuable, and needed, especially in this next phase of your life.

Conclude

As with most rituals, it is good to conclude in gratitude, in silence, or in song. Let the grief and the joy mingle in this moment. The loss *and* the gain. The pain *and* the beauty. A proper marking of what didn't happen *and* what is happening right then and there.

Blow out the candle. And finish this ritual with that something sweet.

Questions for Further Reflection

- What has changed? What am I acknowledging is ending? What is now beginning?
- What is this ritual helping me remember and recognize?
- What does wholeness mean to me?
- What is required for me to feel whole here?

Divorce

Heartbreak asks us not to look for an alternative path,
because there is no alternative path. It is an introduction to
what we love and have loved, an inescapable and often beautiful
question, something and someone that has been with us all
along, asking us to be ready to let go of the way we are holding
things, and preparation perhaps for the last letting go of all.

—David Whyte

Undoing the entanglement. Maybe you've been together for years or even decades. Perhaps you live together, have children together, share a bank account, friends, a last name together. It may be that you can't imagine this person not in your life or you can't wait until they are out of it, or both. Depending on the time in, perchance you don't even know yourself anymore, independent of this other half. The way of life and living have tied you together over and over again, into something quite knotted and tangled. And here you are at this wrecked, necessary moment of divergence and endings. Whether or not it was your choice, the path separates, and you must carry on separately.

If only it could be that easy.

So many cords still bind you, so many ways and things and people overlap you and them. So what do you do to get unbound? How do you untangle your heart, your body, your things from the mired mess that comes with coupling? And in the wretched work that is endings, what needs your attention? What is pleading with you to not turn away from but to turn toward, so you can put this relationship down and untie the knot?

During my research to write this chapter, I interviewed two dozen divorced people, and what became crystal clear was that there are that many ways to end a relationship. I spoke with a seventy-year-old cis man who had four marriages and four divorces. I spoke with a twenty-eight-year-old cis woman who'd been married and divorced by her twenty-fifth birthday. And I reconnected with a divorced couple whose marriage I'd officiated over a decade ago, which ended seven years after it began. And others, many others. Each severance had its own unique, sad story, and some of the stories were still unfolding as I wrote this. A good friend I spoke to, who has been divorced for years, revealed to me that "even though we are divorced, I'm still not ready to say it's over. In reality, we are entangled forever."

There were some I interviewed who got as far away from their exes as fast as they possibly could, while others couldn't, even if they wanted to, because of the children they were raising together. Karina, a dear friend, spoke to me of the "ground zero" she hit while going through this process: "I felt like there wasn't any other place beneath that where I could go. I really felt at that point that I had lost everything. All my health, all my dreams, my love and the level of despair was so intense that I eventually got to a place where I felt there was absolutely nothing more to lose. I had already lost everything. Moving forward, I realized how fragile it all is in every way. I didn't have this false sense of permanence anymore." However each story unfolds, it seems to me that amid the chasm, the pain, the breaking open, despair, darkness, and uncertainty, there's a question that emerges about endings. Specifically, what does it mean to participate in ending something, in putting it fully down, and even more so, what does it take to do that skillfully?

The beginning of every marriage fuses in ceremony. In our modern culture, often devoid of real ways to make meaning, a wedding is actually one of the few life events that still carries some ceremonial heft. It has ceremonial objects, a ceremonial dress, the ceremonial leader, and the ceremonial witnesses. At Jewish weddings there is specific ritual choreography called *hakafot* that has the bride circle the groom seven times, the blessing and drinking of the wine, and the seven blessings, which all culminate with the groom smashing a glass. The movements in a wedding, especially the repetitive motions like the circling, are a forging of sorts. The ceremony serves as a fire that heats and hammers the couple together under the pressure of witness and commitment. Even the folk etymology of the word "wedlock" speaks to an association with fastening, securing, and fusing. So, if a well-wrought ritual fuses the couple together, could it be that it requires a similar heat, pressure, and alchemy to unfuse it? What if the very thing that began in ritual needed some kind of ritual to undo it?

The thing is, divorce happens with or without ritual. There are certain functional and practical milestones that appear to carry a ritualistic function: the last couples' therapy session, packing the home, signing the divorce papers. Each of these conjures a new ending and further undoes the coupling, but what distinguishes them from ritual is that they happen, more often than not, alone. Divorce, like death, can be a very isolating process. It not only splits the couple in half but also divides friendships and communities. One of the divorced women I interviewed asked her ex to stop attending their mutual friend's parties because it had been "her community first." The isolation within divorce also occurs because endings are messy—emotionally, domestically, financially—and it's easier and more convenient to keep them confined.

This is further compounded by our collective compulsion to publicly acknowledge success and privately mitigate failure. With divorces, something that began in witness often ends in withdrawal. I interviewed Ian, who noted about his divorce that "what began as a celebration with many eyes, ended with the stroke of a pen in an office with bad lighting." The community that gathers together to testify to the vows of "in sickness and in health, till death do us part," is conspicuously absent in the releasing of those vows. Most likely, the ending of the marriage is hidden, and the de-unionizing goes unwitnessed.

Here's the thing: You need witnesses for endings just as much as you do for beginnings. Some thresholds are just too hard to cross alone. When the couple I married was considering divorce, I sat down with them around a fire in their backyard with the question "Is it time to end this?" They both had still not made the decision to do it and were desperately trying to find any way around it. This question brought them face-to-face with a choice. As the fire crackled and burned, I listened to them turn it over and over—they spoke of their anger, their blame, their grief, and their fear at what comes next. They went back and forth through the night until the fire died down into shimmering coals, casting a faint light on our tear-streaked faces. The story doesn't end with any neat resolve. We all went to bed that night heartbroken, but in retrospect, my presence and questioning helped to plant a seed for what needed to be done.

Witnessing an ending is the act of staying with it. The author Báyò Akómoláfé ingeniously calls this "with-nessing." This takes an unflagging focus, an unwillingness to turn away, and a gut-wrenching kind of compassion. The kind that says, "Even though this is ugly and uncomfortable, we are seeing this through, we are seeing this done faithfully." Another way of saying it is "staying with the trouble," a phrase coined by ecofeminist author Donna Haraway. The capacity to unflinchingly "stay with" is the true function of witnessing.

These rituals advocate for such a thing. It's not about gathering together the same group of a hundred people that witnessed the wedding, although that could be powerful. Actually, it could just be one other person, as with the fire story. What's more important than how many witnesses is the quality of witnessing. Just like a beginning, endings are disorienting, overwhelming, and quite vulnerable. Every day can feel like an emotional shit storm where you're just trying to get through it. Having witnesses to listen and steady you so that you don't have to cross that threshold alone can be essential to a good ending. It's interesting to consider that the word "witness" contains the word "wit," meaning "intelligence, capacity, sharpness, and cleverness." In other words, the function of the witness is to be the clear-sighted one because being confused is part and parcel to the experience of an ending.

Further, endings are mysterious. They bring us humbly face-to-face with uncertainty. They remind us that what was once so clearly in our grasp isn't anymore. And they ask of us, whether or not we're ready, to loosen our grip and let go. To trust that we can do that may be one of the most challenging aspects of divorce, because we honestly don't know what lies ahead when we do let go. We don't know the relationships that will survive, the places we'll live, or the person we'll become. Instead, divorce simply asks us to cut the cord and trust that this leap of faith will have an outcome in service to a new, unknown, and necessary life.

Cutting the cord is final. Therefore, it's understandable to want to prolong endings, because they also bring you face-to-face with everything you loved and are losing. While some couples attempt to be friends after, others elongate the divorce process so as not to fully let the relationship go. But letting an ending linger too long can often just elongate the pain and suffering. In a way, it can become like a zombie relationship, not alive but not completely dead. A seventy-year-old gentleman, Nigel, who had been through four divorces in his lifetime, refers to the lingering ending as a Gordian knot, a legendary knot that is so tangled, it's impossible to untie. The only way, he says, is to get your sharpest sword and "cut it clean and good." While this might leave your entrails hanging out, it can also be the most loving and compassionate way to end something. And while it is possible to do this alone, having a witness with you in this cutting lets it be real and complete. There is no going back after that. Having an ending marked and witnessed lets time heal the wound and allows the potential for something new to be born from the ashes.

What follows are two rituals, one to do as a couple and one to do solo. Some divorcing couples are capable of still coming together amicably. If this isn't you, don't sweat it. There is no contest for the ideal divorce ritual. If you do want to do something together that would mark this moment, before you begin I encourage you to ask yourself whether this is the right time for this ritual.

If you're in the heat of the actual divorce and there are still strong grievances between you and your ex, consider coming back to this ritual at another time, maybe even years later. This ritual will ask vulnerable questions of and for a generosity toward both of you. Yet with active grievances, it becomes too easy to weaponize those questions and brandish them into more hurt and pain, which is not the point or purpose of this ritual. Be realistic about what you both are capable of doing together and doing apart.

My Friends Are Divorcing

If you are not currently going through a divorce but have still found your way here, I want to ask something of you. Too often we put the burden of a ritual onto those that need it, as if that is something they should ask for. But this may be too much to require of someone divorcing. It's such an emotional struggle that sometimes they are just barely able to get through the day. If you do know a couple divorcing, consider your role—what can you offer them? While these rituals below are meant for the divorcing couple, they are even more effective when brought to them by a friend and witness. That can be you!

THE UNBINDING RITUAL:
With the Ex-Couple

Vows are different than promises. A promise is an assurance about what will occur in the future. "I promise that I will . . . " is often the statement of future intention. Vows, however, are declarations chiseled in the present moment, and they carry the weight of happening in real time. You make a vow during a wedding ceremony, not a promise, because you are committing in the present moment.

Therefore, undoing a vow is also not something "you will be doing" but rather is something "you are doing right now." This relationship is ending and you are undoing that together in real time.

Yet a ritual is not a recipe for any guarantees. Just because you do this doesn't ensure the complete undoing of this relationship. In fact, the untying may need to continue long after the ritual. What this ritual can do, however, is not only mark this important moment but also offer your body a somatic remembering that comes with untying and unraveling. Once you can feel it and be seen doing it, it can arouse a muscle memory so you can continue disentangling long after the ritual ends, until eventually the cord is completely untied.

The inspiration for this ritual comes from the ancient Celtic hand-fasting ceremony, a word loaned or taken into the English language from the Old Norse word *handfesta*, meaning to "strike a bargain by joining your hands together." Within this word are two components, one a noun and the other a verb: The hand is one and the fastening of them or making them solid is the other. We can see a similar intention with the giving of a ring, which also uses the hands and an object that acts to solidify or make whole. Both the hand-fasting and the ring consummate an agreement by bringing two into one.

In this Unbinding Ritual, the hands will begin bound together by ribbon or rope, done by at least one witness, preferably someone who attended the original wedding. Over the course of the ritual, the cords will be slowly untied as each person responds to questions, addressing their answers sometimes to the other person and sometimes to themselves. This employs the ritual technology of repetitive action, of doing something over and over again in order to make it real. So there will be many turns of untying, which acknowledges the many ways these two people have been bound together and the many ways that are needed to undo that.

Prepare

Intentions

May we mark the undoing of our vows before a witness. May we further unbind ourselves and say what needs to be said. May this space let us feel, listen, and be witnessed so we both can set ourselves free.

You Will Need

- About seven feet of rope or ribbon, ideally something natural that can be burned
- A pair of scissors
- One candle and a match or lighter (alternatively, a fireplace or firepit)
- One or more witnesses

Permission

Perhaps you are one part of a divorcing couple, or you are the friend to a divorcing couple who wants to hold space to assist in this ending. Either way, this ritual must have consent first and foremost, and requires everyone's verbal permission and willingness. If you can't get that or it feels untrustworthy, I encourage you not to do this ritual and to reference the Surrendering Ritual (on pages 338–45), which doesn't require your ex's participation. Consent is everything here.

The Invitation

Whoever is making the invitation, keep it clear and concise. Here are some points to consider in the ask:

- *Why them?* Why is this person the right choice to be a witness? Tell them.
- *What for?* State clearly what your intentions are and what the purpose of this ritual is.
- *Why?* Explain the objective of this ritual. For example, "We are already legally divorced but since we put so much effort into coming together, we wanted to do the same with separating."
- *Where?* Choose a place that is private, quiet, and doesn't have any unpredictable activity like children playing or people coming and going. It's even better if it can be outside.
- *How long?* Be clear with how long you are asking for your witnesses' attention. Around two hours is advisable.

- *What to bring?* There are moments during the ritual where beauty might be helpful to soothe the moment. Ask the witnesses to bring a song to sing, a poem to read, or to bring something sweet to eat, like dessert.
- *Ask for clarity.* Ask for a response if they can attend. If someone is a maybe, they are a no. Ask for people's clear yes or no so you can count on their full presence.
- *Restate the intention.* What are you looking to achieve from this ritual? What is its best outcome?

Prior to the Ritual

While it's completely fine for everyone to gather at the time proposed for the ritual, another idea, if possible, is for the "un-couple" to have some time alone before the ritual begins. That could be done by taking a walk together or sharing a meal. The purpose of this is to get them "warmed up" to each other beforehand, so that they can really speak their hearts during the ritual. If they choose this option, the witnesses should already be gathered in advance and welcome them with their presence and by lighting a candle or a fire.

Begin

State the Intention

Before the hand-binding, restate the purpose of the ritual. Why is everyone gathered together? What is being asked of the witnesses? What is being asked of the separating couple? And what is the best outcome for this ritual? State these things, kindly and compassionately. Why? Because by naming them, it gives the ritual half a chance of serving its purpose and everyone the same chance of clearly performing their roles.

The Binding

It is the job of one of the witnesses to bind the couple's hands together. This might be an intense moment, so if there is a song to sing or a poem to read, this is the time to do that.

The un-couple should determine in advance how many rounds they are going to do, and that number should be the number of bindings made.

Once their hands are fastened together, pause. Have everyone take a big breath.

The Unbinding

And so it begins. This part of the ritual is only for the couple bound together. Everyone else's role is to listen and witness, not to give feedback, make suggestions, or share their stories.

However many times the rope or ribbon is wrapped around the un-couple's hands, this is how many rounds you will do. Each round is prompted by a question—a question that isn't meant to be answered but instead to be wondered about. Each person speaking can take as long as they want to respond. Do not rush this. There is no right way to do it. Perhaps memories arise, stories are told, jokes made, tears shed, anger flared, blessings given—whatever it is, it is. When that person is done, they can unwind one wrapping of the cord. This goes back and forth, accordingly.

The Rounds

You can use these questions as your prompts or create your own. Or ditch this structure altogether and invent your own way of untying the binding. However you do it, this is a ritual of the un-couple going back and forth with sharing words to each other and physically unbinding their hands. Each person responds to each round.

> Round 1:
> Begin in beauty and with courtesy.
>> *What can you praise about the person before you?*
> Untie.

> Round 2:
> Reflect on the relationship.
>> *How did you grow as a person? What did you learn about yourself while together?*
> Untie.

Round 3:

Take a hard look and claim your side of things.

> *What is mine in this dynamic? What can I take responsibility*
> *for here?*

Untie.

Round 4:

Ask the other:

> *Is there anything you wish to hear from me?*

Untie.

Round 5:

Harvest and acknowledge the learning from your time together.

> *What qualities am I bringing forward from this relationship*
> *into new relationships?*

Untie.

Round 6:

Let the witnesses name what they are seeing or noticing.

> Witness, please remember, this isn't about you. This is about
> what you are witnessing. Now is not the time to share feelings
> that are coming up for you; remain focused on the un-couple.

> *Witness: What are you seeing here?*

Round 7:

It's the last untying. Offer gratitude and end in grace.

> *What is a blessing you can offer the other person for their jour-*
> *ney ahead?*

Untie.

Burn the Cord

Once the cord is completely undone, it is time to burn it. Whether it's by a candle flame or a fire, the process of burning the rope is the final letting go within the ritual. If you are doing this inside and by candlelight, have each person separately hold one end of the rope and just let the candle burn the middle point until the one rope becomes two. If you have a fire, you can do that as well or put the entire rope into the fire.

Meet this moment with a pause and breath.

If there is another song to sing or poem to read, this is the perfect moment to transition in beauty.

Conclude

This ritual is not just about marking a moment to complete this cycle of separation, but also signifies the turning of a new page of a new life. My advice: End this ritual sweetly, maybe with dessert or wine. Let the sweetness linger on the tongues of all those who gathered together to do the hard, necessary work of unraveling the binding of a relationship. Do not take it for granted that this kind of ritual could even be possible. Celebrate this achievement by feeding the people and the moment with sweetness.

If the candle or fire is still lit, let it be extinguished on its own. Sometimes, there is more to be said or felt after the ritual is over. Linger in the post-ritual and give generous space for the unknown to show itself.

Questions for Further Reflection
- How did it feel to be bound and to unbind?
- What does being witnessed offer this process?
- What can be said or needs to be said before others that is different than if it were just the two of us?
- What does "staying with the ending" bring up for me?

THE SURRENDERING RITUAL: *Solo*

The anger and hate that can accompany a divorce are actually a healthy part of the separating process. The heat from these emotions has a purpose, and it is to help you burn through the cord that connects you to your ex. Anger, sadness, grief—all of it is a necessary part of the alchemy of severance. And severance is needed for the next chapter of life. Even hidden in the word "severance" is the Vulgar Latin word *parare*, meaning, "to make ready or prepare," the underlying purpose of *why* you're severing.

Too often, cords remain unsevered and they sound a lot like grievances: "I don't deserve this," "This is unfair," or "I've been wronged" are common outrages that refuse to end. These remain after the heat of a divorce because our modern culture barely provides any resources or skills to express and transform our grievances, aside from through lawyers. Without doing anything to our grievances, they remain stuck and we stay justified in the story of how we've been wronged. Sadly, our grievances become the relationship's bitter lifeline, the cords we're left holding long after the relationship's over—and maintaining them is what prevents us from fully putting the relationship down.

Where grievances are the festering wounds of affliction, grief is a skill that asks you to get good at loving what you are losing, despite all your best attempts— despite how you want things to be. It is enormously challenging to practice grief in a grief-phobic culture that translates divorce as "you failed me." Instead of grief, we masquerade in anger, blame, judgment, and victimization. Some go kicking and screaming through a divorce, being forced into it rather than choosing and understanding it as a part of the way things are. The belief of a grief-illiterate culture such as ours is that endings are not supposed to happen. They are wrong, and therefore, when we're in an ending such as a divorce, it can easily become "I am wrong." Yet endings are not wrong. They are as much a part of life as are beginnings. My teacher Stephen Jenkinson so beautifully and profoundly speaks of grieving endings as "a love affair in reverse," an understanding that loss and love are two wings of the same bird.

This Surrendering Ritual, like the Unbinding Ritual, asks you to use your hands to sever the cords that tie you to your ex, by naming and releasing the grievances you still hold. As you symbolically surrender objects from your marriage—either by burning them or burying them—you are surrendering your gripes and grievances to the greater mystery that is life, letting them become grief and, in time, healing.

Timing

As with the first ritual, ask yourself, *Is this the right time for this?* Timing is everything with ritual, especially a ritual for divorce. This can be a heated time that rattles your sense of place, survival, and self. Rachel, a divorcee, suggested to me, "It is okay to come back to this ritual when your nervous system has settled and you have some ground to stand on." If you're in the fire and fight of the actual divorce, it's probably not a good time for this.

Prepare
Intentions
May I be heard and witnessed in my grievances. May I physically let go of objects, memorabilia, and gifts that connect me to my ex. May I soften from the anger and hurt while holding the vulnerable parts of myself. May I be held by the place, by nature, by the sun and the moon, and connect to something greater than me.

You Will Need
- One or more witnesses
- Two objects from your ex-relationship (You will need one that can burn and one that can be buried. These objects should be meaningful, such as a love letter or piece of jewelry, but need not have monetary value.)
- One song that you know the tune and lyrics of
- A candle or fire and a lighter
- A trowel
- A filled water pitcher
- A hand towel
- Dessert, like chocolate or fruit

The Witnesses
You can choose as many as you want, but maybe it's enough to just have one good, kind, steady person who will carry your bag for you, bring you food and water, listen to you as you release your anger and tears, and who will embrace you after it's complete and remind you

of how loved you are. Most important, this person is in service to you and your process. They are not there to take for themselves from this experience. They are not there to offer advice or guidance to you or to speak of their own experience. They are, as author Martín Prechtel says, "designated non-grievers,"* holding the space so that you can fully do that grief yourself.

Where

You can do this inside your home, but I don't recommend it. Rather, what I recommend is going outside and letting the sun or moon, the wind or a bird, the shadows and earth help with this release. So much of what you are there to release is personal, so taking this ritual outdoors can help depersonalize it and soften you back to your body and the earth's body.

Consider going to a place in which you already have a relationship. Sure, that could be your backyard, but a backyard is very much like an extension of your home. Instead, go to a place that recognizes you. Perhaps, that is a particular beach where your kids have played every summer or that part of the park you visited when you needed to get away. When interviewing people who have been divorced about their place, many spoke about revisiting the location where they got engaged as a powerful spot to release the marriage. Of course, this all depends on what is available to you, but do make an effort here. Doing this ritual in a place you are already connected to accomplishes half of the work of the ritual.

Begin

When you first get to the place of the ritual, set out all the material you brought with you and then don't do anything else. You and your witness should just sit there, listening to the place. Get a sense of where the sun or moon is in the sky. Feel the earth under your body, always holding you. Observe your lungs breathing in the air of that place. Allow yourself to arrive there and to greet the place with your presence.

---

* Prechtel, *The Smell of Rain on Dust*.

Don't Rush

Don't rush through this section to get to the "real ritual." The secret success of a ritual is really all about the bookends—the approach into it and the approach out of it. To an outside observer, this wouldn't look like anything valuable, but it is in the waiting, the approaching, the lingering, the watching, that the magic can enter. Don't be fooled by the "goal" of getting it done. Orientation is everything, so give yourself plenty of time to arrive and settle in.

The Song

Begin by humming the song you brought. Go slowly. It doesn't have to be fancy singing. The song is an offering so that this ritual can begin in beauty. Sing your song to whoever is there—the trees, the rocks, the clouds, the bugs, the seen and unseen. It's very important that no human is "watching," even the witness, so that you don't have to worry about being self-conscious. Witnessing is not watching. There's no judgment in it. Instead, it is raising up what is happening and making it so.

Say Intentions

When you have finished your song, speak your intention out loud, both to the place and your witness. *Why am I here? What have I come here to do? What do I need help with?* After you have said your peace, listen and observe. Watch the trees rustle or listen to the crow *ka-kaaa*. Everything and everyone is a part of this ritual. After you have spoken and feel ready, begin the rounds.

Round 1: Fire

This round is for you to acknowledge whatever grievance, anger, rage, or wrong is still leftover from this relationship. While it asks you to speak to your anger, it is not meant to reinforce it. You are giving voice to those feelings in order to let them move through you. If you need to yell or pound the earth, do it. Keep expressing your words, wringing them out of you until you have nothing left to say.

1. Light the fire. If it is a candle or a campfire, now is the time to light it. And if you can't have a fire where you are but want to burn the object, use the matches or lighter.
2. Acknowledge the grievances. *What are you still upset about? Where do you still feel wronged by this person? What shouldn't have happened?* Again, do not stop talking until you have all of it out. If needed, ask these questions again and again. Keep saying out loud, "I still feel wronged by," and speak your heart inside out.
3. The witness must ask, "Have you said it all?" If you haven't, keep speaking. When you have finished . . .
4. Burn the object. Do this in silence. Watch the fire take it. Listen to it burn. Smell the smoke. Witness it turn to ash.

When the object is fully ash, sing or hum your song. Beauty soothes the heart. Keep singing the song until you feel settled again.

Round 2: Earth

Take out the trowel.

This round's purpose is for you to claim your side of things. Having burned up your grievances, you are now left with what is yours from this relationship. This is *not* an opportunity to claim your victimhood. Your aim is to reclaim your power from this relationship. The way to do that is by taking responsibility for the role you played so that you can learn from it.

1. Dig a hole. Use your trowel to dig a hole where your object will be buried. Consider putting your hands in the earth too. Feel the dark, cool place where you are laying this object to rest.

2. Claim what was yours in this relationship. Again, keep speaking until everything that needed to be said is said:
   - What was my role in this dynamic?
   - What can I take responsibility for?
   - What did I participate in that gave my power away?
3. The Witness asks: "Have you said it all?" If you haven't, keep speaking. When you have finished . . .
4. Bury the object. Do this in silence. Watch the earth hold it. Listen. Smell. Witness the fresh ground.
5. Again, sing or hum your song. Let beauty return to this moment. Keep singing until the song settles you.

Round 3: Water

This round invites you to soften, release, and receive. Since you just "buried the hatchet," your hands aren't clenched into fists but are open to acknowledge the loss here. This relationship began in love. Can it be ended in love as well? This part of the ritual allows for forgiveness—both of yourself and of all the circumstances that led to the divorce—to clear a way for the new person you are becoming and what is being reborn.

1. Washing. The witness should pour a little water over your hands as you speak to each question. Let it wash over you as you prepare to give voice to empathy and forgiveness.
2. Claim all that can be forgiven here. Again, keep speaking until you've said your peace:
   - What wrongdoing can I forgive, both in myself and my ex?
   - What part of me is still alive and worthy of my love and attention?
   - What have I learned about myself from this relationship?
   - What parts of me are still tender?
   - What aspects of myself do I want to renew?
3. The witness asks: "Have you said it all?" If you haven't, keep speaking. When you have finished . . .

4. Ask for one last hand wash. Do this in silence. Observe the wet earth. Pause. Listen. Smell.

Sing your song again as you dry your hands on the hand towel.

Dessert

The dessert here is meant to be a balm for the wound that comes with loss. Before taking any for yourself, pinch off a piece of the dessert and put it in the earth. Feeding your relationship with the earth is for your own healing and is directly tied to your greater web of relationships, including your ancestors and this place. Speak out loud your gratitude and praise to the land and for life.

Then, share your dessert with your witnesses and speak gratitude to them for so kindly and generously helping you hold space for your process.

And lastly, bless the person you are becoming. Let this prayer carry the sweetness, the curiosity, the wonder and joy inherent in new beginnings.

Questions for Further Reflection

- How do I know this is the right time to do this ritual? What are the signs?
- Who is the person I am asking to be my witness? Why?
- What place do I want to do this ritual? Why?
- What is ending here? What is beginning? How is this ritual carrying me through that?

Death and Dying

Death is the cradle of your love of life. The fact that it ends.

—Stephen Jenkinson

You've lost them. They've passed. They're gone. Whatever euphemism you use, the one you knew is no longer. Maybe you find yourself at the end of a long and arduous road, beyond exhausted and undone as your grief and relief converge into one. Or maybe this death came far too swiftly, unexpectedly even, barely offering a warning sign that they would be stolen away, and that you would have to proceed for the rest of your days without them. Death is the only guarantee that life makes at birth, yet life has a way of helping us forget its inevitability.

When death enters the room, what does it ask of you? Some of us try to hold ourselves together in order to endure our proximity to it. Others of us turn away from it, shielding our eyes from the pain and our hearts from breaking. Maybe we hurry past it, trying to get over it and return to the normal rhythms of our everyday life. But what if death asks us to remember what it means to be a human being, and to know our grief, not as an affliction, but as a way of seeing—a willingness to be awed by the whole of life, which includes it ending. Rather than trying to recover from this death and resist the way it's changing us, we must let it properly mark us, and in return we must mark and praise it back as the great reminder of life's preciousness. And with our hearts full of all the grief, the wondering, the pain and longing that accompany this caravan of despair, we must also find small and beautiful ways to love the one who left, and in turn, to love our whole life even more.

Death, like birth, is messy. During my father's last hours in hospice, I witnessed

too many reasons to turn away and abandon him: his putrid bedsore, his frantic clawing at his oxygen, his pissing himself over and over again. The color, the smell, his
body decaying before my very eyes—all impossibly hard to see. Everything inside of
me wanted anything but to have to witness this. Anything. It was an enormous labor
to stay with him in the mess and keep *my* attention focused on *his* dying. My brother,
Matthew, was there with me in this, and without being told or taught, for twenty-four
hours we became our father's midwives and high priests—lighting candles, singing
songs, playing instruments, holding his hand, and whispering ever so slightly in his
ear, "It's okay, you can go," over and over again, until his breathing got ever so slight,
and then, he did. And when the nurse came in to acknowledge that his body had
failed, we didn't see it that way. There was no failure in this at all. Yes, there was pain
and grief, but they also mixed and mingled with so much beauty. His death was so
mundane yet so mysterious. And as he left his body in the faint light of dawn on that
February morning, my brother and I sat cloaked in our white hospital blankets, in awe
at this birth in reverse, lingering in the enormous grief-love that now overflowed and
surrounded us.

But death isn't always beautiful. I spoke with Kim, who told me the story of her
little sister who died of a drug overdose when she was in her twenties. When her dad
told her how she had died, he couldn't even bring himself to say that she overdosed,
and instead informed Kim that her sister had died of liver failure. For her, his inability
to name what had happened was a portent of the soul-crushing pain he was feeling
and the freight that her whole family now needed to carry. The devastation wrecked
her parents so deeply that the only way they could carry on was to act like nothing
had happened. After the death, her parents would rarely say her sister's name out loud
again or talk about any family memories that she was a part of. In the face of this volcanic pain, her parents froze and let their unattended grief solidify into denial.

This story broke my heart to hear. Not just because it's laden with a shame that
continues to ripple out, but more so because it's a tale of a family refusing to be heartbroken when facing death. The heartbreak masquerades as "everything's fine, we're
moving on" and is not unique to this particular family, but rather is testimony of a
culture that demonizes endings while championing competency, self-mastery, and
potential.

It's amazing how ubiquitous this demonization is. Just this morning, as if the
Facebook gods sensed what I was writing about, an advertisement from an insurance
company popped up, with an image of a very happy family and the words right next to
them that read: "Life is limitless. Never stop." Kind of ironic coming from an insurance

company, but hey, there's the spell itself, unfolding on my screen, just as I set out to write about limits. If you listen carefully, beneath the surface it whispers, "Life doesn't have to end if you don't want it to—so keep going, be all you can be, just do it, break free," and all the other future-promising slogans we've been force-fed over the years. And while this might be a good marketing tactic, it is sourced from a deeper and more pernicious cultural well.

The idea that we can live forever is, of course, a capitalistic shell game, which subversively tells us that endings have no value or purpose, and when it comes down to it, they don't serve you or your life at all—so disregard, ignore, deny, fight, and refuse them. And if and when you inevitably encounter them, there's really no reason for them to impact or change you. The slogan "never stop" becomes another way of saying, "Don't let that heart of yours break too much because it'll slow down your stride."

A few days ago, my cousin contacted me to let me know his uncle was "very sick" with sporadic prion disease, a rare neurodegenerative disease that has no currently available treatment. In just a few weeks, he went from being an active and healthy man to a very weak one, needing a walker and 24/7 home care. To help cover the costs of his care, the family launched a fundraiser. In the description they told stories of all the ways he was living, of all the things he could still do, of what was still working, and of how heroic he was while being sick. They spoke about plans to slow the disease's progression, to provide the highest quality of life, to continue to get him treatments. They even told a story of him sitting on his patio looking at the lake and literally saying out loud to his partner: "Life is not limited." But they didn't once name at all the biggest elephant in the room: the fact that he was dying.

How could that be? With the spotlight only illuminating what's working, then the heartbreak has no place in his dying time. Therefore, what does it mean to love his whole life if it can't include loving it ending as well?

Death asks us to reimagine our understanding of love. To let that pre-morbid way of loving life, of loving our beloved partner or friend, our parent or child, be broken down and broken open so that this new kind of love can emerge, a love that is now in service to the ending. This is challenging emotional labor and can often feel counterintuitive: Loving someone means you would do anything to keep them alive. So how do you love someone while seeing them down—while letting them go? "It occurred to me," Stephen Jenkinson once said, "that the ability to see the end of what you hold dear turns out to be the mothership for being able to hold something dear." That capacity to hold the wholeness of life, its beginning, middle, and end, is made possible by our willingness to grieve that life.

Grief isn't only sadness or sorrow. It is the process of loving what you are losing or have lost. While grief might seem inevitable, as if it will just naturally come with loss, it's not. It's a skill, and like any skill, you must practice it to get good at it. I practice grief every day when I call my ninety-four-year-old grandma, Shirley. She isn't dying and the conversations aren't usually sad. Most of time I'm cracking up from this little old lady's sharp tongue and witty sense of Jewish humor. But when we speak, I can sense that time is always limited. When we say goodbye and *zei gezunt*, which is Yiddish for "be healthy," I wonder each and every time we hang up whether it might be the last. And because of that, my heart breaks a bit more while my love of her overflows. And that love looks like me pleading with her to stick around for as long as she can, as selfish as that might be. I tell her to be careful, to use her walker, to not be so impulsive, to which she usually responds: "I'm doing the best I can, but this old gray mare ain't what she used to be," and we both laugh and the conversation carries on—the love and the longing both there with us.

It mystifies me that my grandma is still alive. It mystifies me that my father isn't. Being mystified by the way things are is a way grief speaks. Of course, there's sadness in there, but grief is more than just a feeling. When I spoke to Brad Wolfe, who founded an organization called Reimagine that helps communities with end of life, he referred to grief as "a Jackson Pollock painting that contains all the colors of the human experience." To get to know all of that takes a willingness to be intimate with life, coming closer to its splattering mess and not turning away from it because you think that's not what it should be. Grief is a way to love it all the more so because it's ending, not in spite of it.

However, to a culture obsessed with problem solving, grief is a sign of a problem. And, therefore, it's something to fix, to get over, or get through so that you can get on the other side of it—so that you can get back to things working out, to shit getting done, and to being on top of it all. In this way of thinking, grief needs closure because it's too disruptive, too costly, too much wear and tear on your heart. A friend's parent recently died, and when I asked them about how much time they were planning on taking to mourn and be with their grief, they said, "Unfortunately, just the weekend. I have too much to do."

Grief isn't something you get over, it's something you get under. The question is, to paraphrase Jenkinson, not what grief does *to* us but what does grief ask *of* us. To grieve well, you have to let go of being the boss of your life, to lay down your belief that you have everything handled, that you have the reins on what's happening, and then to be properly wrecked by the way things are. This isn't a collapse, though that might happen too. It's your humanity chiseled and changed by heartbreak. It's the deep cutting that the poet Hafiz speaks of, that allows your heart to become well fermented and seasoned.

To that end, I want to offer you three rituals to help you linger at this Great Doorway. Someone you love is dying or has recently died and you are needed, whether or not you know it. Their life, their body, their memory is in your hands and requires your whole, broken heart to meet them, to tend to them, to reassure them, to let your life be completely interrupted so that their life won't disappear on your watch. While ritual provides no guarantees, it is a faithful way to navigate this time when your world turns upside down and it seems like the oceans are filled full of your tears. Ritual can help you lean in when you don't know how to, to be gathered in when you feel all alone, and find ways to remember your beloved when losing them is a real proposition.

These three rituals were inspired by the time delineation employed within my Jewish tradition: day of, one week, and one month. These time markings are designed to give you space to fall apart, to be held, and to be protected from the pressures of everyday life. Their purpose comes from the sensitive understanding that grief needs to be sheltered and mourning needs a container so that you can fully surrender into this time. It also understands that grief comes in waves, and what you need a few days after the death might be vastly different than what you need weeks later. These rituals pay attention to that and offer you a safe and unrushed space to be held within. Also, each ritual focuses on a different color of your grief and a different layer of support so that you can eventually return to your everyday life again, changed but also in a new relationship with the one who is on the other side of the veil.

THE TENDING *the* BODY RITUAL:
The Day Of

The body is a vessel that the spirit of life inhabits. And when that breath departs, the same breath this body had been breathing since the moment it came into this world, what happens? While death might make this body look different, smell different, feel different—while our immediate reflex might be disgust or shock—we still have a responsibility to this familiar and yet unfamiliar body.

My culture has a practice for this, and it's done by a quiet band of heroes. They aren't public figures, don't boast of their accomplishments, and have no interest in any kind of reward. They belong to a tradition that's been unbroken since at least the fourth century CE and is most likely even older than that. They are referred to in Hebrew as *chevra kadisha*, or a "sacred society" who oftentimes, late into the night, are called out of the comfort of their homes to gather around a newly deceased body. Their purpose is to perform a ritual called *tahara*, or "purification," and to wash, dress, and prepare this body as a final act of respect, honor, and love.

Over the centuries, the ritual has developed its own choreography. It begins with prayer as those humble humans gather around the body asking forgiveness for any mistakes that might be made performing this service. Then they carefully undress and free the body of anything that would separate it from the cleansing—taking off any jewelry, glasses, or bandages. And then warm water is poured gently over different body parts, starting from the head, while they recite a heartbreaking biblical love poem that ends with: "How fine you are, my love. My perfect one." More water pours over skin, hair, and limbs, until the body is considered pure, and then this holy temple is dressed again in fresh linens, as our high priests once did in ancient times. All of this is our people's way of regarding each tireless human vessel and preparing it to return back to the earth again.

While this tradition might not be available to you, the heart of it is. The inspiration of the Tending the Body Ritual is a way of tending to your loved one's body as a final goodbye. And while it might disturb you to imagine performing a ritual that involves a dead body, it is not just any body. It is your beloved's body.

When interviewing a woman named Melody for this chapter, she spoke about her sisters and her preparing their mother's body for burial. As they assembled around their mom's body, they all realized that this was the first time that they could remember seeing her naked. "[Mom] had scars from the surgeries that we'd never seen. So we honored them. We honored her whole body, her head, hands, and feet, that had cared for us all our lives." They chose to tend to their mother's body like she was royalty—or a goddess. They put flowers around it. Anointed her hands and feet with oil. Put fresh nail polish on her nails, styled her hair. By the time they had finished dressing their mother, they felt a bond between themselves as sisters that they hadn't felt before.

The ritual below might be a big edge for you. It could be that your grief is too great or that tending a dead body is too much. Maybe all you can do is slowly wash your loved one's hands and yours, and that can be more than enough. This ritual isn't about doing it all or doing it right, but about rightfully doing something to bring some beauty and tender care to this body that housed your beloved.

Prepare

Intentions

May I tend to my beloved's deceased body as another way of loving them. May I use water, fire, and earth to honor their body and let my grief be channeled into service and beauty.

You Will Need

- A candle and matches
- A bowl of warm water
- Many towels
- A wash rag or sponge
- A bouquet of flowers or anything beautiful from nature
- Optional: Essential oil, nail polish, makeup

Ask for Support

These things can be too much to do alone. As much as you might think this is a good idea *before* your loved one's death, when you're out there and in it, it might seem unscalable. If you are interested in performing this ritual, ask a friend in advance to support you so that you are not doing it yourself. You can simply hand them this book and earmark this chapter. Then they will be charged with gathering the materials, laying them out, and cleaning them up so that you don't have to.

Also, it's important to note that their role is to be a silent support for you, which means they are there to tend to *your* needs with little to no talking, so that you might tend to the needs of the body.

When

This really depends on what is available to you. Because my father died at a hospice center, we had a very limited amount of time with his body between when the nurse acknowledged his death and when the morgue was called to come pick him up.

Because grief turns time upside down, this would be a good place for the friend assisting to help ensure this happens before the burial. If the body has already been removed from you or it wasn't possible to be in proximity to it, you can skip down to the next section, "The Sheltering Grief Ritual: First Seven Days."

Begin

Before Doing Anything

Pause. This is a holy time. Each second matters, so take care with your approach. This isn't about completing or accomplishing anything, but more so, this is about staying with your beloved in this in-between time.

This pause can happen through lighting a candle, by singing a song, offering prayers, through silence, or just letting those deep rolling sobs move through you. Let the time prior to the ritual become as important as the thing you are intending to do.

Undressing

Again, do what you are able to do. If it's not possible to completely undress the body, then don't. You can simply remove jewelry, bandages, or anything that you feel doesn't belong. For instance, even if you plan to put on fresh nail polish, take time to remove the old paint. Each little thing you do to respect the body and prepare it for burial matters. Again, it's not about doing the whole thing, it's about the level of care you bring to every part of it you do.

Go slow and take your time. There is no rush here.

Washing

Because most of us don't have the equipment that a *chevra kadisha* has, this will be more like a sponge bath.

The assisting friend should have the bowl of warm water already prepared and the towels surrounding the body so that the water can just roll off it and into the towel.

Please note—if you can't or don't want to bathe the whole body, you can refine this ritual to just washing the hands, feet, or face.

With that said, begin by gently bathing the head. This can include the face, hair, and eyes. Go slow. This isn't about getting the body "clean" but about tending to it with kindness, love, and deep reverence. Continue on to the rest of the body, making sure you get the hands and feet.

You can wash in silence or song, but it's also good to offer your grief as praise for this body and life. "Grief is praise, because it is the natural way love honors what it misses,"[*] says Martín Prechtel.

A Guide

You might want to use this as a guide while you wash the body:

As you wash the head, praise it: Name a beautiful way your beloved thought about things. Thank the head.

As you wash the eyes, praise them: Name a beautiful way your beloved saw the world. Thank the eyes.

As you wash the mouth, praise it: Name a beautiful way your beloved spoke about things. Thank the mouth.

As you wash the area over the heart, praise it: Name a beautiful way your beloved loved. Thank the heart.

As you wash the hands, praise them: Name a beautiful way your beloved gave to this world. Thank the hands.

As you wash the feet, praise them: Name a beautiful way your beloved walked in the world. Thank the feet.

And continue on if you choose.

Beautification

After you wash your beloved's body, your assisting friend should remove the water and towels and lay out the flowers, the oil, the nail polish, makeup, or anything else you chose in advance to surround and anoint this body in beauty.

---

[*] Prechtel, *The Smell of Rain on Dust.*

This part should reflect the love and life of the one who died. It should be flowers they loved, smells they wore, colors they adored. It should bring forth another way to honor their personality and preferences.

Make an attempt to speak to the deceased about what and why you are doing this.

For instance, "I am anointing your hands with _____. May this bring you _____ and _____."

Or: "I am doing your nails because I want you to feel _____."

Re-dressing

Even if you only removed their glasses or jewelry, this is the moment to re-dress the body in anything you imagine your beloved would want their body to be buried in. Maybe that is their favorite hat or those socks that they loved so much. You can also adorn their body in flowers or any other beautiful, natural material.

Washing Your Hands

Inspired by my own tradition of ritually washing hands after coming in contact with a deceased body, complete this ritual by washing your hands, pouring water multiple times over each hand. This can be done with another bowl and pitcher that your assisting friend provides or simply in a sink.

As you wash, feel the coolness, the flow, the fresh aliveness of the water. Let that moment of ritually washing your hands ground and revive you and soothe your broken heart.

Questions for Further Reflection

- How was it different to engage with their body dead instead of alive?
- What confronted me about touching a deceased body?
- What was it like to take time to wash and beautify the body?
- What did speaking to my deceased feel like?
- While this is clearly an ending, what is also beginning?

THE SHELTERING GRIEF RITUAL:
First Seven Days

The purpose of this ritual is to give your grief time boundaries. It was inspired by the seven days of *shiva* and the cycle of seven. What that means is that for seven full days, your grief has the space to be sheltered, permitted, encouraged, and welcomed. This time container guards against the need to tend to your normal life, because at this moment life is not normal. For these seven days, if possible, let your whole life stop so that you can reorient to the choppy waters that are your grief and to all the wild ways this loss sways and rocks the stability of your world.

Seven is not a random number. Within the Jewish tradition, it is the number that signifies wholeness and completion—for instance, after six days of work, the seventh is the end of that cycle and the day of rest. The Hebrew word for "seven" is *sheva*, which is also where our weeklong mourning period, called *shiva*, gets its name. Shiva is a time container. For seven days that start immediately following a funeral, the bereaved family takes refuge in their home and is gathered in by their community. During this time, grief is central and anything relating to vanity or self-indulgence is prohibited. Which means, when entering a shiva home, you might notice that all the mirrors are covered, the mourning family sits on low seats or on the ground, and often they walk around barefoot, all to be completely focused on their grief. And the community's purpose is to tend, protect, and bring ease to this space; making meals, answering the doors, offering comfort, reciting mourning prayers, and obeying an etiquette that is based in listening to the stories and needs of the mourners.

It is also customary on the first day of shiva to light a candle that burns for the entire seven days. Lighting candles for our dead is a ritual that is cross-cultural. For this chapter I interviewed Lupe, whose father died in 2020 during the pandemic. With all the restrictions, Lupe and her family could not be at the gravesite when her father was buried and had to stand at a distance watching them put him into the ground. Most of their traditional Mexican rituals couldn't be done, but Lupe made sure a candle was burning for her dad every day. "I would not let it stop burning. I had to have it on. My mom said that when someone dies in our Mexican culture, you must light a candle for them so they can cross over in light and not in darkness."

The sacred action of this Sheltering Grief Ritual is lighting candles, and each candle is accompanied by a question. These questions are intended to offer you opportunities to reflect and remember your beloved and to express your sorrow, your longing for, and, of course, your love for them. It's a very simple ritual that can mark the many faces of this new grief.

As with many of the rituals in this book, please go slow with what is happening. These first seven days are sacred. When my father died, the first few days after his death felt like a dream—mystifying in the sense that the intensity of our grief reminded us of how close he still was to us.

The candles in this ritual serve as a vigil for this holy time and you'll light them, as Kathleen Raine so heartbreakingly points out, "not because they are far, but because so near."*

Prepare
Intentions
May I create a time container for my grief, separate from the busyness of my everyday life. May this ritual offer a way for my community to gather around and support me, and may this ritual help me speak to the different ways my grief is speaking.

You Will Need
- Twenty-eight candles (Twenty-four-hour candles are ideal because they will allow you to carry the flame seamlessly from one day to the next. If you can't get twenty-four-hour candles, use what is available. We're not after orthodoxy here.)
- Matches or a lighter

---

* Jeni Couzyn, ed., *The Bloodaxe Book of Contemporary Women Poets: Eleven British Writers* (Eastbourne, UK: Gardners Books, 1999).

The Non-Mourner

If you are a new mourner, I want to encourage you to hand this book over to a friend or community member, someone other than you whom you trust—what Martín Prechtel calls "a designated non-griever."[*] During this time, it's important to not engage in any kind of organizing, so that you can stay with your grief. And by doing that, you are also providing those that love you a tangible way to support you.

Prepare
Invitations
Work with the mourners to put together a list of whom they would like to invite. When sending out an invitation for this ritual, also encourage people to bring prepared food for the mourners so that they don't have to worry about how they are going to feed themselves. If the gathering is happening online, consider organizing an online document so folks can sign up for a date and order food that is delivered directly to their home.

---

[*] Prechtel, *The Smell of Rain on Dust.*

The Etiquette of Grief

Grief and death make many people uncomfortable. Suddenly, even your most empathic and well-meaning friend is uncertain what to say, how to be, what to do. I find it can be beneficial to offer some guidance to attendees about how to engage with mourners at a ritual. Some suggestions would be respectful ways to offer condolences, such as, "I'm very sorry for your loss," or "They will be missed by all of us," or "I am here for you and we are so heartbroken."

What's especially important is your capacity to listen. When sitting shiva, it's understood that you wait for the mourner to speak first and lead the conversation, even if that leaves silent gaps of space. Tender listening is great etiquette to practice in a house of grief.

Begin

The Candles

Before lighting the candles, ask everyone assembled to take a breath together and maybe even state the intention of *why* you are lighting the candles—it can be to remember, to grieve, to be comforted, etc. Whether it's in person or online, taking a moment to collect the minds gathered with purpose and presence is a good approach for any ritual.

The total number of candles that will be lit depends on what day of the ritual you are in. For instance, if it's the third day since the funeral, three candles will be lit, four candles for the fourth day, and so on. Always use the flame from the previous candle burning to light the subsequent candles. If you have twenty-four-hour candles, use the flame from the preceding day to light the current day's candles; if not, use matches or a lighter.

After you've lit the candles for the day, *pause*. Take a breath and watch the flame. When you are ready, use the prompts below as story-starters. They are not questions, but rather ways to encourage remembering and recollection through story.

Day 1: Light the first candle.
What do you already miss of them?

Day 2: Light the next two candles.
What uncertainties has their death brought?

Day 3: Light the next three candles.
What is a story they would share a million times?

Day 4: Light the next four candles.
What is ending with their death? What is beginning?

Day 5: Light the next five candles.
What is something your beloved left in the world?

Day 6: Light the next six candles.
What have they or their death taught you?

Day 7: Light the final seven candles.
What do you want to remember from this time as you leave these seven days of mourning?

Conclude
The day's previous candles can be extinguished once the new candles are lit.

After the last candle goes out on the eighth day, encourage the mourners to ritually wash their hands as a symbolic gesture of the transition from the first seven days to the first month.

Questions for Further Reflection

- Why must I stop to grieve and not carry on with life as normal?
- What does handing over so many roles to my community or friends grant me?
- What happened when I kept a candle burning for my deceased one over seven days?
- How has this ritual impacted me?

THE MEMORY ALTAR RITUAL:
First Month

The labyrinth of time leads you on, taking you further and further away from the death. What was just a day became a week, and now what was just a week has become a month. How could it be that you've lived a whole month in the world without your beloved? It felt impossible to carry on without them—likely, it still does—and yet here you are. As the current of your everyday life reclaims you and you pass through another gate taking you further from your pain, and therefore further from your beloved, it's important to mark the conclusion of this sacred proximity so that you can ease back into your everyday life with grace.

Within my Jewish tradition, we call this month marker *shloshim*, which in Hebrew means "thirty." For the first thirty days after the burial, the mourners are restricted in what they can do as a way to protect their hearts being so broken. They can't attend parties, wear new clothing, or cut their hair. The restrictions match the intensity of the original mourning, and marking the thirty-day passage helps to slowly reintroduce the normal world, while honoring that an immediate pivot can be terribly jarring.

Whether or not you are Jewish, marking time reminds us to remember. Thirty days becomes the first of many times you will recollect your dead, a harbinger of the birthdays, anniversaries, Father's or Mother's Day, and other holidays that will call you to weave their memory back into the world and to tune in again to your grief and love.

Time scatters memory, and so these dates are opportunities to gather what scatters back into some semblance of togetherness.

This ritual was inspired by the Morning Altars* practice I created. This practice began around the time my father died, as a way for me to assemble some order and beauty out of a chaotic and emotional time. It allowed me to get out of my head and the heaviness that can come with grief, and to wander in nature, renewing my way of seeing the world. It also let me channel my love and longing for my father into something I made with my hands.

What makes this Morning Altars practice potent and appropriate is that you are literally collecting fragments of nature and temporarily arranging them into something symmetrical, ordered, and beautiful, and then letting it all go back to being scattered again. This ritual is a tangible way to recollect the memory of your beloved into something creative, meaningful, and ephemeral.

Prepare
Intentions
May I mark the conclusion of the first month of mourning my beloved and the beginning of a new cycle. May I collaborate with nature and make something with my hands to remember them that is impermanent, that honors and acknowledges my grief.

You Will Need
- A basket or tote bag
- A quiet spot in nature to sit and create

Solo or with Others?
This is completely up to you. This ritual stands independently as a solo endeavor, but if there is another person you'd like to join you, you can easily adjust this to make synchronized altars or create one together.

Wander
The first stage of this ritual is a wander through your neighborhood. Because the whole point is to let yourself wander without a destina-

---

* Day Schildkret, *Morning Altars: A 7-Step Practice to Nourish Your Spirit through Nature, Art, and Ritual* (New York: Countryman Press, 2018).

tion, it's important to set an alarm to reel you back in. Determine the duration: For instance, thirty days after my father died, I wandered for almost three hours, because I just needed that time to be quiet, to not know where I was going, to take in the place around me, and to just let myself go without any kind of destination. That lostness mirrored how I felt in my life without him.

There are no time restraints, but I recommend you set aside at least an hour. Set a timer so that you don't have to watch the clock and can challenge yourself to be present to your surroundings.

As you wander, collect whatever inspires you for your altar (within reason—please don't over-take material, and consider only taking what has fallen to the earth). Remember, this is not a scavenger hunt. Your goal isn't just to gather material for your altar but to exercise your capacity to be awed by the mundane and ordinary: a maple leaf, a clamshell, a mossy rock, a little plantain plant bursting out of the sidewalk. Let yourself take in that time of the day, the way the light hits the trees, the temperature, a slight breeze. Slow down with it all. This is a good practice to let your grief mingle with wonder.

Lastly, you are making an altar for your recently deceased loved one, so it's always a good idea to forage with them in mind. Consider the colors, textures, smells, materials they loved, and forage for them and for you.

Sitting

As your forage ends, find a place where you are going to create this altar. This can be indoors or outdoors, depending on the season and your capacity.

Sit down and give yourself a little bit of time to take in the place: What do you hear? What can you smell? Is anything moving and changing around you? The world is alive and this is about noticing that. Let the world come and go without doing anything to it. Observe it with a kind of gracious generosity, letting it be itself.

Begin

Memory Altar

Your Memory Altar will have four parts, but its design is entirely up to you and your imagination. Reflect on each prompt below and consider how the patterns, symbols, and designs with the natural objects you have can help you capture the thoughts, feelings, and memories that come up for you.

Take your time and build what feels beautiful and true for you (not anyone else, and certainly not for Instagram). This doesn't have to make sense to anyone but you.

Part 1: *What was.*
Begin your altar by remembering life before your beloved's dying or death. What stories, habits, expressions, moments get remembered?

Part 2: *What became.*
Next, remember what the dying and death journey was like. What happened? What was that experience like? What was lost and what was gained?

Part 3: *What is.*
Now, remember the last thirty days of your mourning: The grief and uncertainty. The people that showed up to comfort you. Your world being turned upside down.

Part 4: *What will be.*
Finally, lean into what is to come in the months ahead. What will it be like to walk those days without this person in the world? How do you imagine carrying on with your life without them? How do you plan on remembering them?

Conclude

Praise

As your hands complete the altar, it's time to use your words. Speak directly to the deceased as if you are inviting them to partake in this remembering with you. Walk them through the different stories, feelings, and questions that you wove into the altar. Speak as beautifully as you can, for your words can become an extension of your altar, and your eloquence an extension of your grief. Offer both the altar and your words to your beloved.

Impermanence

When you are ready, walk away but make a commitment to return, at least once. Because the altar is made of living natural material, it too will change, decay, and scatter, and witnessing the impermanence of life is a part of the potency of this ritual. See what becomes of the order and design you made. See how slowly or rapidly it decays, is scattered, eaten, or rots. There is enormous beauty in letting nature unfold, both for this altar as well as for your life.

Questions for Further Reflection

- What happens when I allow myself time to wander without a destination?
- How does making something with my hands impact my grief?
- What do I remember when I look back and forward?
- What was valuable about marking these thirty days of mourning?

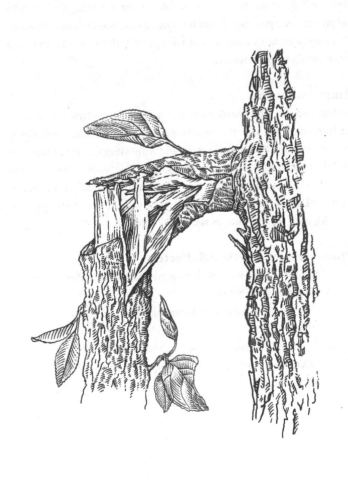

RITUALS
for a CRISIS

Surviving a Near-Death Experience

It takes enormous trust and courage
to allow yourself to remember.

—Bessel A. van der Kolk

I t was not guaranteed in the slightest. It most certainly could have gone another
way. There are ten thousand reasons why it could have ended differently and why
you shouldn't be here at all. And yet, here you are. You've been given the gift of
another chance. Another opportunity to wake up from the haze of believing that this
thing you've called "my life" was so securely in your possession. How forgetful you had
become, thinking that your life was in fact yours. This showed you how threadbare
the whole thing truly is: tenuous and fragile, and entirely ephemeral. And, as quickly
as it was taken, it was given back—the same but different. So what is to be done with
that? What is the evidence that your life has been changed by glimpsing it ending? Is
it enough to be fire-branded by the burning stick of survival or is something more
needed from you? Is life asking for you to brand it back, marking it with the heat of
your love for it, cooling it with the salty tears of your thanks for it, and gazing in awe at
the wound left from it, fresh evidence of how precious and vulnerable this thing called
"life" has always been.

In 1999, I was knocked out of bed by a bus bombing. I was living in Jerusalem
on a junior year study abroad program and had decided that morning, like a typical
college student, to skip my first class and sleep in. I set my alarm to go off just in time
to make it to my next class, but instead of waking up from the beep of my travel clock,
I was jolted to the floor by a deafening explosion. After coming to, I threw on some

clothes and wandered outside, dazed and confused, to the site just up the hill where I would have boarded the bus to the university. The bus stop itself had been blown to bits, with shards of glass cast everywhere, mixed with the shredded remains of a movie poster from the local cinema. Miraculously, there was no one murdered that day, but it was in that moment I realized I could have been. The timing of the bomb was very close to the timing of my commute. That entire day I kept on thinking, *it could have been me*, and for the first time, but not the last, I encountered the fear and awe that comes with surviving an encounter with death. It shattered the fantasy that I was safe. And you know what else left a mark? There was no one at the time who pulled me aside, looked directly in my eyes, and said, "Thank God you're still here."

Accidents displace us. They rip us from being at home in our bodies, our routines, our reality, and cast us out as refugees desperately searching for a new normal—ways to return to these bodies and lives again. But what makes these moments traumatic is not the event itself but how we respond to the event. The essence of trauma, according to psychiatrist Bessel A. van der Kolk, is a wound or injury from an event that is "overwhelming, unbelievable, and unbearable,"[*] or to put it another way, something happening to you that is too vast for your mind to comprehend and that makes no sense at all. Many of these moments happen instantly. One day you have a home, and the next it's burned to the ground. One minute you're cruising down the interstate, and in the blink of an eye your car flips across four lanes and you're hanging upside down by your seat belt. It is in the aftermath of a near-death experience, which could be days, weeks, or even years later, where many struggle to understand why it happened and what to make of it.

Almost a decade ago, I went on a first date with Jared in a regional park near my old home in California. It was the golden hour and we found ourselves at the edge of the Bay, the perfect spot to watch the sun dip and the sky ignite with purples, pinks, and magentas—and frankly, a great spot for a romantic moment. Jared was full of flirt and playfully courted me to climb a tree with him and watch the sunset even higher up. As we both scaled the branches, getting fifteen feet off the ground, Jared wanted to go even higher. Even though the voice in his mind warned him, "Don't do that—it's too risky," Jared reached for one more branch, but never made it. It snapped, and he fell horizontally, landing flat on his back and blacking out.

Miraculously, Jared didn't break his back that day, but it took him many months

---

* Bessel A. van der Kolk, MD, *The Body Keeps the Score: Brain, Mind, and Body in the Healing of Trauma* (New York: Penguin Books, 2014).

to even walk again without pain, and years to heal from that one fall. In retrospect, Jared told me that even though he had a "very accepting attitude" about what happened, that acceptance prevented him from truly grappling with the severity of what *could* have happened and even what *did* happen. He never let himself linger at the edge of those deeper questions trying to uncover what that moment meant and how to understand it as crossing a major threshold in his life. Jared told me: "At first I thought, shit happens. I made a choice and I fell. But at the same time, I realized there was a deeper reckoning available to me that needed to be integrated so I could make more sense of what actually happened." Those unanswered questions, which still stayed with him years later, sounded a bit like *What does this mean for my life?*

Making sense from something senseless is a core function of ritual. Life is unpredictable, messy, and full of accidents. We are distracted, forgetful, and reckless, and sometimes the unexpected happens, and if we're lucky, we're still physically or mentally intact to pick up the pieces afterwards. But that can't be all. Our psyches, bodies, and spirits need ways for us to integrate, wrestle with, grieve, ground, be seen, and understand what our minds can't figure out. According to the ritual scholar Jonathan Z. Smith, "ritual is a way of performing the way things *ought to be* in conscious tension to the *way things are*."[*] What that means is that ritual gives us a controlled and safe place to approach the shattered, overwhelming pieces and temporarily re-collect them into some semblance of order. Social philosopher Daniel Schmachtenberger says that "sense-making is about the exploration into what is real, and what is meaningful is bound to what is real,"[†] and ritual can offer us a unique space to sort through the memory of what happened and distinguish what is meaningful and what isn't, what is a miracle and what is an accident.

August 27, 2012, would be forever deemed "the Dreaded Fucking Day" (DFD), when Beth's partner Michael hit a rock while mountain biking, flipped over, and broke his neck. After forty-five days in the ICU and three subsequent months in the hospital, Michael ended up looking like Frankenstein's monster, with stitches going up and down his neck sewing it back together. The rock Michael hit that morning made him into a quadriplegic, uprooting him from any access to the core of his own body. But that day also marked the end of one life for Beth and Michael, forcing them to give up

---

* Jonathan Z. Smith, "The Bare Facts of Ritual," *History of Religions* 20, no. 1/2 (August–November 1980): 112–27, http://www.jstor.org/stable/1062338.
† Daniel Schmachtenberger, "The War on Sensemaking," Rebel Wisdom YouTube channel, August 19, 2019, https://www.youtube.com/watch?v=7LqaotiGWjQ.

where they thought their life was headed and to reorient toward a totally different way of being in the world and of being together. So much they had taken for granted disappeared. They lost their privacy, with round-the-clock caretakers coming and going. They lost their home and savings, with all the costs that came with Michael's being disabled. And they lost their ability to be intimate through sex and to have a child. "I had to give up the dream of having our own baby. Having a quad as a partner is like having a very big baby," Beth said. Michael wasn't dead, but so much had died.

In the early days, Beth was rageful. She would lash out at strangers in the grocery store or to anyone close to her because she didn't know who to be angry at. She was furious at the bike, at gravity, and at Michael for doing what he loved to do. But her anger was also evidence that this was all too much for her and there wasn't any space to slow down and recognize what had happened—a space to hold her in the grief for the life she had lost. It took a close friend turning to her one day and saying point-blank, "a really fucked thing happened to you," to make Beth realize she needed to be acknowledged for going through this traumatizing initiatory process. She needed help grokking the impossible reality that this was her life now and it was not changeable. She needed to make sense out of something nonsensical—to digest something too big for her mind, body, and soul to metabolize.

So Beth turned to ritual. On the first anniversary of the DFD, Beth and her closest friends went to the exact spot on the trail with the big boulder where Michael broke his neck, in order to mark the place and moment that forever changed their life. She laid her body on the earth, drummed on a hand drum, screamed until her throat was sore, threw rocks at "that fucking boulder," and then poured water on it, which also let the grief pour out from her, all while being witnessed by her closest friends: "I felt like a horse running through a gate," Beth said. "I needed that ritual to move all the emotion so I could finally rage and scream and let my anger and grief be seen and heard." And for many years onward Beth did a lot more grief rituals that let her access the unuttered and unspoken emotion that lived in the depths beneath her rational mind.

Ritual lets us approach the "why of things"—why did this happen, why me, why am I still alive—without demanding an answer. Answers might come, but the questioning itself becomes more powerful and cathartic than any answer that surfaces. Meaning, grief, wonder, memory ride on the back of these questions. And ritual provides the mechanism by which we can, to paraphrase French anthropologist Arnold van Gennep, pivot ourselves toward the sacred. What that means is that ritual gives us the controlled environment to direct questions, objects, and actions into relationship with the Sacred Mystery. Ritually pivoting toward the sacred transformed Beth's experience of throwing rocks from a random act of violence to a meaningful expression of rage. The boulder itself became a sacred, mysterious object to rail against and grieve over. And the ritual housed her question of "why did this happen" in a safe container that let her see and be seen, feel and be felt, question and wonder about how and why the cards fell as they did.

One more story: Sharon survived the Camp Fire wildfire in Butte County in the fall of 2018, but her home didn't. The home that she and her husband had lived in for twenty years burned to the ground in a matter of hours. But it wasn't just her home. Sharon lost the very framework that gave her a sense of belonging, tethering her not just to an address but to her routines, her memories, and her community. The only familiar thing that survived the fire was an iron gazebo. As Sharon and her husband stumbled toward a new beginning, eventually finding their next home filled with all new, unfamiliar things, the iron gazebo remained a link to her past and became a sacred object. On the first anniversary of the fire, Sharon and her husband dismantled the gazebo and brought it back to their new place. But it was the ritualized action of taking it apart, carrying it, putting it back together, and then putting it in a place on the new land that allowed Sharon to find some ground in the groundless. She pivoted toward the sacred by seeing the gazebo as a ritual object, possessing deeper meaning, carrying sacred memory, and being a beloved connection to her pre-fire life. And even though she couldn't reassemble what was before, "finding those pieces, like the gazebo, is helping me try to make something foreign recognizable."

Ritual can temporarily arrange the disordered into some order but it is certainly not a fix-it for the devastation, loss, and injury that can accompany a near-death experience. Rituals aren't meant to fix anything. But they can bring substance to loss. They can help us see what we've been feeling or feel what we've been holding. Ritual can make the unknown not necessarily known but identifiable and present. And by doing that, it helps us relate to the trauma differently. We can slow our approach, listen, and sense our bodies, feel the Earth body, grieve, be witnessed, and begin to make sense of the fact that a "fucked thing happened."

THE RISE *and* FALL RITUAL

Falling is frightening. I've done it many times, and most likely you have too. I've fallen from bikes, trees, ladders, surfboards, and especially from big boulders while rock climbing. Falling is never guaranteed yet always a possibility, and after a lifetime of doing it, it's become one of my greatest teachers. Falling is necessary for learning, needed for growing, and built into the architecture of grief. Yet falling is forever in full retreat in our modern culture. We're okay with babies falling while learning to walk, but we adults are constantly barraged by the seduction of success and the tyranny of recovery. If we're down, the mantra is: stand back up. If we strike out, we're told to get back in the game. And, if we're undone, we're encouraged to pull ourselves together again.

Modernity places enormous value and attention on the holy trinity: stability, productivity, and recovery. Yet what about the wisdom and healing that comes when we "let it fall"? What gets expressed when we can allow ourselves to be wrecked, undone, winded, and humbled without the need to figure it out, to appear collected and/or put together? What if, in the wake of an accident, we gave ourselves the space to fall down and fall apart as a way of being with our losses. Ian, a survivor of many severe accidents, said, "When you finally land on the ground, you can stand back up."

The purpose of this ritual is to let what fell be felt—in your body and with the Earth body. It's a way to tangibly approach the overwhelm, see the inconceivable, and encounter the completely fucked, not through the lens of the intellect but felt, embodied, and experienced by the many dimensions of your emotional and sensual self. It is also a way to be witnessed and loved in your undone-ness, because some things are just too hard to hold on our own.

Sometimes the shame or blame that follows surviving a near-death experience can also bring isolation. The gift that ritual can provide is a space to approach the fall, not alone but together, which is exactly what the etymology of the word "collapse" tells us it means, coming from the Latin *collabi*—"to fall together." Every single human has been fucked up and injured, which means you don't have to feel alone in that.

The inner mechanics of this ritual can be done with words or wordlessly. There are prompts below that can be expressed through speech and reflection, but if they come out in the emotional dialect of rage, grief, shame, or fear, so be it. There is no right way to do this ritual, just as there is no right way to metabolize trauma. There is a wrong way, however, which is to try to force the trauma to change. This ritual is not intended to confront healing head-on, but rather to let what is unexpressed have a diffracting lens to come out and be seen. Whatever happens is enough. The intention is simple: Slow down, fall down, and have the space to find your own pace back into organization and togetherness.

Asking for Help

Almost half of those I interviewed for this chapter said that if they could boil down the challenge of surviving a near-death experience to one thing it would be learning how to ask for help. Very often the kind of care someone needs when healing from trauma is too much to handle alone, which actually reveals the silver lining of these traumatic moments: the layers of potential collectivity and interdependence.

With that in mind, the first thing to do is hand off the responsibility of organizing this ritual. Do *not* pass go and do *not* do this yourself. The process of making meaning from something too vast to understand takes many hands and many hearts. Practice asking for help from someone you trust, someone to whom you can fully give the responsibility. Start by giving them this chapter bookmarked.

Prepare

Intentions

May I slow down with it all and allow myself to revisit this overwhelming experience in a structured, ritualized container. May I be witnessed so that I can feel a sense of connection in the brokenness. May I have the space to, even temporarily, come back into contact with my body, with my emotions, with others. May I let as much information be processed and integrated as wants to be.

You Will Need

- Ten or more large stones
- Charcoal for writing
- A pitcher of water

Invite

Do not over-invite to this ritual. Whoever is doing the inviting, let it be a small list of people that is based in what author Priya Parker calls "thoughtful, concerned exclusion."* What that means is that by severely limiting who can attend, you are actually focusing the ritual's purpose while homing in on the overall commitment from those invited.

Also, please remind those gathering that their role is only to bear witness. They are not there to offer opinions, suggestions, or guidance, and definitely not to make it about themselves. Rather, everyone's role is to be *with* the person whom this ritual is in service to.

Time

Rituals need to operate with a different pace of time—a much slower one. It's like what Báyò Akómoláfé says, "Times are urgent; let us slow down."† Trauma is often recreated and relived in the mind as if it is still happening, which radiates urgency. Slowing down within a ritualized container offers a way to approach overwhelming feelings with spaciousness and focus so that the magnitude of what happened can appear and register. In other words, you need time without the pressure of time. Therefore, resist trying to schedule this in a short window, and instead invite your guests into a generous amount of time. An example of what that could look like is basing the timeline on the sun's movement rather than the clock's: We start at high noon and end at sunset. Those that can't make the time commitment are not the right guests.

Pre-ritual Setup

An altar. On a table or the ground create an altar that can hold all the objects for the ritual. It can be simple, with a beautiful swatch of fabric, the stones, and maybe some candles. Or you can really spruce

---

* Parker, *The Art of Gathering.*
† Báyò Akómoláfé, "The Times Are Urgent: Let's Slow Down," BayoAkomolafe.net, https://www.bayoakomolafe.net/post/the-times-are-urgent-lets-slow-down.

it up with flowers, photos, and other objects that might carry significance to the survivor. Think about what would best serve the person
this ritual is for.

Cushions or seats. Make a circle of cushions or seats in advance
that provides a shape for where people will sit. Don't be shy about establishing clear physical structure, as it will assist the ritual's purpose.

Comforting objects. When someone possesses the courage to approach their trauma ritually, it can take a toll on their body, their
heart. Consider having blankets, hot beverages, and comforting food
to hold that person after the ritual is complete.

Begin

As with all the rituals in this book, go gently. Let people settle in. Consider offering a song, a poem, or a collective deep breath together. Light a candle. Let the
space be filled with a different tenor that is slower, quieter, and less achievement-
oriented. Again, don't overcomplicate this.

After you get a sense that everyone has arrived, welcome them and restate the
intention for the gathering. Consider explaining the value in sharing ritual space
together, the bravery it takes for your friend to be witnessed in their process, and
how needed they are in your life and in the world. And remind the group of their
commitment to bear witness.

Finally, invite the person who survived this trauma to sit in the center of the
circle.

Stacking the Stones

Place the stones and charcoal in the center with the survivor. Each
stone will represent something that was lost or limited as a consequence of this near-death experience. These could range from something tangible and physical, like a home or a part of the body, to
something emotional, like a feeling of peace or security, or even to
an identity and way of being in the world, like being a mother or a
citizen of a country the person fled. The intention is to stack them up
high, one on top of the other, and witness together as the stone tower
collapses. Begin by sharing the overall mechanism of the ritual with
the group but then give space and silence for it to begin on its own.

Step 1

Invite the survivor to begin by writing on one stone a word or symbol that represents what has been lost or limited.

Step 2

Ask them to sit with that stone for as long as they need. Hold it in their lap or hands. Feel the weight of it. Caress it with their fingers. If they are called to speak about that lost thing, invite them to share a story about what they loved about it, how it came to them, or what it meant to them. If they are not called to speak about it, just sitting with the stone is more than enough. If emotions arise, remind them that this is a secure space to express them. If sounds or movement emerge, remind them to let them out. There are no rules or right ways to do this, but be mindful about how you invite them to express themselves.

Step 3

Have them place the stone on the ground.

Step 4

Invite the circle to take a breath together.

Ask the survivor to repeat steps 1 to 4, placing each stone directly on top of the previous one, stacking them high-up like a cairn.

Eventually, the stone stack will fall, which is intentional. The falling is symbolic of the trauma. It's the necessary action of the ritual.

Gently remind the survivor to take as much time as they need with the stones, even re-stacking them and letting them fall multiple times. When they feel complete, ask them to let the group know.

Cleansing the Stones

This section adds the water element as a way to cleanse the stones after they fell, and access forgiveness and grief.

Hand the pitcher of water to the survivor in the center. Invite them to cleanse the charcoal off each stone.

Again, this can be done in silence or with words.

Ordering the Stones

After they have washed the stones, invite the survivor to arrange and order them into a shape, a pattern, or however they see fit. This offers them a hands-on way to reestablish a sense of order from what may have been emotional and chaotic.

Conclude

Conclude this section by surrounding the survivor in all the comfort you brought for them—blankets, pillows, and a hot beverage. Depending on if it would serve the survivor and the ritual, consider having the last moments of the ritual devoted to all those gathered placing their hands on the survivor, offering them a tangible way of feeling held, touched, grounded, and loved.

If the group wants to say something, invite them to share affirmations that remind the survivor how needed and loved they are.

Reflections

Before ending the ritual, give each witness a couple of minutes to reflect on what they witnessed. Very often emotions, actions, or images show up unexpectedly during a ritual, and it's helpful and necessary to have some space to reflect upon that as a way of reintegrating from the experience. Again, be clear about this being a reflection of what the witnesses noticed, and not a time to go into their own personal stories.

The survivor should be the last person to reflect. Give them the space to share what they experienced, what they noticed, what changed—but only if they want to.

Close with gratitude, perhaps offering a prayer or making an offering on a small plate to thank the survivor's ancestors and all that conspired to give this person back their life. Be sure not to forget this part.

Questions for Further Reflection

- What did this ritual allow me to acknowledge or say?
- What could or couldn't happen in the presence of a safe circle?
- What was held that I released?
- What am I learning or remembering about (my) life?

Receiving a Diagnosis

There's a sickness worse than the risk of death,
and that's forgetting what we should never forget.

—Mary Oliver

You never asked for this and yet, it is yours. Your preferences for how things should be have been utterly defeated. Your desire to be able to choose is suddenly irrelevant. No amount of bargaining or pleading can shift the way things are. This moment, the one you didn't ask for, is thrust upon you and you can't ignore the way the knucklebones have rolled. You've received a diagnosis—*your* diagnosis. This horrible, terrible, overwhelming, unwanted news that leaves you speechless and undone yet still pushes you forward, far too exposed for your liking. The minute you accept this, the medical machine kicks into high gear, like heading into a battle: second opinions, research, treatment plans, scheduling, meds. There's no time for anything else. There's only urgency. Yet what if, amid the relentless immediacy, there was allowed a moment, like a shelter in the storm, to adjust to this new reality—a time to catch your breath, gather yourself, and acknowledge all that is changing.

There is such a thing as synchronicity: The morning I set down to start this chapter, Shoshanna, a dear friend of mine, called to share the news that dropped the floor out from under me. A couple weeks ago, she had found a lump in her breast, and even though she told herself, "I'm only thirty-six, it's probably just a cyst," she decided to get it checked out anyway. I answered the phone, and she started with "The tests just came back and"—I could feel her holding back the terror and tears—"I have breast cancer." We both took a breath. It was in that half-a-second pause that I could feel us staring into a wide abyss. I sensed the uncertainty and urgency in the moment. The guarantee of life, of health, of sexy dates with handsome men, and all the ways she had gotten comfortable and familiar with her days, with her body, was now in question. With this diagnosis, that innocence and youthfulness were leaving. "I feel like I've aged so, so much in these last few weeks. Every scan, every biopsy, the news, the talking with doctors, the heart tests, every single time I had any medical experience and every single time I told someone I loved, I got older—I got weaker." Shoshanna's lament was the grief for her love of life and for all that was about to change—her beautiful long hair, her daily walks with her dog, her relationship to her curvy body, her fertility, her belief that she could always do more, her identity as a healthy person. Instead, this diagnosis revealed just how much everything was out of her hands.

Wanting to grasp onto something when the ground falls out from under you is understandable. At times it can feel like you're oscillating between a negotiation and a plea. *Please let this be treatable. Please let the pain be bearable. Please let me be able to keep my food down. Please let my bowels cooperate. Please let me survive.* You are bargaining with your body, with the doctors, with God. "I remember that bargaining so clearly and I was so desperate," Bonnie said about her niece's leukemia diagnosis. "If I could have been on my knees, I would have. These moments you are so useless— where you have no control. You've lost control and there is nothing to do but beg. That's what a diagnosis is."

These moments reveal the fundamental uncertainty that has always underwritten your entire life. You only thought your body was reliable. You only believed you had control. You had only gotten used to having choices. Now this diagnosis draws the curtain back, revealing what the Buddhist nun Pema Chödrön calls "the groundlessness of our situation," the free fall from realizing that nothing was ever secure or guaranteed in the first place. That control was just an illusion. So how do you stand up when there is nothing to stand on?

Ritual can offer a bit of ground in the groundlessness, not necessarily to return to the delusion of safety but to be able to recognize what is changing and to attempt to make sense of it. When Carl got the second major diagnosis of his life, it truly wrecked him. He was born with cerebral palsy, but surprisingly that wasn't what forced him to grapple with his own fragility and mortality. In the summer of 2007, on a thirty-minute commuter flight he caught a norovirus that should have lasted two or three days but, over a decade later, is still with him today.

Prior to this illness, Carl pushed himself to have the same productivity as an able-bodied person, but that was now impossible. The pain from this illness took away the little that was genuinely Carl's—his ability to read and write, his incredibly sharp intellect, as well as his academic ambitions. It was a huge blow to his identity as his body now sets the agenda for what he is able or not able to do on any given day. Carl wrestles with the anger and grief that has come from losing all the ways he understood himself. "It sounds funny to say this as a disabled person, but I didn't grasp my own limits until this chronic illness brought me to my knees. I already had such few areas that were mine and in my control, and the illness said, 'Nope—we're going to take that and turn it on its head and renegotiate everything.'" He longed to be gathered in by his community, to feel that he had various allies, ancestors, energies to sustain him through this impossibly hard time. He craved a way to actually mark how the chronic illness had changed him as a person and to help weave back the tattered threads of his life with the help of those that he loved and who loved him.

A diagnosis can leave us breathless, grasping, undone. It can also be an opportunity to breathe into all that is changing—relenting, rather than relentlessly trying to fix, resist, or run away. Ritualizing this time can offer ground to stand on where you can touch the fleeting, messy, uncertainty of life with reflection, with beauty, with grief, with rage, with community, with courage, and with love.

The following two rituals are simple, imperfect ways to "be in this" while "going through it." One ritual is for the terrible moment of receiving a diagnosis and the other can be performed days or weeks after, as you begin to process the impact it's had on your life. They both are opportunities to gather your people around you, to witness you in your raw humanity so that you can speak to things unsaid, point to things unseen, and transform as much of the shit into nourishment as possible—remembering what we should never forget.

THE EARTH and SKY RITUAL:
The Day Of

The doctor's office is already a cold and sterile place: machines beeping, paper gowns, bright overhead fluorescent lights. Not a space you would choose to be vulnerable in. Yet receiving a diagnosis can be one of the most shockingly vulnerable experiences of your life—in one conversation your whole world flips upside down. As your brain tries to make sense of it, it can feel like the room is closing in on you. Everything

HELLO, GOODBYE

seems suffocating. No air, no space, no movement. Bonnie, a physician, put it to me bluntly: "No one breathes in a diagnosis." And almost automatically, it can switch into mission mode, fueled by the urgency to figure out a treatment plan and put things in motion.

One of the biggest threats to ritual is speed. Because ritual attempts to slow us down and distinguish what is changing, it can appear frivolous and extraneous. Receiving a diagnosis screams urgency. It evokes fear. You've lost control. There's a need for speed to get tested, start the treatment, figure out what to do, make decisions, and it can seem like there is no moment to breathe—no time to stop. But what is the cost of being thrust forward without acknowledging all the change, loss, and emotion that is embedded in this moment?

Marissa's firstborn son had been born with Down syndrome, and at his nine-month checkup he was diagnosed with leukemia, which shook her family to their core. The very next day after diagnosis, they were in the hospital and stepped immediately into the action phase of treatment, which made Marissa feel splayed open by the speed of things. Throughout her son's first year, they had no time for a baby naming, no opportunity for a bris, or to even celebrate his birth. It all went so fast, which left her marriage strained and her nerves frazzled with anxiety. "There just wasn't any time to adjust to this new reality. If I'd had a moment like that, maybe I could have dialed things down a notch."

Diagnosis pushes you into a totally new landscape. Without realizing it, the person you were when you woke up that morning, when you poured your coffee and tied your shoes, is no longer the person you are. Now you are different. You are a new person, with new circumstances, new fears, and new emotions, and there's barely any chance to say goodbye to the person you knew yourself to be before the diagnosis. In a way, the dominant culture and medical industry just expects you to move forward without understanding the need to say goodbye to the life you had before and hello to the life you've now been dealt—a moment to surrender and reorient.

Moments like this need an emergency brake. What would it look like if, amid the deluge that is a diagnosis, you attempted to slow down and mark this moment? Doing something that brings everything to a halt to help breathe space back into the room. Something that, after the wind has been knocked out of you, brings you back to your body, to your heart, and to the present moment.

These junctures where we encounter our mortality are threshold moments, but the thrust from a diagnosis can feel like we are being forced, pushed, and shoved over them, like a riptide. Yet as urgent as things may be, there is always time for a moment to pause and acknowledge how much has changed in an instant. A moment to, as the Greek root of the word *diagnosis* suggests, "distinguish the difference" between who you were and who you now are.

This ritual is that emergency brake. After hearing those unwanted words, this is a way to help you mark this moment in stillness, which is a proper response to encountering the Great Unknown. It has you lie on the earth, look up at the sky, and become silent and watchful—and in that brief silence, remember both what would never be the same and also what would never change.

Prepare

Intentions

May I take a moment to be silent and breathe deeply with the diagnosis before rushing into action. May I mark this moment of change by distinguishing who I was before and who I am now.

You'll Need

- A blanket
- A place to lie on the earth

When

Whether you received your diagnosis in a hospital, doctor's office, or over the phone, try to do this ritual as close to receiving the news as possible. The intention of this ritual is to ground you and give you the space to breathe again so you can return to the urgent decisions that need to be made.

Where

Find a place nearby that is flat and quiet. Maybe that's your lawn, a nearby park, or the beach. Choose to be somewhere where you will not be disturbed.

How Long

Take as much time as you need for each statement. Go slow and don't rush this ritual.

Affirmations

The affirmations below are simple ways for you to find stable ground again when your world is spinning. Use these or make up your own.

Begin

Unfurl your blanket, lie down on the ground, and look up at the sky.
Say out loud: "*I am held.*"
Take some time to feel the Earth underneath you, supporting you.
Say out loud: "*I can breathe.*"
Feel the rise and fall of your lungs and the breeze on your face.
Say out loud: "*I am loved.*"
Put your hands on your stomach or heart and feel the warmth of your body.
Say out loud: "*I am here.*"
Let yourself take in this moment of endings and beginnings. Take some deep breaths.
Say out loud: "*Life is changing.*"
Gaze at the expansive sky and watch the clouds move and the birds fly.

Conclude

Before you conclude, offer a prayer for this moment. Give thanks to your life, to all who will be supporting you, known and unknown, and to the healing of your body. Rise slowly.

Questions for Further Reflection

- Why is it important to slow down after a diagnosis?
- What does lying on the earth do to my energy?
- What did this ritual allow me to feel?
- What did this ritual help me remember?

THE UP *and* OUT RITUAL

Denial can be one of the most challenging yet protective responses to the fear that accompanies a diagnosis. When faced with the loss of health, the loss of control, and the loss of identity, denial can be a strategy to delay having to face an overwhelming reality. Denial can look like not sharing about the diagnosis, delaying or refusing treatment, staying busy, just trying to go on with life as usual, and especially suppressing any feelings that come to the surface.

Isa, who has been through two cancer diagnoses, told me that when receiving the news again, she "went into mission mode and pushed the emotions away and just treated it like any other problem that needed to be solved." Days later, however, the feelings surfaced, and the reality of death became very tangible. She didn't know how much time she had and was swimming in the unknown. So instead of denying it, she chose to turn toward her mortality and let the emotions come up and out. Expressing the sadness, the rage, and the fear also let her get clear about the preciousness of each moment of her life.

The purpose of the Up and Out Ritual is to presence, be witnessed in, and integrate so much of what is happening under the surface—to let it come up and come out and transform into presence and love. There are three parts to this ritual, three distinct ways to work with the roses, each providing you an opportunity to encounter the rage, the grief, and the precious love that this illness has aroused, and bringing your experience to a body much bigger than yours.

A Note on Witnesses

You *can* do this ritual alone. There is certainly nothing wrong with that. But consider this: The process of being diagnosed with an illness can feel alienating and isolating. Since there is already so much pain, labor, worry, and suffering on your shoulders, what if you asked *at least two other people* to gather you in and help hold this space with you. Sometimes when we are in the midst of our suffering, we might not be in a place to see what needs to be seen. This is the purpose of witnesses.

The need for a ritual can also be the glue that binds a group of people together who may not have known themselves to be anything that resembled a "together" in the first place. In other words, when you invite a small group of people to gather and witness you in your pain and prayer, you are also giving them the gift of a purpose as a group. I've seen communities created by coming together around one of their own.

Prepare

Intentions

May I acknowledge what is changing. May I be witnessed in the rawness of my feelings and name and embody the lack of control. May I practice strength, courage, and compassion despite the groundlessness.

You Will Need

- Three bouquets of roses (preferably three distinct colors)
- Items for a small altar
- A warm, cozy blanket
- Hot tea

Where

If you can, bring this ritual to a body of water. It doesn't have to be dramatic, like the Rio Grande or Lake Superior—just some place outside where you can stand before something bigger than you. If that's a local creek or a lake in the park, that's perfectly fine. Why water? Water is life—a healer, a cleanser, a force that can round hard edges. It also moves and can carry your grief, pleas, and prayers back out into the world.

Wherever you choose to be, prioritize privacy. Ritual needs an intimate setting and container for your anger, grief, or love to come on its own without the fear of being self-conscious that someone else might be nosing around.

A Friend at the Reins

Even if there are only two people joining you, hand over this book as well as the responsibilities of this ritual to one of them. Since this is for you, you should not be organizing it, as there is more than enough burden on your shoulders.

From here on out, I will direct my comments to you, the friend, assuming that this book and the organizing role were handed over. Hello.

Altar

Before gathering, consider bringing materials to create a small altar to anchor the ritual. This can be as simple as laying out a small piece of fabric and creating an altar with a couple of special objects or photos you brought from home.

Housekeeping

Again, ease into the ritual. Begin with some housekeeping. Logistics are a great way to step closer in, as they put everyone on the same page with regard to purpose, time, and roles. Here are some questions that can help focus the attention:

- Why are we here?
- What is the ritual's purpose?
- What is the time structure?
- What is the role of the witnesses?
- How will we know it's over?

Time

Set time parameters for each section, twenty to thirty minutes each. A witness can hold the time so that the person who is being witnessed doesn't have to.

How do you get a sense of when each round ends? There might be a point, after the tears flow, where there's a settling down. Or the person with the diagnosis has worked through a layer of the rage, they've expended their energy, and there is just silence. Don't rush this part—just let it be. And always take your cues from the person who this ritual is for.

Advise them to say something like "I'm complete" or "thank you" when they feel finished, to make it clear that they've expressed what needed to be expressed. After they say they are complete, pause and take a collective breath together.

Begin

Speak this section directly to your friend who received a diagnosis.

The First Bouquet: Anger

This round is devoted to the resistance, the anger, the rage at the cards you've been dealt. As you respond to the question, know that some of your response might be expressed in words and other parts might come out through a "FUCK YOU!" "NO!" or a scream. Keep responding until you've got nothing left to express.

The action for this round is to smash, tear, bash, break, throw, and rip apart the bouquet of flowers in order to get into the primal emotion. For each break or tear name something you are furious at losing from this illness.

The first bouquet question:

What are you angry about losing from this illness?

The Second Bouquet: Grief

This round is devoted to the sadness and sorrow at what you are losing from this illness—all that you are yielding, surrendering, and saying goodbye to.

As you respond to the question, know that some of it might be expressed in words while other parts might be expressed in sobs or silence.

The action for this round is to pluck the petals off this bouquet and send them off, one by one, into the body of water. For each petal placed into the water, name one thing you are losing or scared of losing from this illness.

The second bouquet question:
What are you losing and grieving from this illness?

The Third Bouquet: Meaning

This round is devoted to all that gives you strength and meaning beyond this illness: What do you love? What is more valuable than ever right now? What are you devoting yourself to?

The action for this round is to take the flower petals from the bouquet and create any shape you want on the ground. This can be a circle, a heart, a spiral, a diamond—whatever feels right to you. For each petal placed on the earth, name one thing that feeds your soul and gives you life—something you cannot live without.

The third bouquet question:
What gives you strength in spite of this illness?

Conclude

This ritual likely brought up some hard, vulnerable feelings. As the energy settles, it is a good time for a lot of care, both physically and emotionally.

As a witness, gather your beloved friend up in warm blankets and hot tea. Let them feel the gentle safety of being wrapped up and cared for.

A good ending question for everyone gathered to discuss is: *Name something bigger that is holding us right now.*

This question can help everyone remember how much more vast the world is and how many ways our lives are continuously supported, even in the midst of an illness.

And in the same slow way you entered in, don't rush the exit. Take your time. Pour more tea. Tell more stories. Hug. Take good care.

Questions for Further Reflection

- What does this ritual help me express?
- What do I remember from this ritual?
- Why is it important to do this with witnesses?
- What am I more connected to than I was beforehand?

THE ONLINE RITUAL

I'm writing this book in the midst of a pandemic and social distancing. And yet life continues on—babies are born, couples get married, and people are diagnosed with illnesses. So how do you do a ritual when no one can get together in the flesh?

Recently, a friend of mine was diagnosed with cancer. As the medical machine was ramping up, I knew she needed to mark this moment right before her treatment started and her life changed forever. I asked if she would be willing to let me host an online video ritual with a select group of her trusted and beloved friends—a gathering to let her express her heart, feel our support, and mark this moment. She consented, and the ritual below is what transpired. Use it as inspiration for those meaningful gatherings that can't happen in person, but still need to happen.

Prepare
Hand This Off

Do not organize your own ritual. As I stated in the Up and Out Ritual, there is far too much burden on your shoulders to organize your own ritual. Give this over to a trusted friend. You are giving them the incredible purposeful gift of supporting you in a tangible way.

A sample invitation:

"As you know, this moment is unlike any other for our friend _____, as they are entering a new chapter of their life that will be completely focused on healing their body from _____. While speaking recently, we acknowledged the need for them to not rush past this moment but to slow down with it, mark it, and be witnessed in it. Because there is so much uncertainty and change happening—physically, emotionally, existentially—I suggested they ritualize this moment to help ground it and bring it meaning. Everyone here is a very important part of our friend's life and their support circle. Please join us online . . . "

And of course, name the link, the time, date, duration, and what to bring.

You Will Need
- Four candles and a lighter
- A drink of wine, spirits, or anything libation-y
- A one-sentence prayer for the person's healing (Have each friend write this down.)
- An envelope
- A pen

A Buddy
If possible, try to have someone next to you during the online ritual. Even though your support circle is "present," there is still a screen separating you. It's really quite helpful to have a warm hand on your back, someone to fetch some hot tea and pass you the tissues if you need them.

Begin
From here on out, I will direct my comments to you, the trusted friend who is holding the reins of this online ritual.

Housekeeping
As everyone signs into the virtual gathering room, spend about ten minutes orienting everyone to what is about to happen. Because this gathering is online, it really needs you to hold the reins quite firmly, giving simple, clear instructions about purpose, time, and etiquette.

Here are some topics to speak to:
- Why are we gathered?
- Why a ritual?
- What is the structure?
- What are the time parameters?
- What etiquette is permitted and not permitted from everyone gathered? (For instance, no opinions or advice. We are here to witness, reflect, and bless.)

Also, I've found it very helpful to give a special word to the person you are gathering around to help them indicate that they are complete. In many Jewish ritual spaces, we use the Hebrew words *dibarti* and *shamati*, which mean "I've spoken" and "I hear you." Offer two signal words for the whole group to indicate completion. Even saying "thank you" at the end of each share serves that purpose.

Four Rounds

Each question is asked to the person you are gathering around. Ideally, they have around ten minutes to speak to whatever is on their heart.

Before each round begins, invite the participants to each light their candle. This is a simple and accessible ritual action that can give the group something to do together while being apart.

Light the first candle.

First Round

What has changed since you've been diagnosed?

After the person you are gathering around has finished, ask the group to take a collective breath together and light the second candle.

Second Round

What are you losing? What are you scared of losing?

After they have finished, ask the group to take a collective breath together and light the third candle.

Third Round

What do you need reminding of? What do you need support with?

After they have finished, ask the group to take a collective breath together and light the fourth candle.

Fourth Round

What is important to you? What are you recommitting to?

After they have finished, ask the group to take a collective breath together.

Toasting

After the four rounds are over (and maybe even a bathroom break), you are now going to hand the microphone over to each person who is present. I would recommend reminding the group again:

no opinions, advice, or suggestions. Give each person a limited amount of time (I find three minutes tops to be perfect) and ask them to raise a glass to their friend and bless their life, their health, and their healing. Maybe they read from the piece of paper that they wrote in advance or maybe they speak from their heart in the moment.

The Paper

As the group finishes their toasting, invite them to take the paper with the blessing and to put it into an envelope. Write your friend's address on the envelopes and encourage the group to put these in the mail as a tangible way for your friend to feel everyone's support and to be reminded of the ripples of love and prayer that will extend long after this online ritual is over.

Conclude

While lingering is a staple of a post-ritual gathering, it's quite challenging to do this in an online video room. Good thing everyone has a drink. Invite the group to hang around afterward and continue to mingle, drink, make toasts, and tell stories.

Questions for Further Reflection
- What could I acknowledge during this ritual?
- What could I feel when being witnessed by my friends?
- What came to the surface unexpectedly while sharing?
- What important reminders am I taking away from this ritual?

A Global or National Crisis

"I wish it need not have happened in my time," said Frodo.
"So do I," said Gandalf, "and so do all who live to see such times.
But that is not for them to decide. All we have to decide
is what to do with the time that is given us."

—J. R. R. Tolkien

Maybe every generation says this, but we are most certainly weathering the tempest in these turbulent times. I can barely scroll through today's harrowing news without feeling myself shutting down in terror as my nervous system rises up in fear. The day's headlines warn us of a spreading pandemic, a warming climate, racial tensions, political polarization, and a global economy teetering on the verge of collapse. It almost seems like Chicken Little was right and the sky is finally about to fall. There are so many reasons to be worried, and yet so much is out of our control. But is it enough to just carry on with our days and try to live out a normal life amid a crisis or catastrophe? Is there something we can do to not feel so helpless and hopeless in the wake of so much collective upheaval? Can we meaningfully mark these monumental times in order to see our way through them?

In the winter of 2018, there was a shooting at my high school alma mater, Marjory Stoneman Douglas in Parkland, Florida. Seventeen people were brutally killed and seventeen wounded by a nineteen-year-old former student who opened fire with a semi-automatic rifle. Watching the news was surreal those first few weeks as I kept on seeing so many familiar places. Even though school shootings have been happening for years, this one was different—this was *my* high school, my old stomping ground.

And while the rest of the world carried on after sending their obligatory "thoughts and prayers," I just couldn't. It hit too close to home, interrupting the regularity of my days. I kept wondering how a place that was so familiar could be so utterly, catastrophically changed in just a few hours. And how could I carry on with life as usual when it was anything but?

Yet to be completely honest, I did. Perhaps even too quickly. Most of us do after the shock of an event like this. We actually clamber to return to normal—to return to the way things were when life was certain, familiar, comfortable, safe. But it can feel a bit like Humpty Dumpty with things falling apart and no matter how many times we try, we just can't put them back together again. Whether it's a plague, an act of terrorism, a life-changing election, a recession, a shooting, a natural disaster, or a climate catastrophe, these moments throw us from our best-laid plans and remind us of the fragility of our normal lives.

In a way, "normal" is like a trance that prevents us from interfacing with how uncertain and tenuous life really is, and these major national and global crises temporarily obliterate that safety. At the onset of the COVID-19 pandemic, author Charles Eisenstein reported that what was happening felt "like a rehab intervention that breaks the addictive hold of normalcy."* Suddenly, the daily routine is interrupted—that scheduled vacation canceled, the secure job terminated, the stock portfolio decimated. What you once thought was tightly in your grasp isn't anymore, and what was whole a moment ago is broken now. Life unveils her ephemerality.

And the pieces we're left to pick up in the aftermath can instigate panic, denial, confusion, despair, or depression. A feeling of helplessness may prevail as many of the guideposts we rely on for security disappear. Questions like *What should I do now?* or *When will things be normal again?* are common as we grope for some semblance of order or familiarity. Immediately trying to pivot or fix is an understandable reflex, but it can be like grasping at straws. Sometimes the collateral damage is too much.

As I write this, most of the world is desperately trying to emerge from a global pandemic. In the blink of an eye, our lives have changed. We are facing a societal meltdown unlike anything we've seen in our lifetime. Nothing is normal and so much of our daily life is altered. Uncertainty is the air we breathe, and these times are asking something from us, something different than any other time that we can remember. But we can't understand what that is unless we stop running away from this threshold and running

---

* Charles Eisenstein, "The Coronation," CharlesEisenstein.org, March 2020, https://charles eisenstein.org/essays/the-coronation/.

back toward normal, safe, and "how things were." In other words, as author Báyò Akómoláfé asks, "What if the ways we respond to a crisis is part of the crisis?"[*]

The uncertain times we find ourselves in need something from us that may not have been needed before—a different way to approach a different time. If we look at the etymology of the word "crisis," it actually gives us a clue. The root of the word doesn't really have anything to do with catastrophe or cataclysm but rather comes from the Proto-Indo-European word *krei* meaning "to sieve or distinguish." In other words, during a crisis, we must first be able to discern that this time is different than any other time. It is not a normal time. And, therefore, we must become a faithful witness to that.

During Passover, the need to distinguish is so important that it's actually ritualized. Throughout the seder, it is tradition to read from a book called the Haggadah, which recalls the ancient crisis of the enslavement of the Jewish people in Egypt and the enormous struggle they underwent to pass through those narrow times and into liberation. One of the songs traditionally sung by the youngest person at the table is called "*Mah Nishtanah*," which translated from Hebrew means "What Is Different?" In the song, the child asks four questions to understand what makes this night different from all other nights. The lyrics serve as a generational tool to teach the child, and therefore everyone gathered, the importance of making distinctions and especially not treating special times normally, for these times are trying to teach us differently.

If you dove into this chapter, perhaps this is not a normal time for you and for the collective—perhaps something monumental has happened that has left everyone adrift on the great ocean of uncertainty. Perhaps that adriftness has you longing, almost compulsively, to return to the safe shores of certainty. Maybe you've found yourself paddling furiously, trying so desperately to recover that familiar place but unable to find your way back there. And so your little ship floats in the expansive waters of these times, and you wonder if you'll ever return or even want to go back.

So then what? How do we stay together when things are falling apart? What do we do with the broken pieces that once looked like our normal schedule, our income, or our safety? And in the midst of such loss, is there a proper place for our grief? And for healing? Mister Rogers once said, "Sometimes we have to struggle through a tragedy

---

[*] "Dr. Bayo Akomolafe on Slowing Down in Urgent Times," in *For the Wild*, podcast, January 22, 2020, https://forthewild.world/listen/bayo-akomolafe-on-slowing-down-in-urgent-times-155.

to feel the gravity of love. Love is what keeps us together and afloat." And ritual is a way to presence both the undeniable grief and love that accompany the time.

It could be said that all rituals emerge from a need to reduce anxiety and find stability in changing circumstances. However, the real underlying purpose of ritual is to give us a meaningful way of returning to what is meaningful in our lives and in the world, especially in moments of uncertainty—a way that resources us in a language other than fear. In other words, ritual provides a clear, steady, and reliable focus when the world is spinning.

These crisis thresholds define our generations: We must mark them because we have been marked by them. The challenge, though, of defining these crises that have so inexorably defined our collective lives is that it requires us to put aside our impulse to fix, futz, and figure out, and let the brokenness be. We must listen, learn, and be changed from the brokenness of our days. We must slow down long enough to sense the wisdom in not knowing, and value the way that a time of collective struggle humbles us. Perhaps there is something of enormous worth discoverable only here and now that we can't access during those normal times. Maybe these times offer us generational gifts and a purpose that can change a world so desperately needing change.

THE BROKEN WHOLE BOWL RITUAL

The aim of this ritual is to redeem this broken time by breaking a bowl and then making something beautiful with the shards of it. By doing so, you can both acknowledge the real pain, anger, and loss that come with a crisis and eventually transform those emotions by doing something tangible and symbolic with those shards.

The ritual was inspired by the Japanese practice called *kintsugi*, or "golden repair." When a ceramic vessel breaks, it should be repaired with care that beautifies the cracks instead of hiding them. Rather than throwing the bowl away, the fault line of where it cracked is filled with a resin mixed with powdered gold, which, when dried, highlights those places. The mythologist Michael Meade says that "golden repair depends upon a realization that there is something valuable and essentially beautiful that is worth preserving and sharing."[*] In other words, the gold helps to make the place of injury into a place of beauty, of value, and of meaning.

---

[*] Michael Meade, "Golden Repair of the Cracks in the World," Mosaic Voices, December 14, 2017, https://www.mosaicvoices.org/golden-repair-of-the-cracks-in-the-world.

The first part of this ritual, "Breaking," is intended to be performed after the dust has settled from a crisis event. Do not do this ritual when real logistics need to be planned, but when the emotional impact of the crisis starts to set in. The second part, "Shards," is a time devoted to just be with the broken pieces, before you try to repair them. And, the third part, "Healing," is the mending of the shards and of the pain from the crisis.

This ritual has three sections because the process of healing takes time. If we only look at the shattered pieces of our lives, we can easily get overwhelmed and depressed. Yet if we only look to move on and put everything back together without honoring the loss, then we displace our grief and cling to something that doesn't exist anymore. This ritual is a creative way to recognize that the vessel of our lives and our world is broken and yet whole simultaneously. They both need a place at the table because they both are true. And often the most powerful art and the richest lives come from a willingness to bring the broken and the whole together beautifully.

PART 1: BREAKING

Prepare

Intentions

May this ritual give me and my family a way to express grief, to acknowledge loss, and to mark the impact that this crisis has had upon our lives. May I harvest the lessons from this crisis while recognizing my resilience within it. May I remember what's really important about my life, and life as a whole, as I navigate this time.

You Will Need

- One ceramic bowl
- Hammer
- A cloth to wrap the shards within
- Optional: one black marker

> ## What Kind of Bowl?
> ---
> Choose one that you don't mind smashing or feel free to be bold and use one that is especially precious to you. *Why would you do that?* Using something that already matters to you is like putting "skin in the game" and can make the ritual even more meaningful.

Begin

There are four rounds of breaking. Each time you break the bowl, you are acknowledging out loud something or someone that's been impacted by the crisis.

You can smash the bowl either at the beginning of each section or at the end. For example, if you want to acknowledge losing your job due to the crisis, you can smash part of the bowl first and then tell the story, or you can tell the story first and then punctuate it with a smash. You decide what is right for you but whatever you choose, be consistent.

The four rounds are:

1. Name the ways your personal life has been impacted.
2. Name the ways your family/friends have been impacted.
3. Name the ways the environment/nature has been impacted.
4. Name the ways the greater world has been impacted.

If the crisis strongly impacts some or one of these categories but not another, just eliminate the one not impacted. Remember: These creative rituals are just like recipes—so take what works and leave what doesn't.

Start with a Breath

Because you are turning toward loss, this ritual can be rather emotional. Tears are a totally understandable and love-filled response when you're in the presence of what is no longer here. Therefore, before each round, pause. Take in three deep breaths and feel the ground underneath you, supporting you. These still moments between the breaking are as important to the ritual as the breaking itself. Take your time.

Go Deeper

For those of you interested in more structure for a deeper share, you can break down each round into three sections. Each section represents the past, present, or future. This can be a helpful structure in order to follow the timeline of a crisis and how it continues to ripple through your life. Again, these are prompts to facilitate storytelling and witnessing so that we can see more clearly in confusing times.

Breaking down each category into three sections:

1. Speak about what was supposed to be.
For instance, two of my best friends planned their wedding and the date happened to fall during the 2020 global pandemic. They had so much planned, so much excitement and anticipation generated around this event, and the cancellation was completely out of their control. Use this section to name all the ways it was "supposed to be."

2. Speak about what is.
Acknowledge the crisis here and tell the story of how things are now. For instance, these same friends struggled with the decision to postpone the wedding but as the pandemic got more severe, they had to release the date and everyone they'd booked. The original date is coming up, and they are planning on celebrating their "almost wedding" with a weekend alone. Use this section to tell the story of how things are playing out—the unexpected circumstances.

3. Speak about what may happen.
Even though things may still be in the air, it's important to acknowledge what is still uncertain. For instance, my friends are still unsure when the wedding will take place and there is curiosity and anxiety mixed in with that. Feel free to name your worries, concerns, and hopes about the future here.

End with a Breath and a Prayer

Once you're done breaking the bowl, take a breath and a long moment of silence. Letting the silence speak gives a chance for everything to settle.

Conclude

Finish with reflection and/or a prayer. For example, here's something I said recently during the time of this pandemic:

> So much has changed since this crisis descended. So much loss. So much to contend with. May I find courage, perseverance, and a sense of purpose during this time of uncertainty.

Write your own words or just speak from your heart.
Let that be the end of the ritual.

PART 2: SHARDS

Identify the Shards

If you'd like to really remember what each shard stands for, you can take a black marker and write one word on each piece. For instance, if a vacation was canceled, you can write "Iceland" or "travel" on one. If someone was injured or died as a result of the crisis, you can write their name on a shard. This can help distinguish each piece so that the shards can actually carry the memory of that time.

Live with the Shards

Afterward, you should have little bits and pieces of your bowl on the fabric. You are not going to immediately fix the bowl. Instead put these shards in a special place in your home, like on an altar or a mantelpiece. *Why?* Because the broken pieces aren't purposeless but are evidence that this crisis has impacted and affected you. They mean something now. By letting them live in a special spot, the shards not only represent all the loss, the hardship and sorrow, they carry another message: *Life is utterly precious—impermanent even. Do not take it for granted.*

Try to give the shards a bit of your attention every day. If you have a meditation practice, consider sitting in front of them. Maybe at night you can light a candle next to them. Or if life is just too crazy, find a moment or two during the day to just pause in that spot and take in a deep breath.

The reason is simple: Healing happens when attention is given.

PART 3: HEALING

There may be some of you who wanted to jump to this part of the ritual. Having evidence of those broken bits is deeply uncomfortable and your instinct is to fix it fast. Others of you may take years to arrive here, if you get here at all. Maybe the pain is still too great and you're just not ready for any kind of healing.

While only you can decide when you're ready, it may be helpful to choose a certain amount of time to bookend the brokenness so you can begin the third part of the ritual. This time container is a way to slow down those who want to move on too quickly and speed up those who tend to linger too long in grief. The limit allows a person to fully inhabit their emotions and be with what has happened.

Choose the amount of time to begin this section that is relevant to you. For instance, if I were performing this ritual after the school shooting at Marjory Stoneman Douglas High School in Florida, I might choose seventeen in honor of the number of people who died. This could become seventeen days, weeks, or months. Whatever number of days or weeks you choose, do choose one. Counting is a fundamental part of ritual, and counting time helps the ritual to continue.

Repurpose the Shards

Sometimes we can't or shouldn't put our life back into the same shape it was in before. This might be true with the bowl too. If you're inspired to repurpose the shards into something other than a bowl, go for it. Maybe you want to make a mosaic or scatter them in a garden path. If your inner artist is saying "I have a better idea!" listen to them! What's most relevant is that the shards don't remain as shards but are re-created into something new.

Prepare

You Will Need

- Ceramic glue or Gorilla glue
- A colored marker, glitter, or pigment (Metallic colors like gold, silver, or bronze are my favorites, but you can use any color that you love.)
- A pair of scissors
- Paper
- Pen

Begin

Put It Together

1. *Hold a shard in your hand.* Feel the sharp, ragged edges. As you feel it, let yourself remember something broken by this crisis. Close your eyes and take a breath.
2. *Say what you are doing.* Acknowledge that you are simultaneously remembering the pain caused by the crisis and are also healing from it. If you need a prompt, you can say something like "When I broke this bowl, so much had

been changed by this crisis. Specifically, I remember when _____ was canceled/lost/interrupted/injured."

3. *Glue the pieces together.* Recognize that this is a time for healing and reconciliation and consider saying: "I am healing the _____ part of my life and am putting it back together."

4. *Repeat for each piece or just do this once.*

5. *Let the glue dry.*

6. *Pause, breathe.*

Conclude

The bowl is back together. It's not perfect and can't/shouldn't look exactly as it did before you broke it. That imperfect, scarred edge is what you are about to beautify. *Take out the colored marker or glitter and highlight/color the cracks.*

As you are colorizing the cracks on the bowl, it's also crucial to acknowledge this for yourself and your life. This has been a time of struggle and pain, but that is not all. Maybe you've been on the receiving end of learning what's important and unimportant, strengths you didn't know you had and new behaviors, capacities, and mindsets that were born from the crisis. This bowl can hold both the pain and the praise.

Ask yourself: *What are the gifts I'm carrying only as a result of this crisis?* Here are some examples:

- Resilience
- Forgiveness
- Adaptability
- Self-care
- Rest
- Being with what is

If you are doing this ritual with your friends/family, this can be spoken aloud. If you are doing this solo, give yourself time to journal.

Bring the bowl to your altar or the mantelpiece the shards once occupied. Or use the bowl in your kitchen as a meaningful object marked by a particular time of your life.

This bowl is now a ritual object—evidence of not just your capacity to turn toward your pain and recognize the brokenness but also your willingness to make something beautiful from it. Let it serve as a reminder of your resilience during a troubled time.

Questions for Further Reflection

- What is the purpose of "time boundaries" on this ritual? How does that help the healing process?
- Why not toss the shards? What's the purpose of highlighting the cracks?
- What gifts can a crisis offer us? Why is it important to acknowledge them? And how can they help our lives and our generational purpose?

GOODBYE.

E very hello is a goodbye and every goodbye, a hello. Births and deaths, departures and arrivals, endings and beginnings—there cannot be one without the other. We wave our hands to welcome and wave them the exact same way to bid farewell. Even though at times we may believe that life only moves in one direction, if we can step back and broaden our gaze, we can see that these hello, goodbye moments hinge on a door that swings back *and* forth.

This has been a book about rituals. Rituals place us right at that door's threshold, and their purpose is to help us acknowledge that something happened, something has changed: We are no longer the person we were. We no longer have the relationship we did. We no longer call this place home. Our child is not the same, our body is not the same, this time is not the same. Rituals mark distinctions—helping us recognize what was and what is—so that we can wonder how it came to be: *How did my child become a teenager? How did I just survive cancer? How did I get to be fifty years old?* To wonder like this takes real courage and a deeper vulnerability because to see change is to be changed.

This book understands ritual as a way to return to our human capacity as beauty- and meaning-makers. Over the centuries, rituals have been claimed by the realm of religion, but they actually predate religion—their roots are much older and far deeper. From my perspective, they belong to the people, and most especially to the people's imagination. Anything can be ritualized and made holy. For instance, a bath can just be a bath, but it can also be transformed into a healing oasis, a cleansing immersion, or a sanctuary for grief. Reimagining and reawakening the spirit of a ritual in any moment is to remember that the only thing that separates the divine and the mundane is our willingness to make it so.

From the start, I have always seen this book more akin to a cookbook than anything else. While I have served as the ritual chef, bringing you inspired ritual recipes from my own imaginative kitchen, my greatest hope is that this book empowers you to cook for yourself. There have been too many threshold moments that tried their hardest to make it into these pages and, due to a lack of space, were crowded out. But just because you don't find them here doesn't mean you can't open your creative cupboard, choose your own ritual ingredients, and try your hand at making a meaningful meal. The worst that can happen is that it comes out bland or burned, so you simply refine the recipe and try again. This is how any delicious dish came to exist.

Also, it's perfectly fine to make and eat this meal alone. I do plenty of rituals by myself. But we already live in a lonely and isolated culture—one that has forgotten the real value of belonging. I hope that throughout this book, you have been inspired to turn your transitions into not just nourishment for yourself but food that can feed your people too. Being human is to forget, and rituals are ways we can remember to remember. Sometimes remembering is to recognize that other people have been here before us and that we don't have to cross this threshold alone. When we can allow ourselves to invite others into these ritualized spaces, even handing them over so we can be held and witnessed inside of them, then we are taking the scattered and broken pieces that naturally happen and making them whole again, which is what "to remember" truly means.

Beginnings and endings rouse wonder. They can wake us from the slumber of the familiar and the spell of the inevitable and remind us that life is forever ephemeral and fleeting. Seeing our life this way is to stop taking it for granted and receive it as a gift that is always coming and going. To greet life this way is to unclench our hands and let our hearts break over and over again, because then we can remember that the gift was only borrowed and was never ours to begin with. This book is a brokenhearted love letter to these holy moments of comings and goings. And the rituals within this book are a way to feel how precious it is to be so close to, so intimate with our lives that we can't help but make beauty from our losses and joys so that life can continue on.

I began this book with a Jewish prayer, and I will end it with a Hebrew folk song that is sung at moments of arrival and departure. The song centers around the shape-shifting and quite queer word "shalom," which, depending on the moment, can transform itself into hello, goodbye, or peace. A perfect word for this book and a perfect prayer for a time of endings and beginnings.

> *Shalom, chaverim,*
> *shalom, chaverim,*
> *shalom, shalom.*
> *L'hitraot, l'hitraot,*
> *shalom, shalom.*
> *Hello, friend.*
> *Goodbye, friend.*
> *Peace, peace.*
> *'Til we meet again, 'til we meet again,*
> *Hello, goodbye.*

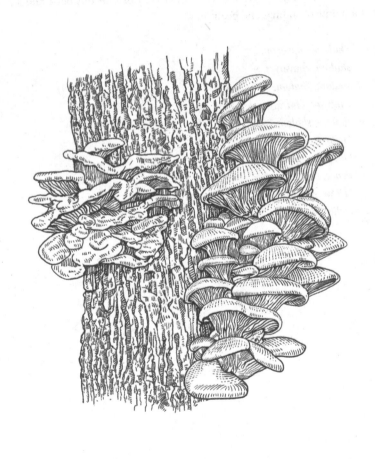

DEEP BOWS

Birthing a book during a pandemic came with no guarantees. There were many moments that tested my faith, dissipated my resolve, and activated my anxiety. And each time I was convinced this book would never come to be, another midwife arrived right by my side to keep calling it forward. I was enormously fortunate to be held by so many people and places during this process, and it would be impossible to thank everyone, but there are a few hands to kiss and heads to adorn for giving so generously.

Firstly, to my Salt Spring Island family who welcomed in this wandering American just as the border closed, and specifically to Tali Weinberg, Natasha Kong, Christopher Roy & family, Jenessa Lenore, Jon Pulker & family, Christine Hrvatin & family, Michael Mann, Malgosia Rawicz & family, Ophir and Dana Bruck, John Wolfstone and Laryssa Tamara, Natalie Baack, and others (you know who you are). And, of course, to Jocelyn and Jarvis Lukow & family and their tiny home sanctuary which became my faithful shelter in the storm.

I have been fortunate to have studied at the feet of the salient and legendary storyteller Stephen Jenkinson and Nathalie Roy of the Orphan Wisdom School, who above all sparked my love of learning, my understanding of grief, and a profound wonderment at how so much came to be.

A special thank-you to the delightful wellspring Tyla Costgrove, who was the first to lay eyes on the newborn manuscript and reminded me to not expect anything but observe everything.

To my agent, Katherine Latshaw of Folio Literary Management, always my steadfast champion, whose resolute guidance steadied me so skillfully through another birth.

To my editor, Ronnie Alvarado of Simon Element, thank you for rising to meet this book so graciously and to all those from what was Tiller Press—my first editor, Hannah Robinson, and my second editor, Anja Schmidt, under the leadership of Theresa DiMasi. Thank you to all for believing in this book's needed-ness in the world and giving it a place to call home.

To the growing Morning Altars team, who not only supported me through this labor but also tended to my first baby when I just didn't have the capacity. To my eagle-eyed Illana Burk, my bacon-loving assistant Jessica Sala, my man of the books Ryan Dematteo, and my wizard of trainings Tim Fife. And to the growing cohort of Morning Altars certified practitioners committed to bringing this practice to communities all over the world. I couldn't have asked for better aunties and uncles to tend to my firstborn.

To my family, alive and dead, whose healing this book is devoted to—to my big-hearted mother, Wendy Schildkret, and my spark plug, beloved granny Shirley Schildkret, to my magical sister-in-law Kaci Diaz, and, most notably, to my noble brother, Matthew Schildkret, who is now my most trusted ally in healing our family line.

To the each and every person who volunteered to open a window into their life and share their sacred story with me and you, giving this book its flesh and bones. Bless your lives: Lilli Weisz, Kyia Downing, Joti Levy, Suzannah Sosman, Sarah Marshank, Steve Marshank, Trevor Oswalt, Nigel Seale, Rachel Kaplan, Ian MacKenzie, Shoshanna Howard, Tali Weinberg, Karina Towers, Shuly Goldman, Zach Fredman, Zivar Amrami, Wendy Lukas, Brian Lukas, Avi Steinhart, Jenessa Lenore, Natasha Kong, Reva Navah, Yigal Deutscher, Karren Reppen, Linda Kriss, Taya Shere, Sige Weisman, Kelly Butler, Patricia DiRenzo, Lori Gale, Aoife Nally, Diane Palmason, Lela Davia, Becky Longardner, Teresa Vincent, Rachelle Padgett, Kelly, Kait Singley, Matthew Stillman, Yaniv Snir, Nickie Kromminga, Raven Miller, Dominique Lando, Christin Ament, Graham, Cynthia James, Judy Williamson, Diane Rudebock, Ahri Golden, Kelly McRee, Kim Chestney, Kimberly Johnson, Barb Phillips, Pavrita, Rebecca Roveto, Dania Morris, Jessica Neafsey, Carl Rabke, Jordankin Dworkin, Jocelyn Lukow, Eleanor Burke, Mariah Agee, Kathy Abbott, Vicki Rosenberg, Ashley Riegler, Audrey Beerman, Lily Datnow, Rae Abileah, Keshira HaLev Fife, Jeanne Carbone,

DEEP BOWS

Michele Faia, Gigi Cachard, Elizabeth Horstmann, Janeta Kobes, Jane Hanson, Beth Erlander, Jeanie Wright, Anne Pittman, Sharon Garcia, Jared Wood, Eyen Zak, Tad Hargrave, Michelle Haviar, Elena Berliner, Lily, Rivka, Karin Sabbeth, Gintare, Marissa Upin, Kristen Reed, Heather Ware, Kayla Rayson, Eric Chisler, Erin Pillman, Carter McGuigan, Andi Last, Michelle Triella, Isa, Kala Wright, Marsha Rosenblatt, Bonnie Vastola, Jen Myzel, Simcha Schwartz, Qristine Hrvatin, Rachel Ruach, Zelig Golden, Lauren Ashley, Rachel Stern, Peter Sabbath, Miriam Rubin, Rachelle Lamb, Dan Dan Schindelman, Eli Marenthal, Michael Mann, Tyla Costgrove, Lupe Wurth, Carol Coogan, Peggy Acott, Tassia Schreiner, Monica Thomas, Elizheva Hurvich, Tamuz Shiran, Melody LeBaron, Lindsay Coulter, Alexandra Mait, Rachel Rose Reid, Tara Elson, Sara Beth Berman, Amanda Nube, Julie Wolk, Melita Silberstein, Jeanne Marie, Rabbi David Steinhardt, Simon Abramson, Ian Holloway, Becky Longardner, Catherine Fixe Chapin, Lauren Anderson, Brad Wolfe, Collin Morrow, Christian Holden, Anthony Porter, Geo Case, and Kyle Lemle.

Last but not least, to the unceded and ancestral territories of the SȾÁUTW (Tsawout) First Nations, where this book was born. HÍSW KE to your generous hospitality, your unceasing beauty, and the unseen mystery singing in your shores, trees, creatures, and waters. You gave this weary traveler a place to call home for some time, and this book is your book too.

BIBLIOGRAPHY

"Ageing Without Children." AWWOC.org, accessed May 28, 2021, https://www.awwoc .org/statistics.

Akómoláfé, Báyò, and Marta Benavides. "The Times Are Urgent: Let's Slow Down." BayoAkomolafe.net, https://www.bayoakomolafe.net/post/the-times-are-urgent-lets-slow -down.

"Ancient Greek Funeral and Burial Practices." Wikipedia, accessed May 28, 2021, https:// en.wikipedia.org/wiki/Ancient_Greek_funeral_and_burial_practices.

Argetsinger, Kathryn. "Birthday Rituals: Friends and Patrons in Roman Poetry and Cult." *Classical Antiquity* 11, no. 2 (October 1992): 175–93, doi: 10.2307/25010971.

Backman, Maurie. "Why I'm Weaning More Carefully This Time Around." Kveller, February 22, 2016, https://www.kveller.com/why-im-weaning-more-carefully-this-time -around/.

Barry, Ellen. "A Peculiarly Dutch Summer Rite: Children Let Loose in the Night Woods." *New York Times*, July 21, 2019, https://www.nytimes.com/2019/07/21/world /europe/netherlands-dropping-children.html.

"Basic Goodness." Wikipedia, accessed August 10, 2021, https://en.wikipedia.org/wiki /Basic_goodness.

Becerra, Maricela. "From the Cuarentena to the Faja: Postpartum Wisdom from My Abuelita." *Academic Mami* (blog), July 5, 2017, https://academicmami.com/www .academicmami.com/2017/07/from-cuarentena-to-faja-postpartum.html.

Bell, Catherine. *Ritual Theory, Ritual Practice*. New York: Oxford University Press, 2009.

"Bengkung Abdominal Binding: Traditional Malay-Indonesian Postnatal Treatment." TraditionalBodywork.com, July 16, 2021, https://www.traditionalbodywork.com /bengkung-abdominal-binding-a-traditional-indonesian-postnatal-treatment/.

"Berakhot 7b." Sefaria, accessed May 28, 2021, https://www.sefaria.org/Berakhot.7b.10?la ng=bi&with=About&lang2=en.

Berry, Beth. *Motherwhelmed: Challenging Norms, Untangling Truths, and Restoring Our Worth to the World*. Revolution from Home Publishing, 2020.

"Better Mental Health." TheCoddling.com, accessed May 28, 2021, https://www.thecod dling.com/better-mental-health.

"Birth and Childhood Rituals." African Tribes, May 2012, https://africantribesuws .wordpress.com/birth-and-childhood-rituals/.

"Birthday Parties: A Torah 'How to' Guide." Torch, accessed May 28, 2021, https://www .torchweb.org/torah_detail.php?id=293.

"Birthing from Within for Parents." Birthing from Within, accessed May 28, 2021, https:// birthingfromwithin.com/birthing-from-within-for-parents/.

Bogaard, L. V. D. "Leaving Quietly? A Quantitative Study of Retirement Rituals and How They Affect Life Satisfaction." *Work, Aging and Retirement* 3 (2017): 55–65.

Bond, Sarah. "The History of the Birthday and the Roman Calendar." *Forbes*, October 1, 2016, https://www.forbes.com/sites/drsarahbond/2016/10/01/the-history-of-the -birthday-and-the-roman-calendar/?sh=27cc904b7bdc.

Boss, Pauline. *Ambiguous Loss: Learning to Live with Unresolved Grief*. Cambridge, MA: Harvard University Press, 2000.

Bowerman, Su. "Ayurveda for Childbearing Years." Ayurveda Vancouver, October 1, 2019, https://www.ayurvedavancouver.com/ayurvedablog/ayurvedaforchildbearing.

Brach, Tara. "Part 1: Trusting Your Basic Goodness." TaraBrach.com, January 11, 2012, https://www.tarabrach.com/part-1-trusting-your-basic-goodness-audio/.

Brooks, Alison Wood, et al. "Don't Stop Believing: Rituals Improve Performance by De-creasing Anxiety." *Organizational Behavior and Human Decision Processes* 137 (2016): 71–85, https://www.hbs.edu/ris/Publication%20Files/Rituals%20OBHDP_5cbc5848-ef4d-4192-a320-68d30169763c.pdf.

Bryant, Miranda. "Maternity Leave: US Policy Is Worst on List of the World's Richest Countries." *Guardian*, January 27, 2020, https://www.theguardian.com/us-news/2020/jan/27/maternity-leave-us-policy-worst-worlds-richest-countries#:~:text=0%20weeks%20total)-,The%20US%20is%20the%20only%20OECD%20country%20without%20a%20national,60%25%20of%20workers%20are%20eligible.

Bumgarner, Norma Jane. *Mothering Your Nursing Toddler*. Raleigh, NC: La Leche League International, 2000.

Burg-Schnirman, Deborah. "A Weaning Ceremony for Joshua Ruben and Eli Nathaniel and for Me." Ritualwell.org, accessed May 28, 2021, https://www.ritualwell.org/ritual/weaning-ceremony-joshua-ruben-and-eli-nathaniel-and-me.

Bushnell, Britta, PhD. "'This Is My Body': Poems by Postpartum Mothers #3." Britta Bushnell.com, accessed May 28, 2021, https://brittabushnell.com/this-is-my-body-3/.

———. *Transformed by Birth: Cultivating Openness, Resilience & Strength for the Life-Changing Journey from Pregnancy to Parenthood*. Boulder, CO: Sounds True, 2020.

Cameron, Catherine M. *Hopi Dwellings: Architectural Change at Orayvi*. Tucson: University of Arizona Press, 1999.

"Caroline's Story." Miscarriage Association, accessed May 28, 2021, https://www.miscarriageassociation.org.uk/story/carolines-story-2/.

"Chevra Kadisha." Jewish Museum London, video, August 24, 2018, 5:54, https://jewishmuseum.org.uk/schools/asset/chevra-kadisha/.

Chzhen, Yekaterina, Anna Gromada, and Gwyther Rees. "Are the World's Richest Countries Family Friendly? Policy in the OECD and EU." UNICEF Office of Research–Innocenti, June 2019, https://www.unicef-irc.org/family-friendly.

Couzyn, Jeni, ed. *The Bloodaxe Book of Contemporary Women Poets: Eleven British Writers*. Eastbourne, UK: Gardners Books, 1999.

Crosby, Joy. "Liminality and the Sacred: Discipline Building and Speaking with the Other." *Liminalities: A Journal of Performance Studies* 5, no. 1 (April 2009): 1–19, http://liminalities.net/5-1/sacred.pdf.

Day, Jody. "The Lost Tribe of Childless Women." TEDx Talks YouTube channel, June 2, 2017, 17:00, https://www.youtube.com/watch?v=uufXWTHT60Y.

"Death Around the World: Obon Festival, Japan." Funeral Guide, September 2, 2016, https://www.funeralguide.co.uk/blog/death-around-world-obon-festival-japan.

Dettwyler, Katherine A. "Breastfeeding and Weaning in Mali: Cultural Context and Hard Data." *Social Science & Medicine* 24, no. 8 (1987): 633–44.

"*Dies lustricus.*" Wikipedia, accessed May 28, 2021, https://en.wikipedia.org/wiki/Dies_lustricus.

Directo-Meston, Danielle. "Why I'm Not Sharing My Baby's Birth Announcement on Facebook." Brides.com, May 25, 2021, https://www.brides.com/reasons-not-to-share-pregnancy-birth-announcements-5112039.

Eisenstein, Charles. "The Coronation." CharlesEisenstein.org, March 2020, https://charleseisenstein.org/essays/the-coronation/.

"Ellen Bass: The Human Line." Jaxxengine YouTube channel, November 2, 2007, 2:39, https://www.youtube.com/watch?v=PaIMlzergm8.

Elliot, Diane, Rabbi. "Elohai Neshama: Breathing the Soul Alive." My Jewish Learning, accessed May 28, 2021, https://www.myjewishlearning.com/article/elohai-neshama-breathing-the-soul-alive/.

Erskine, Richard G., and Rebecca Trautmann. "Methods of an Integrative Psychotherapy." Institute for Integrative Psychotherapy, accessed May 28, 2021, https://www.integrativetherapy.com/en/articles.php?id=63.

Feit, Shir Yaakov. "Handwashing: Cleanliness, Holiness, Godliness." Sefaria.com, accessed May 28, 2021, https://www.sefaria.org/sheets/223839?lang=bi.

Fletcher, Alice C. "A Pawnee Ritual Used When Changing a Man's Name." *American Anthropologist* 1, no. 1 (January 1899): 82–97, http://www.jstor.org/stable/658836.

Frankl, Viktor E. *Man's Search for Meaning: An Introduction to Logotherapy.* New York: Simon & Schuster, 1984.

Freidenfeld, Lara. *The Myth of the Perfect Pregnancy: A History of Miscarriage in America.* New York: Oxford University Press, 2020.

Garrick, David A. "Ritual Self-Disclosure in the Coming-Out Process." *Journal of Ritual Studies* 11, no. 2 (Winter 1997): 1–19, http://www.jstor.org/stable/44368982.

"A General Outline of Taharah Procedures." Kehillah Synagogue, accessed May 28, 2021, https://kehillahsynagogue.org/wp-content/uploads/2012/05/TAHARA.pdf.

Gibran, Kahlil. *The Prophet*. New York: Alfred A. Knopf, 1923.

Gino, Francesca, and Michael I. Norton. "Why Rituals Work." *Scientific American*, May 14, 2013, https://www.scientificamerican.com/article/why-rituals-work/.

Gionet, Linda. "Breastfeeding Trends in Canada." Statistics Canada, November 27, 2015, https://www150.statcan.gc.ca/n1/pub/82-624-x/2013001/article/11879-eng.htm.

Golinkin, David, Rabbi. "When Should Baby Girls Be Named?" Schechter Institutes, Inc., November 11, 2005, https://schechter.edu/when-should-baby-girls-be-named/.

Goodman, Leslee. "Between Two Worlds: Malidoma Somé on Rites of Passage." *Sun*, July 2010, https://www.thesunmagazine.org/issues/415/between-two-worlds.

Gordon, Martin L. "*Netilat Yadayim Shel Shaharit*: Ritual of Crisis or Dedication?" *Gesher: Bridging the Spectrum of Orthodox Jewish Scholarship* 8 (1981): 36–72, http://www.zootorah.com/RationalistJudaism/netilat.pdf.

Granger, Byrd Howell. "Naming: In Customs, Beliefs, and Folk Tales." *Western Folklore* 20, no. 1 (January 1961): 27–37, https://doi.org/10.2307/1496513.

Groth, Leah. "A 'Frida Mom' Commercial Aimed at Postpartum Women Just Got Banned from the Oscars for Being 'Too Graphic.'" *Health*, February 11, 2020, https://www.health.com/condition/pregnancy/frida-mom-commercial-banned-oscars.

Gustafson, Ellen. "Why I Didn't Post a Single Photo of My Pregnancy on Social Media." *Cosmopolitan*, June 29, 2017, https://www.cosmopolitan.com/sex-love/a10235827/pregnancy-social-media-birth-announcements/.

Haidt, Jonathan, and Jean Twenge. "Is There an Increase in Adolescent Mood Disorders, Self-Harm, and Suicide Since 2010 in the USA and UK? A Review." Unpublished manuscript, 2021, https://docs.google.com/document/d/1diMvsMeRphUH7E6D1d_J7R6WbDdgnzFHDHPx9HXzR5o/edit?ts=5c80262c#.

———. "Social Media Use and Mental Health: A Review." Unpublished manuscript, 2019, https://docs.google.com/document/d/1w-HOfseF2wF9YIpXwUUtP65-olnkPyWcgF5BiAtBEy0/edit#heading=h.5ec16tpt0qi4.

Hall, Marika Reid. "The Ancient Art of Mother Roasting." MarikaReidHall.com, October 22, 2018, https://marikareidhall.com/the-ancient-art-of-mother-roasting/.

Hammer, Jill. "Holle's Cry: Unearthing a Birth Goddess in a German Jewish Naming Ceremony." *Nashim: A Journal of Jewish Women's Studies & Gender Issues*, no. 9 (2005): 62–87, doi: 10.1353/nsh.2005.0003.

Harvey-Jenner, Catriona. "19 Celebrities Who Got Real about Their Post-Baby Bodies." *Cosmopolitan*, June 23, 2021, https://www.cosmopolitan.com/uk/body/health/g12764048/celebrities-honest-opinion-post-baby-body/.

Heaton, Tim B., Cardell K. Jacobson, and Kimberlee Holland. "Persistence and Change in Decisions to Remain Childless." *Journal of Marriage and Family* 61, no. 2 (May 1999): 531–39, doi: 10.2307/353767.

Heaney, Seamus. "Blackberry-Picking." Poetry Foundation, accessed May 28, 2021, https://www.poetryfoundation.org/poems/50981/blackberry-picking.

Heilman, Samuel C. *When a Jew Dies: The Ethnography of a Bereaved Son*. Berkeley: University of California Press, 2001.

Helsel, Philip Browning. "Witnessing the Body's Response to Trauma: Resistance, Ritual, and Nervous System Activation." *Pastoral Psychology* 64 (2015): 681–93, https://www.ictg.org/uploads/1/2/9/5/12954435/phil_helsel_dec_2014_article.pdf.

Hingston, Michael. "Don't Tell the Kids: The Real History of the Tooth Fairy." *Salon*, February 9, 2014, https://www.salon.com/2014/02/09/dont_tell_the_kids_the_real_history_of_the_tooth_fairy/.

Hirschman, Charles, and Marilyn Butler. "Trends and Differentials in Breast Feeding: An Update." *Demography* 18, no. 1 (February 1981): 39–54.

Hobson, Nicholas M., et al. "The Psychology of Rituals: An Integrative Review and Process-Based Framework." *Personality and Social Psychology Review* 22, no. 3 (2018): 1–25, doi: 10.1177/1088868317734944.

Hogan, Jojo. "Jojo Hogan's Slow Postpartum." SlowPostpartum.com, accessed May 28, 2021, https://slowpostpartum.com/.

Homans, George C. "Anxiety and Ritual: The Theories of Malinowski and Radcliffe-Brown." *American Anthropologist* 43, no. 2 (April–June 1941): 164–72, http://www.jstor.org/stable/662949.

Homepage. Pulling at Threads, accessed May 28, 2021, https://www.pullingatthreads.com/.

Horowitz, Juliana Menasce, and Nikki Graf. "Most U.S. Teens See Anxiety and Depression as a Major Problem among Their Peers." Pew Research Center, February 20, 2019, https://www.pewsocialtrends.org/2019/02/20/most-u-s-teens-see-anxiety-and-depression-as-a-major-problem-among-their-peers/.

Hüsken, Ute, and Donna Lynne Seamone. "The Denial of Ritual and Its Return—An Introduction." *Journal of Ritual Studies* 27, no. 1 (2013): 1–9, http://www.jstor.org /stable/44368860.

"The Importance of a Name with Meaning." Mi Yodeya, accessed May 28, 2021, https://judaism.stackexchange.com/questions/79302/the-importance-of-a-name-with-meaning.

Jensen, Derrick. "Singing to the Dawn: Thomas Berry on Our Broken Connection to the Natural World." *Sun*, May 2002, https://www.thesunmagazine.org/issues/317/singing -to-the-dawn.

Kimmerer, Robin Wall. *Braiding Sweetgrass: Indigenous Wisdom, Scientific Knowledge, and the Teachings of Plants*. Minneapolis: Milkweed Editions, 2013.

Kirkpatrick, Elise. "The Blessingway: A Complete Guide to Honoring the Mother." *The Birth Hour* (podcast), accessed May 28, 2021, https://thebirthhour.com/blessingway/#:~:text =The%20History%20of%20the%20Blessingway%20or%20Mother's%20Bles sing%20Ceremony&text=In%20Native%20American%20tradition%2C%20 (Dine,the%20way%20ahead%20for%20her.

Koontz, Katy. "Listening in with . . . Grandmother Flordemayo: Seeding the Future." *Unity Magazine*, May/June 2020, https://www.unity.org/publications/unity-magazine /articles/listening-grandmother-flordemayo.

Krohn, Paysach J. "What's in a Name?" Torah.org, February 19, 2004, https://torah.org /interest/name/.

"Kwanzaa." Disciples Home Missions, accessed May 28, 2021, https://www.disciples homemissions.org/wp-content/uploads/2016/05/Kwanzaa-2017.pdf.

Lee, Kyung Hee, MA. "Journey to Remain Childless: A Grounded Theory of the Decision-Making Process among Voluntarily Childless Couples." Dissertation, August 2011, https://ttu-ir.tdl.org/bitstream/handle/2346/ETD-TTU-2011-08-1872/Lee_kyunghee _DissREVIEWED.pdf?sequence=3.

Lertzman, David Adam. "Rediscovering Rites of Passage: Education, Transformation, and the Transition to Sustainability." *Ecology and Society* 5, no. 2 (2002), https://www .ecologyandsociety.org/vol5/iss2/art30/.

"Life at Home." MyDomaine.com, accessed June 12, 2021, https://www.mydomaine .com/life-at-home-5112980.

Lunde, Stein Erik. *My Father's Arms Are a Boat*. Brooklyn, NY: Enchanted Lion Books, 2013.

Madden, Janet. "Leaving Shloshim." Ritualwell.org, accessed May 28, 2021, https://www.ritualwell.org/ritual/leaving-shloshim.

Mahdi, Louise Carus, Nancy Geyer Christopher, and Michael Meade, eds. *Crossroads: The Quest for Contemporary Rites of Passage*. Chicago: Open Court Publishing Company, 1998.

Mary. "After Weaning: How It Feels After Stopping Breastfeeding." Mom Friend, December 31, 2020, https://themomfriend.com/after-stopping-breastfeeding/.

———. "Tonight I Nursed You for the Last Time." Mom Friend, May 14, 2020, https://themomfriend.com/tonight-i-nursed-you-for-the-last-time/.

Meade, Michael. "It Takes More Than a Village." Mosaic Voices, May 11, 2015, https://www.mosaicvoices.org/it-takes-more-than-a-village.

———. *The Water of Life: Initiation and the Tempering of the Soul*. Seattle: Green Fire Press, 2011.

Morgan, John D., and Pittu Laungani, eds. *Death and Bereavement Around the World: Major Religious Traditions*, vol. 1. Abingdon-on-Thames, UK: Routledge, 2002.

Mowry, Tia (@tiamowry). "7 weeks #postpartum." Instagram, June 24, 2018, https://www.instagram.com/p/BkZwUaClmRE/?hl=en&taken-by=tiamowry.

Mull, Amanda. "A New Sign That Teens Know They Aren't Struggling Alone." *Atlantic*, February 25, 2019, https://www.theatlantic.com/health/archive/2019/02/teen-mental-health-worries/583531/.

Nathoo, Tasnim, and Aleck Ostry. *The One Best Way? Breastfeeding History, Politics, and Policy in Canada*. Waterloo, ON: Wilfrid Laurier University Press, 2009.

National Research Council Institute of Medicine. *Adolescent Development and the Biology of Puberty: Summary of a Workshop on New Research*. Washington, DC: National Academies Press, 1999, https://www.ncbi.nlm.nih.gov/books/NBK224692/.

Nelson-Becker, Holly, and Kimberly Sangster. "Recapturing the Power of Ritual to Enhance Community in Aging." *Journal of Religion, Spirituality & Aging* 31, no. 2 (2019): 153–67, doi: 10.1080/15528030.2018.1532858.

Nicholas, Chani. "Summer Solstice: A Testimony of Light." ChaniNicholas.com, accessed June 20, 2021, https://chaninicholas.com/summer-solstice-testimony-light/.

O'Donohue, John. *Anam Cara: A Book of Celtic Wisdom*. New York: Cliff Street Books, 1998.

Oliver, Mary. *American Primitive*. Boston: Back Bay Books, 1983.

"Oscars Ban Postpartum Commercial for Being 'Too Graphic.'" ET Canada YouTube channel, February 7, 2020, https://www.youtube.com/watch?v=1q9leHVgecw.

Parker, Matt, DMD. "International Tooth Fairy Tales: Lost Tooth Myths from Around the World." AZ Family Dental, February 27, 2017, https://www.azfd.com/blog/lost-tooth-myths-around-world/.

Parker, Priya. *The Art of Gathering: How We Meet and Why It Matters*. New York: Riverhead Books, 2018.

Penner, Hans H. "Functions of Ritual." Britannica.com, accessed May 28, 2021, https://www.britannica.com/topic/ritual/Functions-of-ritual.

Perel, Esther, and Mary Alice Miller. "Rituals for Healthy Relationships at Every Stage." EstherPerel.com, accessed June 20, 2021, https://estherperel.com/blog/rituals-for-healthy-relationships#:~:text=Routines%20get%20us%20through%20the,ground%20us%20and%20create%20familiarity.

Poirot, Lissa Harnish. "10 Hardest Things about Being a New Mom." *Bump*, October 12, 2020, https://www.thebump.com/a/life-with-a-newborn.

Prechtel, Martín. *The Smell of Rain on Dust: Grief and Praise*. Berkeley, CA: North Atlantic Books, 2015.

Premberg, Asa, and Ingela Lundgren. "Fathers' Experiences of Childbirth Education." *Journal of Perinatal Education* 15, no. 2 (April 2006): 21–28, doi: 10.1624/105812406X107780.

Preston, Elizabeth. "What's a 'Normal' Amount of Time to Breastfeed?" *New York Times*, September 3, 2019, https://www.nytimes.com/2020/04/15/parenting/baby/how-long-should-you-breastfeed.html.

Quack, Johannes, and Paul Töbelmann. "Questioning 'Ritual Efficacy.'" *Journal of Ritual Studies* 24, no. 1 (2010): 13–28, http://www.jstor.org/stable/44368818.

Rameswaram, Sean. "Netflix Has No Chill." *Today, Explained* (podcast), July 6, 2020.

Reid, Kohenet Rachel. "Mekonenet: Soul Candles." Accessed May 28, 2021, https://docs.google.com/document/d/1vhNrozCsEg1AnoV_KIDByocz7PPZiWRcj_UBuSBGrAE/edit?ts=5ed68e59.

Rippeyoung, Phyllis L. F., and Mary C. Noonan. "Is Breastfeeding Truly Cost Free? Income Consequences of Breastfeeding for Women." *American Sociological Review* 77, no. 2 (2012): 503.

Safransky, Sy. "By Fire and Water: An Interview with Michael Meade." *Sun*, January 1994, https://www.thesunmagazine.org/issues/217/by-fire-and-water.

Saile, David G. "The Ritual Establishment of Home." In *Home Environments*, vol. 8, Irwin Altman and Carol M. Werner, eds. New York: Springer Science+Business Media, 1985.

Savage, Maddy. "Why Do Women Still Change Their Names?" BBC, September 23, 2020, https://www.bbc.com/worklife/article/20200921-why-do-women-still-change-their -names#:~:text=In%20the%20US%2C%20most%20women,they%20still%20 follow%20the%20practice.

"Saying Hello to Everything." Returning to Earth, January 25, 2016, http://www .returningtoearth.com/blog/2016/1/25/saying-hello-to-everything.

Schildkret, Day. *Morning Altars: A 7-Step Practice to Nourish Your Spirit through Nature, Art, and Ritual*. New York: Countryman Press, 2018.

Schorsch, Ismar. "Why Jews Light Candles." Jewish Theological Seminary, February 19, 2005, https://www.jtsa.edu/why-jews-light-candles.

Scott, Will. "Rites of Passage and the Story of Our Times." School of Lost Borders, accessed May 28, 2021, https://test.schooloflostborders.org/content/rites-passage-and -story-our-times-will-scott.

Sellen, Daniel W. "Comparison of Infant Feeding Patterns Reported for Nonindustrial Populations with Current Recommendations." *Journal of Nutrition* 131, no. 10 (October 2001): 2707–15.

Sendrey, Eileen. "The Child Who Is Not Embraced by the Village Will Burn It Down to Feel Its Warmth." EileenSendrey.com, August 6, 2019, https://www.eileensendrey.com /blog/2019/8/6/the-child-who-is-not-embraced-by-the-village-will-burn-it-down-to -feel-its-warmth.

Shaw, Martin. "Mud and Antler Bone: An Interview with Martin Shaw." *Emergence Magazine*, June 4, 2018, https://emergencemagazine.org/interview/mud-and-antler -bone/.

Simmons, Shraga, Rabbi. "Naming a Baby." Aish HaTorah, accessed May 28, 2021, https:// www.aish.com/jl/l/b/48961326.html.

Smith, Jonathan Z. "The Bare Facts of Ritual." *History of Religions* 20, nos. 1/2 (August– November 1980): 112–27, http://www.jstor.org/stable/1062338.

Spitzer, Juliet I., MSEd. "Dignity in Life, Dignity in Death: One Perspective on the Chevra Kaddisha." Ritualwell.org, accessed May 28, 2021, https://www.ritualwell.org /ritual/dignity-life-dignity-death-one-perspective-chevra-kaddisha.

Stanford University, accessed June 4, 2014, https://web.stanford.edu/class/e297c/war_peace/media/hpsych.html.

Stephenson, Barry. *Ritual: A Very Short Introduction.* New York: Oxford University Press, 2015.

Strauss, Norbert. "Hollekreisch Ceremony." Jewish Link, February 28, 2019, https://jewishlink.news/features/29831-hollekreisch-ceremony.

Sturme, Ashlee. "A Time to Heal: Mother Blessing..." Home Birth Matters, February 2015, https://homebirth.org.nz/magazine/article/a-time-to-heal-blessingway/.

"Sunbeams." *Sun,* July 2010, https://www.thesunmagazine.org/issues/415/sunbeams-415.

"The Surgeon General's Call to Action to Support Breastfeeding." Centers for Disease Control and Prevention, May 11, 2021, https://www.cdc.gov/breastfeeding/resources/calltoaction.htm.

Towsley, Lanie. "How to Prepare for the New Role: Big Brother!" Baby Chick, April 12, 2016, https://www.baby-chick.com/fischers-new-role-big-brother/.

Turner, Victor W. "Betwixt and Between: The Liminal Period in *Rites de Passage.*" In *Reader in Comparative Religion: An Anthropological Approach,* 4th edition, William A. Lessa and Evon Z. Vogt, eds. New York: HarperCollins, 1979, http://hiebertglobal center.org/blog/wp-content/uploads/2013/03/Reading-20-Victor-Turner-Betwixt -and-Between.pdf.

Twenge, Jean M. "Have Smartphones Destroyed a Generation?" *Atlantic,* September 2017, https://www.theatlantic.com/magazine/archive/2017/09/has-the-smartphone-destroyed -a-generation/534198/.

Van der Kolk, Bessel, MD. *The Body Keeps the Score: Brain, Mind, and Body in the Healing of Trauma.* New York: Viking, 2014.

Van Gennep, Arnold. *The Rites of Passage.* Chicago: University of Chicago Press, 1960.

"The War on Sensemaking, Daniel Schmachtenberger." Rebel Wisdom YouTube channel, August 19, 2019, https://www.youtube.com/watch?v=7LqaotiGWjQ.

Wasilenko, Ashley. "I Am Sad to End Our Breastfeeding Journey—but So Ready, Too." Motherly, May 3, 2018, https://www.mother.ly/life/i-am-sad-to-end-our-breastfeeding -journey-but-so-ready-too.

"What Really Helps You Bounce Back After Pregnancy." Johns Hopkins Medicine, accessed May 28, 2021, https://www.hopkinsmedicine.org/health/wellness-and-preven tion/what-really-helps-you-bounce-back-after-pregnancy.

"Why Breastfeeding is a Political Issue." Graduate Institute Geneva, August 10, 2018, https://www.graduateinstitute.ch/communications/news/why-breastfeeding-political -issue.

Wiessinger, Diane, Diana West, and Teresa Pitman. *The Womanly Art of Breastfeeding.* New York: Ballantine Books, 2010.

Wotherspoon, Dan. "Pivoting the Sacred." *Sunstone,* November 2006, https://sunstone .org/wp-content/uploads/sbi/articles/143-07-08.pdf.

"Wudu." Wikipedia, accessed May 28, 2021, https://en.wikipedia.org/wiki/Wudu.

Young, Ayana. "Dr. BAYO AKOMOLAFE on Slowing Down in Urgent Times." *For the Wild* (podcast), January 22, 2020.

———. "Homebound: The Roots and Shoots of Earth-Based Community with STAR-HAWK." *For the Wild* (podcast), May 15, 2020.

"Your Stories." Miscarriage Association, accessed May 28, 2021, https://www.miscarriage association.org.uk/your-feelings/your-stories/.

"*Zeved habat.*" Wikipedia, accessed May 28, 2021, https://en.wikipedia.org/wiki/Zeved _habat.

INDEX

INDEX

ABOUT THE AUTHOR

Day Schildkret has devoted his life to inspiring people of all ages the world over to connect deeply, be awed, and make meaning with nature, art, and ritual. His award-winning work *Morning Altars: A 7-Step Practice to Nourish Your Spirit Through Nature, Art and Ritual* (Countryman Press, 2018) has sparked an international movement and has been featured on NBC and CBS and in *VICE, BuzzFeed*, Well+Good, *Spirituality & Health* magazine, and more. In addition to *Morning Altars*, Day is the author of *Hello, Goodbye: 75 Rituals for Times of Loss, Celebration, and Change* (Simon Element, 2022). He is also host of the podcast *Hello, Goodbye.* He is blessed to be claimed by many homes, including the San Francisco Bay Area; New York City; Portland, Oregon; and Salt Spring Island, Canada. He travels extensively, bringing his creative whimsy and heartfelt wisdom to wherever he plants himself. For details on Day's trainings, workshops, and current projects, visit DaySchildkret.com.